Three Burlesque Plays of

THOMAS DUFFETT

Three Burlesque Plays of
THOMAS DUFFETT, *fl. 1678.*

The Empress of Morocco

The Mock-Tempest

Psyche Debauch'd

Edited with an Introduction by
Ronald Eugene DiLorenzo

UNIVERSITY OF IOWA PRESS
IOWA CITY   1972 Ψ

Library of Congress Catalog Card Number:
72–81173

University of Iowa Press, Iowa City 52240
© *1972 by The University of Iowa. All rights reserved*
Printed in the United States of America
ISBN 87745–033–1

Ad Patrem

Contents

Plates

Introduction

Little is known about Thomas Duffett: we do not even know the dates of his life. Langbaine refers to him as "An Author altogether unknown to me but by his Writings," [1] and Gildon is only somewhat more informative: "He was before he became a Poet, a Milliner in the New Exchange." [2] In May 1677 someone named Thomas Duffett confessed to and received a pardon for forgery; [3] perhaps the former milliner turned to more than playwriting in his search for a new career,[4] but even this suspicion has never been confirmed. Yet we do know that Duffett tried his hand at a variety of projects related to the theatre: two comedies, a masque, and a book of poems.[5]

Duffett's turn to burlesque was occasioned by the sagging fortunes of the King's Company during the period 1672–75, at which time the Duke's Men had particular success with productions emphasizing spectacle and music. Since the King's Men could not compete with these opulent productions, a simpler revenge was taken by having Duffett burlesque them. It is likely that his effort was directed primarily toward winning over a part of the audience from Dorset Garden, and also to having a bit of intramural fun. After the printing of *Psyche Debauch'd* in 1678 his writing career seems to end. It might be pleasant to know more about Duffett.

Having decided to ridicule the spectacular productions by the Duke's Men at Dorset Garden, what kind of burlesques did Duffett write? Burlesque drama usually takes one of two forms: plays whose actions include or lead up to the rehearsal or production of another play, such as *A Midsummer Night's Dream*, *The Knight of the Burning Pestle*, *The Rehearsal*, and *The Critic;* and plays

---

[1] Gerard Langbaine, *An Account of the English Dramatick Poets* (Oxford, 1691), p. 177.

[2] [Charles Gildon], *The Lives and Characters of the English Dramatick Poets* (London, 1699), p. 48.

[3] *Calendar of State Papers, Domestic Series, 1677-78*, pp. 108, 117.

[4] John Harold Wilson has concluded that Duffett the forger and Duffett the playwright are one and the same. See *Mr. Goodman, the Player* (Pittsburgh, 1964), p. 54.

[5] The two comedies are: *The Spanish Rogue* (London, 1674); and, *The Amorous Old-Woman: or, 'Tis Well if it Take* (London, 1674). The latter play was ascribed to Duffett by Langbaine (p. 526). It was reprinted in 1684 with a different title (*The Fond Lady*). Duffett's masque is *Beauties Triumph* (London, 1676); and his book of poems, *New Poems, Songs, Prologues and Epilogues* (London, 1676), which was reprinted the following year with a different title page.

in which the action is single in itself, involving no break in the dramatic illusion, such as Cibber's *The Rival Queans*, Fielding's 1730 version of *Tom Thumb*, Carey's *Chrononhotonthologos*, and W. B. Rhodes's *Bombastes Furioso*. The former type could be called a "frame-play," and in its structure we can see the outline for a particular burlesque view: the object to be ridiculed is presented in the "rehearsal" material, usually in the form of a pretentious tragedy; the ridicule is reinforced and directed by "outside" characters who are identified as men of wit and intelligence. Burlesques of the second type, in which the action is single, present the object to be ridiculed solely in the play itself, while the ridicule is derived from the particular style employed. Duffett's burlesques are of this latter type.

In creating his burlesque style, Duffett did not have to look far for precedents. Material was readily available in Restoration burlesque poetry. A work that demonstrates quite well the characteristics of this kind of poetry is Charles Cotton's *Scarronides*.[6] In his version of Book I of the *Aeneid* (p. 60), Cotton describes Venus after she has given advice to Aeneas:

> With that she turn'd to go away,
> And did her freckl'd Neck display;
> By which, and by a certain Whiffe,
> Came from her Arm-pits, or her Cliffe,
> And a fine hobble in her pace,
> *Aeneas* knew his Mothers grace.[7]

The burlesque here derives from the shock of straight-forward debasement. For Virgil's "rosea cervice" (which Dryden translated as "neck refulgent") Cotton gives "freckl'd Neck," which has the lumpy charm we associate with Gay's *The Shepherd's Week*. But Cotton is more noted in this poem for unsubtle renderings like "Arm-pits," "Whiffe" and "Cliffe" in place of "ambrosiae comae" and "divinum odorem" (which Dryden combined into "dishevel'd hair" and "ambrosial scents"). Cotton's treatment of the death of Dido (IV, pp. 146–47) is even more crude:

---

6 *Scarronides: or, Virgile Travestie. A Mock-Poem. Being the First Book of Virgils Aeneis in English Burlesque* (London, 1664). Cotton followed this with *Scarronides: A Mock-Poem. In Imitation of the Fourth Book of Virgils Aeneis in English Burlesque* (London, 1665). Cotton's source was Paul Scarron's *Le Virgile Travesti*, which began appearing in 1648. Scarron eventually completed the full twelve books. His poem is much less crude than Cotton's; at times he achieves a playfulness and wittiness lacking in Cotton's vulgarization.

7 Compare with the above this parallel passage from Book I of Scarron's poem:
> Notre pauvre messire Énée,
> La voyant grandir à l'instant
> De quatre pieds et d'un empan;
> Sentant de son corps diaphane
> Sortir odeur de frangipane.

(Paul Scarron, *Le Virgile Travesti*, Nouvelle Édition par Victor Fournel, Paris, 1876, p. 68).

Introduction

Down fell she
She capr'd twice, or thrice, most finely;
But th' Rope imbrac'd her Neck so kindly
Till at the last in mortal Trance,
She did conclude the dismal dance.
A yellow aromatick matter
Dropt from her heels, commixt with water,
Which sinking through the Chamber-floor,
Set all the house in sad uproar.
All at the first that they amiss thought,
Was that her Grace had mist the piss-pot.[8]

Cotton's verses might have appeal to the reader who has had a forced diet of Virgil and who would welcome the chance for a little nose-thumbing; the enjoyment is clearly in the debasement itself. This kind of burlesque is usually called travesty.

What Duffett did was to appropriate the verbal debasement of this kind of style and apply it to the writing of burlesque plays. The play to be ridiculed, therefore, whether it was an heroic drama or operatic romance, was mocked by the creation of another play which degraded all of the elements of the original play: plot, character, situation, dialogue, and language. Duffett works, then, by means of travesty; and, until evidence is discovered, one can only speculate as to what extent Duffett travestied aspects of the target-plays other than what we can discern from his text. However, it seems reasonable to suppose that many facets of the particular productions at Dorset Garden could have been travestied when Duffett's burlesques were performed: costumes, scenery, music, dancing, stage-business, and individual performances.[9]

Though Duffett uses travesty as his chief strategy, his burlesques show a growth in comic significance away from the narrowness of travesty. *The Empress of*

---

[8] Compare the above with the following from Book IV of Scarron:

> Ayant parlé de cette sorte,
> On la vit tomber demi-morte,
> Sans dire un seul mot d'*In manus*,
> Un glaive entre ses tetons nus
> Avait fait un large passage
> Par où cette dame peu sage
> Répandit de bon sang humain
> Par terre, non pas plein la main,
> Mais plein une bonne écuellée;
> Et son âme, parmi mêlée,
> S'en alla je ne sais pas où.
>
> (*Le Virgile Travesti*, p. 185)

[9] In connection with this possibility, V. C. Clinton-Baddeley has commented that Duffett's burlesques "were founded in high spirits and visual wit" (*The Burlesque Tradition in the English Theatre After 1660*, London, 1952, p. 42). This point is elaborated by Peter Elvet Lewis in "The Three Dramatic Burlesques of Thomas Duffett," *DUJ* 58 (1966), 149–56.

Introduction

Morocco comes closest, of his three burlesques, to being pure travesty. The two later burlesques, *The Mock-Tempest* and *Psyche Debauch'd,* can be called travesties, but are much more extravagant creations. However, if Duffett's burlesques do, willy-nilly, end in making an appeal to humor over and above the level of travesty, such does not seem to have been appreciated by any of his contemporaries. This is partly a result of the growing prejudice against burlesque as being an inherently unethical genre, and quite probably of a prejudice against Duffett himself as an unfortunate hack who turned to scurrility. Unfairness, of course, seems to be the rule of the game in most burlesque. This attitude is reflected in James Sutherland's comment on *The Rehearsal:*

. . . in our amusement at the sardonic comments of Smith and Johnson we probably do not pause to reflect that many of them are quite unfair, and that some of them could be equally well, or ill, applied to *Hamlet* or to *Paradise Lost*.[10]

This remark applies particularly to travesty. Langbaine called Duffett "a Wit of the third Rate," and quoted the following lines from the Soame-Dryden translation of Boileau's *L'Art poétique:*

> The dull Burlesque appear'd with Impudence,
> And pleas'd by Novelty for want of Sence.
> All except trivial points, grew out of Date;
> Parnassus spoke the Cant of Billingsgate:
> Boundless and Mad, disorder'd Rime was seen;
> Disguis'd Apollo chang'd to Harlequin.
> This Plague which first in Country Towns began,
> Cities and Kingdoms quickly over-ran;
> The dullest Scriblers some Admirers found,
> And the *Mock-Tempest* was a while renown'd;
> But this low stuff the Town at last despis'd,
> And scorn'd the Folly that they once had priz'd.[11]

The main point to consider here is that burlesque was equated with travesty in the late seventeenth century. As a result, Duffett was probably regarded as a kind of literary Neanderthal man, a fit example of bad taste, and (with deadening frequency) succeeding discussions of him have involved the faithful reproduction of the lines quoted by Langbaine.

Yet, if Duffett's burlesques were regarded contemptuously, it is important to

---

10 *English Satire* (Cambridge, 1958), p. 146.

11 *An Account of the English Dramatick Poets,* pp. 177, 178. The Soame-Dryden translation can be found in *The Poetical Works of Dryden,* ed. George R. Noyes, rev. ed. (Boston, 1950), pp. 916–25. The lines quoted above may imply that *The Mock-Tempest* had some success ("was a while renown'd"). The Soame-Dryden translation appeared in 1683, almost a decade after *The Mock-Tempest* was produced. It may be noted that in the *L'Art poétique,* Boileau's example of low burlesque was "d'Assoucy" (i.e., Charles Coypeau d'Assoucy, 1605–77), who wrote a burlesque of the *Metamorphoses* called *Ovide en belle humeur.*

note that Butler's *Hudibras* was exempt from this censure. The Soame-Dryden translation of Boileau goes on (Canto I.93–96) to claim for *Hudibras* a "buffooning grace" that is above "so mean a style" represented by *The Mock-Tempest*. Richmond P. Bond distinguishes *Hudibras* from travesty by calling it a "Hudibrastic." [12] While Butler's poem does use debasement as a principle of style, it is not confined, as travesty is, to a specific literary target; and further, it makes use of a variety of styles. When Butler *is* vulgar ("As if divinity had catched / The itch on purpose to be scratched"), there is often a pointed insight involved. Vulgarity in travesty, in comparison, seems merely to call attention to itself. Duffett's burlesques, though rooted in travesty, show a growth beyond its confines. In this respect Duffett occupies a chair between Cotton and Butler.

Duffett's *The Empress of Morocco,* for example, consists of a brief skit made up of two scenes surrounded by a cluster of additional burlesque devices which give the whole piece a quality of playfulness and surprise. More telling, though, in *The Mock-Tempest* and *Psyche Debauch'd,* is the frequent use of realistic prose rather than burlesque verse, the development of memorable characterizations, and the inclusion of material extraneous to the ostensible burlesque purpose. As a result, Duffett creates in the two later burlesques an exuberant low-life world that is interesting in and for itself.

Duffett's basic method in *The Empress of Morocco* can be described as an "inversion of values": the kings, queens, and dignitaries of Settle's *Empress* are converted in Duffett's version into pimps, prostitutes (queans), dray-men, porters, and corn-cutters. Suitably ridiculous parallels for the action are then added to this first transformation. Instead of being assembled at court, the main characters play at "hot cockles"; the language becomes splay-footed tetrameter couplets with feminine endings. Such elements combine to reinforce the intended image of raucous irreverence.

While Duffett's skit ridiculing Settle's play is slight in itself, there are a few other features of Duffett's *Empress,* which strengthen the satire, and which deserve consideration. The main skit of two scenes ridiculing Settle's *Empress* is prefaced by a "prologue" of fifty-three lines which is itself in the form of a skit. The first twenty-one lines, comparing pretentious plays to overdressed wenches, seem ordinary enough; but the prologue opens up at that point into a brief scene in which the ghost of Muly Labas appears before the sleeping Morena "and does not sing (lest it should be thought that the rare Fancy, was stolen from that singing Ghost of *Pompey*) but speaks." In the ensuing sequence the ghost of Labas refers to himself as "Great P——y's injur'd Ghost," and, after warning Morena that she too will be as slighted and forgotten as he, she wakes and says, "*Is not my P——y here?*", at which point the prologue ends. The references to Pompey allude to an earlier theatrical skirmish. In the early 1660s there were two translations of Corneille's *Pompée.* One was, *Pompey, a Tragedy,* in a version by "the Matchless Orinda," Mrs. Katherine Philips, produced in Dublin in 1663 and printed in Dublin and London the same year. The other

---

12 *English Burlesque Poetry 1700–1750* (Cambridge, Mass., 1932), p. 145.

was *Pompey the Great*, translated by Buckhurst, Sedley, Waller, and Sidney Godolphin, produced and printed in London in 1664. Duffett's prologue alludes to the former of these productions. Mrs. Philips's version included songs by various of the characters following each act. The last thirty-one lines of Duffett's prologue are a fairly close parody of the song by Pompey's ghost to Cornelia at the end of the third act of Mrs. Philips's play. One function of Duffett's prologue, then, may have been to inform the audience that Settle's *Empress*, like a previously pretentious production (Mrs. Philips's *Pompey*), is doomed to be forgotten.

However, Duffett's prologue may allude to more than Mrs. Philips's *Pompey*. It may also have been intended to remind the audience of a burlesque of *Pompey* that Davenant included as the fifth act of *The Play-house to be Let*. Langbaine claimed that he saw Mrs. Philips's play performed at the Duke's Theatre with Davenant's burlesque performed as an afterpiece.[13] Davenant's burlesque is based on Act III, scenes ii and iv, of *Pompey,* which are concerned with an argument between Caesar and Ptolomy, and with Cornelia's appearance bearing the ashes of Pompey. Davenant's piece has a close similarity with Duffett's skit attacking Settle's *Empress* both in its brevity and in the spirit of its burlesque verse. In the following passage, Caesar is quizzing Ptolomy about his part in the death of Pompey:

> *Caesar.* Know tender Springal (I'll not chide but frump ye)
> You play'd at Trap, when Traps were lay'd for *Pompey*.
> With finger in eye his wife had not wept here
> If stead of Trapstick you then had us'd Scepter.
> *Ptol.* When Fortune frumpish is, who e're withstood her?
> *Caesar*, this bus'ness makes too great a pudder:
> I would not slander *Pompey* now he dead is;
> Yet let me tell, what by my people said is,
> You'll say the pratling people falsly charge men;
> But all report that *Pompey*'s Barge and Bargemen
> Had plunder'd *Nilus* banks till there was scarce one
> Turky or Pigg left for the tyth of Parson;
> Of which even *Pompey* muncht his share in Cabin,
> Where, from the shore, he becken'd many a drab in:
> Under the *Rose* I speak't, he was a Dragon
> When he brown Damsel got with scarce a rag on;
> And came not here for rescue, but to rob us;
> Yet we at last bob'd him who meant to bob us.[14]

Alfred Harbage's comment on this skit applies equally to Duffett's *Empress:* ". . . although utterly pointless in plot if the truth be told, it is remarkable for the vigor with which august tragic figures are pushed from their pedestals." [15] Although Davenant's *The Play-house to be Let* was first produced in 1663, it

13 *An Account of the English Dramatick Poets,* p. 405.
14 *The Works of Sr William Davenant K^t* (London, 1673), p. 116.
15 *Sir William Davenant, Poet Venturer 1606–1668* (Philadelphia, 1935), p. 220.

was not printed until the Folio edition of Davenant's works appeared in 1673. The possibility that Duffett may have gotten his inspiration from Davenant's skit, if true, would raise the pleasant irony of the faltering King's Men attacking the more successful Duke's Men and using as their ammunition Davenant's own technique of ten years' vintage.

Both Davenant and Duffett, in their respective skits, achieve brevity by alluding to central sequences in the target-plays rather than attempting to burlesque scene by scene. Duffett's first scene burlesques the banishing of Muly Hamet, which takes up Acts II and III of Settle's play; similarly, the second scene burlesques in rapid order several parallel actions in Settle's play, telescoping them into a drunken orgy in the midst of which Muly Labas falls down "dead drunk." The Duffett and Davenant skits share still one further quality worth mentioning. Unlike Cotton's burlesque, they feel free to incorporate material that is extraneous to the burlesque purpose, that is, they include characters and actions that have no parallel in the target-plays. Davenant's use of Antony and Cleopatra in his skit is not warranted by Mrs. Philips's play. Justification for their inclusion was more than likely "the more the merrier"—if we're going to have Caesar, Pompey, and Cornelia, why not the others? Duffett is somewhat more flagrant in this regard, concluding his skit with fifty-three lines which violate the satiric parallel by bringing in completely extraneous material: there is a "Hamlet-Laertes" ranting scene between Muly Hamet and Muly Labas over who shall win Miriamne (who in Settle's play is Muly Labas's sister!); her denunciation of them; and, finally, their duel, won by Muly Labas with Muly Hamet concluding the skit with an exasperated speech. In short, the two skits are very much of a piece, and Duffett's prologue may well be intended as an announcement of intention as well as an acknowledgment.

Two other features of Duffett's *Empress* deserve mention. Following the main skit ridiculing Settle's play, is the "Macbeth Epilogue," a series of songs with connecting recitativo which burlesques the witches' songs from the recent "operatic" version of Davenant's *Macbeth* in 1673. However, this burlesque "epilogue" also provides a pointed conclusion for Duffett's main skit attacking Settle's *Empress*. For the "Macbeth Epilogue" is actually a defense of the skit preceding it; at least, that is how Heccate's last remark (90–92), before the concluding songs, can be interpreted:

> He that wou'd damn this Farce does strive in vain
> This charm can never be o'ercome by man,
> 'Till Whetstones Park remove to Distaff Lane.

Here, "this Farce" can be referring to the preceding attack on Settle, and "This charm" to the "Macbeth Epilogue" itself insofar as it is supposed to be casting a protective spell over the main skit. Its purpose is to defend the main skit and to challenge the audience to see that the gaudy spectacles at Dorset Garden were really just as brainless, only more pretentious. Duffett's witches, who are represented as a bawd ("Mother Heccate") and her prostitutes, do more than debase Shakespeare, and do more than gossip about the actual bawds of London: they also act as guardian angels from Duffett's Newgate-pastoral world of pimp, punk and bawd, drayman, porter, and corn-cutter, who cast a protective spell around the skit ridiculing Settle. I believe this notion is supported by the general air of devil-may-care gaiety that pervades the coarse and vulgar carryings-on reflected in prologue, main-skit, and epilogue. They are all rooted in the same world of exuberant and impudent low-life.[16]

Finally, mention should be made of the frontispiece to Duffett's *Empress*, a striking detail designed to mock the six "sculptures," or engravings, included in the 1673 quarto of Settle's *Empress*. Representing various scenes, and causing the price of the quarto to rise to two shillings, the sculptures were included to give a spectacular impression.[17] Duffett's frontispiece was designed to ridicule this specific feature of the printed play, and the inclusion of it in the quarto indicates that Settle's sculptures probably had the desired effect. The "Aunt Jemima" aspect of Duffett's frontispiece has caused one commentator to suggest that all of the performers in Duffett's burlesque wore blackface.[18]

Duffett's *Empress*, then, for all its obvious crudity, is quite inventive. Rather than being a shapeless hodge-podge, I think it may be argued that it was arranged deliberately as a burlesque variety-package with frontispiece, prologue, main-skit, and epilogue working together as a unit. In this respect it is worth noting that Duffett's *Empress* differs from two other Restoration burlesque plays. John Wright's *Mock-Thyestes* was printed with a translation of Seneca's *Thyestes*,[19] and may have been intended as a reading entertainment since there is no evidence that it was ever performed. It is one-fourth as long as the original, and has the raucously base idiom that seems to be at the heart of travesty. Here (pp. 100–01), Megara threatens Tantalus:

> Well, since I can't this way prevail,
> I'le try now to perswade your *Tail*,
> Your *Toby* I'le so seaze with this
> Rod that has lain three weeks in piss,
> That you shall begg the thing to do . . .

---

[16] Mention should be made of a type of attack on Settle's *Empress*, quite different from Duffett's, which also appeared in 1674. This was Notes and Observations on *The Empress of Morocco*, usually attributed to Crowne, Shadwell, and Dryden. It is a lengthy refutation of Settle's play, sometimes proceeding line-by-line, emphasizing (sometimes in a rather hard-headed way) Settle's lack of grammatical and metaphorical consistency. Settle answered in kind with a pamphlet of his own, attacking *The Conquest of Granada*. Facsimile reprints of both pamphlets, as well as Settle's *Empress*, and Duffett's *Empress*, can be found in Maximillian E. Novak's *The Empress of Morocco and Its Critics* (Los Angeles, 1968).

[17] A good discussion of these engravings can be found in Novak, pp. xx–xxi.

[18] John Harold Wilson, *Mr. Goodman, the Player*, p. 30.

[19] *Thyestes A Tragedy, Translated out of Seneca. To which is Added Mock-Thyestes, in Burlesque* (London, 1674).

Introduction

Later (pp. 123–24), the Chorus reflects on the nature of destiny:

> O what a *Jilt* is *Gammer Fortune?*
> No Weather-cock is more uncertain.
> A Spinster of so rough a hand,
> That when her work seems at a stand,
> She gives her Wheel a whisk o' th' suddain,
> And stirs all round like Hasty Pudden.

While this is the same sound as Duffett's *Empress,* the *Mock-Thyestes* is more faithful to its original. This is also true of a later burlesque, Cibber's *The Rival Queans.*[20] For the most part Cibber tries to avoid using rhymes—in deference to his original. The debasement he achieves is evidenced in this passage modeled on the famous sequence in which Alexander quarrels with Clytus (p. 34):

> *Alex.* . . . O that thou wert Young again,
> That like a Mill-stone
> I might fall, souse upon thy Head;
> Grind thee to Dust, and dash thy Teeth out
> For this damn'd Lye, thou pitious Bastard.
>   [*Throws Drink in his Face.*]
>   *Clyt.* What's that for, Ha! what do you drench me
> Like a Pick-Pocket!
> I know the reason that you Use me so,
> Because I sav'd your Life at Billings-Gate;
> And when your Back was turn'd, ventur'd my Bones,
> Among a thousand Clubs and Prongs, you hate
> Me for't: you do proud Prigg.
>   *Alex.* Away, your Breath's too strong.
>   *Clyt.* You hate the Benefactor, tho' you took the Gift,
> Your Life, from this affronted *Clytus,*
> Which is the black and blue Ingratitude.

Finally, Alexander loses control, saying, "Give me a Mop-staff," and several lines later a stage-direction reads, *"Runs a Mop in's Face."* This is of the same order as the game of hot cockles at the beginning of Duffett's *Empress.* However, while similar in tone, Duffett's *Empress* differs from these burlesques by Wright and Cibber in that it occasionally departs from the bounds of its target-play. Although it is a slight difference, it is important, for it becomes a major factor in making Duffett's next two burlesques, *The Mock-Tempest* and *Psyche Debauch'd,* more independent comic creations rather than grotesque caricatures.

Why Duffett's burlesques do not remain wholly faithful to their originals can be reasonably conjectured. Travesty, if it is to remain pure, must stay with its original; the only variety it can admit and still remain "true" to the original is selectivity. The burlesques of Cotton, Wright, and Cibber could be called "pure"

---

[20] The Dublin quarto of 1729 has been reprinted in *Lake Erie College Studies,* 5 (Painesville, Ohio, 1965).

travesties. Davenant's *Mock-Pompey* includes some extraneous material; while Duffett's *Empress* gets downright erratic. The former three, however, refer to their originals and to them alone, and in this regard they maintain a strict and rather narrow focus. One certain danger in this kind of form is the possibility of its becoming tedious if maintained too long. Would one want, for example, a word-for-word, scene-by-scene travesty of a five-act play? It was to avoid this danger that Wright and Cibber utilized an economic principle of selection (Cotton tends to stay with his original). Duffett, however, in his *Empress,* and more so in his two later burlesques, adds actions and characters that are extensions of the original plays, and he also frequently adapts the basic material itself.

If Duffett's *Empress* is flimsy, yet clever, *The Mock-Tempest* gives an impression of much greater solidity. It is written predominantly in prose, which creates a more "realistic" tone than the splay-footed couplets of the *Empress,* which give a more deliberately wooden effect. Also, *The Mock-Tempest* is a full-length play, a highly detailed piece of work, often parodying its original scene-by-scene and line-by-line.

It should be emphasized, however, that the target *The Mock-Tempest* was aimed at was the extravagant and successful production of the operatic *Tempest* in 1674 and not, as some interpretations have suggested, at Shakespeare's *Tempest.* The fact is that the operatic *Tempest* is itself based on the Dryden-Davenant adaptation of Shakespeare's *Tempest.*

While the operatic *Tempest* retains a good deal of Shakespeare's play, it is based entirely on the Dryden-Davenant version. The most notable alterations Dryden and Davenant made are the absence of the Sebastian-Antonio conspiracy to kill Alonzo (Sebastian being dropped completely), and the addition of two characters, Dorinda, a sister to Miranda, and Hippolito, a ward to Prospero. The addition of these two characters gives the play an extra set of lovers which thickens the romantic plot by permitting some crisscrossing of affections.[21] There are several other changes, which are small when considered individually, but which add up to an impressive sum of difference.[22] The result is that, in spite of the retention of a good deal of Shakespeare's *Tempest,* the Dryden-Davenant version is a complete reworking of the original. The operatic *Tempest*

---

[21] In Shakespeare's *Tempest* 256 lines are given to the lovers; in the Dryden-Davenant version there are 1,227.

[22] Some of these changes and omissions are: the absence of Gonzalo's "ideal commonwealth" speech (II.i); the transposing of Caliban's conspiracy to undo Prospero into a struggle for dominance between the various low-comedy characters; the absence of Caliban's "This isle is full of noises" speech (III.ii); the absence of Ariel's lengthy speech (III.ii), "You are three men of sin," in which he reprimands the nobles for their crimes; the absence of Prospero's famous speech (IV.i), "Our revels now are ended"; and the absence of the masque (IV.i) involving Iris, Ceres, and Juno.

of 1674 [23] simply takes over the Dryden-Davenant version with only minor changes.[24]

Although Duffett parodies the operatic *Tempest* quite closely, he avoids some of the tedium that such a close parody risks by creating some memorable characterizations, which are a result of a willingness to add comic material that is extraneous to the burlesque purpose. The place in which to see these qualities admirably working together is the opening scene of *The Mock-Tempest*, which is the most inspired piece of sustained clowning in the whole play. Duffett changes the storm at sea into a raid on a bawdy house. The sailors become prostitutes, a pimp, and a bawd; the noblemen become the customers; and the instigators of the raid, Prospero and Ariel, are changed by Duffett into the keeper of Bridewell and his chief henchman.

The scene consists of the reactions inside the brothel to the onslaughts of the raiding party (set on by Ariel and Prospero) trying to get in. Duffett wryly adds lines like, "More noyse and terrour then a Tempest at Sea" (I.i.68), and, "They break in like a full Sea upon us" (I.i.225). Even more pointed are the parodies of last-ditch efforts to stave off disaster and "save the ship." These include the call to fill the "Sweating Tub" with stones and to set it against the door (I.i.33-35); to empty chamber-pots on the raiders' heads by bringing out all the "Jourdans full of Water" (44-45); to "go down to the Sellar Windows" to search for full chamber-pots (50); to urinate on the raiding party from the upstairs windows (57-58); and to shoot off corks from wine-bottles at the raiding party (92). These various calls to action refer to their counterparts in the operatic *Tempest*. The opening scene of *The Mock-Tempest*, as a whole, is full of boisterous energy, and is a far cry from the game of hot cockles at the beginning of Duffett's *Empress*. It is interesting in and for itself.[25]

The extensiveness and ingenuity of the parody in *The Mock-Tempest* is further enhanced by characterization. Mother Stephania dominates and unifies the first scene; [26] she is a real presence, quite unlike the cartoons from the *Empress* skit. Duffett manages to suggest in her portrait the quality of an aging-but-indefatigable bawd; and, at times, it is an engaging portrait. In particular, her unwillingness to give up the "ship," in the opening scene, makes her attractive; but more telling is her long speech (III.i.68-95), which is unique in the play. The speech occurs in the midst of a sequence in which two of her prostitutes, Beantosser and Moustrappa, are having difficulty accommodating

---

23 Recently edited by Christopher Spencer in *Five Restoration Adaptations of Shakespeare* (Urbana, 1965). All quotations from the operatic *Tempest* are taken from this edition.

24 For a brief summary of the scholarship, see Spencer, *Five Restoration Adaptations of Shakespeare*, pp. 18-20.

25 Act I, scene i, of *The Mock-Tempest*, has 241 lines; the operatic *Tempest* 103; and Shakespeare's 72.

26 In the operatic *Tempest*, Stephano is the "ship's master"; in Shakespeare's he is a "drunken Butler."

themselves to life in Bridewell. The girls begin to feel sorry for themselves, but Stephania breaks in with a long reminiscence of her past experiences, and concludes with a lusty song. The tone of the passage is that of the social realist. Stephania's account of the "close thriving Tradesman," for example, sounds like a sequence from Wycherley. As in the opening scene, this passage resonates a quality of satire that distinguishes it from the doggerel and caricature of the *Empress* skit, and helps sustain the whole play by giving it some depth and variety. It is too bad, in this respect, that Mother Stephania reappears only momentarily after Act III, scene i; she would have been an ideal person to pronounce the final benediction.

Not all the characterizations in *The Mock-Tempest* are as winning as Stephania's. The girl-and-boy scenes, and those with Prospero, maintain an amusingly coarse parallel with the original, but are rather flat in comparison. The sequences involving Gonzalo, Alonzo, and the "noblemen" are considerably redeemed by the use of song as burlesque. There is some notable close parody evidenced in several of the songs, particularly in, "Arise, Arise ye Subterranean Fiends," at the end of Act II. More interesting in terms of characterization, although not as fully realized as Stephania, is Duffett's treatment of Ferdinand, who is transmogrified into Quakero, a canting, hypocritical rogue. The explanation for this side-satire into contemporary religious extremism is probably that Duffett felt the need to give some added variety to the burlesque.[27]

Before turning to *Psyche Debauch'd,* one further consideration helps shed light on the way in which Duffett's *The Mock-Tempest* resembles a practical joke. The recent discovery of the pamphlet, *The Songs and Masques in the New Tempest,*[28] suggests the possibility that, just as there was a "mock-sculpture" included in the quarto of Duffett's *Empress* to ridicule Settle's six sculptures, there was a mock-libretto printed to accompany *The Mock-Tempest* and intended to ape a libretto printed for the operatic *Tempest.* The pamphlet reprints almost all of the song-material from *The Mock-Tempest.* This discovery was announced shortly after Professor J. G. McManaway identified a similar pamphlet entitled, *Songs and Masques in the Tempest,* as a libretto

---

[27] Montague Summers noted that the quarto of *The Mock-Tempest,* p. 50, line 17, and p. 51, line 1, both have as speech-prefixes, "Foran," and "Faran," respectively. Summers suggests that "In Duffett's first draft of his burlesque Quakero was probably called by some name that closely resembled Ferdinand . . . and when our author rechristened the character he, no doubt, forgot to alter the speech-prefix in these two instances" (*Shakespeare Adaptations* [London, 1922], pp. xii–xiv). An earlier name for Quakero that is close to "Ferdinand" may have been "Farendino," or "Farendine," after the cheap fabric. The word occurs in *The Mock-Tempest* twice (I.i.76, and III.i.52).

[28] Charles Haywood, "*The Songs and Masques in the New Tempest:* An Incident in the Battle of the Two Theatres, 1674," *HLQ* 19 (1955), 39–55. This is a discussion and reprint of the pamphlet.

based on the song-material in the operatic *Tempest*.[29] McManaway claims that the pamphlet "was prepared for the benefit of the audience, rather than the reading public," which leads him to refer to it as "perhaps the earliest English libretto." [30] Professor Charles Haywood came to a similar conclusion about *The Songs and Masques in the New Tempest:*

> The King's Company not only employed the talents of Thomas Duffett to burlesque and ridicule Shadwell's *Tempest*, but they also published a similar libretto, giving the texts of the songs in the play, and sold it no doubt at the entrance to the Theatre Royal in Drury Lane, as their rivals had been doing at Dorset Garden.[31]

This kind of evidence suggests an impish, pre-Scriblerus quality about Duffett's mock-projects: they are conceived in a spirit of foolery.

The strong points of *The Mock-Tempest* are present to a greater degree in *Psyche Debauch'd*, the longest, funniest, and most neglected of Duffett's burlesques. The central action which closely parallels Shadwell's *Psyche* is concerned with Mother Wossat's (Venus') effort to get the attractive None-so-fair (Psyche) out of circulation. Spurred on by None-so-fair's two jealous sisters, Sweetlips (Aglaura) and Woudhamore (Cydippe), Mother Wossat evolves a plan to undo Nonsy by having a phony fortune-telling device, a "Wishing-Chair" (Apollo's oracle), tell her that she must marry the "White Bear of Norwich" (the Serpent). The complication comes when Mother Wossat's man, Bruine (Cupid), who is to play the part of the bear, falls in love with None-so-fair. The climax and resolution follow in order. What is distinctive about this plot is that it is so arrestingly funny in and for itself, apart from the burlesque parallel with Shadwell's *Psyche*. *The Mock-Tempest* achieves this quality tellingly, but sporadically; *Psyche Debauch'd* attains it much more consistently. The only lapse I find is the curiously conventional masque at the end, which is given over to classical deities singing praises to the power of love. Duffett surely could have done better than this!

The liveliness that Duffett achieves can be seen in terms of characters and of language. There are at least a dozen characters who emerge clearly; they fall into small groupings that revolve around the central figure of None-so-fair. And while they have interest as absurd counterparts to the originals in Shadwell's *Psyche,* they have just as much interest in themselves. Toward the end of the play (V.i), for instance, when Bruine is pleading with Mother Wossat to have mercy on None-so-fair, Mother Wossat's retort to Bruine (350–52) points up the very real actions these characters have been involved in:

29 J. G. McManaway, "Songs and Masques in 'The Tempest' [ca. 1674]," in *Theatre Miscellany: Six Pieces Connected with the Seventeenth-Century Stage* (Oxford, 1953), pp. 69–96.
30 "Songs and Masques in 'The Tempest' [ca. 1674]," pp. 73, 71.
31 Haywood, p. 40.

Introduction

Woss. For her you did neglect my Trade,
And when to *Wishing-Chair* I call'd for aid,
You wheedl'd him to be your Bawd.

These lines emphasize that Wishing-Chair's allegiance has been a factor of some import, and they also remind the reader that Wishing-Chair (he is also called "Apollo") is a character as well as a device. He is the operator of a much sought-after titillating machine which also serves as a fortune-telling device. As a parallel to Apollo's oracle the wishing-chair idea was a stroke of obscene genius, but it is also pleasant to see how Duffett allows this comic touch to function in the plot. In *The Mock-Tempest,* for example, Duffett's Prospero and Ariel function mainly in their capacities as debased counterparts of the originals. Yet, we know that they are also the keeper of Bridewell, and his lackey, respectively. In this latter aspect, we don't come to know them very well.

Another memorable character in *Psyche Debauch'd,* Mother Redstreak, is an example of how Duffett was able to include material that was extraneous to his main plot, and do it with more artistry than he showed in the two earlier burlesques. There is no parallel character for Mother Redstreak in Shadwell's *Psyche.* There is a lengthy sequence, for example, in which she is discovered sitting in the wishing-chair (III.iii), a scene full of coarse innuendo, but which doesn't burlesque anything particular from Shadwell's play. However, she is made to fit very well into the plot of the play. In Act IV, for example, when princes Nick and Phil cut off Mother Redstreak's head—mistakenly thinking that she is the White Bear of Norwich—this *is* a parallel to the long sequence Shadwell included in Act IV of *Psyche* when his princes cut off the head of the serpent and lead a triumphal procession. It is at this point that Duffett is able to incorporate Mother Redstreak quite effectively into his plot. He has the princes decapitate her because they apparently assume from her relations with Wishing-Chair that she is also involved in the plot to undo None-so-fair. Their mistake causes Mother Wossat to be terribly upset, for it turns out that Mother Redstreak is one of her dearest crones. This is different from Duffett's burlesque of Ferdinand as the ranting Quakero in *The Mock-Tempest,* and also from the zany, but irrelevant, conclusion to his *Empress.*

Characterizations in *Psyche Debauch'd* are effective partly because the language employed is so expressive. An instance of this can be seen in Act I, when, after None-so-fair has commanded princes Nick and Phil "after me no more to sniff" (429), the two love-lorn suitors are suddenly confronted with None-so-fair's impetuously eager sisters. While this sequence parallels a similar one in Shadwell's *Psyche,* the most amusing part of it is Duffett's own addition (I.i.443–54):

> *Woud.* . . . Love us, Princes, here's your true beauty.
> *Phil.* There's your Anchovies.
> *Woud.* Here's a Cherubimical Face, mark how my Eyes roll.
> Here's a Languishing look, Ah!—
> *Phil.* Odzboars, my Stomach begins to wamble at her.
> *Woud.* Here's a foot like a Fairy, and a leg like a
> Lapwing.

> *Phil.* Look, Prince *Nick,* chil wager a Groat there's
> zomething at the end of thick leg,—there's your
> Anchovies.
> *Sweet.* Here's your white Hounds Tooth.
> *Woud.* Here's your Illustrious *Persian* Hawk-nose.
> *Sweet.* Here, here's your generous wide Nostrils,
> you may see my Brains work through 'em when I'm in
> passion.

The dialogue here clearly indicates an attempt on the part of the princesses to assume what is, to them, sophisticated postures and facial expressions. At this point, language is implying comic actions which stage-business and the performers' talents can seize on and express in terms of visual humor, but the kernel of amusement is in the text.

This expansion of burlesque material with respect to character and language is only one of varying degrees of parody employed by Duffett. The amount of verbal parody that Duffett included is astonishing, especially when one realizes that he could not be sure his audience would recognize particular passages, unlike Cotton, who could assume his readers' familiarity with the *Aeneid.* This suggests that Duffett may have had his readers in mind as well as the theatregoers. At times, passages are burlesqued in part, telescoped with others, or entirely neglected; close line-for-line parody, however, is often the most striking of the various types employed. In Act I, when None-so-fair urges Prince Nick to refrain from pursuing her, a sustained close parody begins. The parallel sequence in Shadwell's *Psyche* runs to over fifty lines, in which Prince Nicander and Psyche debate the question of just what constitutes the proper way to follow Nature's promptings. Duffett follows this long sequence almost line-for-line (I.i.356–403) by including ingenious substitutions throughout: "Butter," in Duffett's version, stands for sexual consent, and is the equivalent for "Nature" in the Shadwell passage; "Ciss," apparently a prudish milkmaid who refuses to yield, is the counterpart to the "Priest"; and "Dame" seems to be a substitute for "the Gods." Prince Nick's lyric cry at the end of the passage—"Butter, Oh sweet Butter; ease my hissing smart, / And Butter *None-so-fairs* unbutter'd heart"—is surely Duffett's most obscenely poignant moment.

The distance Duffett travels in his burlesques can be measured by comparing this "Butter" sequence and its original with the only two passages of sustained parody in the *Empress* skit: in the first scene (7–21) he burlesques the speech describing the onset of Muly Hamet (Settle's *Empress,* beginning of Act II); the second scene of Duffett's *Empress* opens with a parody of the speech by Hametalhaz (Settle.IV.ii). The foolery here seems quite pedestrian when compared with the "mock-reasoning-in-verse" of the "Butter duet."

The variety of parodic methods used in *Psyche Debauch'd* is unified and strengthened by Duffett's structuring of the plot on the extended debased sexual metaphor of a world of blustering prostitutes, bawds, and pimps. While the over-all effect, ultimately, is interest in this "world" in and for itself, it is important to realize that this very interest itself springs from the sense of satiric judgment against the inflated world embodied in Shadwell's opera.

This judgment is literally suggested in Act V when None-so-fair is put on trial. This sequence cleverly exploits the parallel section in Shadwell's version in which Pluto and Proserpine allow Psyche to go free. Duffett (V.i) makes this into an elaborate trial scene in a prison, in which the princes, princesses, and None-so-fair are tried by a draggle-tailed court. Tagrag, spokesman for the court, delivers sentence upon None-so-fair (210–14):

> . . . *Psyche* the 2d. also Miss *Nonsy* shall be freed,
> because her Predecessor *Psyche* the first was, though
> both (for running from their Fathers; and practising
> publickly what their Sisters did but wish well to)
> deserve more punishment than they.

Besides the obvious level of reference to sexual delinquency, the sense here is also that plays like *Psyche* exploit certain obvious advantages, "practising publickly what their Sisters [i.e., the wicked sisters, but also in the sense of "other plays"] did but wish well to"—these practices being gaudy ostentation in general, and more particularly, the extra-literary trappings that surrounded the operatic production. If *Psyche Debauch'd* ridicules a specific target, it is the pretentiousness of *Psyche*.

However, Duffett does more than create a debased world that ridicules the pretentiousness of the originals. The most impressive comic effect that emerges in his burlesques is the creation of a world that gradually rivals the world of the originals, and threatens to supplant it. For the Duffettian world, albeit debased, has the effect of being more real in comparison with the inflated world of heroic play, operatic romance, and pastoral opera. This sense of comic triumph can be partly explained by Duffett's addition of characters like Mothers Stephania and Redstreak, who call more attention to themselves than to any parallel with the original plays. Similarly, Duffett's principle of selection of passages to burlesque, and his treatment of them, at times help to reinforce the image of a fallen world while only lightly glancing at the originals. In Act V of *Psyche Debauch'd*, Duffett really does nothing with Pluto and Proserpine; instead, he includes a prison scene which is quite believable in itself, but which only roughly parallels its original.

One may well ask how deliberate all this is. Duffett must have known that his burlesques were undergoing a substantial change of emphasis. Perhaps the best answer lies in the limitations of travesty. In a sense, the only direction in which it can grow is up. And if Duffett was encouraged to write something more elaborate after his *Empress* appeared, he may well have been consciously trying to widen his comic focus when he came to write the two later burlesques. The quality that emerges when Duffett's low-life characters come to life may well be described as a precursor of the "Newgate-pastoral": the use of characters from the dregs of society for a variety of satiric purposes, but who have a distinctive and vital life of their own. In making note of the fact that *The Mock-Tempest* concludes with a musical sequence that deals with the freeing of prisoners, Edward J. Dent commented, "Possibly Gay had some knowledge of Duffett's works when he wrote *The Beggar's Opera*." [32] Aside from this interesting possibility, the important fact about Duffett's burlesques is the way in which they move from narrow travesty into a wider range of low comedy.

This kind of genre-hopping, if such it be, is particularly endemic to low comedy. A play which resembles Duffett's burlesques in this regard is Fielding's *The Covent-Garden Tragedy* (1732). The subject matter consists of the same boisterous world of pimp, bawd, and doxie; and the language, although sometimes "mock-heroic" in style, is frequently as low as the characters themselves. In particular, Fielding's Mother Punchbowl, and Duffett's Mothers Stephania and Redstreak, not only share a common calling, but also speak similar sentiments in a similar idiom. Where Fielding goes farther than Duffett, however, is in completely eschewing any close parallel with his ostensible target, Ambrose Philips's *The Distrest Mother* (Fielding's preface, which is apparently ironic, claims that Philips's play is being attacked). As the bickering and brawling between Mother Punchbowl, Bilkum, Lovegirlo, Stormandra, and Brickdusta ensues, there is no immediate way of knowing which characters or actions in Philips's play are being ridiculed. In Duffett's burlesques, the originals are followed much more closely. Fielding resembles Duffett very strongly, however, with respect to the kinds of names he gives his characters. They tend to resemble Mother Stephania, Hectorio, Beantosser, and Moustrappa, the only characters in *The Mock-Tempest* (with the exception of Quakero) to whom Duffett gives names not synonymous with the originals. In *Psyche Debauch'd*, of course, Duffett rechristened the entire cast. This kind of alteration shifts the emphasis away from the target-play. In spite of differences, Fielding's *The Covent-Garden Tragedy* shows the same interest in rough-and-tumble low-life characters that distinguishes Duffett's three burlesques.

The sense of transformation into something rich and strange, from travesty towards Newgate pastoral, that emerges from Duffett's burlesques results in great measure from the thoroughgoing spirit of gaiety in which they were conceived.[33] Duffett was apparently amused enough with his material, and aware of the narrowness of travesty, to let it grow beyond the limits prescribed by his original intention. In this regard, two comparisons outside the area of burlesque drama come to mind. Gay's *The Shepherd's Week* comically alludes to pastoral tradition in general and in particular to Philips's "rustic" pastorals.

---

[32] *Foundations of English Opera* (Cambridge, 1928; reprint ed., New York, 1965), p. 146n. The prison sequence at the end of *Psyche Debauch'd* also supports Dent's contention. The possibility of a link between Duffett and Gay is also mentioned by E. M. Gagey in *Ballad Opera* (New York, 1937), p. 19.

[33] Cf. Clinton-Baddeley's comment that they were "founded in high spirits" (*The Burlesque Tradition in the English Theatre After 1660*, p. 42), and Montague Summers's reference to their "rollicking vitality" (*Shakespeare Adaptations*, p. lxx).

However, *The Shepherd's Week* can be read with enjoyment aside from these burlesque intentions, for Gay's bumpkins have a clumsy charm that makes them more real, and therefore more interesting, than many of the characters in serious pastorals. As with Duffett, Gay *uses* his mock-characters for more than mere debasement of burlesque targets. At a much more self-conscious level, Fielding moved from *Shamela* (which could be called a travesty in prose) to the world of *Joseph Andrews,* which uses the "Pamela" material as a point of departure. Again, the point is the use made of the burlesque material. Certainly, the lasting impression given by Duffett's burlesques is their movement toward a broadening and deepening of comic significance.

It is probably the combination of the opprobrium attached to travesty, and Duffett's lack of stature, that has caused him to be disparaged for nearly three centuries. This has earned him the reputation of a "vulgar beast," [34] with a "personal ill-nature," [35] whose "productions are beneath criticism." [36] Reacting to the "Macbeth Epilogue" and *The Mock-Tempest,* one writer commented, "Duffett . . . exercised his talent for throwing dirt at Shakespeare." [37] A hint that times were changing came when, a year later, Edward J. Dent pointed out that *The Mock-Tempest* was primarily directed at its operatic target [38] and, in general, spoke kindly of Duffett. Montague Summers's estimate of Duffett is notable for the dramatic change it underwent. In 1914, Summers wrote of Duffett with the massive condescension that was becoming customary.[39] However, eight years later, Summers's view had completely changed:

In some sense we may say that only the dry bones of his travesties remain. And yet, even for those who have no very specialized acquaintance with Settle's tragedy and Shadwell's opera, enough is left to vindicate for these burlesques more serious consideration and more particular mention than they have hitherto received.[40]

Following Summers, writers like Dent and Clinton-Baddeley have found Duffett's

---

34 Joseph Furnivall, ed., *New Shakespeare Society Papers,* Fourth Series (London, 1886), p. 242.

35 *Biographia Dramatica,* 3 vols., ed. David Erskine Baker, Isaac Reed, and Stephen Jones (London, 1812), 1:211. *Psyche Debauch'd* is described as "nothing but a mass of low scurrility and abuse, without either wit or humour; and (which) soon met with the contempt it merited" (3:186). Yet, in connection with Duffett, Cotton's *Scarronides* is granted the accolade of "great genius" (1:211)!

36 *Dictionary of National Biography,* 16:132.

37 Hazleton Spencer, *Shakespeare Improved* (Cambridge, Mass., 1927), p. 95.

38 *Foundations of English Opera,* p. 146. One might add that Montague Summers's inclusion of *The Mock-Tempest* in a volume entitled, *Shakespeare Adaptations,* was a bit awkward, in spite of Summers's accurate discussion of the play's intention and his general enthusiasm for Duffett.

39 George Villiers, Duke of Buckingham, *The Rehearsal,* ed. Montague Summers (Stratford-upon-Avon, 1914), pp. xx–xxi.

40 *Shakespeare Adaptations,* p. lxx. Clinton-Baddeley noted Summers's shift in attitude (*The Burlesque Tradition in the English Theatre After 1660,* p. 40n).

burlesques to be intelligible (assuming some familiarity with the originals) and to have genuine interest.[41]

Duffett deserves a better hearing than he has had. His burlesques are consistently lively and inventive. At their best, they present an ever-expanding metaphor of a low-life world that celebrates its own coarseness and vulgarity, and in doing so, puts down the inflated world of the original plays by supplanting it. *The Mock-Tempest* and *Psyche Debauch'd* suggest both the Newgate pastoral world of Gay's *The Beggar's Opera* and the hardened gaiety of Burns's *The Jolly Beggars*. Duffett's burlesques are amusing in themselves, show how the genre of travesty develops, and give evidence of variety in the Restoration theatre.

For assistance in putting together this edition I wish to thank Professor Carl H. Klaus, who offered many helpful suggestions concerning Duffett's particular contribution to low burlesque. I am grateful also to Professor O M Brack, Jr., who "initiated me into the mysteries of fallen print," and who is responsible for the effort to decipher the meaning of the press-variants in *The Mock-Tempest*. For advice concerning the annotations, and for friendly encouragement through the years, I wish to thank Professor Curt A. Zimansky. I owe a hearty thanks to all of the above for reading the manuscript in various stages of its preparation. To these friends and former mentors from The University of Iowa, I am delighted to express thanks; but there is one other, to whom I wish to make a belated acknowledgment: my thanks to Professor Charles B. Woods, who inspired me to take on such a project, and helped me to formulate its initial scope and design, but who did not live to see its completion. And finally, I would like to thank my wife, Bernadette DiLorenzo, for constant help and encouragement through the years.

---

[41] Dent, pp. 144, 146; Clinton-Baddeley, p. 42.

A Note on the Texts

The copy-text used for each play is the Yale copy. No substantive change is made silently. Punctuation is altered when a reader familiar with seventeenth-century practice would be misled; and to bring it in line with modern form in printing. Emendations are recorded in the Textual Notes, but are also recorded in the Annotations when discussion of them is needed. Each of the burlesques went through only one edition; therefore editorial problems are minimal. In the case of *The Mock-Tempest,* where there are some notable differences within various copies of the quarto, such differences are recorded and discussed. Misspellings are recorded when they are unusual (*The Mock-Tempest.*IV.iii: 18 friends] fiends). Characters' names are not regularized within the text.

A number of changes are made silently. Long "s" and "VV" are modernized throughout. Display capitals, ornamental initials, factotums and ornaments are not retained; similarly, capital letters which customarily follow display or ornamental letters are silently reduced to lower case. Faulty italicization, obvious misspellings, and turned letters are silently corrected. The first letter of a word that begins a line of verse is capitalized silently; question marks at the end of obvious questions are added silently. Characters' names are spelled out in the stage-directions. In addition, stage-directions that occur after a speech-prefix have been put in brackets and italicized, as have stage-directions which occur in the middle of a speech without any break in lineation. Act and scene designations are corrected when in error. When scene designations are added, they are put in brackets. Line-numberings for text have been added. Act and scene designations are added in the running heads of each text page. When stage-directions are referred to, the letters "SD" are used either before or after the relevant text line-number. Thus, "182SD" refers to the stage-direction following line 182. The corrections in the Errata List for *The Mock-Tempest* have been silently incorporated into the text.

Information concerning the appearance and performance of each play is given in a note preceding the text of each play. The Textual Notes consist of: a signature collation; a finding list of extant copies; a table of press variants (this for *The Mock-Tempest* only) ; a list of substantive variants, widely divergent readings resulting from differences within the quarto, or any substantial change of my own (few of the latter); and a list of accidental variants, lesser changes, mainly of punctuation added or removed. In the case of *The Empress of Morocco* all changes are discussed in the note preceding the text, since they are so few.

The Empress of Morocco

The Performance

Information concerning the production of Duffett's *The Empress of Morocco* remains somewhat hypothetical. *The London Stage* (I, p. 212) comments:

It is difficult to assign a date to this burlesque, but it is obviously a satiric thrust at Elkanah Settle's *The Empress of Morocco,* which had been acted on 3 July 1673, and on *Macbeth,* which had been most recently acted (probably) on 9 August 1673. As the title page of Duffett's burlesque does not name a theatre, it is not known whether it was acted before the King's Company left Lincoln's Inn Fields for the new theatre in Drury Lane. But the fact that Settle's *Empress of Morocco* was acted again at Dorset Garden on 6 Dec. 1673 makes December 1673 a likely month for the King's Company to play its burlesque, although it may have been given in the late summer or early autumn, as many lesser actors are in the cast.

Duffett's *Empress* might well have been successful, for he was called upon to perform the same service with regard to two subsequent spectacular productions at Dorset Garden. Furthermore, the two later burlesques, *The Mock-Tempest* and *Psyche Debauch'd,* are full length productions. Perhaps Duffett's *Empress* made enough of a splash to make Duffett's wit in demand for a short while.

The Text

There was only one edition of Duffett's *The Empress of Morocco.* Its publication was noted in the *Term Catalogues* for 26 May 1674, Easter Term (I.170). I have examined copies of the quarto at the Newberry Library (ICN); Butler Library, Columbia University (NNC); Folger Library (DFo); Princeton University Library (NJP); Houghton Library, Harvard University (MH); Library of Congress (DLC); and Beinecke Library, Yale University (CtY). The copies at Yale and the Library of Congress lack the frontispiece. In the Newberry copy leaf B2 is reversed, with the verso, "Actors Names. Women.," coming first. I have made only two changes worthy of notation. In scene ii, line 236, I have given as speech-prefix, *"Muly Lab.,"* instead of the quarto's *"Muly Ham."* The previous speech is Muly Hamet's, and the context clearly justifies the change. Second, in the final Epilogue, line 34, I have added a comma after "cloy'd." Montague Summers twice refers to his edition of Duffett's *The Empress of*

Morocco,[1] but I have been unable to locate such an edition, or any information concerning it. Perhaps this was a case of a project announced as completed which was in fact only intended. Duffett's *Empress* was included as part of Anne Therese Doyle's doctoral thesis, "The Empress of Morocco: A Critical Edition of the Play and the Controversy Surrounding It." [2] Miss Doyle says (of her reprint of Duffett's *Empress*), "The text presented here is simply a copy of that at Harvard University."

The edition of Settle's *The Empress of Morocco* that is currently the most accessible is Bonamy Dobrée's *Five Heroic Plays* (London, 1960), which includes a reprint of the 1673 quarto; Davenant's *Macbeth* has been recently edited by Christopher Spencer in *Five Restoration Adaptations of Shakespeare* (Urbana, 1965), which is the edition utilized in the annotations. Also, facsimile reprints of Settle's *Empress,* Duffett's burlesque, Crowne, Shadwell, and Dryden's *Notes and Observations on the Empress of Morocco,* and Settle's reply to the latter, *Notes and Observations on the Empress of Morocco Revis'd* can be found in Maximillian E. Novak's *The Empress of Morocco and its Critics* (Los Angeles, 1968).

---

[1] See his *A Bibliography of the Restoration Drama* (London, n.d.), p. 15; and *The Restoration Theatre* (London, 1934), p. 93.

[2] University of Illinois, 1963.

THE
EMPRESS
OF
MOROCCO.

A Farce.

ACTED
By His MAJESTIES Servants.

LONDON,
Printed for *Simon Neal*, at the Sign of
the three Pidgeons in *Bedford-street*
in *Covent-Garden*. 1674.

William Harris(?), the actor, represented as Morena, in the burlesque The Empress of Morocco. *From the copy in the Butler Library, Columbia University.*

PROLOGUE.

As when some dogrel-monger raises
Up Muse, to flatter Doxies praises,
He talks of Gems and Paradises,
Perfumes and Arabian *Spices:*
Making up Phantastick Posies   5
Of Eye-lids, Fore-heads, Cheeks and Noses,
Calling them Lillies, Pinks and Roses.
Teeth Orient Pearl, and Coral Lips are,
Neck's Alabaster and Marble Hips are;
Prating of Diamonds, Saphyrs, Rubies,   10
What a Pudder's with these Boobies?
Dim Eyes are Stars, and Red hairs Guinnies:
And thus described by these Ninnies,
As they sit scribling on Ale-Benches,
Are homely-dowdy Country Wenches.   15
So when this Plot quite purg'd of Ale is,
In naked truth but a plain Tale is;
And in such dress we mean to shew it,
In spight of our damn'd Fustian Poet,
Who has disguis'd it with dull Histr'i's,   20
Worse than his Brethren e're did Mistress.

THE

SCENE OPENS.

Morena *the Apple-woman Empress of* Morocco *discovered*
sleeping.

Thunder and Lightning.

The Ghost of *Labas* the Corn-cutter ascends and does
not sing (lest it should be thought that the rare
Fancy, was stolen from that singing Ghost of
Pompey) but speaks.

The Empress of Morocco

From Tuttle Fields full speed I came
To tell you all y'are much to blame.
Great P——y's injur'd Ghost I am.

Sister Morocco *pine no more,*   25
Behold the man they lov'd before,
Though slighted now like common Whore.

When to Elyzium *they shall come*
Where all submit to Poets doom,
Wee'l be reveng'd on all and some.   30

Hectors shall take their Oaths away,
Poets their Wit they steal from Play,
Wenches their Claps—then what are they?

When thus the swelling thing's brought low,
How will poor naked Critick show;   35
Think Ladies, for you best do know.

As dull and cold you'l find his zeal,
As heart of Mob *that home does steal,*
Forc'd to leave Cloaths in pawn for Ale.

Then hungry Jilt that rails at Play,   40
'Cause Cully will not bite to day,
And's eager grown for want of prey,

Shall still in sight have Jolly Robin,
But all her tricks shan't make him bob in.

When passion's up, t' allay the flame o' t,   45
Wee'l tickle her to death with straw moat.

But I must go—

When Pullen swell and rustle so,
And Critick Cock prepares to Crow,
All Ghosts but his unwelcome grow.   50

The Ghost descends.

Morena the Apple-woman wakes and speaks.

Is not my P——y here? then sure hee's gone,
How long his speech was and how soon 'twas done!

ACTORS NAMES.

Men.

Muly Labas *a Corn-cutter, Empe-*
    rour of Morocco.   }   *Mr.* Coysh.

Muly Hamet *a Dray-man, and Ge-*
    neral of the Emperours Armies.   }   *Mr.* Kew.

Crimalhaz *a Strong-water-man,*
    and Gallant to Queen-Mother.   }   *Mr.* Watson.

Hamet Alhaz *a Country Vicar,*
    and Friend to Crimalhaz *the*
    Strong-water-man.   }   *Mr.* Powel.

Abdrahaman *a Chimney-sweeper,*
    and Rival to Muly Hamet *the*
    Dray-man.   }   *Mr.* Bird.

Abdelcador *a Porter and Em-*
    bassador from Taffalet *to* Muly
    Hamet *the Dray-man.*   }   *Mr.* Carlton.

Messenger, *a Coffee-man.*   *Mr.* Kempton.

Eunuch, *a Tapster.*   *Mr.* Venner.

Women.

Laula *an Hostess, Queen-Mother.*   *Mr.* Griffin.

Mariamne *a Scinder Wench,*
    Daughter of the Empress,
    and Mrs. of Prince Muly
    Hamet *the Dray-man.*   }   *Mr.* Goodman.

The Empress of Morocco

Morena *an Apple-woman, young Empress and Daughter of* Taffalet.   Mr. Harris.

Bum-bailyes, Morris-dancers, Tapsters, Gypsies, Tinkers, and other Attendants.

THE

EMPRESS

OF

MOROCCO.

A FARCE.

SCENE OPENS

and discovers the Court at

HOT-COCKLES.

Muly Labas *the Corn-cutter being taken, and about to lay
down his Head in* Morena *the Apple-womans Lap.*

Muly La.   *Oh Morena* I am took napping
          And must lay my head thy blew Lap in,
          And my poor fist upon my Rump lay
That ev'ry one of these there thump may.
          Morena. Is my Lap then such ill abiding   5
That you should need make all this chiding?

Enter Hamet Alhaz *the Country Vicar, and speaks to* Muly Labas
          the Corn-cutter.

          Ham. Al. Great Sir, your Hector *Hamet*'s coming:
From Car-men and stout Butchers thrumming
At the Bear-garden, he is crossing
From Bank-side on billows tossing: 10
River bright does change complexion
With his tatter'd Flags reflexion:
Boat does move as man does pull her,
In greater State you ne're saw Sculler:
Drum does rattle and Boys do bellow   15
Hamet up, for a pretty Fellow.

He all the way Tobacco puffing,
And in the smoak your praises huffing:
As School Boys use with little trouble
From Walnut-shell to blow up bubble;   20
Or as Nurse pleases Child in Cradle
With the dim smoak of an old Ladle.

    Muly Lab. This matter that you are relating
Does not merit half this prating.

Lays his Head down again in Morena's *Lap.*

    Q. Moth. Come about the business roundly   25
And be sure you strike him soundly.

As Crimalhaz *the Strong-water-man strikes with his Slipper,*
    Muly Hamet *the Dray-man Enters.*

    Morena. Who was that?

        He rises up and looks about him.

    Muly Lab. It was some Brangler
That struck with Slipper, like a Wrangler:
By *Jove* if I knew who's the author   30
I in his porridg wou'd pour Water.
    Ham. Alhaz. **Labas** though you be in such dudgeon
Yet you must swallow me this Gudgeon.
These are new Shoes, as I was saying
I came just now from *Cudgel* playing   35
Where from all the mad rout I won them,
So you may take them there, and don them.

        Throws the Shoes.

    Q. Moth. Think'st thou with Shoes to beg thy pardon,
Those Shoes with which thou layd'st so hard on?

    Ham. Alhaz.—Who I?

    Q. Moth.—I thou.

    Ham. Alhaz.—O errant Lyer!   40

Q. Moth. Stand all away, let me come nigher
That I may scratch his copper Nose off.

Ham. Alhaz. Peace Beldame, or I'le shake your Shoes off.

Muly Lab. Good Mother peace, you make a squabble
In very truth abominable,   45
And with your bawling put the Youth out,
So I shall never find the truth out.

Ham. Alhaz. Sir I came in but very newly,
Old Mother Bunch does not say truly.

Muly Lab. Peace sawse-box, know it is Queen Mother.   50

Ham. Alhaz. 'Twas *Crimalhaz* made all this pother.

Crimalhaz. It was not I, no in good sooth Sir.

Morena. He tells you not one word of truth Sir;
When Bum was turn'd up I did watch it,
And I do say, 'twas *Crimalhatchet.*   55

Q. Moth. But you may spare him tho' *Morena*
You know well enough what I mean a.

Morena. Fye, Fye, Fustilugs, be not yellow
For he is but a dungy Fellow.

Q. Moth. Marry come up, my durty Cozen,   60
He may have such as you by th' Dozen,
And therefore make not such a bustle
For you are but an errant pussle.

Morena. Mother *Shipton* been't so testy,
You may perhaps find me as resty;   65
My *Labas* struck by *Muly Hamet!*
You may all be asham'd to name it.

Q. Moth. *Eunuch* tell truth, for you stood by it;
Since they so shamefully deny it.

Eunuch. Tut all this scolding is but Non-sence,   70
'Twas *Crimalhaz* upon my conscience.

Q. Moth. Out from my sight thou base mishapen
Ugly Dastard, Craven, Capon.

Abdra. How *Crimalhaz!* upon my credit
'Twas *Muly Hamet* there that did it.   75

Crimalhaz. Now, I will haste me to our Village
And there look after Sheep and Tillage.   (aside)

Crimalhaz *the Strong-water-man steals off.*

Muly Lab. Is *Crimalhaz* so good at sneaking
To steal away thus without speaking?

[*Turns to* Muly Hamet *the Dray-man.*]

Hamet since thou hast caus'd this brabble   80
Converse hereafter with the rabble:
From Court and City I thee banish
Presto be gone, why dost not vanish?

Muly Ham. In troth Sir I am verry sorry
So soon to quit your territory;   85
Tho' in it I must make no figure,
With all my heart I wish it bigger.

Muly Lab.—How bigger!

Muly Ham.—Yes indeed and longer.

Muly Lab. I find my Choler waxing stronger.

Mariam. Labas were you ten times my Brother,   90
My love I can no longer smother;
Your anger now grows too unruly,
For my part I'le go with my *Muly.*

Muly Lab. Mariamne I don't think it proper
That you so soon shou'd turn Hedg-hopper;   95
But since you are in such a taking,
As you do brew you may be baking.

[*Exeunt* Muly Hamet *and* Mariamne.]

Q. Moth. Oh Son you have now quite undone us
If *Crimalhaz* does thus outrun us,
For we the Parson must be feasting   100
And with him there will be no jesting,
He'll be so cross, who can abide him
If we a Sheeps-head don't provide him?
He's such an errant Mutton-monger:
Wherefore let us stay here no longer,   105
But after *Crimalhaz* be creeping:
Who has got all the Sheep in's keeping:
And when we are all there together,
Be sure with him you make fair weather.

Muly Lab. But *Laula* you who are his doxie   110
Had best bespeak him by your proxie;
For he'l be vapouring and bragging
If I go after him a begging.

Q. Moth. No *Labas,* there you are mistaken,
We shall have Coleworts, Beans and Bacon,   115
Fat Mutton boil'd and Chestnuts roasted,
Parcht Pease, Potatoes, and Cheese toasted:
And fully to end all the quarrel,
Of humming Ale a lusty barrel.

Muly Lab. If this be more than meerly Cogging,   120
Let's talk no more but straight be jogging.

Q. Moth. 'Tis very true, you need not doubt it.

Muly Lab. Then Come away, let's go about it.

Exeunt omnes.

Scene the second.

Enter Hamet Alhaz *the Country Vicar.*

Ham. Alhaz. Sweet Gentiles all, I am that Parson
       They lay the fault of all this Farce on,
       And thus most basely do belye me
Having no Friend here to stand by me,
Saying this Journey they were put on   5
Only to feast my Chops with Mutton.

Although the scandal on our Coat lies,
Who ever says it in his throat lyes;
As though I'de keep a Jewish pascal.
But I may thank *Hamet* that Rascal,   10
For he, and that same Jackadandy
Emperour, came here for Ale and Brandy;
Laula, Morena, and t'other Gipsy
Came hither only to be tipsy:
And when spent *Crimalhaz* his store is   15
They will come out, and dance the *Moris:*
And I myself the Hobby-horse am;
Thus treated I without remorse am.

Enter a Messenger, *viz. the Coffee-man.*

   Messen. Hamet they have drunk all the fuddle
And straight will come here on a huddle.   20

   Ham. Alhaz. Then till they come I'le tell a story,
The strangest too, e're came before ye.
To day as I the wheat-Field stood in
The sky was alter'd on a suddain,
And look'd as thick as hasty pudding: 25
For lo, behold the Aiery Region
Had water in't to drown a Legion
Of Flies, had they been buzzing in it,
If you will credit one has seen it:
Then presently our goodly Sun shine,   30
Was grown almost as dusk as Moon shine;
And which did more encrease our wonder,
It did both lighten, rain, and thunder;
And wet to the skin poor I, and *Hamet,*
But now it is too late to blame it: 35
Quoth I, let's find some place to sleep in,
This is no weather to keep Sheep in.
See what it is to be no Scholler,
This made the Woodcock grow in choller,
And at the gods to huff and spatter,   40
Swearing they were all drunk with water;
When I that stood just behind him,
Besought their worships not to mind him:
Parson quoth he I'me not so silly,   } *[changes his place*
Though you do strut in *Piccadilly* } *and voice.]*   45
And are a greater cheat than—   }

E're to be frighted with your canting,
More than you are at all my ranting:
Then he began to stare and goggle
Like skittish Jade about to boggle.   50
Then straight cry'd I, *Hamet* I'le leave ye,
Still praise the Gods though they deceive ye:
Yet I no Parson with starch't face am,
But in good sooth *Hamet Alhaz* am.

The Scene opens.

A Table furnished with Brandy, Ale, and Tobacco-pipes. Enter King,
Queen, &c. with Attendants; their Trains supported by Porters and
Gypsies; a Heathen dance is presented by Tinkers and Jack-
puddings, who bring in an artificial broad spreading broom about
which they dance to Drum-stick and Kettle, Tongs and Key, Morish,
Timbrel and Salt-box, &c. In the Intervalls of the Dance, this
Song is sung by the Court, and the Chorus excellently perform'd
by all the voices and instruments.

SONG.

Stanza I.

Your North-down Ale is muddy,   55
French Wine quite spoils your studdy,
'Twill make your Brains so addle,
As any jog i' th' Cradle.
        'Twill make your &c. Chorus.

Stanza II.

All strong Beer makes you duller,   60
Than Porter, Groom, or Sculler:
Excess of Sack does dull some,
And Chocolate is fulsome,
And Coffee now does gull some.
        Excess of Sack, &c. Chorus.   65

Stanza III.

It elevates the Reason,
No higher than damn'd Treason;
Which makes the Saints to love it,

And all new lights approve it.
Which makes the &c. Chorus.   70

Stanza IV.

Brumsick *Mum's meer puddle,*
And Rhenish Wine base fuddle,
But Brandy is the Liquor,
Makes all your veins flow quicker:
Brandy the best of Nectars,   )
Makes us bolder than Hectors,   }   75
Fearing no Ghosts nor Specters.   )
Brandy the best &c. Chorus.

After they have Danced a while, Muly Labas *the Corn-cutter*
falls down, being dead drunk.

Morena. Woe and alas, help, help some Brandy;
Oh help me some body that's handy.   80

Q. Moth. Pernicious Woman tho hast kill'd him,
And with base tipple over fill'd him.

Morena. Mother it makes me more astonisht
To be by you now thus admonisht.
Did you not cry, Ply him with liquor,   85
Yawling out fill, fill, Daughter quicker?

Q. Moth. Was I of drink so very craving?
I pitty her, this is meer raving,
She rages worse than huffing Players;
Go try if you can say your Prayers.   90

Morena. I'le wing'd by love for you be groping.
Nor can I miss where you lie moping.

Turning to Muly Labas.

Crimalhaz. What's the cause of all this rumble?
What was it ho, did make him tumble?

Morena. You need not ask me what he aileth,   95
Do not you see his memory faileth?
Then thus in short, the all and sum is

My poor *Labas,* so drunk, as drum is:
Though he thus sweetly seems to slumber,
His Breeches are bedight with scumber: 100
Oh drunken Sister, Maudlin Mother,
Thus to disguise your Son and Brother.

Muly Labas *wakes and speaks.*

    Muly Lab. When Gods are in Olympus fluster'd,
And for a while half hufft and bluster'd:
Breeches for Petticoats they're chopping   105
In Masquerade to come hedg-hopping
Amongst us here to bellow.
Jove in disguise has been a Sculker
On Earth, to find him out a Bulker;
You know he once came down a trulling,   110
The shape of beastly great Town Bull in;
And so in twenty other dresses,
In Villages to find out Misses;
Which shews no Game i' th' upper Region,   ⎱
Can be compar'd to the sweet Pidgeon,   ⎰ *chucks* Morena *the Apple-*   115
Who e're disputes this is a widgeon.   *Woman under the chin.*

Lies down and sleeps again.

Crimalhaz *the Strong-water-man addresses himself to* Morena
the Apple-woman.

    Crimalhaz. Sweet blouz you make us all look sadly,
To see you still take on thus madly;
But shou'd you blubber till to morrow,
There's no drink left to ease your sorrow.   120

    Morena. Oh *Crimalhatchet,* you are cruel
To use him thus, loves you but too well.

    Crimalhaz. Fresh as the Honey-suckles flower,
Say wilt thou be my Paramour.

    Morena. Stand off, bold impudent Invador,   125
Thinkst thou I am of Copper made, or
Brass, that I my *Labas* shou'd wrong thus,
Now he but sleeps Dog-sleep among us.

– 19 –

Crimalhaz puts by her hood.

Crimalhaz. Just so the blushing Morn appeareth,
When from behind black Cloud it leareth: 130
So falling rain doth look on Cherries,
When baskets full come here in Wherries,
Thus Orange looks new rub'd with piss-clout,
Or scullions face besmear'd with Dish-clout;
Such looks the Welkin puts on even   135
When Cuckolds are going to Heaven.

Morena. Though on my shoulders you are leaning,
Yet I don't understand your meaning.

Crimalhaz. So when *Aurora*'s Dew doth scatter,
Rose-buds do smile quite through her water;   140
And whilst your Roses are distilling
Of their sweet Liquor, I'le be swilling.

> Crimalhaz *the Strong-water-man, offers to kiss* Morena *the
> Apple-woman, and bites her Pendents which are two Pears.*

Morena. Fie, get you gon you nasty swabber,
For I do hate your ugly slabber.

Crimalhaz. I gave ye wherewithal to paint ye,   145
Therefore you need not be so dainty.

> *flings away and comes again.*

Against all these I'le fight your battle,
And give each of them a sound rattle;
One Brandy bottle is behind yet
And hid, where none but I can find it.   150
    Morena. Indeed?

Crimalhaz. And you shall have your share on't,
Before your company is 'ware on't;
Come tell me now, will you not love me?

Morena. I'le do in that as shall behove me.   155

Crimalhaz. Then stay not here, but let's together.

Morena. I will do both—I can do neither.
Revenge says go, honor does no say,
Truly I do not know what to say.   [*whispers.*]

> Laula *the Hostess strikes at* Crimalhaz *the Strong-water-man,*
>   *and hits* Morena *the Apple-woman, they make a great*
>   *scuffle and* Hamet Alhaz *the Country* Vicar *runs out with*
>   Mariamne *the Scinder Wench,* Muly Hamet *the Dray-man a*
>   *little after at another Door.*

Q. Moth. Out fornicator are you billing,   160
And is your Franion too so willing?

Ham. Alhaz. Come thou with me thou pretty Harlot,
And I will be thy loving Varlot.

> *They all fall in confusion, tumbling one over another,* Muly
>   Hamet *the Dray-man Enters as they go out.*

Muly Ham. That I my baggage now shou'd lose so,
Does make me wilder than *Furioso:*   165
I shou'd have kill'd all that came near me,
Nay even those that did but hear me,
Made all the Furies stand affrighted,
Like trembling Children when benighted.
But they most basely have outrun me,   170
Alas, alas, they've quite undone me;
And left so many woes to grieve me,
That Divine Brandy can't relieve me;
If you'd describe grim *Pluto's* dwelling,
'Tis done by my sad Story telling.   175

> *Enter* Abdelcador (*a Porter, smoaking a Pipe of Tobacco*)
>   *Ambassador from* Taffilet *to* Muly Hamet *the Dray-man.*

Abdelcad. Kind *Taffilet* hearing your praises,
Has turn'd his army to pick Daysies;
And gives to you our great Metropolis
With all Excises and Monopolies;
Swearing I pray you Sir observe it,   180
That your stout drinking does deserve it;
And soon he'le privately come hither,
That you two may be drunk together.

Muly Ham. All this alas, to me's no blessing;
Now my kind *Bona Roba*'s missing;   185
For neither conquest, thrones, nor treasure,
Without a Wench, yield any pleasure.

    Enter Hamet Alhaz *the Country Vicar, Bound.*

Thus stript of thy black gowns protection,
I order thee Gentle correction;
Tyed up to post, instead of Gaunches,   190
Thou shalt be drubb'd on both thy haunches.

  Ham. Alhaz. Princox, I scorn thee, and thy malice;
And in thy Guts, wish all thy Tallyes.

    Hamet Alhaz *is led off to Execution.*

    Enter Abdrahaman *the Chimney-sweeper, leading* Mariamne *the*
      Scinder-Wench.

  Abdrah. I found your Trull behind yon Bushes,
Sleeping upon a Tuft of Rushes;   195
Strecht out at length on her back lying,
Some warm thoughts thereby signifying:
Louder, than any Porpus snoring;
Oh, what man cou'd forbear adoring?

  Muly Ham. Thanks brave Heroick Chimney-sweeper;   200
Hold, thou shalt be my Tally keeper.

  Abdrah. How? I keep your Tallyes! no such matter,
She in my chops makes too much water;
I'le fly from her for all this pother,
Yet I scarce know, where's such another.   205

    Abdrahaman *the Chimney-sweeper offers to go, but is stay'd*
      by Muly Hamet *the Dray-man.*

  Muly Ham. Oh stay and drink some Ale that's nappy,
And make me just as th' ast made he happy.

  Abdrah. I'le not stay, though you had the Town full,
But will suppose I have my Crown full;
And my self banish from her presence,   210

Of all my joys the verry Essence;
And to what place so e're I blunder,
I'le think I see this Cole-yard wonder.

     Exit Abdrahaman *the Chimney-sweeper.*

    Muly Ham. I do not value all their talking,
Now I have got agen my Maulkin;   215
Then since thou art my only dowdy,
Fie, do not wear thy face so cloudy.

    Mariam. Abdrahaman, I must not forget yet,
For I am sure y'are in his debt yet.

   Hamet Alhaz *the Country Vicar discover'd, tyed to a Post.*

    Muly Ham. My justice on yon scoundrel ended,   220
I with a Crown shall be befriended;
Pish, what are Crowns to a fine Woman,
Though most of them are very common;
All blessings not compar'd with drinking,
Aretine shews, (to my thinking)   225
Drink in the first place I adore thee,
Next Woman, I fall down before thee;
Therefore I'le take thee my sweet Trallop
Behind me, and so homeward gallop:
Empire's but toil, though Commons wou'd leave grumbling,   230
And age in that's not worth an hour in fumbling.
                                  [*going out.*]

    Enter Labas *the Corn-cutter hastily, with his Sword drawn to*
        Muly Hamet *the Dray-man.*

    Muly Lab. Turn scoundrel turn thee and thy Trull resign,
Know I will have her, if she will be mine.

    Muly Ham. Labas—
Come from my Punk, why dost thou tempt thy fate,   230
She's my concern—

    Muly Lab.—this shall the brawl debate
                         [*means his Sword.*]
Who can the toughest Fox and longest show,
Will find all doxies his, or make them so.

Muly Ham. Are you not asham'd? de'e come here to brawl?
Begone—I'le tear thee from my Natural.   240

Mariam. Unhand me, Caitiffs, for I hate you both.

Muly Lab. Both—Both—did you say? [*spreading his arms.*]
O murrain luck! [*thumping his breast.*]
Can *Jove* hear this? I'le to prevent this wrong,
Scold with my Eyes, and blubber with my tongue. [*weeping.*]   245

Muly Ham. Dost thou come here to whine—
What wilt thou dare to do for her, wou't weep,
Wou't drink, wou't swear, wou't rant, wou'd sleep,
Wou't toss a Bottle, eat a Custard, or Mince-pye,
Wou't go to bed with her, why so will I.   250

Muly Lab. Ha, ha, he.—
Dost thou know what th' ast said now? If I do
Not do all this, and a thousand things more—
Nay if I do not eat, drink, sleep, go to bed with her,
Play at Scotch-hoppers, chuck-farthing, or anything   255
And all that, I am the verry'st Son of a Whore breathing.

                Spoken laughing, but very positively.

Muly Ham. O Villain dost thou grin, dar'st thou believe
After my Drab is gone, that thou shalt live?

Muly Lab. What—am I slighted, then I will not die,
Till I from you obtain what you deny.   260

        They fight, and after several Passes Muly Hamet *the Dray-*
            man falls, and Muly Labas *the Corn-cutter full of re-*
            morse beating his Brest speaks.

Muly Lab. What Murrain luck, did urge me to contend
Against this honest Fellow, my old Friend?
And yet the baggage I must still pursue,
Let Quean which made the brawl, excuse it too.

                Exit Muly Labas *the Corn-cutter.*

        Muly Hamet *the Dray-man rises and speaks.*

Muly Ham. Doxie! Doxie!   265
O thou hast a tender thing!
I'de rather lose a bit of both my Eares,
Did I her warlike Pimp full fourteen years,
Outswear her Hectors, and outface her Dun,
While the vile Girl to Coverlet did run;   270
Out-cheat the Ale-house when we run o' tick,
Out-last the Beadles Penetential whip;
Out-eat old *Mariot*—out-huff Bottle Beer,
Out-cant the Gypsie and the Maunderer;
And there where last Night's reck'ning was unpay'd,   275
When Watchmen furr'd like Bears made all afraid:
I did with hands in Pocket door maintain,
'Gainst show'res of marrow bones and Piss pot Rain,
Have I made Wives secur'd by Husbands yield,
Sent snotty Rascals cursing from loves Field;   280
Must I for fop *Labas* all this forgo,
For which I did so impudently throw?
He steales my Doxie e're my job is done,
Who can but dream of Claps that I have won.   [*Exit.*]

EPILOGUE.

Being a new Fancy after the old,
and moſt ſurpriſing way

O F

MACBETH,

Perform'd with new and coſtly

MACHINES,

Which were invented and managed
by the moſt ingenious Operator
Mr. *Henry VVright*. P. G. Q.

LONDON,
Printed in the Year 1674.

THE

ACTORS NAMES.

Heccate. .... *Mr.* Powel.
1 *Witch.* .... *Mr.* Harris.
2 *Witch.* .... *Mr.* Adams.
3 *Witch.* .... *Mr.* Lyddal.
Thunder. .... *Mr.* Goodman.
Lightning. .... *Mr.* Kew.
      Spirits, Cats, and Musicians.

AN

EPILOGUE

Spoken by

Heccate and three WITCHES,

According

To the Famous Mode of

MACBETH.

The most renowned and melodious
    Song of *John Dory*, being heard as
    it were in the Air sung in parts by
    Spirits, to raise the expectation,
    and charm the audience with
    thoughts sublime, and worthy of
    that Heroick Scene which follows.

The Scene opens.

Thunder and lightning is discover'd,
    not behind Painted Tiffany to
    blind and amuse the Senses, but
    openly, by the most excellent way
    of Mustard-bowl, and Salt-Peter.

Three Witches fly over the Pit
    Riding upon Beesomes.

Macbeth Epilogue

Heccate descends over the Stage in a
Glorious Charriot, adorn'd with
Pictures of Hell and Devils, and
made of a large Wicker Basket.

Heccate and 3 Witches.

Hec. What, you have been at Hot-Cockles I see,
Beldames! how dare you traffick thus, and not call me?
'Tis I must bear the Brunt—
Where's *W*——?

Within. Here.   5

Hec. Where's *W*——?

Within. Here.

Hec. Where's Mack'rel back and Jilting-Sue?

All the three
Witches. } We want but you: We want but you.

Hec. You Lazie Hags! What mischief have you done?   10

1. *Witch.* I was with Templer lock'd from Night till Noon,
My case he open'd thrice and once
Actions he entred three and one,
But grown with study dull as dunce
His deeds I burnt, his Fees I spent;   15
And till next Term or quarters Rent
I left him poor, and Male-content.

    Hec. Thou shalt have a Spirit—What hast thou done?

2. *Witch.* I pick'd Shop-keeper up, and went to th' Sun,
He Houncht—and Houncht—and Houncht;   20
    and when h' had done,
      Pay me quoth I,
Be damn'd you Whore! did fierce Mechanick cry,
And most unlike a true bred Gentleman,
Drunk as a Bitch he left me there in Pawn.   25
Hec. His Shop is in *Fleetstreet*—

Macbeth Epilogue

2 *Witch.* In *Hackney* Coach, I'le thither sail,
Like wanton Wife with sweeping Tail;
    I'le do! I'le do! and I'le do!

3 *Witch.* A running Nag I'le thee lend;   30
2 *Witch* Thou art my Friend;
1 *Witch.* I'le give thee Shancker and Buboe.
2 *Witch.* I can have all the rest of Friends below.

pointing to the Pit.

To sweating Tub I'le youth confine,
Where he shall dwindle flux and pine,   35
Though white Witch Surgeon drench and noint,
    I'le have at least a Joint.

Hec. And what hast thou done?
3. *Witch.* With Cock of Game I fought a Match,
While his————my————did catch,   40
I stole his money and Gold Watch.
Hec. Thou shalt have an *Incubus;*
Come to our Friends to make their charms more quicker,
Here's six go-downs of humming Stygian Liquor.

*Enter two Spirits with Brandy burning, which
        drink while it flames,* Heccate *and the
        three Witches Sing.
    To the Tune of, A Boat, a Boat,* &c.

Hec. *A health, a health to Mother* C——   45
From Moor-fields *fled to* Mill-bank *Castle,*
She puts off rotten new rig'd Vessel.
    1. Witch. *A health, a health to* G—— *that Witch,*
She needs must be in spight of fate Rich,
Who sells tough Hen for Quail and Partridg.   50
    2. Witch. *A health, a health to Sister* T——
Her Trade's chief beauty and example,
She'll serve the Gallant, or the Pimp, well.
    3. Witch. *A health, a health to* Betty B——
Though she began the Trade but newly,   55
Of Country Squires there's not a few lye.

Chorus.

Macbeth Epilogue

But of all the brisk Bawdes 'tis *M*—— for me,
    'Tis *M*—— the best in her degree;
      She can serve from the Lord, to the Squire and Clown,
From a Guinny she'll fit ye to half a Crown.   60
1. Witch. *Fie! Fah! Fum!*
      By the itching of my Bum,
Some wicked Luck shou'd that way come.

                 pointing to the Audience.

    Hec. Stand still—by yonder dropping Nose I know,
That we shall please them all before we go.   65

      Heccate *speaks to the Audience.*

    Hec. Hail! hail! hail! you less than wits and greater!
Hail Fop in Corner! and the rest now met here;
Though you'l ne're be wits—from your loins shall spread,
Diseases that shall Reign when you are dead.

                Deed is done!   70
                War's begun!
            Great Morocco's *lost and won.*

Bank-side Maulkin thrice hath mew'd, no matter
If puss of t' other house will scratch, have at her.
T' appease your Spirits and keep our Farce from harm,   75
Of strong Ingredients we have powerful charm,
To catch Bully Critick whose wit but thin is:
Yonder sits empty *Cully* stuft with Guinnies,
Then for the wary squeamish Critick Lover,
A Dainty Virgin Pullet sits above there,   80
And those two Vizards hide a brace of Jinnyes,
Enough to hamper all the Critick Nynnyes:
Besides all this, our charm is stronger made yet,
With Dock of Harlot hasht and grylliaded,
Carcass of Country Girl that's fresh and wholesome,   85
Haunch of whetstone Doe, but that is fulsome.
Moreover Friends! In ev'ry place to fit ye,
Goose Giblets, Rumps, and Kidneys for the City.

Heccate *and* ⎫
all the three ⎬ Huff no more! ⎰ *a Hellish noise*
Witches. ⎭   ⎱ *is heard with-*
                                            in.

Macbeth Epilogue

Hec. He that wou'd damn this Farce does strive in vain   90
This charm can never be o'ercome by man,
'Till Whetstones Park remove to Distaff Lane.

Within Singing.

Heccate! Heccate! Come away.
Hec. Heark I am call'd—

She Sings.

I come; I come; *Alack and well a-day.*   95
      Alack and well a-day.
  Within.
The pot boyls over while you stay—

  Heccate.
    Vanish—

In Basket Chariot I will mount,
'Tis time I know it by my count.   100

Thunder and Lightning: while they
    are flying up *Heccate* Sings.

The Goose and the Gander went over the Green,
They flew in the Corn that they could not be seen.

Chorus.

  They flew, &c.

The Three Witches Sing.

Rose-mary's green, Rose-mary's green,
          derry, derry, down.   105
When I am King, thou shalt be Queen,
          derry, derry, down.
If I have Gold, thou shalt have part,
          derry, derry, down.
If I have none thou hast my heart.   110
          derry, derry, down.

F I N I S.

An

EPILOGUE.

This Farce—
    Not like your Country Girl made proud at Court,
    Because she there first learn'd the naughty sport,
    She'd now take place of all and's grown so haughty,
    Those that debauch'd her, dare not say she's faulty,   5
    Asham'd to own she jilted them with low dress,
    As stroling Punk did once in Somers progress:
    No, this like Sutlers Doxie, came from *Black-heath,*
    Long'd but to be as fine as Witch in *Mackbeth.*

    High though it looks 'twill stoop to all good fellows,   10
    As most proud Women will for Story's tell us,
    They now will do from Room of State to Ale-house.

    Like blith Scotch Maggy Cloaths in River bucking,
    T' has shew'd you all the flowers it had worth plucking,
    It thinks you Gentle-folks, are all for—looking.   15

    Farce and Heroick tale use but one fashion,
    Love and affection Layes the first foundation
        Then Gyant noyse and show set cheating Glass on.

    So little cruising punk and first rate Harlot,
    Though one Don's stuff t' others clad in Scarlet,   20
    Use but one Mouse-trap to catch trading Varlet.

    Those that adore the Ghosts and Devils yonder,
    The Powder Lightning and the Mustard Thunder;
    Who though they can't of Plot and Language prattle,
    Can mew like Cats, and roar like Drum in battle.   25

Macbeth Epilogue

When scourged Vermin from the Stage do Crall
    Whipp'd off—
As some are from Estates with Lusty Tail,
    Those we shall hardly please—

When *Heccate* calls, they thither swarm till full 'tis,   30
Like humours drawn to boil by old Wifes Poultice,
Because at yon Show-house you lik'd such doings,
We thought to purchase Cake-bread and stew'd Pruines;
But you look all like Lovers cloy'd, fie on ye,
When deed is don you should not grudg your money.   35

Have we not seen, O whorson Rogue *John Dory?*
You that Damn most, you know not wherefore nor why,
Catch'd ten times o're with one old new dress'd Story.

Be to this joy thus kind you'l rouse up yet,
Much better Farce, one more Heroick Puppet;   40
When little Worm is prais'd it will so brag o't,
That 'twill set Tail on end of bigger Maggot;
Since with success great Bard's grow proud and resty,
To get good Plays be kind to bad Travesty.

FINIS.

ANNOTATIONS

All quotations from Settle's *The Empress of Morocco* in the annotations which follow are taken from the facsimile reprint of the 4to in Maximillian E. Novak's *The Empress of Morocco and Its Critics,* Los Angeles, 1968. The quotations from Davenant's *Macbeth* are taken from the edition by Christopher Spencer in his *Five Restoration Adaptations of Shakespeare,* Urbana, 1965.

Frontispiece.

See "Introduction" above (p. xviii), for comment on the burlesque intention of this picture. The artist has been identified as Wenceslaus Hollar (1607–77), the engraver [W. Carew Hazlett, *Second Series of Bibliographical Collections and Notes on Early English Literature 1474–1700* (London, 1882; reprint ed., New York, 1961), p. 691]. Hazlett identifies the picture as a representation of "Harris the actor . . . in the character of Morena, the burlesque Empress of Morocco." The picture is reproduced facing page 282 of Summers's *The Restoration Theatre* (1934), where Summers identifies it as a portrait of "William Harris." It may be argued, though, that the portrait might just as well be intended to represent, not Morena, but Laula, who more powerfully dominates the play. The card in the Yale library card catalogue for Duffett's *Empress* includes the notation: "Frontispiece (portrait of Griffin the actor) wanting." Philip Griffin took the part of Laula. More mystery was added when John Harold Wilson included the portrait as the frontispiece to his book *Mr. Goodman, the Player* (1964) with the note that it is "possibly Goodman as 'Mariamne a Scinder Wench.'" Whoever the portrait represents, its inclusion suggests that a hit at Settle's "sculptures" was in order.

Prologue.

See "Introduction" above (pp. xv–xvi), for general comment on the significance of this sequence. Duffett's prologue ridicules, sometimes rather closely (compare Duffett's second stanza with the third stanza of the following), the song by Pompey's ghost to Cornelia between the third and fourth acts (pp. 35–36, F1) of Mrs. Katherine Philips's *Pompey, A Tragedy* (1663):

> After the third Act, to Cornelia, asleep on a Couch,
> *Pompey's* Ghost sings this in Recitative Air.

The Empress of Morocco

From lasting and unclouded Day,
From Joys refin'd above allay,
And from a Spring without decay,

I come, by Cynthia's borrow'd Beams,
To visit my Cornelia's Dreams,
And give them yet sublimer Theams.

Behold the Man thou lov'dst before,
Pure Streams have wash'd away his Gore,
And Pompey now shall bleed no more.

By Death my Glory I resume;
For 'twould have been a harsher Doom
T' outlive the Liberty of Rome.

By me her doubtful Fortune try'd,
Falling, bequeaths my Fame this Pride,
I for it liv'd, and with it dy'd.

Nor shall my Vengeance be withstood,
Or unattended with a Flood,
Of Roman and Egyptian Blood.

Caesar himself it shall pursue,
His days shall troubled be and few,
And he shall fall by Treason too.

He, by Severity Divine,
Shall be an Off'ring at my Shrine;
As I was his, he must be mine.

Thy stormy Life regret no more,
For Fate shall waft thee soon a-shore,
And to thy Pompey thee restore.

Where, past the fears of sad Removes,
We'll entertain our spotless Loves,
In Beauteous and Immortal Groves.

There none a guilty Crown shall wear,
Nor Caesar be Dictator there,
Nor shall Cornelia shed a Tear.

After this a Military Dance, as the continuance of her
      Dream, and then Cornelia starts up, as waken'd
      in amazement, saying,

      What have I seen? and whither is it gone?
      How great the Vision! and how quickly done!
      Yet if in Dreams we future things can see,
      There's still some Joy laid up in Fate for me.
                      [Exit.]

16. *when this Plot quite purg'd of Ale is.* "When Settle's plot in his *The Empress of Morocco* is stripped of pretentiousness."

19–20. *our damn'd Fustian Poet, / Who has disguis'd it with dull Histr'i's.* Settle, in his dedication to the Earl of Norwich, says of his play, ". . . the story of which, I owe to your hands, and your Embassy into Africa."

22. *Tuttle Fields.* Tothill Fields, Westminster, used for drilling troops, duels, archery and sports; Bridewell House of correction and a bear garden were there. Pompey's ghost might come from there as an allusion to the fact that Tothill Fields was used for common graves during the plague.

Actors Names.

Corn-cutter. One who cuts corns on the feet.

Strong-water-man. A liquor-dealer.

Scinder Wench. A girl who rakes cinders from the ashes.
Bum-bailyes. Bailiffs of the meanest kind; that are close to the debtor's back, or that catch him in the rear.

Scene i.

SD 1. *Hot-Cockles.* A rustic game in which one player lay face downwards, or knelt down with his eyes covered, and after being struck on the buttocks by the others in turn, guessed who struck him.

2. *Lap.* Skirt. *Blew Lap* here most likely refers to the blue apron or uniform of a menial.

7–22. These lines parody the speech announcing the arrival of Muly Hamet, which opens the second act of Settle's *Empress* (II.i):

> *The Scene opened, is represented the Prospect of a large River, with a glorious Fleet of Ships, supposed to be the Navy of* Muly Hamet, *after the Sound of Trumpets and the Discharging of Guns.*

> *Enter* King, Young Queen, Hametalhaz *and Attendants.*

> *Hamet.* Great Sir, Your Royal Fathers General
> Prince *Muly Hamet's* Fleet does homward sail,
> And in a solemn and triumphant Pride
> Their Course up the great River *Tensift* guide,
> 5   Whose guided Currents do new Glories take
> From the Reflection his bright Streamers make:
> The Waves a Masque of Martial Pageants yield,
> A flying Army on a floating Field.
> Order and Harmony in each appear,

10   Their lofty Bulks the foaming Billows bear.
    In state they move, and on the Waves rebound,
    As if they danc'd to their own Trumpet sound:
    By Winds inspired, with lively Grace they roul
    As if that Breath and motion lent a Soul.
15   And with that Soul, they seem taught Duty too,
    Their Topsails lowr'd, their Heads with Reverence bow;
    As if they would their Generals Worth enhance,
    From him, by instinct, taught Allegiance.
    Whilst the loud Cannons eccho to the shore,
20   Their flaming Breaths salute You Emperor.
    From their deep Mouths he does your Glory sing:
    With Thunder, and with Light'ning, greets his King.
    Thus to express his Joys, in a loud Quire
    And Consort of wing'd Messengers of fire
25   He has his Tribute sent, and Homage given,
    As men in Insense send up Vows to Heaven.

The writers of *Notes and Observations on The Empress of Morocco* comment extensively on this speech (Novak, p. 14 ff.).

The speech itself draws some specific comment. Lines 1–2 of Settle's (quoted above) are charged with faulty syntax: "Here he makes *Muly-hamets* Fleet to be the Old Emperours Generall; and Generall of a Prince that is dead" (Novak, p. 14). Line 9 is similarly charged: "In each? In what? in the Flying Army, the Waves, the Masque, or the Floating Field?" (Novak, p. 14). *Notes and Observations* leaves the "Great Sir" speech with a brilliant line-for-line parody of it, which is usually ascribed to Dryden (it can be found in Novak, p. 18; and in Noyes's *The Poems of John Dryden,* p. 913).

8. *thrumming.* Pressing or crowding in.

20. *From Walnut-shell to blow up bubble.* The allusion appears to be to a bubble-pipe.

28. *Brangler.* Brawler.

32–53. This sequence emphasizes Muly Labas's inability, amid the mutual accusations, to suspect Crimalhaz.

33. *Gudgeon.* Bait. "Swallow me this Gudgeon" might have the sense here of "Accept this excuse."

42. *copper Nose.* The condition caused by excessive drinking.

49. *Mother Bunch.* A noted London ale-wife of the early seventeenth century.

55. *Crimalhatchet.* Miss Doyle suggests (p. xxiv) that this is possibly a deliberate corruption of "Crommelhaiche," a name that appears in one of Settle's possible sources. However, "Crimalhatchet" is close to "Crimalhaz," and the rhyme ("watch it") might have helped turn up the name.

58. *Fustilugs.* A fat, frowzy woman.

63. *pussle.* Pucelle, a slut.

64. *Mother Shipton.* Allegedly, a prophetess said to have lived in the reign of Henry VIII, and to have foretold the deaths of Wolsey, Cromwell, Lord Percy, and others.

80. *brabble*. Noisy quarreling.

80–83. Cf. Settle's *Empress* (III.ii) when Muly Labas banishes Muly Hamet:

> Be gone, and fly to some infected air,
> Where poysons brood, where men derive their Crimes,
> Their Lusts, their Rapes, and Murthers from their Climes:
> And all the Venome which their Soils do want,
> May the Contagion of your Presence grant.

Notes and Observations is rather harsh on this passage:

The whole is thus; Go to infected Airs, and there Piss Poyson like a Toad, till the Contagion fills the Soyl of their Climes with Venome; and for the Letchery thou hast shewn, mayst thou infect infected places with all the Rapes and Murders they want. A most wise doom (Novak, pp. 32–33).

84–87. Cf. Settle's *Empress* (III.ii):

> Since in your kingdoms limits I'm deni'd
> A seat, may your great Empire spread so wide,
> Till its vast largeness does reverse my doom,
> And for my Banishment the world wants room.

Notes and Observations, although faulting them, singles out these lines as the best in Settle's play:

There are but these lines that have any tollerable fancy throughout the whole Play: But like good Cloaths sent to a Botcher to finish, the fancy is so bungled together, so filled with Bombazeene stiffning that one abhors it in the shape he has put it . . . Bombazeene in abundance. . . . May your great Empire grow so great, till its great greatness, . . . or till its vast vastness, or large largeness (Novak, p. 33).

96. *taking*. A disturbed or agitated state of mind.

98–123. In the forthcoming "feast" which Laula mentions, Muly Labas is to be undone by becoming "dead drunk," but the parallel with Settle's *Empress* does not emerge with precision. These lines fail to suggest why Laula would want to undo Muly Labas. Similarly, lines 110–13 make a considerable break with the parallel, for Muly Labas acknowledges that Laula is Crimalhaz's "doxie."

103. *Sheeps-head*. Simpleton.

104. *Mutton-monger*. Whore-monger.

107. *Sheep*. Whores.

115. *Coleworts*. Cabbage.

117. *Parcht*. Dried.

120. *Cogging*. Cheating, wheedling.

Scene ii.

Although this second (and last) scene of Duffett's *Empress* burlesques incidents

in the fourth and fifth acts of Settle's play, the main parallel scene from Settle's
Empress is IV, ii.

SD 1. *Enter Hamet Alhaz the Country Vicar.* In Settle's *Empress* (IV.ii),
Hametalhaz comes to a mountain encampment disguised as a priest with the
intention of killing the banished Muly Hamet.

9. *As though I'de keep a Jewish pascal.* "As though I'd give no party at all."

19. *fuddle.* Liquor.

23–33. Cf. Settle's *Empress* (IV.ii):

> This morning, as our Eyes we upward cast,
> The desart Regions of the Air lay wast.
> But strait, as if it had some penance bore,
> A mourning garb of thick black Clouds it wore.
> But on the sudden—
> Some airy Demon chang'd its form, and now
> That which look'd black above look'd white below,
> The Clouds dishevel'd from their crusted Locks,
> Something like Gems coin'd out of Chrystal Rocks.

Notes and Observations comments on the fourth line from the above: "Penance
is done in White, and that White is no Garb, besides Garb includes Motion and
Mien; but this it seems is a Black Penance"; and of the last two lines—"Besides
the non-sense of Crusted Locks of Clouds, dishevel'd is never made a Verb, but
if it were, to dishevel Gems from Locks is non-sense" (Novak, p. 40).

46. I am unable to determine the missing rhyme-word here.

SD 55. Cf. Settle's *Empress* (II.ii):

> *A State is presented, the King, Queen, and* Mariamne
> *seated,* Muly Hamet, Abdelcador, *and* Attendants, *a*
> Moorish *Dance is presented by* Moors *in several*
> *Habits, who bring in an artificial Palm-tree, about*
> *which they dance to several antick Instruments of*
> *Musick; in the intervals of the Dance, this Song*
> *is sung by a Moorish Priest and two Moorish Women;*
> *the Chorus of it being performed by all the* Moors.

A contemporary observer, Roger North, commented that the sequence in Settle's
play was "but scandalously performed" (*Roger North on Music*, ed. John
Wilson, London, 1959, p. 306). *Notes and Observations* twice refers to the
"artificial Palm-tree" as "a Dancing Tree" and "a dancing Palm-tree" (Novak,
pp. 44). *Kettle.* Kettle-drum. *Tongs and Key, Salt box.* Instruments used
in burlesque music. The salt-box, a box for keeping salt for domestic use, was
used like the marrowbones and cleaver. *Timbrel.* Tambourine.

55–78. Duffett's song here in praise of the power of liquor is roughly parallel
to the song in Settle's *Empress* (II.i) in praise of the virtue of loyalty.

55. *North-down Ale.* A popular drink, good enough for Pepys to serve to his
relatives on New Year's Day, 1661 (*Diary,* ed. Latham and Matthews, vol. II, p. 2).

71. *Brumsick Mum.* A kind of beer originally brewed in Brunswick.

The Empress of Morocco

78 SD. The parallel is in Settle's *Empress* (IV,iii) where Morena is tricked into killing Muly Labas.

79–90. Cf. Settle's *Empress* (IV.iii):

> *Morena.* Mother, it does a much less wonder seem,
> That I've kill'd him, than that you blame the Crime.
> Was it not You that arm'd me to this guilt,
> Told me I should a Ravishers blood have spilt?
> No 'twas by your design my Husband fell;
> You in this Masque have over-acted Hell.
>   *Laula.* Alas! she Raves. See how her rage begins,
> But madness always ushers in great sins.

100. *scumber.* Excrement.

101–02. Cf. Settle's *Empress* (IV.iii): "No, barb'rous stepmother, 'Twas you alone / Guided that hand that kill'd your King and Son."

109. *Bulker.* A Prostitute.

110. *trulling.* Prostituting.

111. *Town Bull.* The myth of Zeus and Europa is alluded to. Interestingly, *Notes and Observations* refers to Settle's Muly Hamet as "this Town Bull" (Novak, p. 31).

117. *blouz.* Wench.

117–59. These lines parallel Crimalhaz's attempt to seduce Morena in Settle's *Empress* (IV.iii).

125. *Invador.* Cf. Settle's *Empress* (IV.iii): "Hold, e'er the pleasures of Revenge I'll want, / Invader, here whate'er you ask I'll grant."

133. *piss-clout.* Diaper.

137–38. Cf. Settle's *Empress* (IV.iii): "That breath I cannot, must not understand."

146 SD. *flings away and comes again.* This see-saw technique of characters starting to exit but then staying is employed three times by Settle in IV, iii. Morena is described as *"Retreating from him"* and soon after Crimalhaz *"offers to go"* once, and then again.

159 SD. The commotion here described is parallel to the sequence in Settle's *Empress* (V.i.) where after Laula stabs Morena she *"Runs to stab* Crimalhaz *but being stopt by the Guards, stabs her self."*

161. *Franion.* Gallant.

166. The return of Muly Hamet to the confusion of the drunken party is parallel to his return in Settle's *Empress* (V.i) to the palace of Morocco after the deaths of Muly Labas, Morena, and Laula.

165. *wilder than Furioso.* i.e., Ariosto's hero.

176–83. Cf. Settle's *Empress* (IV.i), where the parallel lines are spoken by Abdelcador:

> Kind *Taffalet*—
> Concern'd to owe this Conquest to the Charms

The Empress of Morocco

Of your Victorious presence, not his Arms:
Scorning to wear that which his Arms ne'r won,
Frankly surrenders you *Morocco*'s Crown.

184–87. Cf. Settle's *Empress* (V.ii): "It does a larger happiness afford, / To have a Mistress, than a Crown restor'd."
188–93. Cf. Settle's *Empress* (V.i):

> *Muly Hamet.* . . .
> See him convey'd to Execution straight:
> He as he rose in blood, in blood shall set.
> *Crimalhaz.* . . .
> My Grave may dart forth Plagues, as may strike death
> Thro' the infected Air where thou draw'st breath.

190. *Gaunches.* The gaunches were the apparatus employed in the execution of criminals which let the criminal fall (as in a strappado) on sharp stakes pointed with iron. In Settle's *Empress* (V.i) Crimalhaz is executed by being "cast down on the Gaunches."
193. *Tallyes.* A tally is a notched stick used to record debts.
194–99. Cf. Settle's *Empress* (V.i):

> When her hard fate and her bright Charms I saw,
> These did my homage, that my pity draw,
> Something so kind I to that face did pay,
> That to serve her I could my trust betray.

206–13. Cf. Settle's *Empress* (V.i):

> *Muly Hamet.* Stay I conjure you; stay you shall, you must:
> You've made me great; let me not be unjust.
> Speak what command, what power, what Crown you'll choose.
> *Hametalhaz.* Crowns, no, such little favours I refuse.
> None but the place you hold my wish can bound.
> But since I have your free offer to be crown'd,
> It is accepted: I a King will be,
> And of my Reign make this my first decree,
> This Criminals Banishment, and to pursue
> My state, a Conqueror and a King like you;
> To whate'er place my wandring steps incline,
> I'll fancy Empires for I'll think her mine.

Hametalhaz refers to himself when he says "This Criminals Banishment." Miss Doyle considers the conversion of Hametalhaz as one of the significant features of Settle's *Empress* (see Doyle, pp. xlvi–l). Of Duffett's passage she comments:

Duffett exposes the lack of a basic morality underlying the conduct idealized in the heroic tragedy . . . by his ruination of the supreme moment of beauty and virtue in Settle's play wherein Hametalhaz renounces Mariamne, with whom he had fallen in love hardly an act before (p. lviii).

Macbeth Epilogue

215. *Maulkin.* A slattern.

220–31. These lines are close to those of Muly Hamet at the conclusion of Settle's *Empress:*

> My Justice ended: now I'l meet a Crown:
> Crowns are the common Prizes I have won.
> Those are entail'd on Courage. No, 'tis you
> Can only yield a bliss that's great and new.
> The charm of Crowns to Love but dull appears:
> Reigning a whole life's toil, the work of years.
> In love a day, an hour, a minute's Bliss,
> Is all Flight, Rapture, Flame and Extasies.
> Love's livelier Joys so quick and active move;
> An Age in Empire's but an hour in Love.

225. *Aretine.* Pietro Aretino (1492–1556) wrote plays and satires, and poems of a licentious character to accompany obscene pictures.

232–84. These concluding lines have no parallel in Settle's *Empress.* With line 231, Duffett came, in effect, to the conclusion of Settle's *Empress.*

236. *Muly Lab.* The quarto (1674) gives as speech-tag *"Muly Ham.",* but the context warrants an obvious change.

240. *Natural.* Mistress, wench.

246–56. Cf. *Hamlet* (V.i.297–303).

255. *Scotch-hoppers.* Hopscotch. *chuck-farthing.* A tossing game in which coins were pitched at a mark, and then tossed at a hole by the player who came nearest the mark, and who won all that alighted in the hole.

271. *run o' tick.* Run into debt.

274. *Mariot.* Apparently, a notorious glutton. Pepys (4 February 1660) worried about his own eating habits, and compared himself to "Marriòtt, the great eater" (*Diary*, ed. Latham and Matthews, vol. I, 40–41).

274. *out-huff.* Out-swell, out-brag. *Maunderer.* Professional beggar.

The "Macbeth Epilogue."

Title page. "The whole of this imprint, down to the mystic intials, sounds like a jeer at some grandiloquent announcement made by the rival theatre" (W. J. Lawrence, *The Elizabethan Playhouse,* first series, London, 1912, p. 219). Downes's comments on the 1673 production of *Macbeth* suggests its gaudiness:

The Tragedy of *Macbeth,* alter'd by *Sir William Davenant;* being drest in all it's Finery, as new Cloath's, new Scenes, Machines, as flyings for the Witches; with all the Singing and Dancing in it: The first Compos'd by Mr. *Lock,* the other by Mr. *Channell* and Mr. *Joseph Preist;* it being all Excellently perform'd, being in the nature of an Opera, it Recompenc'd double the Expence.

(*Roscius Anglicanus,* reprinted, London, 1886, p. 33.)

Macbeth Epilogue

SD 1. *Song of John Dory.* Song about the career of John Dory, captain of a French privateer. Words and music reprinted in Thomas Ravenscroft, *Pammelia, Deutromelia, Melesmata,* ed. MacEdward Leach, reprint of the first editions of 1609, 1611 (Philadelphia: The American Folklore Society, Inc., 1961), p. 59. *sung in parts.* Sung with voices joined in a concerted piece. *Thunder and lightning.* They appear as characters. This is similar to their appearance in *The Rehearsal,* I, ii, where they perform a prologue in dialogue. *Tiffany.* A kind of thin transparent silk. "That transparencies were used in blinding storm effects is indicated in Thomas Duffett's burlesque Macbeth" (George C. D. O'Dell, *Shakespeare from Betterton to Irving,* 2 vols., New York, 1920, I, 151–52). *Mustard-bowl and Salt-Peter.* The latter is the chief ingredient of gunpowder. A mustard bowl is a wooden bowl in which mustard seed was pounded, proverbially referred to as the instrument for producing stage-thunder. *Three Witches fly.* Cf. Davenant's *Macbeth* (I.iii.SD 1): "*Enter three Witches flying.*"

1. *Hot-Cockles.* A children's slap-and-tell game, but here, the sense suggests the slang meaning of the phrase: sexual manipulation.

1–44. The summoning and bawdy catechism of the witches parallels Davenant's *Macbeth* (I.iii.1–28) where the witches meet, are questioned, and plan to torment a sailor's wife.

8. *Mack-rel back.* Refers to Betty Mackeral, a famous prostitute of the day. *Jilting-Sue.* "Sue Flavel, a well-known prostitute" (Summers, *Shakespeare Adaptations,* p. 262).

18–37. Cf. Davenant's *Macbeth* (I.iii.3–24):

> *3rd Witch.* Sister; where thou?
> *1st Witch.* A Sailor's wife had Chestnuts in her lap,
> And mounch'd, and mounch'd and mounch'd; give me quoth I;
> Anoint thee, Witch, the rump-fed Ronyon cry'd,
> Her Husband's to the Baltick gone, Master o' th' *Tyger.*
> But in a sieve I'll thither sail,
> And like a Rat without a tail
> I'll do, I'll do, and I will do.
> *2nd Witch.* I'll give thee a wind.
> *1st Witch.* Thou art kind.
> *3rd Witch.* And I another.
> *1st Witch.* I my self have all the other.
> And then from every Port they blow;
> From all the points that Sea-men know.
> I will drain him dry as hay;
> Sleep shall neither night nor day
> Hang upon his pent-house lid;
> My charms shall his repose forbid,
> Weary sen-nights nine times nine,
> Shall he dwindle, waste, and pine.
> Though his Bark cannot be lost,
> Yet it shall be Tempest-tost.

19. *th' Sun.* There were several Sun Taverns in London.

32. *Shancker.* Chancre, an ulcer occurring in venereal disease. *Buboe.* Inflammation of the groin and armpits.

34. *sweating Tub.* Formerly used in the treatment of venereal disease.

35. *flux.* Purge, regurgitate.

36. *white Witch.* A beneficent witch or wizard. *drench.* A dose of medicine administered forcibly. *noint.* Anoint. Cf. Davenant's *Macbeth* (III.viii.31): "I will but Noint, and then I mount."

44. *go-downs.* Draughts, gulps, or swallows.

SD 45. *To the Tune of, A Boat, a Boat.* Cf. Shadwell's *The Miser* (III) where Timothy Squeeze says: "We can i'faith, and sing, *a Boat, a Boat,* or *here's a health to his Majesty.*" This latter was the title of a popular loyalist song; a stanza from it is reprinted in Peter Cunningham's *The Story of Nell Gwynn* (London, 1908), p. 169.

45. *Mother C——.* Mother Cresswell, a noted bawd and courtesan of the time.

46. *Moor-fields.* Located from the wall of the city between Bishopsgate and Cripplesgate to Finsbury and to Holywell, and noted for wrestling, cudgel players, drawers, and cheap book-stalls. The old Bedlam was located there. *Mill-bank Castle.* Millbank penitentiary, Westminster.

48–50. Mother Gifford, another well-known madam, is alluded to. Cf. Dryden's *Sir Martin Mar-all* (IV.i.213–16), when Lord Dartmouth says:

> . . . every night I find out for a new maidenhead, and
> she has sold it me as often as ever mother *Temple,*
> *Bennet,* or *Gifford,* have put off boil'd Capons for
> Quails and Partridges.

51. *Sister T——.* Another bawd (cf. previous note).

54. *Betty B——.* Betty Buly, a prostitute of the day.

57. *M.* Mother Mosely, a bawd often linked with Shaftesbury in the literature of the period.

62–63. Cf. Davenant's *Macbeth* (IV.i.61–62): "I by the pricking of my Thumbs, / Know something Wicked this way comes."

64. *dropping Nose.* A dripping or running nose.

66. Cf. Davenant's *Macbeth* (I.iii.65): "Lesser than *Macbeth,* and greater."

68–69. Cf. Davenant's *Macbeth* (I.iii.67): "Thou shalt get Kings, thou shalt ne'r be one."

70–72. Cf. Davenant's *Macbeth* (I.i.3–5):

> *2nd Witch.* When the Hurly-burly's done,
> When the Battle's lost and won.
> *3rd Witch.* And that will be e're set of Sun.

73–74. *no matter If puss of t'other house will scratch, have at her.* I can find no indication of whether the Duke's Men retaliated in any way as a result of Duffett's travesties.

81. *Jinnyes.* Wenches.

84. *Dock.* The solid fleshy part of an animal's tail. *grylliaded.* Grilled or broiled.
86, 92. *whetstone Doe, Whetstones Park.* The latter refers to a narrow lane between Lincoln's Inn Fields and Holborn, well known for its prostitutes; a whetstone doe is a whore.
90–92. Cf. Davenant's *Macbeth* (IV.i.84–87):

> *Heccate.* Be Confident, be Proud, and take no care
> Who wages War, or where Conspirers are,
> *Macbeth* shall like a lucky Monarch Raign,
> Till *Birnam Wood* shall come to *Dunsinane.*

Distaff Lane. Distaff Lane proper has been absorbed by Cannon Street, but the name is preserved in a subsidiary street known as Little Distaff Lane.
93–95. Cf. Davenant's *Macbeth* (III.viii.19–20): *"Heccate, Heccate, Heccate!* Oh come away; / Hark, I am call'd."
99–100. Cf. Davenant's *Macbeth* (III.viii.30–31): "Come away make up the Count. / *Heccate.* I will but Noint, and then I mount."
101–02. There is a general resemblance between Duffett's folk-song ending the skit and the parallel sequence in Davenant's *Macbeth* (III.viii.43–49):

> *3rd Witch.* O what a dainty pleasure's this,
> To sail i'th' Air while the *Moon* shines fair;
> To Sing, to Toy, to Dance and Kiss,
> Over Woods, high Rocks and Mountains;
> Over Hills, and misty Fountains:
> Over Steeples, Towers, and Turrets:
> We flye by night 'mongst troops of Spirits.

Final Epilogue.

Although Summers refers to this last epilogue as "A somewhat shambling epilogue in more ordinary fashion" (*Shakespeare Adaptations,* p. lxv), there is considerable close parody in it of Settle's "Epilogue" to *The Empress of Morocco.*
1–2. Cf. Settle's "Epilogue" (1): *"This Play, like Country Girl come up to Town."*
5. Cf. Settle's "Epilogue" (13): *"Tis barb'rous to defame what you debauch."*
8. *Sutler.* One who follows an army or lives in a garrison town and sells provisions to the soldiers. *Black-heath.* Located in the southern suburbs of London, chiefly in the parishes of Greenwich and Lewisham, and noted for military reviews.
10–15. Cf. Settle's "Epilogue" (14–18):

> Nay, now you've cast it off, yet do not frown:
> Tho' like the Refuge of a Miss o' th' Town,
> It is turn'd common, yours for half a Crown.
> 'Twas generous at Court and did for Love,
> But does for profit to the Stage remove.

Macbeth Epilogue

16–18. Cf. Settle's "Epilogue" (19–21):

> *Women and Wit on equal scores begin;*
> *Love and Affection first may make 'em sin,*
> *They trade for interest when they're once got in.*

22–25. Cf. Settle's "Epilogue" (22–26):

> *But for you, Sirs, who censure but not Write;*
> *Who do in Wit, as some in War, delight;*
> *Whose Courages do not much care to fight:*
> *But tho' you can't of Scars nor Conquests vapour,*
> *You can draw Sieges and take Towns in Paper.*

29. Cf. Settle's "Epilogue" (27): *"You it will be hard to please."*
36–38. Cf. Settle's "Epilogue" (33–37):

> *Have we not seen* (Oh loves almighty Powers!)
> *A Wench with tallow-Looks and winter-Face,*
> *Continue one Mans Favorite seven years space?*
> *Some ravishing knack i'th' sport and some brisk motion,*
> *Keeps the gilt Coach and the gallants Devotion.*

39–44. Cf. Settle's "Epilogue" (38–43):

> *Be to this toy thus kind, and you will raise*
> *Much better Fancies to write better Plays.*
> *When meaner Faces are us'd kindly by ye,*
> *What power have greater Beauties to deny ye?*
> *So your kind smiles advance the Scribling Trade.*
> *To get good Plays you must excuse the bad.*

TEXTUAL NOTES

Location File of Extant Copies

Title page: THE EMPRESS OF MOROCCO (*see facsimile*)

Signature collation: 4°: A^4, B^2, C–G^4, H^2

Copies are in the following libraries: British Museum (BM); Bodleian Library (O); Worcester College Library, Oxford (OW); Signet Library, Edinburgh (ES); William Andrews Clark Memorial Library, Los Angeles (CLUC); Henry E. Huntington Library (CSmH); Beinecke Library, Yale University (CtY); Folger Library (DFo); Library of Congress (DLC); Newberry Library (ICN); University of Chicago Library (ICU); Houghton Library, Harvard University (MH); Butler Library, Columbia University (NNC); University of Pennsylvania Library (PU); Princeton University Library (NJP); University of Texas Library (TxU).

The Mock-Tempest

The Performance

The only recorded performance of *The Mock-Tempest* was on Thursday, November 19, 1674.[1] However, as *The London Stage* puts it, "There is no certainty that this is the premiere, but the frequency of the performance of *The Tempest* [i.e., the operatic *Tempest*] during Sept–Oct–Nov would make November 1674 a suitable time for a burlesque of this sort" (I, p. 224). The operatic *Tempest* was performed November 11, 17, and 18, which gave the November 19 performance of *The Mock-Tempest* a close vantage-point from which to display its ridicule.[2] It is likely that many viewers had seen the operatic *Tempest* by the time *The Mock-Tempest* appeared. One of Nell Gwynn's biographers reports that "In, September to December 1674 she saw *The Tempest* four times."[3] Perhaps Nell also saw *The Mock-Tempest;* she was in a position to appreciate it!

The possibility of a performance of *The Mock-Tempest* as late as March 2, 1681–82, has been suggested on the basis of the following announcement in *The Protestant Mercury*, 25 February–1 March 1681–82: "Tomorrow, we hear his Majesty is to be there (DL) to see the Mock Tempest."[4] Langbaine "heard that when one of his [Duffett's] Plays, *viz. The Mock Tempest* was acted in *Dublin*, several Ladies, and Persons of the best Quality left the House" (p. 177). I can find no further mention of this performance.

Although there is no cast included in the quarto, it seems probable that Joe Haines and Mrs. Betty Mackarel, who speak the introductory "prologue-in-dialogue," had roles in the play. In Duffett's last burlesque, *Psyche Debauch'd*, Haines played the lead role of Princess None-so-fair.

The Text

Publication of the quarto of *The Mock-Tempest* is recorded in *The Term Catalogues* for 15 February 1674–75 (I, p. 197). It is the only one of Duffett's

---

1 Mentioned on the Lord Chamberlain's list, 5/141, p. 116; this is reprinted in *Nicoll*, I, 345.

2 The next performance of the operatic *Tempest* was Saturday, December 28 (*The London Stage*, I, p. 225). It had first appeared in the Spring of 1674.

3 Peter Cunningham, *The Story of Nell Gwynn* (London, 1908), p. 201.

4 *The London Stage*, I, p. 307.

three burlesques that bears his name: "by T. Duffett." An examination of the text suggests that this quarto is either one edition with stop press corrections, or two impressions of the same edition. Copies examined were the following: British Museum (BM), 644.h.5, from a photo copy; Columbia (NNC); Library of Congress (DLC); Folger (DFo); Yale (CtY); and Harvard (MH). Particular problems were noted at $F1^r$, $F3^v$, $F4^r$, $G1^v$, $G2^r$, $G2^v$, $G4^r$, $G4^v$, and $H1^r$. Additional copies partially examined for these problems and compared with the above-mentioned copies include: Clark Memorial Library (CLUC); Huntington Library (CSmH); Newberry Library (ICN); University of Chicago (ICU); Williams College (MWiW); University of Cincinnati (OCU); and University of Texas (TxU).

For gathering F there are two uncorrected copies: Columbia and Newberry. At some point stop press corrections were made in the outer form of the sheet and all other copies have these corrections. In gathering G things become much more difficult. In this case we have four uncorrected copies: Chicago, British Museum, Columbia, and Harvard. Presumably, the error on $G1^v$ line 16 ("hath he is sweetly" instead of "hath it sweetly") was not discovered until copies like the Chicago, British Museum, and Columbia had already been printed. The Harvard copy is the only one corrected with an errata slip; the remaining copies were corrected in the press. If $G1^v$ and $G2^r$ of the inner form are carefully examined, they show that all of $G1^v$ and at least the top half of $G2$ (down to the song) have been entirely reset. The group of variants represented by the Chicago copy and the group of variants represented by the Texas copy, on these pages, are not the same type setting. This resetting was necessary because of the addition of the two lines ("*Ari.* Thou art the very Devil." added as line 26 to $G1^v$; and "*Ari.* Alas Poor Codshead." added as line 11 to $G2^r$). As a result of the resetting, in which they corrected most of the previous errors, they introduced two new ones by setting "snatch'd" as "snach'd" and "right" as "write" (lines 3 and 17 of $G1^v$). In the outer form, $G2^v$ shows stop press corrections, as does $H1$ (outer form of gathering H).

There are several peculiarities in the Columbia copy; $A4$ comes before $A3$. In addition, $A4$ is torn and has been mended, but the list of errata on the bottom of the verso is lost. More curious, though, is the insertion of an extra page after $A3$. A pencilled notation reads: "This sheet belongs to Love and Revenge by Elkanah Settle (our copy incomplete)." The recto of this inserted sheet contains the Prologue to Settle's play, while the verso has the first part of the Epilogue. Following $B1$ is a second inserted sheet, the recto containing the conclusion of Settle's Epilogue, and the verso giving the actors' names. A final oddity in this copy is that $B3$ comes before $B2$.

In the Yale copy $A4$ is missing. With a more awkward gap than this, the Library of Congress copy lacks $G3$ and $G4$, which is particularly unfortunate since this is the copy reproduced in Readex Microprint's series, *Three Centuries of British Drama: 1500–1800.*

The Mock-Tempest was reprinted and edited in 1922 by Montague Summers in his *Shakespeare Adaptations*. This is in the main a faithful reprint of the quarto, and includes a number of silent corrections. Summers noted several of the differences within the quarto, and included full annotations for idiomatic expressions, place names, and other proper nouns. There was no attempt made to cite passages in the original that are parodied. One must be grateful to Summers for starting to make Duffett available again after nearly 250 years.

More recently, facsimile reprints of the operatic *Tempest* and Duffett's *The Mock-Tempest* have been made available in George Robert Guffey's *After the Tempest* (Los Angeles, 1969).

THE
MOCK·TEMPEST:
OR THE
Enchanted Caſtle.

ACTED AT THE
Theatre Royal.

Written By T. Duffett.

Hic totus volo rideat libellus. Mart.

LONDON,

Printed for *William Cademan* at the *Popes-Head* in the lower
Walk of the *New Exchange* in the *Strand.* 1675.

THE

INTRODUCTION,

Spoken by Mr. Hains, *and Mrs.* Mackarel.

Mr. Hains *Enters alone.*

You are of late become so mutinous,
Y'ave forc'd a reverend Bard to quit our House.
Since y'are so soon misled to ruin us,
I'le call a Spirit forth that shall declare,
What all your tricks and secret Virtues are.   5
What? ho *Ariel!*

Enter Betty Mackarel.

Here's *Betty*—Now rail if you dare:
Speak to 'em *Betty*—ha! asham'd, alass poor Girl,
Whisper me!—Oh I'le tell 'em—Gentleman! she says,
Y'are grown so wild she could not stay among ye,   10
And yet her tender heart is loath to wrong ye.
Spare 'em not,
Whom kindness cannot stir, but stripes may move.
     Bet. O Mr. *Hains!* I've often felt their Love.
     Ha. Poh, felt a Pudding that has taken vent,   15
Their love cools faster, and as soon is spent.
Think of thy high calling *Betty,* now th'art here,
They gaze and wish, but cannot reach thy Sphere,
Though ev'ry one could squeeze thy Orange there.
     Bet. Why this to me, Mr. *Haines* (d'ee conceive me) why to me?   20
     Ha. Ay, why this to *Betty?*
O Virtue, Virtue! vainly art thou sought,
If such as *Betty* must be counted naught:
Examins your Consciences Gentlemen!
When urg'd with heat of love, and hotter Wine,   25
How have you begg'd, to gain your lewd design:
Betty, dear, dear, dear *Betty,*
I'le spend five Guinnyes on thee, if thou'lst go:

And then they shake their (d'ee conceive me) *Betty* is't not
so, their yellow Boyes?   30

    Bet. Fie Mr. *Hains,* y'are very rude (d'ee conceive me).

    Ha. Then speak your self.

    Bet. Gentlemen! you know what I know.

        If y'are severe, all shall out by this light:

        But if you will be kind, I'le still be right.   35

    Ha. So that's well—make thy Cursy *Betty.*

Now go in Child, I have something to say to these
Gentlemen in private.

                                [*Exit* Betty.]

PROLOGUE.

Spoken by Mr. *Hains.*

Since Heroes Ghosts, and Gods have felt your spight:
Your She Familiars, and your dear delight;
The Devils shall try their power, w'ee to night:
Some do believe that Devils ne'r have been,
Because they think, none can be worse then them: 5
But Female Sprights by all are felt and seen.
    You see our Study is to please you all:
Lets not by stiff Tom Thimbles *faction fall;*
Whose censures are meer ign'rance in disguise,
The noyse of envious fools, that would seem wise.   10
If Bacons *Brazen-head cry—that won't pass,*
Strayt all the little Fops are turn'd to brass,
And Eccho to the braying of that Ass:
Although we take their shapes and senseless sounds,
Lets not be worryd by our own dull Hounds: 15
Let not their noyse that got your Money there,
Deprave your Judgements, and your pleasure here.
    Ye men of Sense and Wit, resume your Raign.
Th'are honour'd who by noble Foes are slain;
Such comforts wounded Lovers have who swear,   20
When their tormenting pains are most severe,
Dam'ee!
It does not vex me to be Clapp'd by her:
Gad she was handsome, though the sport is dear.
But who in your sight at their mercy lyes,   25
Much like an Eastern *Malefactor dyes,*
Expos'd i' th' Sun to be devour'd by flyes.
    Let Language, Wit and Plot, this Night be safe,
    For all our business is to make you laugh.

Persons Represented.

Prospero .... a Duke, Head-keeper of the Enchanted Castle.
Alonzo .... a Duke, his mortal Enemy.
Quakero .... Son of Alonzo.
Gonzalo .... a Subject of Alonzos.
Antonio .... his Friend.   5
Hypolito .... Infant Duke of Mantua, Innocent and ignorant.
Hectorio .... a Pimp.
Miranda   ....⎫
Dorinda   ....⎬ the harmless daughters of Prospero.
Stephania .... a Baud.   10
Beantosser ....⎫
Moustrappa ....⎬ Wenches.
Drinkallup ....⎭
Ariel .... a Spirit waiting on Prospero.
A Plenipotentiary.   15

Wenches, Bridewell-Keepers, Spirits, Devils, Masquers, and Prisners.

The Scene in LONDON.

THE

NEW TEMPEST

or the

ENCHANTED CASTLE.

Act I, scene i.

A great noyse heard of beating Doors, and breaking Windowes,
   crying a Whore, a Whore, &c.

Enter Beantosser, *and* Moustrappa.

Bean. What a noyse they make!
Mous. A roaring noyse, we shall have
foul weather.

Enter Drinkallup.
Drink. The Dogs have us in the Wind, 'twill go hard.

[*Exeunt* Beantosser *and* Moustrappa.]

Enter Stephania.

Steph. Hectorio! Hectorio!   5
All. Hectorio! Hectorio! Hectorio!

Enter Hectorio.

Hect. Here here Mother, what cheer, what cheer.
Steph. Never worse, never worse, barr up the Doors, barr up
the Doors: Oh! Oh! [*She whistles, Wenches run on and off again.*]

Enter Moustrappa.

All. Barr up the Doors, barr up the Doors.   10

Mous. Let's make all fast enough, and let'm roar the Devils head off.

Steph. Beantosser, Beantosser.

All. Beantosser, Beantosser, Beantosser.

Steph. Why where is this damn'd deaf flunder mouth'd drab?   15

Enter Beantosser.

Bean. Here, here, a pox o' these full mouth'd Fox hounds.

Hect. They hunt devilish hard, I'me affrai'd they'l earth us.

Steph. Give *Hectorio* a dram of the Bottle, the Whey-Blooded Rogue looks as if his heart were melted into his Breeches.

[*Exeunt* Beantosser *and* Hectorio.]

[*Enter Wenches arm'd with Spitts, Forks, Tongs, Chamber-Potts,*
&c. *They pass over the stage.*]

Steph. Bear up, bear up my brave *Amazons,* y'ave born Ten   20
times as many men in your times: heigh my Girles, stand fast my
stout bona Robas, run, fly, work nimbly, nimbly ye Queans, or all's
lost.   [*Exeunt all.*]
                                                  [*A great noyse again.*]
                Enter Hectorio, Alonzo, Gonzalo, Quakero.

Alon. Good friend, stand to thy tackling, and play the Man:
where's Mother *Stephania?*   25

Hect. Pry'thee old Goat, tye up thy Clack, and move thy hands.

Quak. Friend, friend, look thee, bridle thy unruly member—to
wit, thy tongue.

Hect. Work, work, my hearts of Gold.

Quak. Ha, ha, ha, my Father to whom thou spakest so unadvisedly   30
is Duke of that building which do-eth sustain my Lord Mayors
Cattle, *Vidicilet,* his Doggs.

Hect. Fill the sweating Tub with Stones, and set it against the
Door, quick, quick.

Within—The Sweating Tub, the Sweating Tub! Stones,   35
Stones!

Quak. He is moreover perpetual Whiffler to the Worshipful
company of *Pin-makers,* as I my self am.

Hect. Confound thy Father and thy self.   [*A noyse within.*]
What care these Roarers for the worshipful *Pin-makers?*   40
Silence, and to work, or I'le ram thee into a Chamber-pot, and
throw thee out at Window.   [*Exeunt all.*]
                Enter Stephania, Beantosser, Moustrappa, *and* Drinkallup.

Steph. Stir, Wenches, stir, bring out all the Jourdans full of
Water.

All. The Jourdans, the Jourdans, &c.   45

Beantosser, Drinkallup, *and* Moustrappa *run off several wayes
    crying the Jourdans.*

[*A great noyse within, all crying a Whore, a Whore, a Whore,* &c.]

Steph. Send a Legion of Devils down their yelling throats to
pluck their lungs out. —Out ye bauling Curs, ye ill-bred hounds,
here are Whores enough for you all, All, if you would behave
your selves like civil Gentlemen, and come one after another.

                             She Whistles, Enter Wenches.

Down, down, down to the Sellar Windows.—   50

All. The Sellar Windows, the Sellar Windows.   [*The Wenches run
                             down the Trap Door.*]

Enter Beantosser, Moustrappa, *and* Drinkallup *hastily one after
    another.*

Bean. Undone, undone, not one drop of Water in the house.

Mous. With hard labour all their moisture turns into sweat.

Drink. Th'are dryer then hung Beef, and almost as black too.

Bean. Your advice, your advice Mother.   55

Drink. Dispatch, or w'are ruin'd.—

Steph. Get up in the Windows, you musty Queens, make water in
their Eyes, and burn e'm out, I'me sure y'are hot enough.—

                             Enter Hectorio.

Hect. Turn out, turn out all hands to the Back-door: is this a
time to prate, ye spurr-gald jades, ye over-rid Hackneys?—   60

Mous. O you huffing Son of a Whore.

Drink. You rotten Jack in a box.

Bean. You foul mouth'd Nickumpoop.

Hect. Prate on, prate on, d'ee hear how it Thunders? —stand
still and be damn'd, I'le shift well enough for one.   65

                        [*The noyse renew'd.*]

                          [*Exit* Hectorio.]

Steph. Turn out, turn out Seditious mutiners, flye or I'le have
ye all flead—Out, out!

              [*Exeunt* Beantosser, Moustrappa, *and* Drinkallup.]

              Enter Gonzalo, Alonzo, *and* Quakero.

Gonz. More noyse and terrour then a Tempest at Sea.

                 Enter Beantosser.

Bean. The green Chamber, the green Chamber.   [Stephania
    whistles, the Wenches come up from the Trapp-door.]

Steph. Aloft, aloft, to the green Chamber, all to the green   70
Chamber—Aloft, aloft.—   [*Exeunt* Beantosser *and* Wenches.]

Alon. My Honour, my Reputation.—

Quak. Yea! Reputation, Reputation! —Woo man, ah! ha!

Steph. Reputation! ye crop-ear'd whelps, Reputation! is not my
Reputation dearer to me then your lives, and Souls? Down with the   75
Close stool upon their heads.

You louzy farandinical Sots, Reputation! I have had Lords—
Lords! thou whey-bearded Ananias, and then I had a blessing on my
endeavours; but this is justly fall'n upon me, for dealing with
such zealous Whore-masters, thin gutted 3d. Customers—Out of   80
my sight, and to work, or by the beards of my renowned Predecessors
I'le have you hung out like Wool-sacks to defend my Walls. See if
thou canst preach the Rabble to Silence, thou canting Hypocritical
Abednego.

Quak. Yea, thou babylonish Whore in grain, thou Harlot of   85
a *London* dye, thou shalt see the strength of the power of a
um—Thou shalt see, I say, look ye Friends, Brethren and
Sisters—Give heedful attention, and a, and I say a um—
[*A shout within, and dirt thrown in his mouth.*] [*Exeunt all.*]

            Enter again Stephania *and* Beantosser.

Bean. We are gone, we are gone, th'are all broke in the Closet
Window.   90

                Enter Hectorio.

Hect. Hell, and Devils, th'are untiling of the House.

                Enter Wenches.

Steph. Let off the Bottles of Stepony, they may think th'are Guns.

Bean. Clap up the middle hatch with Iron spikes.

Hect. Take down the false Stairs.

                Enter Moustrappa.

Mous. Open the Trap-door, that falls into the Common-shoar.   95

                Enter Drinkallup.

Drink. Hang up the tenter Hooks.—

Steph. Set the great Chest against the stair Door.   [Stephania
                                        Whistles, Enter Wenches.]

All. To the great Chest, the great Chest.

                            [*Exeunt all but* Stephania.]

Hect. [*within*] Heave all together, heave Cats, Heave.
            Heave Cats, heave—cheerily, cheerily.   100

        Enter Alonzo, Gonzalo, *and* Quakero.

Alon. Gonz. Quak. —Murther, murther, murther.

Steph. Oh, you obstreperous Woolves, a Rot consume your
Windpipes, y'are louder then the rabble.

Alon. O, this base, this cursed business!

Steph. Cursed bus'ness, thou invincible Fop, thou Brazen headed   105

Ignoramus—Hast thou a mind to be limb'd? one word more, and
all the Doors shall fly open: Cursed bus'ness, with a pox to ye.

[*She whistles.*]

Enter Wenches—And go off again.

Come tag-rag and long-tail, Old Satin, Taffaty, and Velvet, rouze
about, charge 'em briskly, showr the Coals on their pates. —He
calls Wenching base cursed bus'ness—Oh you rake Hells, sons   110
of unknown Fathers.

Enter Beantosser.

Bean. Hell take 'em, they clime the Walls like Cats.

Steph. Down with the Tables and Stools upon 'em. [*Exit* Beantosser.]

[*The noyse renew'd.*]

Enter Hectorio.

Hect. Sound a Parle, sound a Parle, or they'l break in upon
us—There's no hope left.   115

Steph. A Parle, thou impudent miscreant! false hearted Caytiff,
I'le rather like a noble Roman *Virago,* make my House my Funeral
pile.

Hect. All are resolv'd not to fight a stroak more, sound a
Parle but to gain time.   120

Steph. To delude the Foe I consent, but never to yield.

[*She whistles.*]

Enter Drinkallup, Beantosser, *and* Moustrappa.

Sound a Parle, and hang out the White Flag.   [*A Horn sounds
within, and one passes over the Stage with a Flannel Peticoat on a Stick: another
Horn sounded on the other side.*]

Hect. Hark, they answer us.

Steph. Go you *Drinkallup,* and see what they will demand.

[*Exit* Drinkallup, *and returns immediately.*]

Drink. Here's a Plenipotentiary desires admittance.   125

Steph. Let him be blinded, and introduc'd by the Postern—
Casement—Come fellow Souldiers, lets sit in State, and
receive him with undaunted Countenances, as blustring Warriours
do, though we are like to dye for fear.

A Guard of Wenches Enter.

Master of our Ceremonies, introduce the Plenepotentiary.   130

[*A dirty fellow led in between two Wenches.*]

Fellow Souldiers 'tis a Maxim in Warr to treat with our
Arms in our hands— (Guard, deliver us your Weapons) —and
while we talke of peace to prepare for a Battle; therefore Guard
go you and mend the backs of the Chairs.   [*Exeunt Guard.*]

Plenipotentiary, be not dismaid with the glittering Splendour   135
of our Court, but boldly deliver what thou hast in Charge.—

Plen. My Master, the many-headed-monster-Multitude, to save the

– 67 –

great effusion of Christian Chamberly, will grant you peace on
these terms.

Steph. Say on.   140

Plen. First, they demand the Dominion of the Straights mouth,
and all the Mediterranean Sea—That every Frigot, Fireship, you
have, shall strike, furle up their sail, and lye by to the least
of their Cock-boats, where-ever they meet, and receive a man aboard
to search for prohibited Goods, and permit him to romage fore and   145
aft without resistance.—

Steph. Umph. —My friends, this is very hard.

Plen. Secondly, That all their Vessels shall have and enjoy a
free-trade into and out of all your Ports without paying any
Custom.—   150

Steph. The duties of Importation are my greatest Revenue, and
must not be parted with.

Bean. But though your People pay for import, we will engage to
pay them at going off.

Mous. As we have always done heretofore.   155

Plen. Lastly, That you re-imburse the charge of the War, pay
for the Cure of the wounded, and the recov'ry of those that have
surfeited on your rotten Ling and Poys'nous Oyl, and allow Pensions
for those that are dismembered—What say ye, Peace, or
War?   160

Steph. War.

All. War, War, War.

Steph. Return for answer, that we will rather dye at their Feet,
then submit to such dishonourable Conditions: —Begon: —And
so she pray'd me to tell ye.   165

Plen. Though you refuse peace, I scorn to carry back my
present,—there.   [*Throwes out a bunch of Carrets.*]

Drink. We scorn their Courtesies, and their dry toyes.

Plen. Are ye so fierce? if the Seige continue, you'l Petition
for 'em: look for Fire and Sword—And so she pray'd me to   170
tell you.   [*Exit* Plenipotentiary.]

Steph. Arm, Arm, give the word, Arm, Arm.

All. Arm, Arm.

Within. Arm, Arm, Arm.   [*Exeunt All.*]
                                  [*The noyse of the assault renew'd.*]

        Enter Stephania, Beantosser, *and* Moustrappa.

Steph. Many a brush have I gon through in my time, but never   175
was any so sharp.

                        Enter Hectorio.

Hect. S'death, our Ammunition's spent, the dear dear dyet-
drink's gone.

Steph. And yet these Canibals, more insatiate then the Sea, are
not satisfi'd with our best goods; pull up the Harths, and down   180
with the Chimnies.

           Exeunt Beantosser *and* Moustrappa.

Hect. 'Tis in vain to strive.

Steph. Thou Cow-hearted cormorant, shall we be all lost for thee?

Hect. No, 'tis for thy obstinacy, thou insatiable shee-Woolf.

Steph. Rot your Sheeps blood.   185

Hect. Confound your brutish heart and bacon face.

Steph. Nounz, stir about, or I'le beat thy brains out with my
Bottle.

Hect. One word more, and by the Lord, *Harry.*

Steph. Thou dar'st not for thy Blood, thou dar'st not.   190

                      [*She Whistles.*]

       Enter all the Wenches.

For shame let not the Army see our difference, or thy
Cowardise.—

Hect. Pull down the House, and bury them in the Ruines: come
along boldly, my dear hearts, follow me, I shall find a time.—

           [*Exeunt Wenches.*] [*Exit* Hectorio.]

Steph. To be hang'd—I don't doubt it.   195

       Enter Beantosser.

Bean. O save the Syring and the Pot of Turpentine-pills for my
sake.—   [*Exit* Beantosser.]

Steph. Save nothing, cut off your Leggs and throw at 'em. Out
with the Exchange Womans Trunk of Perfum'd Linnen which the
Old Knight us'd to play hey Gamer Cook in—Out, out; save   200
nothing.   [*Exit* Stephania.]

       Enter Hectorio, *and* Moustrappa.

Hect. Fill the old Justices greazy Night-Cap with the Rosary of
Beads the Fryer pawn'd here but last Night, and down with 'em.

Mous. I wish they were all Cannon-bullets for their sakes.

                   [*Exit* Hectorio.]

       Enter Stephania, *hastily.*

Steph. Hold, hold, if you throw out the Beads, they'l take us   205
for Papishes, and then there's no Mercy; otherwise we may still
hope for pity because we are all of one Religion.

       Enter Hectorio.

Hect. Set the Led Cistern against the Door; all hands to the
Cistern, to the Cistern.   [Stephania *whistles.*]

       Enter all the Wenches.

Steph. My Girles, my Daughters.   210

Hect. Fellow Souldiers, dear hearts now for the last push.

Steph. All hands to the Cistern, away.—   [*Exeunt all.*]

Enter all, pulling at a Rope.

Hect. Hoa up; hoa up; cheerily, cheerily, pluck all together.—

All. Hoa up! hoa up! hoa up!

Enter Stephania *whistling.*

Steph. Down, down, all hands down, th'are going to spring a   215
Mine.   [*All run down.*]

Enter Beantosser, *and* Moustrappa.

Bean. There's a fresh Brigade of sturdy Blood-hounds come from
the Butcher-row.

Mous. The Barr of the Door's broke.—

[*Exeunt* Beantosser *and* Moustrappa.]

Steph. Barr it with the Constables staffe that lay here last   220
Night.

Enter Drinkallup.

Drink. O Mother, save your self, save your self.

Steph. Must our mouths be cold then?   [*She whistles.*]

Enter Hectorio.

Hect. All's lost, all's lost.—   [*Exit* Drinkallup.]

Enter Beantosser *and* Moustrappa.

Bean. They break in like a full Sea upon us.   225

Mous. O Mother, Mother, shift for your self.

Steph. Name not me: the Justices, and Jaylors, are my very good
Friends, and Customers.

All. Ah, there's no trust to Friends now.

Steph. If I dye, I dye, but I pity your tender backs, and   230
grieve for the present want all these young Gallants will have
of so many excellent Beauties.   [*Exeunt* Hectorio, Beantosser,
                         Moustrappa, *and* Drinkallup, *and return presently.*]

Hect. Yet, Yet, you may 'scape perhaps.

Bean. The poor hearts fight as if they were all *Scanderbegs.*

Mous. Yet, shift Mother, in two minutes 'Twil be too late.   235

Steph. No, here will I stay, and like a *Phaenix,* perish in my
Nest, the Fates so Decree.

Bean. Then let's among 'em, and dye all together, or break
through.—

All. Agreed, agreed.   [*Exeunt all.*] 240

A great noyse of fighting, crying Fire, Murther, &c. The Rabble,
and Wenches enter fighting. It Rains Fire, Apples, Nuts. —
A Constable and Watch enter, and drive all off.

Act I, scene ii.

[*The Scene chang'd to* Bridewell.]

Enter Prospero, *and* Miranda.

Pros. Miranda, where's your Sister?

Mir. I left her on the Dust-Cart-top, gaping after
the huge noyse that went by.—

Pros. It was a dreadful show.

Mir. Oh woe, and alass, ho, ho, ho! I'm glad I did not see it   5
though.

Pros. Hold in thy breath, and tell thy Vertuous Body, there's no
harme down, th'are all reserv'd for thine, and thy Sister *Dorindas*
private use.

Mir. And shall we have 'em all, a-ha! that will be fine i'fads;   10
but if you don't keep'em close, pray Father, we shall never have
'em long to our selves pray; for now ev'ry Gentlewoman runs
huckstring to Market, the youth are bought up so fast, that poor
Publicans are allmost starv'd, so they are so.

Pros. Leave that to my Fatherly Care.   15

Mir. And shall we have 'em all, ha, ha, he! O good dear hau,
how the Citizens Wives will curse us.—

Pros. Miranda, you must now leave this Tom-rigging, and learn
to behave your self with a grandeur and state, befitting your
illustrious Birth and Quality. —Thy Father, *Miranda,* was 50   20
years ago a man of great power, Duke of my Lord Mayors Dogg-
kennel.—

Mir. O lo, why Father, Father, are not I *Miranda Whiffe,* sooth,
and arn't you *Prospero Whiffe,* sooth, Keeper of *Bridewell,* my
Father?   25

Pros. Thy Mother was all Mettle. —As true as Steel, as
right's my Legg, and she said thou wert my Daughter; canst thou
remember when thou wert Born, sure thou canst not, for then thou
wert but three days old.

Mir. I'fads, I do remember it Father, as well as 'twere but   30
yesterday.

Pros. Then scratch thy tenacious Poll, and tell me what thou
findest backward in the misty back and bottomless Pit of time.

Mir. Pray Father had I not Four, or Five Women waiting upon
top of me, at my Mothers groaning, pray?   35

Pros. Thou hadst, and more *Miranda,* for then I had a Tub of
humming stuff would make a Cat speak.

Mir. O Gemine! Father how came we hither?

Pros. While I despising mean and worldly bus'ness, as mis-
becoming my grave Place, Quality, did for the bett'ring of my   40
mind, apply my self to the secret and laudable study of Nine-pins,
Shovel-board and Pigeon-holes—do'st thou give ear Infant?

Mir. I do, most Prudent Sir.

Pros. My Brother, to whom I left the manage of my weighty

state, having learn'd the mysterious Craft of coupling Doggs, and   45
of untying them; and by strict Observation of their jilting
carriage, found the time when *Venus,* Countess, Lady, Beauty, and
the rest of my she subjects, were to be oblig'd, by full allowance
of their sports, soon grew too Popular, stole the hearts of my
currish Vassals, and so became the Ivy-leaf, which cover'd my   50
Princely Issue, and suck'd out all my Juice. Dost observe me Child?

    Mir. Yes, forsooth Father, this story would cure Kib'd-heels.

    Pros. This Miscreant, so dry he was for sway, betray'd me to
Alonzo, Duke of Newgate; and in a stormy and dreadfull Night
open'd my Kenell Gates, and forc'd me thence with thy young   55
Sister, and thy howling self.

    Mir. Father! did they kill us then, pray Father?

    Pros. Near the Kenell they dar'd not for the love my dogged
Subject bore me. —In short to Newgate we were carry'd,—
And thence all in a Cart, without a cov'ring, or a Pad of Straw,   60
to Hyde Park-corner, we were hurṛi'd there on the stubbed Carkase
of a Leafeless Tree, they hoysted us aloft to pipe to winds,
whose murm'ring pity whistling back again, did seem to show us
cursed kindness.

    Mir. O poor Father! —But whereof, how did we 'scape, Father?   65

    Pros. Some Friends we had, and some Money, which gaind the
assistance of a great man called *Gregoria Dunn,* appointed master
of that black design: now luck begins to turn. —But ask no
more; I see thou grow'st pinck-ey'd, go in, and let the Nurse lay
thee to sleep.   70

    Mir. And shall she give me some Bread and Butter, Father?

    Pros. Ay, my Child,—Go in.— [*Exit* Miranda.] —So she's
fast. —*Ariel,* what ho my *Ariel?*

Enter Ariel *flying down.*

    Ari. Hayl most potent Master, I come to serve thy pleasure
Be it to lye, swear, steal, pick pockets, or creep in at Windows—   75

    Pros. How didst thou perform the last task I set thee?

    Ari. I gather'd the Rabble together, show'd them the Bawdy
House, told e'm they us'd to kill Prentices, and make mutton pyes
of 'em—I led them to the Windows, Doors, backward, forward,
now to the Sellar, now to the House top—Then I ran and call'd   80
the Constable, who came just as the Rabble broke in, and the
defendants were leaping from the Balcony, like Saylers from a
sinking Ship. The Duke and his Trayn I clap'd into a Coach.

    Pros. Are they all taken and safe?

    Ari. All safe in several parts of this thy enchanted Castle of   85
Bridewell, and not a hair of 'em lost.

    Pros. Twas bravely done my *Ariel!* Whats a Clock?

Ari. Great Tom already has truck ten:
          Now blest are Women that have men,
          To tell fine tale, and warm cold feet,   90
          While lonely lass lyes gnawing sheet.

Pros. We have much to do e're morning come: follow me, I'le
instruct thee within.

Before the gorgeous Sun upon House top doth Sneer,
The Laud knows what is to be done, the Laud knows where.   95

                                          [Exeunt.]

               The End of the First Act.

                  Act II, scene i.

           Enter Miranda *and* Dorinda.

Dor. Oh Sister Sister, what have I seen, pray?

Mir. Some rare sight I warrant.

Dor. From yonder dust-cart-top, as I star'd upon the noyse, I
thought it had been fighting, but at last I saw a huge Creature,
for ought I know.   5

Mir. O, whereof you mean the Coach.

Dor. Coach! i'fads, I thought it had been a Fish, I'm sure it
was alive, and it ran roaring along, and all the People ran away
from it for fear it should eat 'em.

Mir. O lo, O lo Sister, O lo! —ha ha he—   10

Dor. Why d'ee laugh at one, Sister? indeed it had eaten men,
for just by our gate it stood still and open'd a great Mouth in
the belly of it, and spit 'em out all whole.

Mir. Oh but Sister, whereof I can tell you news pray, my Father
told me in that Creature was that thing call'd Husband, and we   15
should see it shortly and have it pray, in a Civil way.

Dor. Husband, what's that?

Mir. Why that's a thing like a man (for ought I know) with a
great pair of Hornes upon his head, and my father said 'twas made
for Women, look ye.   20

Dor. What, must we ride to water upon't, Sister?

Mir. No, no, it must be our Slave, and give us Golden Cloaths
Pray, that other men may lye with us in a Civil way, and then it
must Father our Children and keep them.

Dor. And when we are so Old and Ugly, that no body else will   25
lye with us, must it lye with us it self?

Mir. Ay that it must Sister.

Dor. You see my Father gets men to lye with us, is not he a
Husband then?

Mir. No, you see he has no Hornes.   30

Dor. May be he sheds 'em like a Buck, or puts 'em in his pocket
like a rich Citizen, because he won't lye with us himself when he
can get no body else.

Mir. Fie Sister; no! Fathers and Mothers are kinder and wiser
now then they were heretofore look ye; for when they see their   35
Daughters will be modish and kind, they provide 'em Gallants
themselves to lye with.

Dor. But if we must take those our careful Parents get, only
for profit, 'tis as bad as marrying.

Mir. They doe it only 'till they get us Husbands to ease them   40
of the trouble.

Dor. O whereof Sister, my Father may spare himself of that
trouble, for I am old enough to shift for my self in a civil way,
for I was 13. last quarter Sessions, ay and wise enough too.

Mir. So we all think i'vads, but they can get us Coaches and   45
Settlements, whereof if we were left to our selves, we should
creep into holes, and get nothing but Bastards.

Dor. If our fathers don't get us Husbands quickly, wee'l make
him lye with us himself, shall we, Sister?

Mir. Ay, ay, that we will, but lets goe in now, He's about   50
something I long to see the end of, come lets not despair, the
flesh is strong.

Dor. O for a Husband, Sister, how I long.

[*Exeunt* Miranda *and* Dorinda.]

Act II, scene ii.

Enter Alonzo *and* Gonzalo, *affrighted.*

Alon. Gonzalo, Oh—my lodging is inchanted.

Gon. Mine with a Devil and like your Grace is haunted,
    Which plays more tricks then e're the witch my Aunt did.

Alon. First doleful groans at both my ears were lugging.
    Then whistling voyce like wind in empty muggin.   5

Gon. Shrieks as of switcheld lass I heard, and anon
    Sighs of enchanted ghost like roaring Canon.

Alon. With Princely hoof I knock'd, and noyse did follow,
    By which I find, O, Heavens! the House is hollow.
    My bed of state—   10

Gon. Of straw you mean—now good my Lord doe not lye.

Alon. Millions of devils mov'd, black, white, and motley,
    Six legs a piece, sharp claws.

Gon. Aye mine were so Sir,

Each tooth a needle, and each eye a saucer. 15
They stole my shooes, and in a hole I found 'em.
The white possest, black Armies did surround 'em.
Feircely the black attaqu'd, and white defended,
Horrour and death in ev'ry Seam attended.
The nimble black like hopping Devils ventur'd, 20
Mounted the works, and on the half moon enter'd.
But here the white serty'd as thick as sawdust,
And beat them off.
Then march'd up the red listed Reformadoes,
But what they did I dare not tell for fear. 25

Alon. Sage matrons say, where such kind Foes appear,
The Lord o'th' pasture shall not dye that year.

Gon. Unless he's eaten out—

Alon. On large deal board by prudent vermine chosen,
Two Armies more were fighting for my hosen. 30
If I but offer composition for my sock,
All leave the field, and to my Carkass flock.
No Fairy pinches half so close, nor no Witch.

Gon. 'Tis worse then nettle, sting of Wasp, or Cowitch.

[Alonzo *pulls a Louse out of his neck.*]

Alon. Treason treason, O here's one of the white devils, 35
treason treason, my guard my guard, Oh ho hoe.
Fortune has cheated me of all, pize on her,
I am no Duke now, but a poor Prisoner.

[*A noyse of horrid Instruments.*]

Gon. Oh what horrid noyse is this assaults our ears?

Devils rise and Sing.

1 Dev. *Where be those boyes,* 40
That make such a noyse,
And won't eat their bread and butter?

2 Dev. *Without all doubt*
Th' are hereabout,
Wee'l teach 'em to make such a Clutter. 45

3 Dev. *Who are the ring-leaders, who rules the Roast?*

4 Dev. Alonzo *the Duke, and another old* Toast.

1 Dev. *Wee'l put water in their porridge,*
And straw in their beds,

2 Dev. *Shooes on their feet, and a Comb in their heads.* 50

Chorus. *Wee'l put* &c.
And straw &c.
Shooes &c.

Alon. O save me, save me, *Gonzalo.*

Gon. I would give him the best member I have, to save my self.   55

Alon. These great He Devils will hearken to no such Composition.

The Devils Sing again.

1 Dev. *Rogues that from their Liquor shrink,*
       Shall scorch to death for want of drink.

2 Dev. *And who with false glass good fellows betray,*

3 Dev. *And tipple small beer in stead of their wine,*   60

4 Dev. *Then bubble their poor weak brothers at play,*
       To the whip and the stocks wee'l confine.

1 Dev. *So poor, so poor, they still shall remain;*
       Mirth, or good Wine, they shall ne'r have again,
       Nor never, oh never, be eas'd of their pain.   65

Chorus. *So poor,* &c.—
        Mirth—
        Nor never—

Gon. Never, oh never, eat Custard again!
       Oh murthering Sentence—Oh, ho, ho!   70

Alon. Never, never—O Inhumane Correction!
        Oh, they begin again—Oh.—

The Devils Sing.

1 Dev. *Who are the pillars of the wenching Trade?*

2 Dev. *The zealous professor, and brisk City blade.*

3 Dev. *The Gallants, and Bullies,*   75
       Do often grow poor, and bare, and bare.

4 Dev. *But these Canters, and close City Cullies*
       Are ne'r without Money, or Ware.

1 Dev. *What Slave permits*
       Such Hypocrites   80
      In peace to tast of all our sweets.

2 Dev. *In the midst of their joyes, they discoveries fear,*

3 Dev. *And their Wives, if th'ave any, shall make the score clear.*

4 Dev. *With Claps, and with Duns, we torment them all day,*
       And at night we take them and their Doxies away.   85

Chorus. *With Claps* &c.—
        And at night &c.—

Alon. Pox o'the Devil, 'tis too true, they did take our Doxies
away.

   Gon. Ay, and I would procure 'em a whole Regiment, for my   90
Ransome.

Alon. Alass, they were but Oysters before their meale; besides
they were so rotten, they would melt in their mouthes, all their
bones were turn'd to gristle: We are kep'd for the standing Dish.

Gon. Nay, then I am safe enough, for I have no more standing   95
Dish, then a post, my hearts no bigger than a Pins-head.

Alon. My poore Boy *Quakero*'s gone too, Oh, ho, ho!

The Devils Sing.

1 Dev. *Say, say,*
     Shall we take up these Rogues, and Carry them away,
     With a tory, rory, Tory, rory, rory, Red-Coats?   100
2 Dev. *Aye, aye.*
3 Dev. *Aye, aye.*
4 Dev. *Aye, aye.*
1 Dev. *Aye, aye.*
Chorus. *With a Tory, rory, Tory, rory, rory, rory.*   105
2 Dev. *No, No,*
     'Till we show them their Crimes, let e'm stay.
     With a Tory, rory, Tory, rory, rantum, scantum.
3 Dev. *Let 'em stay.*
4 Dev. *Let 'em stay.*   110
1 Dev. *Let 'em stay.*
2 Dev. *Let 'em stay.*
Chorus. *With a Tory, rory, Tory, rory, rory, rory.*

1 Dev. *Cabbage is windy, and Mustard is strong,*
     But a Lass with a wide Mouth, and a liquorish Tongue   115
     Will give thee the Palsie, though never so young.
     Then first let their Pride, let their Pride come along.
Chorus. *Cabbage.—*
     But a Lass—   120
     Will give—
     Then first—

Enter *Pride,* represented by a Painted, gaudy Woman, with a
    Glass in her hand.

She Sings.

Pride. *Lo here, here is Pride, that first left them aside,*
     An honest true Trojan, *and then she dy'd.*

Enter *Fraud,* a female Quaker. *Sings.*

Fraud.   *With upright look, and speech sincere,*
       In publick, I a Saint appear.   125
      But in private I put out the light,
      And I serve for a Whore, or a Baud.
      I have taught them to cheat, Swear, and Fight,
      For by Yea, and by Nay, I am Fraud.

Enter *Rapine,* drest like a Padder, with a Pistole in his hand.

Sings.

Rapine. *Send out a Scout*   130
   To yonder Hill.
   Stand, and deliver.
   You dogg, must I wait?
   I'm thy fate:
   Dispatch, or I'l send thee to Hell.   135
   From Fraud, *they thus proceed to force.*
   And then I, Rapine, *guide their Course.*
       Enter *Murther.*
A man drest all in Red, with two Bloody Daggers in his hands,
  and his Face and Hands stain'd with blood.

Sings.

Murther. *Wake* Duncan! *would thou couldst.*
   Disguis'd with blood, I lead them on,
    Until to Murther they arrive.   140
   Then to the Gallows they run.
    Needs must they go, whom the Devils drive.
       1 Devil *Sings.*
   Alass poor Mortals.
   They gape like the Earth, in the Dogg-dayes.
   What a rare life the Frogg has?   145
    Drawer, Drawer.
2 Dev. *Anon, Anon.*
1 Dev. *Give 'em drink, or they'r gone,*
   E'r their torment's began.
   Pour, pour, pour, pour.   150
    Heark, heark, how it hisses,
     See, see, how it smoaks:
   Who refuses such Liquor as this is,
   May he pine, may he pine, may he pine
     'Till he choakes.   155

Chorus. *Heark, &c.*

The Devils sing, and Dance round *Alonzo,* and *Gonzalo.*

Chorus. *Around, around.*
        Around, around, around.
        Let's sing, and tear the ground,
        There's no such sport below,   160
        Where sinfull mortals go.

                              [*Exeunt all the Devils.*]

Gon. Oh, oh, are you alive, my Lord Duke?

Alon. I cannot tell, Ah, ha,—Feel me, feel me, what a
drench they gave us, sure 'twas Spirit of Brimstone. —I am all
in a flame.   165

Gon. Their design, is to roast us as some do Geese, by putting
a hot Iron in their bellies, I begin to drip, they may make a
Sop in the Pan already.

Alon. Anon they'l cut off slivers from us, as they did from the
whole Ox, in St. *James*'s Fair.   170

Gon. Oh, 'tis intollerable: methinks I hear a great she Devil
call for Groats worth of the Crispe of my Countenance. —They
are all for Gristle.

Alon. Another cries Six-peny-worth of the brown, with Gravy,
Shalot, and Pepper, Oh there's a Collop gone!   175

Gon. Shalot, and Pepper, was well thought of, for if I am not
well season'd, there's no eating of me.

Alon. Indeed old Lord, you have a kind of Ven'zon haugou.

Gon. How can it be otherwise, my Lord, when I'me roasted
with the guts in my belly?   180

Alon. If *Shat'lin* or *Locket* had us, what *Olio's,* Raggous, and
Pottages, would they make?

Gon. So new a Dish never came from *France,* they would get the
Devil and all by us.

Alon. We should out-stink *French* Cheese.   185

Gon. O help help, here's Raw-head and Bloody bones, the Master
Cook of Hell.   [*A noise of horrid Musick; a Devil arises*
                                          with a Crown of Fire.]

                        Sings.

Arise, arise, ye Subterranean Feinds,
        Come claw the backs, of guilty hinds:
        And all ye filthy Drabs, and Harlots rise,   190
        Which use t' infect the Earth with Puddings, and hot Pies;

Rise ye who can devouring glasses frame,
By which Wines pass to th'hollow Womb, and Brain;
Engender Head-akes, make bold elbows shake,
Estates to Pimples, and to desarts turne.   195
And you whose greedy flames mans very entrals burne,
   Ye ramping queans, who ratling Coaches take,
   Though y'ave been fluxed 'till Head and Body shake.
   Come Clap these Wretches 'till their parts do swell:
   Let Nature never make them well.   200
   Cause Leggs, and Arms to pine, cause loss of hair,
   Then make them howl with Anguish, and sad groans.
   Rise and obey, rise and obey, Raw head and bloody bones.

                                      [Exit Devils.]

Devils arise with Bellows, and blow *Alonzo*, and *Gonzalo*, off the
    Stage.

A Dance.

The End of the Second Act.

Act III, scene i.

Enter Stephania, *with a Pitcher,* Beantosser, *and* Moustrappa, *all*
    drunk.

Steph.   *There was a noble Marquess,*
          Took up his Maidens carkass,
          Fast by the Fire side.
        A very homely Damsel,
        Her lips were soft as Lambs wool,   5
          Or marrow Pasty-fri'd.
    This is but a kind of a doleful Tune, to beat Hemp to, but hang't
lets squeeze the Picher, here's to thee my doughty *Amazon.*
    Bean. Right reverend Trot-up-and-down, I'le do thee reason
here *Moustrappa.*   10
    Steph. Come bouze it about, and a fico for the Justice. Fortunes
a Whore, and will be kind to her Sisters.
    Mous. Of the first Five men, we met Three were *Johns,* and Four
of those were Cukolds,—Which is a good sign, and so squeez the
juice.—   15
    Bean. A strong point of Consolation, let me kiss thee for that,
thou pretty, pocky, well favour'd Crack.

Sing.

Steph. *Fill the Dish* Molly,
     And think of a Cully.
     Here's a health to the best.   20
  Give us more Drink, a Surgeon that's jolly.
     And a pox take the rest.
     Molly *fill.*
     We cry still,
   Fill again, and drink round.   25
 'Till we empty the Pitcher, and fill up the Crown.
  Bean. Hold, hold, our Sister is grown hollow hearted, and like
a jilting Quean, forsakes us in our Tribulation.
  Mous. 'Tis ev'n what I look'd for,—The last Dish came as
slow, and frothy, as the last words of a declaring *Quaker.*   30
  Bean. When the Spirit sinks down his Throat, and rattles like
the departing Water in a leaky Pump.
  Steph. Blame her not, you hear she is sound still, ha! wilt
thou so? [*Knocks the Pitcher.*] Why that's very fair,—She
sayes, she will do w'ye for a Groat a time, 'till you are not   35
able to stand: I'le be hang'd if the worst Jugg in Town, will
do cheaper.
  Bean. Look, *Moustrappa* Weeps,—Hang losses, though our
Dancing Schooles ruin'd, we have sav'd our Instruments: And as
long as Men drink, and Women paint, we shall still jog on.   40
  Steph. There are more of our Dulcimers thump'd ev'ry Night in
Covent-Garden, then there are Ghittars scrap'd in a Week, in *Madrid;*
therefore I say, staunch thou false hearted misbeleiving Jewes-
Trump, do not many industrious Females live well by bidding
Gentlemen welcome to Town, singing at their Chamber doors?   45
  Bean. And trucking their *English* small Wares, for *French* Toyes.
  Mous. O this was a dreadful bout for poor *Moustrappa.* In robbing
me, they pillag'd six Brokers: ruind my Credit and quite kill'd
my old dealer, honest Jack the *Mercer;* for just as I had brought
his Body to such a state, that none else would touch him so that   50
I could set my own rates, they took me from him; the *French*
Farendine he gave me for a Gown is gone too. —But let the
World rub, when 'tis at worst 'twill mend.
  Bean. The devil take thee, for putting me in mind of my losses:
hang me if I can forbear weeping too.   55
  Steph. Then thou art in danger of drowning, for the water's
above thy mouth, and there's no passage by the Nose, for the
bridge was down long ago; and so she prai'd me to tell ye.
  Bean. My friend is a brisk *French* Merchant, I knew him a
Taylors Trotter: but from 3 Ounces of Jessimy-butter, halfe a   60
Pound of Powder, and 6 pair of Jessimy-Gloves, by cheating the

King of his Customes, and his fellow Subjects of their Money,
he's come to his beaten Farendine Suit ev'ry day: had not this
befall'n me, I had reduc'd him to his first being, and I had
hazarded the saving of his Soul, by the ruine of body, and   65
estate. —But he is but repreiv'd,—the pox will take him,
for he is a Termagant at laced Mutton.
    Steph. Mischeif light on ye both, for minding me of my losses;
there was scarce a Manchild in Town, gentle, or simple, from
Fifteen to Threescore, that did not pay me Tribute. —When I   70
walk'd the Streets, the Shop-keepers bow'd, the Prentices wink'd;
If five, or six Gallants stood in the way, Lord what rustling and
cringing was there to Madam *Stephania?* —Aunt, cries one, how
does my little Neece? —The Aunt, and the Neece, may both be
damn'd, for any thing you care to please: me he slips a Guinny.   75
When shall we cut up the Giblet Pye? cryes another. —Go y'are
a wag, cry I: there's halfe a Peece. Saies a third, is there never
a fresh Runlet tap'd? yes quoth I, but you shall be hang'd e're
you lick your lips with it; and so she praid me to tell ye: still
something's coming, for every now and then slips in a close   80
thriving Tradesman, look ye Mrs. quoth he, I do not use these
things, but the case is thus, I'le be at a word, I want a Wench,
give me good sound ware, here's your Money, ready Money: I won't
build Sconces, and bilk you, as your Gentlemen Bullies do, let me
have weight and measure, one words as good as a thousand. Well   85
quoth I, put your bus'ness into my hand, I'le use a Conscience,
aye, and I did too, for as I hope for freedome; sometimes I have
hardly got 8*d.* in the Shilling. But such were sure Customers, they
never left me for fear of discovery. Oh! I could tell you such
stories of Vestry-men, and Burgesses, as would make the Bells   90
ring backwards, i'faith,—Me, and my bus'ness, was the whole
talke of the Town, but all was kep'd secret, not a word mention'd,
unless 'twer in some Coffee-house, or the Streets. —But now
they all forsake me—but 'twill rub out when 'tis dry, and so
I squeeze.—   95

Sing.

Tough Hemp must we beat?
Dry Bread must we eat,
And be bumbled, and jumbl'd, and grumbl'd at too, too, too.
And drink nothing, but Wat, Wat, Water that's cold?
Then Harry, *and* Mary, *be merry and cheery, as long's we can do,*
*   do, do.*   100
And drive away sorrow, untill we are old.

Come bouze it about, and lets squeeze out the Pitcher.
He's a Rogue that stands out, and shall ne'r be the Richer.

Bean. Heres Ten go downs upon Re. *Moustrappa.*
Mous. Put *rem* to't or I renounce thee.   105
Bean. Renounce me Puss, not pledge me, thou salt Suburbian
Hackney, not pledge me.
Mous. Well Mrs. *Beantosser,* I hant stood three years at Livery,
and been hyr'd for 6*d.* a side on Holydaies, by Chimny-Sweepers,
and Coblers 'Prentices, I hant so.—   110
Bean. Who has, Mrs. Gillian flirt! Mrs. To and agen, who has?
Mous. I name no body, but touch a gall'd Horse, and he'l
wince.
Bean. But I know who has been taken up in the common, and rode
so many heats that they got the *French,* fashions that was ev'n   115
your own sweet Monkey face, I scorne to go behind your crooked
back to tell you so.
Steph. Fight Dog, fight Bear, still here's the juice of life.
Mous. I never danc'd naked at the *French* house for Mild-
Sixpences, goody Lerry-come-twang.   120
Steph. Out, out, that's old, that's old.
Bean. Nor I never walk'd the Streets at Night, stark naked in a
Buckram Suit, trim'd with black Ribons at the Codpeice, Mrs.
Gincrack, Mrs. Nimble-go-through.
Steph. No, no, that thou didst not old Tru-peny, that was the   125
Tailors Wife. —but 'tis old too.—
Bean. Who dress'd her self in mans cloathes to commit with
another Womans Husband under his natural Wifes nose, not you?
Mous. Who goes ev'ry Night upon Water to see men swim on their
backs, and show beastly triks, not *Beantosser,* no?   130
Bean. Who uses to be drunk at Tavernes tear her friends Wigs,
and then give all the Money she has for a frisk with the Drawer,
not Mrs. Betty *Moustrappa?*
Mous. Who storms the Fort in private with a Leathern Gun?
Bean. Go y'are a mean spirited Crack, to be kep'd by a Club of   135
Prentices: and so she praid me to tell ye.
Mous. 'Tis better to receive small ware then give broad Gold,
as thou doest like a silly Trapes.
Bean. The foul names thy own, and I'le dash it down thy Throat.
Mous. Help, help, murther, she'l murther me.   140
Steph. Hold, hold, hold, keep the Kings Peace, I say keep the
Peace, do you not tremble to use such bug words, if any body
should hear you it would bring a scandal on the house, and make
'em think us Whores, Restore her nose *Moustrappa,* and you

Beantosser, give back her Eye-brows: I say squeeze the juice,   145
and let acts of Hostility cease, I was governaunt at home, and
I will be justice of Peace here.

    Bean. I will have no Justice.—

    Steph. *Beantosser* be orderly, and thou shalt be my Clerk.

    Mous. No private bribery to Corrupt Justice, and to show that   150
I desire all things may be done without favour or selfishness, let
Beantosser be hang'd, and give me her cloathes, and so I squeeze.

    Bean. Justice, an't please your Worship, I'le swear the peace
against her.

    Steph. Bear back, bear back, good People don't press upon the   155
Court. —Constable stand by me, and go fetch the offender
before me.

    Bean. I command thee to come before my Lord Justice.
No—good people will ye ayd and assist me. —We are
resolved to assist Mr. Constable *Beantosser* to the death.—   160
La you there now.

    Mous. The Justice is an Ass, the Constable a Sheepshead, and
all the good People a Whore, and a Baud: and so she pray'd me
to tell ye.

    Bean. Grant me a humming Warrant to compel her to come before   165
you volens nolens of her own accord.

    Steph. How, how, thou art an evil Counsellor, and a Traytor;
thou seekest to deprive me of my honourable Imployment by force
quoth'a, no, some wiser than some: I am a Justice of peace, and
must keep the peace. But if I grant a Warrant to compel, I break   170
the Peace. If she comes, she comes, all must be done in a
peacefull way: Volens nolens quoth'a.

    Bean. Right Worshipfull, 'tis a common way to grant a Warrant.

    Steph. Ay, ay, 'tis so common that we Magistrates are all the
worse for't, it makes justice so cheap that no People of fashion   175
care for using any.

    Bean. An't please your Worship,

    Steph. Please me, and please thy self, I say still.

    Bean. To accept this small present?

    Steph. Hay! more Plots, how darst thou corrupt Justice, thou   180
Treacherous Strumpet! devour the bowels that gave thee Suck?
Now do I know she wants Justice, because she would buy it—
Clerk, take up the Bribery, and give it to the poor: since my
Clerk is absent I will vouchsafe to do it my self. —But did
this audacious Tatter-de-mallion declare with her own Corporal   185
voyce, that she would not come before us?

    Mous. I did, and I do again send thee word by my self, that

thou shalt come before me,—If thou wilt not, I command thee
to stay there,—and so I squeeze.

    Steph. Does the Rebel send word, her self being present, that   190
she will not appear?—it stands not with our high place to put
up such affronts. —Head-Constable, knock her down, and keep
the Peace.   [Beantosser *and* Moustrappa *fight.*]

    Steph. So now the whole Courts in an uproar, fight, 'till the
Devil part you. —Hold, hold, fall off, and unite against the   195
common Enemy.

      Enter Hectorio, *and* Drinkallup, *drunk and Singing.*

Drink.   Francky, *was his name a,*
        And Francky *was his name a;*
     His Beard was black, and his Gills were Red,
     And his Bill was all of the same a.   200
   With weapon full sharp, he fought 'till he was dead,
     With a Heycock of the game a,
      And Francky *was his name a,*
      And with weapon &c.

Hect.   Francky's *dead, and gon a,*   205
     Poor Francky's *dead, and gon a:*
    Thy browes are black, and thy lips are Red,
    And thy bellies soft as the down a.
   Let me be thy Worm, and at every turn,
    I will tickle thy flesh, and bone a.   210
      Then prithee cease thy moan a,
      Since Francky's *dead, and gon a.*
   Let me &c.—

    Steph. Silence in the Court, to keep a sound Peace, I make you
both my High-Constables of *Westminister.*   215
    Bean. ⎫
          ⎬ Agreed, agreed.
    Mous. ⎭
    Steph. Then by Virtue of my Warrant, which shall be made when
we are at leasure, bring those disturbers of the Peace before me.
    Bean. Woman, leave thy babbling, and come before the Justice.
    Mous. Hectorio, be uncover'd in the Court, and obey the Officers.   220
    Hect. What Court? what Officers?
    Bean. Why *Stephania* is Justice of Whorum, and we are both Head-
Constables.
    Hect. Then Officers, look to your Throats, for there will be

above Ten thousand up in Armes to Night. [*Sings.*] *And their*   225
bellies soft as the down a.
 Steph. He has confest, and shall be hang'd 'till he's dead.
Come thou Rake-hell, villain, dog, where are they, what's their
design, who leads 'em on, who brings 'em off, make his *Mittimus,*
before he answers, and send him to *Tyburn.*   230
 Hect. Old touch and go, why so hasty? —My Lord *Bacchus* leads
'em on: my Lady *Venus* brings 'em off: their design is to rise up in
their Beds, at midnight, to stab all the Women, and behead all the
Virgins they Catch.
 Drink. [*Sings.*] *With a Hey-cock of the game a.*   235
 Bean. O inhumane *Canibals!*
 Mous. Let 'em do their worst, the Women will be hard enough
for 'em, man to man.
 Steph. And I believe the Virgins had notice of their design, for
there is not one left in my Liberties: Head-constables, dispatch   240
this *Westminster* Wedding, I say, tye 'em up.
 Bean. Won't your Worship examine the Woman?
 Steph. I say, take her away, shes a Pick-pocket I know, by her
lac'd Shooes: besides, heark ye, she's a Witch, she carries an
enchanted Ring about her which turns Rich men to beggers, and   245
makes an Ass of a Justice of Peace.
 Drink. Gentlemen of the Jury, this Villain is no honester then
he should be, he rob'd me of a dozen of precious Turpentine guilt
Nutmegs, and a Pewter Squirt.
 Hect. Which is flat felony, for that's the Iron work to her   250
Plough, without which it must stand still, and her Familiars must
starve: and so she prayd me to tell ye.
 Drink. But because the old Rogue is a true friend to the Chuck-
office, I care not much if I save him, therefore you may bring in
the Fellony, Man-slaughter.   255
 Hect. Gentlemen, I am a Witness for the King, and so lets
squeeze all round.
 Mous. Art thou her Cozen after the flesh?
 Drink. No, he is my Husband's Brother, for they tumbl'd both in
one Belly.   260
 Bean. Then thy Husband has a whole Legion of Brothers, for halfe
the Town have tumbl'd in the same place: and so she pray'd me to
tell ye.
 Steph. Woman, put me in good Bail, or take her away, Jaylor.
 Hect. Hold, hold, what Bail dost thou demand?   265
 Steph. Two substantial Citizens, Aldermens fellowes, or
common Councel men, but no Cuckolds.
 Drink. No Cuckolds, Jaylor take me away,—hold, heark

you, If you'l take a Hundred that are Cuckolds, by the help of my
friends here they shall be produc'd presently. —Nay don't   270
bob down your heads, I did but try him.

    Steph. No, no! no Cuckolds.

    Hect. This is flat Tyrany, thou maist as well demand a Tribute
of Maiden-heads in the Teens: but Miracles are ceas'd.

    Steph. What is this notorious talking Rogue in for?   275

    Mous. For Robbing of the Vestry.

    Steph. How Sirrah, who made you a Church-Warden?

    Mous. 'Tis but a Vestry matter, and may be agreed at the next
Tavern.

    Bean. Who will pay Scot and lot, as they say, and serve in all   280
under Offices of trouble, if every Rascal shall usurp that very
Office, where they may reward themselves?

    Steph. Ay, without Authority, or paying a farthing for't, when
'tis well known substantial House-keepers have given hundreds
for't.   285

    Bean. Yes, and thriv'd upon't too, with a blessing on their
pious endeavours.

    Steph. Head Constables, take 'em away to *Limbo.*

    Hect. We defie thee, and thy Head-Constables, to mortal battle.

    Steph. Then blood will ensue: and so she prai'd me to tell ye.   290
--Sound a charge, and keep the Peace.

                        [*Musick plays, they dance, and Exeunt.*]

Act III, scene ii.

Enter Ariel, *and* Quakero.

Ariel *Sings.*

    Follow me, follow me, hey jolly Robin.
        The Moon shines bright,
        And Women are light,
    And most men had rather eat then fight.
        Then leave off your Coging.   5
    And follow me, and follow me hey jolly Robin.

    Quak. Four corners on my bed,
        Four beauties there ly spred.
        If any evil come to me,
        O goodness sweet deliver me.   10

    Blessed be thanked, it is now again departed; this Charme I
learn'd in the days of my *Paganis-me,* before I attain'd to the

inworking and the bowel-yearnings of the outgoing of the over-
flowings; but now that I am mounted into the Saddle, and exalted
to the House top, and lifted on the sounding Tub of reformation,   15
I am above the Fruit-mongers of the hard Streets of stony-
heartedness: and I am above thee Satan—ha it cometh again.
> *Four corners on my bed.*

> Ariel *Sings.*

> *Turn thy Stocking, and tye thy Shooe hard.*
> *Thy mouth being wash'd, and wip'd thy beard.*   20
> *Come away, come lets be jogging.*
> *Bo, bo, bo, bo,*
> *Heark, heark, how the Bettern bellows:*
> *Now is the time for good fellows.*
> *To it—to it—to it—to it.*   25
> *The Citizens Wife,*
> *Leads a merry, merry life,*
> *While her Husband at homes does grunt and groan.*
> *Whoo whoo oo oo oo—whoo ooo oo.*
> *Alass poor man he is sick of the yellowes.*   30
> *Cuckoe, cuckoe.*
> *Heark, heark, what the little birds tell us.*
> *Cuckoe, cuckoe, cuckoe.*

Quak. Torment me no more thou Hobgoblin, thou *Robin*-good-
fellow, thou *Will* with a wisp, thou Spright, thou Fairy, thou,   35
thou nothing, thou something—ha, what should this be,
assuredly here hath been some Crouder slain against his consent,
or murther'd wrongfully, or else 'tis the Soul of some profane
Singing-man that rejoyceth and gibeth at the death of the Duke
my father, Oh! O! O! it comes again.   40
> *Four corners on my bed,*
> *Four beauties—*

> Ariel *Sings.*

> *Youth, youth of mortal race, give ear,*
> *Thy Daddies dead, thy Daddies dead.*
> *To Stocks his feet, to Pillory his Ear,*   45
> *To whip of thong his flesh is ay turned;*
> *And tough battoon does thump his bone.*
> *O hone, O hone, O hone, O hone.*
> *Then little youth Nandy,*
> *Drink Ale and Brandy.*   50
> *His knell is hourly rung on his back.*
> *Heark now I hear it, thwick, thwick, thwack,*
> *Thwick &c.—thwack.*

Quak. This dolefull madrigal sayes my Father is in *Limbo,* that
is *Mortus est,* that is, he is dead, that is, he is departed, he   55
is gone, he is fled, he is no more; he is, he is, I say, he is,
that is, he is not.

> *His feet Stock-fish, his ears Pilchards, his flesh*
>   *Thornback, and Tough Battoon does thump his bone.*
> *O hone, O hone, O hone, O hone.*   60

Friend *Quakero,* this is no mortal business, though thou hast
done Satan right noteable service in perverting many, believe him
not, I say believe him not: hast thou forgot how it was resolv'd
in a full dispute, where a friend, ev'n *Guly Penno,* declared that
Satan was a lyer, nay thou hast not forgot, believe him not, yet   65
I will go to find out and be satisfi'd in the truth of the lye.

Ariel. [*Sings.*] *Thwick, thwick, thwick,* &c. [*Exit* Ariel.]

Quak. Hark, it is there again, it luggeth me by the Ears, even
as a Swine is lugged by a Mastiffe dog: or as one of your wicked
Idolatrous Misses is led by the rattling of a guilt Coach, or as,   70
as I say, or as ah ha em, or as ah a aa.

So much for this time.   [*Exit* Quakero.]

The End of the Third Act.

Act IV, scene i.

Enter Prospero, *and* Ariel. Prospero *eating a peece of Bread
    and Butter.*

Pros.   Now does the charm'd impostume of my Plot
                        Swell to a head, and begin to suppurate,
                    If I can make *Mantua's* Infant Duke,
                    Switchel my young giglet *Dorinda.*
                    Sincere *Quakero* to my power bends,   5
                    And shall with my discreet *Miranda* yoak,
                    Or be tormented ever here,
                    In my enchanted Castle of *Bridewellow.*
                    Great pity 'tis—for he's a pretty fellow.
                    Ariel!   10

Ari. What says my mighty and most potent Master?

Pros. How do these right puissant Ragamuffins bear their durance?

Ari. The Duke with haughty meen, for lack of food,
              Sits cracking Fleas, and sucking of their blood.
              With him is good *Gonzale.*   15

Pros. Is he so, Adsbud.   [*Throwes away his Bread and Butter,*
                                              in passion.]

Ari. From eyes of Glass the gummy tears that fall

– 89 –

           Down Iv'ry beard like Christal vermine crawl.
           The rest are picking strawes, and so that's all.

Pros. Where is *Quakero,* that young Princely Sprout?   20

Ari. Like Lanthorn-jack I led him all about,
           And now he's blowing of his nailes without.

Pros. Alass poor Trout.

Ari. I have so gally'd 'em, 'twould make your Graces hair stand
on end to see how they look; though your heart more stony was   25
then Coblers wax i'th dog days, 'twould make it in your mouth
dissolve like Culvers dung.

Pros. Do'st thou think so Spirit?

Ari. It makes mine open and shut, open and shut, like a fat
Hostesses greazy Pouch, so it does: and then the poor old   30
Gentlewoman and her daughters have almost torne one another
to peeces—I pity them.

Pros. And I will—hast thou that art so young a Spirit, so
little too—had a touch, a feeling of their Case, and shall not
I have a relish? —Well, *Ariel,* go let a Table be brought to   35
them furnish'd with most sumptuous Cates, but when they try to eat,
let two great Babboons be let down with ropes to snatch it away.

Ari. O Sir *Punchanello* did that at the Play-house.

Pros. Did he so? —then bend thy ayry ear.   [*Whispers.*]

Ari. More toyle—I pry'thee now let me mind thee of thy   40
promise then—where is my Two-penny Custard?

Pros. Ho now moody, doe'st thou murmure?

Ari. No my Lord!

Pros. Thou ly'st, Malignant thing, thou dost.

Ari. I pri'the my Lord, ben't so touchy.   45

Pros. Hast thou forgot the hairy Woman I freed thee from, who
sent thee ev'ry morning down her Gormandizing throat with a Candle
and Lanthorn, to tread the Ooze of the salt deep? —At other
times she made thee pass up against the strong Northern blasts,
when the capacious Bay was bak'd with brandy 'till thou hadst   50
clear'd thy passage to her nose, on whose sulph'rous top thou
sat'st Singing like a little Chimny Sweeper, hast thou forgot her?

Ari. No my dread Lord.

Pros. If thou more murmur'st, in some small dimple of her Cheek
I'le peg thee, where Twelve Sommers more thou shalt lye stewing   55
like a Maggot in a *Holland* Cheese.

Ari. O pardon great Sir this once, and I will be a good Boy,
and never do so more.

Pros. Then do as I commanded, but make hast least the Conjurers
of to'ther House steal the Invention—thou knowst they snatch   60
at all Ingenious tricks.

Ari. I fly most potent Sir.   [*Exit* Ariel *flying.*]

Pros. Now for the infant Duke of *Mantua. Hypolito* my Child
come forth.

Enter Hypolito *playing with Nickers.*

Hyp. Anan, anan, forsooth—you Sir, don't you stir the   65
Nickers, I'le play out my game presently.

Pros. Come gentle youth, exalt thy ducal chin, for thou shalt
have a Wife my boy.

Hyp. A Wife Sir! what's that, I never saw it?

Pros. No my boy, but they are now so common, young men can   70
hardly walk the streets for them.

Hyp. Don't go away, you Sir, I do but stay for a Wife, and then
I'le play out my game—O good Sir, let me have it quickly.

Pros. And so thou shalt, for my daughters sake; if he should know
Wives were growing out of fashion, I fear he would not marry, for   75
the stripling has a gentile fancy, I see by the neatness of his
cloathes.

Hyp. Will it play at Bullet with me?

Pros. Ay and Cat, and Trap-ball too.

Hyp. What is it like Sir? what is it like?   80

Pros. 'Tis so inconstant I scarce know what to liken it to, 'tis
still unsatisfi'd, restless and wrigling like an Eel.

Hyp. O pray let me have it then; I love Eels mightily.

Pros. But like an Eel 'twill slip from thee.

Hyp. But I'le bite it by the tail then, and shake it 'till it   85
lies still.

Pros. A shrew'd youth! well thou shalt have it, 'tis beautiful
as a Colly-flower, but like that too, when 'tis kep'd long, nothing
is more unpleasant.

Hyp. O Sir! I won't keep it long.   90

Pros. A very hopeful Lad! —But it won't part from thee.

Hyp. Then I'le beat it, and kick it, and run away from't.

Pros. Modishly said y'gad, still hopeful—but she'l save
thee that trouble, and leave thee as soon as any other will keep
her; for she's wild and skittish as an unbackt Colt.   95

Hyp. Is it like a Colt? O Lemine! then I'le ride upon't.

Pros. Alass poor youth! thou wilt soon be tir'd, and thrown off.

Hyp. No Sir, I shall never be weary of Riding; and I'le hold so
fast by the Mane and the Tail, that I won't fall off.

Pros. O fie, you must not use it like a Beast.   100

Hyp. What must I do with it then?

Pros. Why you must eat and drink with it.

Hyp. What is it, a Fork, and an Earthern-Pot then?

Pros. No, but she may make Forkes, and crack too many Pots.

Hyp. Then she shall teach me to make Forks.   105

Pros. Hold there,—you must enjoy none but her.

Hyp. Enjoy, ah ha! enjoy! what a word is there? enjoy! O
rare!—what is enjoy Sir?

Pros. Why, that is to be happy.

Hyp. Enjoy to be happy, then I'le enjoy all the Wives in the   110
World; —For I love to be happy Sir: enjoy!

Pros. I'le tell you more hereafter; go in and read your Horn-
book, that Treatise of Abstruse Philosophy I gave you last.

Hyp. I go forsooth.   [*Exit* Hypolito.]

Pros. Now by my best hopes, a shrew'd youth, a very shrew'd   115
youth, and a notable head-peace—I'm glad he's grown so
prudent. If all that Marry in this Age of liberty were so
Politick, we should see better times.

                        Enter Hypolito *crying.*

Hyp. O lo! o lo! o lo! Oh, ho, ho, ho!

Pros. What's the matter? what grand intrigue of Fate can reach   120
to the disturbance of thy manly Soul?

Hyp. Manly Soul, quoth a, 'twould disturb any mans Soul: I'me
undone Sir, while I was talking with you about a Wife, Tom *Bully*
stole away my stones.

Pros. Hah, thy stones, what stones?   125

Hyp. Why my bowling stones. O ho ho, now I can't teach my
Wife to play Nickers.

Pros. I'me glad 'tis no worse; O fie, fie my Lord, you must
leave off this boyes Play now, and learn to play with Children;
go, go in.   130

Hyp. By never, I'le pay that Rogue Tom *Bully,* when I catch him.

                                          [*Exit* Hypolito.]

Pros. Now I must instruct my Daughters.

   Long sleeps and pleasures follow ev'ry Novice:
   But plots and cares, perplex grave men of Office.
   Ye Gods!   135
   More blest are men of mean and low condition,
   Then *Bridewell*-keeper is, or sage *Magician.*

                                          [*Exit* Prospero.]

                        Act IV, scene ii.

                Enter Miranda, *and* Dorinda.

Dor. Oh Sister! I have such a twittering after this Husband,
   And my mouth doth so run in a civil way.

Mir. Are you not breeding Teeth Sister?

                              − 92 −

Dor. Zooks, if I am, the King shall know't.

Mir. 'Vads Sister, ever since my Father told me of it, which is   5
at least six Hours ago, I can't rest Day, nor Night, for ought I
know.

Dor. Its hole's hereabout, whereof looky' my Father said that it
should get me with Child pray.

Mir. O lo! get you with Child, what's that?   10

Dor. I can't tell, but I do shake and laugh when I think of't.

Mir. Heigh ho! whereof Sister you are affraid? —Let it come
to me, vads Sister I won't be affraid.

Dor. Zooks Sister, if my Father should send a hundred to get me
with Child in a civil way, I wouldn't be affraid.   15

Mir. O but Sister, whereof looky', my Father said that a Husband
was wild as a Cock-Sparrow or a Curl'd-Lamb, that he did now pray.

Dor. Then I would chirrip to't, and make it hop, and stroak it,
and make it wag its tayl and Cry blea, 'til it 'twas as tame as a
little Lap-dog, but my Father says they are always gentle at home: 20
and wild abroad.

Mir. Whereof Sister heark ye, now lets leave this idle talk, and
play the *Scotch* Morice.

Dor. Then I'le play forward, and backward, for that's the way   25
now.

Mir. No I won't play Boyes play,—I'le tell you what, you
should be a School Mistris, and—

Dor. No Sister, no I'le tell you what. You should be a Citizens
Wife pray, and so I should be a Lord looky', and I should come in   30
a Golden-Coach and be your Husbands Customer.

Mir. Ay 'vads that's pretty.

Dor. So I should meet you at the Play-House, and say Madam
looky' 'tis a thousand pitties such a glazing Di'mond of beauty
should be the Slave of a dull Mechanick Cit. and cry what d'ee   35
lack? Whereof you should cry then, O Lord Sir, you are mistaken
Zooks.

Mir. O Lord Sir, you are mistaken Zooks!

Dor. Then I should say Dam'ee Madam! you are a necklace for a
Prince, I'le settle Three Pounds a Year upon you, and you shall   40
have a Silver Baby, and a Silver house, and eat nothing but
Golden Custards, and Silver-Stew'd-Pruines: then you should say
whereof you have got a Wife of your own, my Lord?

Mir. Then you should say whereof you have gotten a wife of your
own my Lord.   45

Dor. Then I should throw my Wig, and say, Oh Madam! if you
love me, name her not. She's so dull and musty, the very thought
of her will make me swoun, Dam her. But you I doat upon. So then

you should let me lye with you in a Civil way.

    Mir. O ay, ay, I love that y'vads!   50

    Dor. And then another should lye with you, and another, so at
last you should be catch'd in a Baudy-house with your Husbands
under 'Prentice looky', and so be brought to *Bridewell* as Mrs.
Tweedlebum was t'other day.

    Mir. No, no, Sister, I won't play so—I'le tell y'what, lets   55
play Truss-fayl, do pray now Sister.

    Dor. Come then, I'le lye down first.

    Mir. Truss.

    Dor. Fayl.

    Mir. Send me well upon my Grey Nags taile. O Sister, Sister!   60
here's the Husband thing coming.

            Enter Hypolito *reading gravely in a Horn-Book.*

    Dor. Looky', looky', O sweet Father its Leggs are twice as long
as ours.

    Mir. What's that before so trim'd up with yellow Pissabeds, and
green Blew Bottles.   65

    Dor. See, see it pulls off half its head.

    Mir. Run Sister, run, I'me so affraid 'twill pull your head off
too.

    Dor. Zooks! I would rather lose a hundred Heads if I had 'em,
then stir a foot.   70

    Mir. Oh! it looks angry, I'me so affraid for you, Sister.

    Dor. Fear not me, if I offend it, I'le ly down and paw it with
my Four-feet, as our Shock does when we beat it.

    Pros. [*Within.*] *Miranda, Miranda!*

    Dor. O Sister! my Father calls you,—whereof she sayes she   75
won't come for'oth.

    Mir. She fibs, she fibs Father,—I wou'd come, but I am not
here for'oth—you spiteful pissabed Slut.

    Dor. But you are here for'oth.

    Mir. I wonder y'are so simple Sister, as if I could not tell   80
where I am better then you—for ought I know.

    Dor. I will take Husband first that I will.

    Mir. Hussey, am not I the Elder?

    Dor. Then you shou'dn't set your Wit against a Child.

    Mir. Well then Sister, I'le tell y'what, wee'l play heads or   85
tails, who goes first, that's fair now, e'nt it?

    Dor. Ay, and she that don't win shall lose and keep the door.

    Mir. Well ther's a good Girle, now toss up.

    Dor. A ha! my tails turn'd up, you must watch.

    Mir. Good dear Sister have done quickly, prithee do for because   90
you know why Sister.   [*Exit* Miranda.]

Hyp. Prospero has often told me, Nature makes nothing in vain,
why then is this kip kap here—tis not *aw* nor *e* nor *ee* nor *oo*,
nor *lm n o-q-py* you—it strangely puzles me; I'le ask him when
I see him next.   95
    Dor. Thing, thing, fine long thing.
    Hyp. Bessy come bunny, come buy me some lace Sugarcandy, Cloves
and Mace. Sure I am ready for a Wife now, I can read my abstruse
Horn *Philosophy.*
    Dor. O Rare thing, it talkes just like one of us.   100
    Hyp. Ha—what thing is that? Sure 'tis some Infant of the
Park, drest in her Mothers gayest beams of Impudence, and sent
down here to play at Hemp and Beetle; but stay, is not this that
thing call'd Wife? What art thou, thou fleering thing?
    Dor. Alass I am a Woman, and my Father says I must be a Wife   105
in a Civil way, pray thing don't be angry.
    Hyp. Angry, no, I'le sooner break my Trapstick; mun if thou
art that thing call'd Wife, which troubles poor men so that they
can't Wench in quiet—*Prospero* says that I must enjoy thee.
    Dor. If thou art that thing call'd Husband which art alwayes   110
sullen and niggardly at home, but merry and expensive abroad,
which feedst a Wife with tripe and Cowes heels, and treatest a
Mrs. with Woodcock and Teale, and fine things, and at last turnest
off a Wife with just enough to buy Bread and Cheese and worsted
Farendine, but maintainst thy Miss like a Princess, my Father   115
says thou must get me with Child for ought I know.
    Hyp. Get thee with Child, O lo! whats that?
    Dor. Whereof I can't tell, but I think you must dig it out of
the Parsly-bed.
    Hyp. Show me the Parsly-bed then.   120
    Dor. I won't, you ha' got nothing to dig with: you said you must
enjoy me, what's that pray?
    Hyp. Why *Prospero* says you are like a Colt, and then you should
be backt.
    Dor. Phoe, I won't play so.   125
    Hyp. Won't you, then look to't, for you are but a Colly-flower,
and though y'are so proud to day you'l stink to morrow.
    Dor. Zooks this is the silli'st Husband-thing I ever saw: I'le
run into the Garden, and teach him more wit in a civil way.
    Hyp. Nay if you run from me like an Eel, I'le bite you by the   130
tail.   [*Exeunt running after each other.*]
    Pros. [*Within.*] *Miranda! Dorinda!* Daughters, Daughters!
                  Enter Miranda *hastily.*
    Mir. Oh I'me glad my Father comes, for when Fire and Flax are

together, none knows how soon mischeif may be done. *Dorinda,*
Dorinda, my Fathers coming.   135

        Enter Dorinda *and* Hypolito *hastily.* Hypolito *runs off.*

Dor. O Sister pray lets Dance our new Heroick Song that our
Father mayn't know who was here.

        They Sing and Dance. Enter Prospero *observing them.*

Mir. Here comes a lusty Wooer, my dildin, my darling.
        Here comes a lusty Wooer Lady bright and shining.

Dor. I Wooe for one of your fair Daughters, my dildin, my
          darling.   140
        I Wooe for &c. —*Lady bright* &c.

Mir. I'm glad I have one for you my dild, &c.
        I'm glad &c. —*Lady bright,* &c.

Dor. She looks too brown upon me my dild, &c.
        She looks, &c. —*Lady* &c.   145

Pros. Enough, enough, all this won't blind me, come, come, come
stand, stand you here, and you there, nay, nay, nay, no
whim'pring.

Mir. Indeed, and indeed, pray Father, I did but keep the door.

Pros. Didst thou keep the door for thy younger Sister?   150

Mir. Yes forsooth, pray Father, that I did.

Pros. Blessing on thy pretty heart, cherish that gentile
Motherly humour, thou hast a generous Soul; and since I see thy
mind so apt to take the light impression of a modish Love, I will
unfold a secret to thee—That Creature, that thou saw'st, is a   155
kind of a Creature which is much like another Creature that shall
be nameless, and that's *Quakero.*

Mir. But Father, pray Father, shall that *Quakero* Creature be my
Husband? You said I should have a Husband before she, that you
did.   160

Pros. Shortly my *Miranda* thou shalt see the flower of this bud;
this Chit, chit, chit, chit, Cock-sparrow husband may serve thy
Sister well enough, thou shalt have a ho-ho-ho-ho-Husband, a
Horseman, go in I'le provide for thee.

Mir. Let me have the ho-ho, quickly then pray Father.   165

               [Going out she returns again.]

Father, Father, I forgot to make my Cursy; b'wy Father.

                  [Exit Miranda.*]*

Pros. Come hither *Dorinda,* why saw you this Husband without my
order?

Dor. Who I! truely I didn't saw'd him 'twas he saw'd me.

Pros. Come, come, your Sister told me all.   170

Dor. Then she fibs for ought I know, for she would ha' seen him
first, if I would ha' let her.

Pros. Tell me what past between you?

Dor. Nothing pass'd between us but our great dog Towzer.

Pros. What did he do to t'ee? come confess.   175

Dor. He did nothing, but I am affraid he wou'd if you hadn't come.

Pros. Why, why? speak out.

Dor. Because he came towards me with his tail up as stiffe as any thing.   180

Pros. Ha, I thought as much; wha what did he do then? the truth, I charge you.

Dor. Why he did nothing but walk to his Kennel.

Pros. Walk'd to his Kennel—who?

Dor. Why our great dog Towzer.   185

Pros. Pho, thou understandst me not, what did the Husband-thing do to thee?

Dor. Why nothing at all, for just as we got to the Parsly-bed, you frighten'd it away.

Pros. I charge you see it no more, 'twill Poyson you, and make   190
you swell as big as a house.

Dor. Not see it, I'le run th'rough Nine Walls, but I'le see it, and have it too, though it make me swell 'till I break in peeces.

Pros. Go get you in, y'are a naughty Girle.

Dor. The World's come to a very fine pass for ought I know,   195
one can't play with a thing an hour or two alone, or be in bed
with a man, but one must be naught: I won't endure it much long,
that I won't so.   [*Exit* Dorinda.]

Pros. So—my wishing Pipe
    Has swell'd my hopeing Cistern to a Flood.   200
    Dorind' and *Polito's* agreed, that's good.
    Now for *Miranda,* and the youth *Quakero;*
    When they are coupl'd too—there ends my Care'o.
                        [*Exit* Prospero.]

Act IV, scene iii.

Enter Alonzo, Gonzalo, *and* Antonio.

Gon. My hands are so tyr'd with stareing about for meat,
that my feet can look no further—I must rest
my old bones.

Alon. Old Lord I cannot blame thee, for I am seiz'd with such a
griping, that I cannot rest. —My Courtyers us'd to tell me I   5
had no humane imperfection; But here I will put off my hose and
keep it no longer for my Flatterers.   [*Musick as in Air.*]

Gon. Ha, these are a sort of doggish greedy Devils, come to devour the meat e'r 'tis dish'd up.

Anto. Do not for one repulse forgo the great design you were   10
about to act.

Gon. Oh help, help, something unseen has ty'd my hands behind me.

Alon. Mine are stollen away too, and 'tis well for 'em, for my mouth is grown so angry for want of meat, that if they should   15
again appear empty it would devour them.

Anto. Sure tis the Devils hock-tide, for mine are bound too.

Musick.

Alon. O hoark my friends,
      I fear we shall behold another horrid sound.

Gon. The Devil takes his time when we are bound.   20

Alon. He thinks to save his Bacon, feeble feind,
      But with bound hands our hands we will unbind.

Enter Ariel *Singing.*

Song.

Dry your eyes, and cease your howling:
For your Broath is set a Cooling.
While y'are in this Castle staying,   25
Eat and Drink, ne'r talk of paying.
Wine and Women here are plenty,
You shall tast of ev'ry dainty.
And as soon as you are weary,
Here are Crowds to make you merry.   30

                                     [*Exit* Ariel.]

Alon. I marry this is comfortable.

Anto. No Musick like that which powder'd Beef Sings,
      A consort of Carrets with hey ding a ding.

Gon. Wee'l dye for our meat, then our lives shall maintain.
      No butt'ring of Parsnips like long live and raign.   35
      O for a dainty vision of butter'd *Neptunes Tritons*
      And *Nereides.*

Two Devils descend, bringing down a Table with meat and drink on it.

Anto. See my Lord a stately Banquet, adzooks!

Gon. First come, first serv'd.

Alon. Happy man catch a Mackarell—But stay is not this meat   40
and drink brought to Poyson us?

Gon. Here may be more Spirit of Sulphur: but hungers sharp, and I will tast in spight of the Devil.

Anto. And I will have a Soop.

Alon. If both resolve, I'le take my part; Devil do thy worst.   45

As they try to eat, Gonzalo *and* Antonio *are snatch'd up into the*
Air, and Alonzo *sinks with the Table out of sight.*

The End of the Fourth Act.

Act V, scene i.

Enter Quakero, *and* Ariel.

Quak.   I Will be no longer seduced by Yea and Nay, I defie
                 thee.

Ari. I defie thee.

Quak. Thou art a Torch of Darkness, and a Snuff of the Candle
of the Socket, of the Dominion of Darkness.   5

Ari. O minion of Darkness.

Quak. Thou liest, I am no minion of Darkness, for look thee, a
lye is a lye, but the truth is not a lye, and therefore thou art
a lyer because thou lyest, as one of us hath it sweetly in his
Scourge-stick of Prophanishness, he is a right precious one,   10
truely, truly.

Ari. You lye, truely.

Quak. Out thou reproacher of friends, thou Bearward of the Bull
and Mouth, thou Lambskinner of *Lumbard-street,* thou waspish
Woolf of *Westminster,* thou a a, I say thou um ah a, thou-avaunt,   15
begone, fly, vanish, I defie thee, I abhor thee, I renounce thee,
yea, I will scare-crow thee, I will top and scourge thee, and I
will humguig thee, for I see by thy invisible Hornes that thou
art the very Devil.

Ari. Thou art the very Devil.   20

Quak. Out *Dagon, Bell* and the *Dragon,* I knew thee long agone.

Ari. I knew thee long agone.

Quak. What dost thou know of me? Speak, say thy worst, what
dost thou know of me? —I may fail, but I cannot fall, for I am
a Friend—a Chosen—One of Us.   25

Ari. A Chosen one of Us.

Quak. None of thy Usses, Satan, none of thy Usses; therefore
cease to torment me, for I will not speak one word more.

Ari. One word more.

Quak. Nay but I will not—I will Padlock my lips with   30
Patience, and set the Porter of peaceisness at the Wicket of my
Mouth, who shall knock thee down with the Silver head of saving-
gableness which is on the long Cane of Conscientious Reproof:
So that thou shalt no more enter into the Meeting-House of my
heart, look thee—*Obadiah Cod,* one of Us, who now sleep-eth   35

did declare soundly what thou wert, and I find it all as Poor
Cod said.

    Ari. Alas poor Codshead.

    Quak. Mock on, mock on, I will try if thou wilt answer me while
I sing my Sorrows to the snapping of my Thumbes: thy gibing is   40
all but nonsense.

    Ari. All but nonsense.

                 Quakero *Sings.* Ariel *answers like an Eccho.*

    Quak. *How dost do?*

    Ari. *How dost do?*

    Quak. *What's that to you?*   45

    Ari. *Whats* &c.

    Quak. *Pull out thy whistle, and tune up thy Pipe.*

    Ari. *Pull* &c.

    Quak. *Under yonder hollow Tree,* Nan *lyes asleep.*

    Ari.*Under* &c.   50

    Quak. *Her thing is her own, and I'le bounce it anon.*

    Ari. *—and I'le bounce* &c.

    Quak. *What care I for treasure, if* Nanny *but smile?*

    Ari. *—if* Nanny &c.

    Quak. *Within this shining place,*   55
             There's not a better Face;
      Faith now she's down, there I'le get her with Child.

    Ari. *Kind* Nanny *smiles, and she*
           Does sigh and snore for thee;
           O strange Simplicity,   60
           Follow me, follow me, and thou shalt see.

    Quak. Does *Nanny* sigh and snore for me, O Lo! umph, I ham
mollified: *Nanny* snore for me—think of thy Soul *Quakero,* I say
think of thy Soul; if the flesh prevail, thy Soul is but a dead
man.   65

    Ari. Follow me, follow me, and thou shalt see.

    Quak. Heark I am called again—this voyce may be a good Vision—
go *Quakero,* I say go—but it may be a snare, a trick to draw
me into derision, go not *Quakero,* nay, but I will not go—*Nanny*
sigh and snore for me, O dear!   70

    Ari. Follow &c.

    Quak. Again—Well I will go and advise with Friends, but why
shouldst thou advise, look thee, thy intention is good, though the
Action may wander, it matters not, I say, it matters not.—
Nanny sigh and snore for me, I will go—yea assuredly I will.   75

    Ari. Follow &c.

    Quak. Nay but I will not, it shall not be said *Quakero* follow'd

the Devil. —But look thee, go thou before, and I will come
after,—if that will do.   [*Exeunt.*]

Act V, scene ii.

Enter Prospero *and* Miranda *at one Door.* Ariel *and* Quakero *at another.*
    Ariel *goes off immediately.*

Pros. Advance the frizled frouzes of thine Eyes, and glout on
                    yon fair thing.
Mir. O dear sweet Father, is that a ho ho ho a Horse-man,
Husband?
Pros. It is my Girle, and a yerker too; i'faith were he not   5
tir'd with seeking of his Company, he would play thee such Horse-
tricks, would make thee sneer again.
Mir. 'Tis a most crumptious thing; i'vads if you'l let me have
it, I'le make no more dirt Pies, nor eat the Chalk you score with,
nor spoil your Garden to play with the Carrets before they are   10
ripe—pray sweet honey Father.
Pros. Well I'le leave ye together. But I charge you let him not
touch your honour.
Mir. My honour O lo! pray what is that father?
Pros. 'Tis a kind of fluttering Blood, which haunts the head and   15
hinder parts of men, some call it life-Blood, because death often
ensues when those tender parts are touch'd: in Women its seat is
on the nose, and on the ———
Mir. Where else pray tell me, that I may defend it.
Pros. That's the ready way to make it be betrai'd. —No, Child   20
of my bowels, thou shalt never know thy honour from me.
Mir. Now I do long to have this secret of my honour open'd:
prythee now, Father tell me where 'tis.
Pros. Why,—I know not what to say—On thy Elbow.
Mir. My Elbow, O lemine! fear it not then, for my honour is so   25
hard with being thump'd and leand upon, that a hundred touches
can't hurt it.
Pros. All falls out yet even as my Soul would wish, but I must
watch, I don't like this leering *Quakero,* such zealous youthes are
very Tyrants in secret.   [*Exit* Prospero.]   30
Quak. Assuredly Satan thou hast told truth, for she is here; But
yet thou art a lyer Satan, for she is not here, that is to say, she
sleepeth not, I will declare before her umph a ha h.—
    Most finest, most delicatest, and most lusciousest Creature,
whose face is more delicious then a Pot of Ale with Sugar and   35
Nutmeg, after a long Exercise.

Mir. Ha.

Quak. The savour of whose breath is more comfortable then the
hot steam of a Sundays Dinner.

Mir. O Lo!   40

Quak. Whose Paps are whiter then two Norfolke-dumplins stufft
with Plums—and softer then Quaking-puddings.

Mir. Why, did you ever feel my Bubbies?

Quak. Nay assuredly, but I hope I shall—Whose soft Palmes
are pleasanter then a warm cloath to my Sweaty-back, or a hot   45
Trencher to an akeing Belly.

Mir. O rare!

Quak. Whose Legs are smoother then my Chin, on a Saturday-night,
and sleeker then thy Elbowes.

Mir. O my honour, my honour, my Father sayes you must not touch   50
my honour pray.

Quak. Nay Sister, far, far be it from me to soyl thy honour. Thy
nature is more inviteing then a Christn'ing-Bowl of warm red Wine
deckt round with Lemon-peel.

Mir. Oh my dear ho, ho, ho, I can no longer forbear.   55

                                        [*She imbraces him.*]

Quak. Ah Sister mine; Now I ham even like unto that little
Creature called a Cat, when his back is stroaked, he longeth to
play with his tail.

Mir. And what are I like then, tell me what I are like?

Quak. Why thou are like a pretty little Mouse verily. —But   60
then I ham two-fold luck thee: first I ham like a Cat, and
secondly I am not like a Cat. —First, I ham like a Cat, for
when the Cat smells the pretty Mouse, he is restless and eager;
Nay, he cannot stand still, but frisketh, and jumpeth, and
dance-eth 'till he hath devoured hit; —In like sort, firstly,   65
I ham like a Cat, look thee, for I am inflamed, and eager truely:
nay, I am even ravenous after the pretty tender Mouse, as a Bear
bereaved of her Whelps. But secondly, I ham not like a Cat, look
thee; for that seeketh the destruction, and the nothingness of the
Mouse, but I thirsteth for the Propagation, look thee, and the   70
somethingness, yea the fullness of hit—ha, ha, hae.

Mir. And am I like a Mouse i'vads?

Quak. Unfeignedly.

Mir. Then I'le run into my hole.

Quak. And I will pursue even unto thy very hole, till I have   75
overtaken thee.   [*Exeunt.*]

                    Enter Prospero *hastily.*

Pros. Ah how nimble this zealous youth is—*Miranda!*—
Miranda!   [*Enter* Miranda, *and* Quakero.]

And you *Quakero,* come back, or I'le throw you over the Balcony,
and try if you have as many lives as a Cat.   80

    Mir. Zooks, Father you have spoiled the rarest play of Cat and
Mouse.

    Pros. Thou shalt be mouz'd my Girle, but every thing in season,
Rome was not built in a day, go in and trust me.

    Mir. Shan't my Puss go with me? come Puss, come little Puss.   85

                                       [*Exit* Miranda.]

    Pros. Hypolito my Child!   [Enter *Hypolito.*]
Come hither, discourse this trusty *Nicodemus,* 'till my return, you
must be acquainted with him.   [*Exit* Prospero.]

    Hyp. Pray Mr. *Nichodemus,* what did your Periwig cost you?

    Quak. Ha, ha, ha, he!

    Hyp. Ha, ha, he, how much is, ha, ha, he!

    Quak. I will be avenged of thee Satan!

    Hyp. Sa-tan, my name is *Hypolito!*

    Quak. I will no more stir up friends to despise Government, and
teach them 'tis a great point of Faith, rather to beleive an   95
ignorant upright Taylor, or a precious enlightened Weaver, then a
Book-learned Tythmonger verily.

    Hyp. Hey brave Boyes you Rogues Mr. *Nichodemus,* will you play
at Nickers you Sir, or Spand-farthing?

    Quak. Out thou lew'd scoffer, I ham a Professor.   100

    Hyp. A Professor, what's that?

    Quak. That is a friend.

    Hyp. And what is a friend?

    Quak. Why a friend is one of Us.

    Hyp. And what is one of Us?   105

    Quak. Why one of Us is a—I say is a—um a—ha, ha, ha,
he.

    Hyp. Pray Mr. *Nichodemus,* let me be one of Us, ha, ha, ha, he.

    Quak. I would thou wert, I say, I would—thou wert, but thou
knowest not the Splendour of the obscurity of the revealed   110
secret, umph-ha, thou understandest not?

    Hyp. Yes I understand you well enough, but only I don't know
your meaning.

    Quak. What Religion art thou of?

    Hyp. Religion? why I am a Duke.   115

    Quak. What Faith dost thou profess?

    Hyp. Why Faith and Troth, and adznigs, and by this Cheese.

    Quak. Ah thou art a beast, and shouldest be chastised; —
therefore provoke me not: —I say provoke me not.

    Hyp. Not provoke thee—but I will provoke thee: take that.   120

                                     [*Kicks him.*]

Quak. I ham not provoked.

Hyp. Then have at thee again.

Quak. I ham not provoked yet.

Hyp. There, then there.   [*Kicks him.*]

Quak. Nay, but I ham not yet provoked.   125

Hyp. No then I'le wear out my Shooes, but I'le provoke thee;
there, there, there, and there.   [*Kicks him.*]

Quak. Hold, hold, I say hold, for I ham provoked, and I will
chastise thee.   [*The* Quaker *throwes off his Coat, and beats*
                                        Hypolito *'till he lyes as dead.*]

Hyp. O murther, murther, I'le fight no more: you pull by the   130
hair Mr. *Nichodemus.*

Enter Prospero.

Pros. What dismal noyse is this—ha! *Hypolito* dead, then all
my toyl's in vain: —O thou unlucky chit, I wish I'de been
betwattl'd, when I had to do with thee.

Quak. Unfeignedly I was provoked, therefore I say have   135
Patience, that is to sayo be pacified.

Pros. Out thou stinking, sneaking Bastard, he's quite dead: If
ever thou serv'st me so again, I'le whip thee 'till the Blood
drops at thy heels.

Quak. Dead! then by Yea, and Nay, I never saw him in my life.   140

Pros. O cruel luck! *Ariel,* what ho my Spirit *Ariel.*

Enter Ariel.

Ari. What says my mighty, and most Potent Lord?

Pros. Most potent Lord! most Potent Fiddle-stick! See thou lazy
droan of a Spirit, what mischief here is done.

Ari. O lo! O lo! O Laud! Ah poor *Polly,* how sadly his finger's   145
scratch'd; but I'le fly to Mother Damnables, and fetch some
Pilgrim salve to cure it.   [*Exit* Ariel.]

Pros. Miranda! Dorinda!   [*Enter* Miranda, *and* Dorinda.]
O my Girles, we are all undone, look there *Dorinda,* thy poor
Polly's dead.   150

Mir. O my dear Puss-cat, shall us play Cat and Mouse?

Pros. Touch him not you Harlotry baggage, why when I say—
come away.

Dor. Alass! What's worse then ill luck?

Enter Alonzo, Gonzalo, *and* Antonio, *as driven in by Spirits.*

Alon. Never were Hogs so driv'n to *Rumford,* as we are hunch'd   155
along.

What, my Boy *Quakero,* and alive? touch my Flesh.

Quak. My Father after the Flesh, O sorrowfull joy.

Pros. You stare as if you had never seen me: have so short a
time as 50 years made you forget *Prospero?*   160

Gon. How, my good old Neighbour Duke *Prospero!*

Alon. The Devil 'tis: O strange, I thought he had been hang'd
long ago.

Anto. Laud, how a little time will change folkes, I had quite
forgot him, and yet I remember him as well as if 'twere but   165
yesterday.

Pros. Had I liv'd 'till now where you sent me, I had been dead
20 years ago—Know 'twas I trappan'd you to this my enchanted
Castle of *Bridewello,* where I yet govern, and am Lord Paramount.
I meant to be friends with you all, and Marry that strippling to   170
my eldest Girle; but see what he has done to the Infant Duke of
Mantua.

Gon. Never stir, if it be not honest little Duke *Polly.*

Anto. Alass poor Duke, as towardly a Child as ever broke bit of
bread.   175

Alon. And what dost thou now intend? we fear thee not.

Pros. *Quakero* shall be hang'd, and you shall be all tortur'd;
ho within there, prepare the Pillory, the Whipping-post, the
Stocks, and Cat of Nine tailes—entreat me not, dispatch.

Mir. I can hold no longer, O, ho, ho-ho-ho.   180

Quak. Ah, ha-ha-ha-e.   *[Enter Devils.]*

Pros. Away with them, See it done.

> *The Scene of* Bridewell. Ariel *flyes down.*

Ari. Stay, my most Potent Master, I come from the sage *Urganda*
of *Wildo streeto,* that renowned Enchantress, who has disarm'd all
the Knights of the White Spear and Nut-brown Shield: And that   185
most mighty Necromancer *Punchanello Alquiffe,* who with one breath
puffs Candle out, and in Rains Fire, makes Sea of painted Clout
to move, and Devils dance: by their ayd I have compos'd a
Suppositorial Ligneous puffe and blow, which would recal life
though Nine days lost, see here 'tis come.   190

> *Enter Devils with a great pair of Bellows.*

Pros. 'Tis joyful newes.

Ari. All must assist in the Ceremony.

Pros. Come then let's about it.

Ari. Help, help Lordlings, and Ladies help
To raise up great Heroick whelp.   195

> Ariel *Sings.*
> Prospero, Prospero
> *Looks feirce as a Hero;*
> *If* Polly *should dye, poor I shall be killed I fearo.*

Chorus. *Then blow the Bellows, blow the Bellows, blow the
Bellows blow; blow and puff, blow and puff, puff, puff, and*   200
blow, blow, blow.

     Let not his Soul,
     Get out of the hole
   And all shall be well I tro, tro, tro, &c.

Pros. *We conjure thee to wake*   205
    By a Two-peny Cake,
Alon. *By a Ginger-bread-role,*
Mir. *By a thing with a hole,*
Dor. *Which thou lov'st with thy soul;*
Gon. *By a Rattle and Drum,*   210
Anto. *By a great Sugar-plum,*
Quak. *As big as thy Thumb.*
Chorus. Polly, Polly, Polly,
    O Polly, Polly, Polly!
    To dye is but folly.   215
    For shame lye not there,
    While thy Doxie is here.
All. *How is't?*
Ari. *By th' Mass*   220
   As 'twas.
All. *Alass.*
Ari. Prospero, Prospero,
   Looks, &c.— [As before.]
Chorus. *Then blow the Bellows,* &c.— [As before.]
Pros. *We conjure thee agen*   225
    By a hobby Horse fine,
Mir. *By thy Bullets and Cat-stick,*
Dor. *By thy Rearer and Trap-stick,*
Alon. *By thy stealers and Pickers,*
Gon. *By thy Marbles and Nickers,*   230
Anto. *By thy Top and thy Gigg,*
Quak. *By thy Beard, and thy Wigg.*
Chorus. Polly, Polly, &c.— [*All as before. Then* Hypolito *rises.*]
Ari. Victoria, Victoria! He lives, he lives, he lives.
        [*They Dance confus'dly round him.*]
  Chorus. *Then let's hugg him, and lugg him, and tugg him, and* 235
smugg him: with a hey brave Polly, *and ho brave* Polly *and take*
him, and shake him, and wake him, and never forsake him, with a
hey brave Polly, *and ho brave* Polly.

  Pros. So, so, so, wellcome to life again, now the man shall
have his Mare again, and all friends.   240

  Alon. Thanks *Prospero,* and gentle *Ariel.*
  Gon. Thanks *Ariel,* and gentle *Prospero.*
   Enter Stephania, Beantosser, Moustrappa, Drinkallup, *and*
      Hectorio.

Steph. Ha, is it so, more Officers then head Constables, you
may dismiss the Pris'ners and adjourne the Court.

Bean. What, to the old place in *Moor-fields?*   245

Mous. Ay, ay, and make Proclamation that all good Religious
People may take notice of it.

Steph. No, no, wee'l meet here again to morrow. And so she
pray'd me to tell ye.

Drink. If any forget the place, that man in black may instruct   250
them, for he's Chaplain to the Society.

Pros. Set open the Gate, you may march off, y'ave had
punishment enough for once.   [*Exeunt Baud, and Whores.*]

Now to wipe out the remembrance of all past sorrow, I'le
show you the pleasures of my enchanted Castle. —*Ariel,* see it   255
done, and then be free.

Ari. I'le about it strait.   [*Exit* Ariel.]

M U S I C K.

The Scene drawn discovers Bridewell *with Prisners in several*
    postures of labour and punishment, then a Baud and Pimp drawn
    over the Stage in a Cart follow'd by a Rabble; then arise
Caliban, *and* Sycorax.

Sycorax. *My Lord great* Cac-Cac-Cac-Cac-Calyban.

For my sweet sake,
Some pity take   260
On beauteous Nimph in Caravan:
And check with seemly snout,
The Rabble rout.

Calyban. *Sweet* Sycorax, *my Mopsa dear,*

My Dove, my Duck,
My Honey suck-
-le which hast neither prick nor peer,
I'le do't, take tail of Shirt,
Cleanse Eye from Dirt.

Syc. *Give all the rest of this fair Crew,*   270

A play day too;
Let Pillory
And Stocks agree,
To set all free:
Let the Beetle and Whip, be both laid to sleep,   275
And Pris'ners Condemn'd, live for want of a slip.

Cal. *Dear* Dowdy *be jocund, and sleek*

The dainty fine furrowes of thine Olive Cheek:
I cannot deny
My pretty Pigs nye,   280

— 107 —

> *With a Nose like a Rose,*
> *And a lip as green as a Leek.*
> *Be calme ye great Parents of the Punch, and the Pad,*
> *While each Bully and Lass sing and revel like mad.*

Chorus. *Be calme, &c.—*   285
> *While each, &c.—*

Pimp. *Compel this roaring rout to fly.*
Baud. *And wee'l obey you by and by.*
Chorus. *Compel, &c.—*
> *And wee'l, &c.—*   290

Rabble. *Give's something to drink, and wee'l go hence,*
> *For we meant your honours no offence.*

Cal. *Here, here ye dogs, here's Eighteen-pence.*
Syc. *But ere you go, lets have a Dance.*
Chorus. *Here here, &c.—*   295
> *But ere you, &c.—*
> > [They Dance, and Sing this *Chorus.*]

> *Be calme ye great Parents of the Punch, and the Pad:*
> *While each Bully and Lass, sing and revel like mad.*
> > [Exeunt Rabble.] [The Prisners make a noyse.]

Cal. *Head-keeper, let Correction cease,*
> *Let ev'ry back and bum have peace.*   300
Syc. *Do not the noble Crew beguile,*
> *They came to sing and dance a while:*
> *And you of pleasure make a toyle.*
Cal. *Be still, be still, ye whips, and ye backs,*
> *Obey, obey, my lovely* Sycorax.   305
Chorus. *Be still, &c.—*
> *Obey, &c.—*

The Head-keeper flyes down and sings.

Head-k. *Her I'le obey whose breath's so strong, one blast*
> *Sent from her Lungs would lay my Castle wast;*
> *Come down my furies, lash no more,*   310
> *But gently poure in*
> *Salt and Urine,*
> *To cleanse their crimson Lace from gore:*
> *Whatever they are, or what'ere their transgressions,*
> *Free all in the Castle, free all;*   315
> *Make it as quiet, as at quarter Sessions,*
> *When they make visits to* Westminster-Hall.

Here Four Keepers fly down.

> *To the Houses you know,*
> *Round, round, must you go,*
> *And search ev'ry place where their Revels they keep:* 320
> *But no more 'till I call, shall ye handle the whip.*

Chorus. *To the Houses,* &c.—
    Round, &c.—
    And search—
    But no more—   [Exeunt Keepers.] 325
Cal. *Now the Tyrants are gone that made ye affraid:*
    Let each Daughter and Son,
    Make hast to come on;
   And be merry, be merry, be merry,
    Be merry, as a Maid. 330
Chorus. *Now the Tyrants,* &c.—

While the *Chorus* is Singing the Prisners are freed, and make
  ready for a Dance. The Scene shuts. A dance with Bottles in
  their hands.
Pimp. *Bullies my Lads, your Bottles sound.*
Baud. *And let sweet Eccho from each Lass rebound.*
Chorus. *Bullies,* &c.—
    And let, &c.— 335

A Dance.

Chorus. *Drink up all.*
    Drink up all.
    Drink up all.
    —Up all.
    Drink up all. 340

The Scene opens, discovers the Sea; —The Night going down;
  Aurora, and the Sun rising—the Musick sitting in an Arch
  of Chariots.

Cal. See, see black Queen of Night, is sneaking down,
    And under sable Arm, she hides pale Moon.
    And Dame *Aurora,* yonder with eyes grey,
    Shedding Od'rifferous dew, and breaking day.
    Behold the Skies Head-Waggoner, the Sun, 345
    With Firy steed up yonder Hill does run.
    Miss *Thetis* would from Watry Bed pursue.
    Begone fond Minx, must none have Sun but you?

Sing.

Cal. *Now your drink, and your Drabs you shall safely enjoy.*
Syc. *No Constables or Watch, shall your quiet destroy.* 350
Chorus. *Now, &c.—*
　　　No Constable, &c.—

Pimp. *Wee'l closely convey you by a private back door:*
　　　Your Ale and Stepony wee'l fill on the Score.
Baud. *Wee'l treat ye great lubbers, as ye sail in the Straits,* 355
　　　With Trumpets and Cymbals, and loud City Waits.
Syc. *In each room a soft Bed, or a Couch we will lay,*
　　　To please you all Night, and delight you all day.

Chorus. *In each room, &c.—*
　　　To please you, &c.— 360

A Dance.

Ariel *appears in the Air, and Sings.*

Song.

　Where good Ale is, there suck I,
　In a Coblers Stall I lye,
　While the Watch are passing by;
　Then about the Streets I fly,
　　After Cullies merrily. 365
And I merrily, merrily take up my clo'se,
Under the Watch, and the Constables nose.

Pros. Henceforth may our Enchanted Castle be,
　　　From Ign'rant Sprights, and sullen Devils free:
　　　May beautious *Nymphs* like little Lambkins play, 370
　　　While Swains with am'rous Pipes drive care away,
　　　Our harmless mirth shall still attend you here:
　　　'Tis mirth that makes you Youthful brisk and fair.
　　　That our Mock-Tempest, then may flourish long,
　　　Clapp all that would seem beautifull and young. 375

F I N I S .

EPILOGUE by *Miranda.*

Gentlemen look'ee now, pray, my Father sayes that I and my
        Sister must have ye all i'fads:
Whereof I can't tell what to do, I'le swearo;
If I take you, I lose my dear Quakero:
His things are precious, and his love is true;   5
But there's no trust in ought you say or do:
Yet for ought that I know,
My self could serve you all as well as any;
But my Father says, pray,
One Dish of meat can never serve so many;   10
For though you all agree in one design,
To feed like Schollers on the tender Loyn;
In this you differ with them, pray;
One little Chop, and one plain Dish will do.
You must have Sause, warm Plates, fresh hau-gou's too;   15
The large Pottage of glitt'ring show and dress,
Must cheat you to the little bit of flesh.
My Father says,
Since with such charge we purchase your Contents,
He thinks 'tis fit we should have Settlements: 20
For when you have enjoy'd, what that is, I can't tell i'vads; but
I beleive you can,—
Y'are dronish, cold and dull as any thing;
Just like a Bee, when he has lost his sting:
And though with all our tempting sweets we strive,   25
We ne'r shall catch you more within our Hive.
Then must our sinking joyes ne'r rise again?
Must we be kind, and show all in vain?
You lov'd the jilting Mother much and long;
She's old, the Daughter's active brisk and young: 30
If you neglect us still, pray,
May all your stony Pride unpiti'd fall;
And may our harmless Devils take you all.

ANNOTATIONS

All quotations from Shadwell's operatic *Tempest* in the annotations that follow are taken from the edition by Christopher Spencer in his *Five Restoration Adaptations of Shakespeare,* Urbana, 1965.

Hic totus volo rideat libellus. Martial, *Epigrams* (XI.xv.3): "I wish this little book to laugh from end to end."

The Introduction.

Mrs. Mackarel. Betty Mackarel, the actress who apparently played Ariel. The ensuing innuendo suggests that she dispensed favors on the side.
2. *Y'ave forc'd a reverend Bard to quit our House.* Of this Nicoll says: "This cannot apply to Dryden, but shows that he was not alone in abandoning the Theatre Royal" (I.328). Nicoll places Dryden's walkout during January or February 1677–78.
15. *a Pudding that has taken vent.* A cold sausage; or, possibly, a burnt-down fuse, a dud.
30. *yellow Boyes.* Guineas.
35. *right.* Fit, ready.

Prologue.

2. *She Familiars.* Familiar spirits, demons, or evil spirits, supposed to attend at a call.
8. *Tom Thimble.* A professional sharper or trickster; one who operates a thimble-rig (i.e., the old shell game). Tom Thimble is one of the characters in *The Rehearsal* (III.i).
11. *Bacons Brazen-head.* If Friar Bacon heard the enchanted head of brass when it spoke, the legend went, he would succeed in his projects; if not, he would fail. While Bacon slept, the head spoke—and shattered. The sense intended here seems to equate the brass head with the influential fault-finding critic.

Half-title page.

The New Tempest. The Mock-Tempest is generally not referred to by this alternate title.

The Mock-Tempest

Act I, scene i.

One wonders whether a case should be made for *The Mock-Tempest* as a Shrove Tuesday play, for it was customary for London apprentices on holidays, and especially on Shrove Tuesday, to search out prostitutes and to confine them during the season of Lent. Pepys (24 March 1667–68) saw young men in tow by soldiers "and overheard others that stood by say, that it was only for pulling down the bawdy-houses" (*Diary*, ed. H. Wheatley, 10 vols, London 1895–99, VII, 374).

1–12. Cf. operatic *Tempest* (I.i.1–8):

> *Enter* Mustacho *and* Ventoso.
>
> *Vent.* What a Sea comes in?
> *Must.* A hoaming Sea! we shall have foul weather.
> *Enter* Trincalo.
> *Trinc.* The Scud comes against the Wind, 'twill blow hard.
> *Enter* Stephano.
> *Steph.* Bosen!
> *Trinc.* Here, Master, what say you?
> *Steph.* Ill weather! let's off to Sea.
> *Must.* Let's have Sea-room enough, and then let it blow
> the Devils head off.

15. *flunder mouth'd*. Large-mouthed; i.e., like a flounder.

17. *earth us*. Force us into hiding.

SD 20. Cf. operatic *Tempest* (I.i.SD12): *"Enter marriners, and pass over the Stage."*

24. Cf. operatic *Tempest* (I.i.13–14): *"Alon.* Good Bosen have a care; where's the Master? / Play the men."

25. *Clack*. Tongue.

33. *the sweating Tub*. Cure for venereal disease.

33 ff. There begins here a series of efforts to prevent the raiding party from entering the brothel. For comment on how this parodies the original see "Introduction" above, pp. xxi–xxii.

37. *Whiffler*. An armed attendant employed to keep the way cleared for a procession.

40. Cf. operatic *Tempest* (I.i.20–21): ". . . what care these roarers for / the name of Duke?"

43. *Jourdans*. Chamber-pots.

54. *hung beef*. Drying beef.

66–67. *flye or I'le have ye all flead*. This is my own emendation for the quarto's "ye or I'le have ye all flead." Perhaps a word has been omitted before the first "ye." Changing it to "flye" helps maintain the context, sounds like one of Stephania's utterances, and is done without too much fuss.

72–73. Since lines from Shakespeare pop into the play every so often, it might not be too far-fetched to see here a glance at Cassio's lines in *Othello* concerning reputation (II.iii.262–63).

77. *farandinical*. Cheap, second-rate. Farrandine was a cloth used in the 17th century made partly of silk and partly of wool or hair.

78. *Ananias*. A generally used name for a Puritan. Cf. Jonson's *The Alchemist*.

82–83. Cf. operatic *Tempest* (I.i.24–25): ". . . if you can advise these Elements to silence, use your wisdom."

84. *Abednego*. A scriptural name (*Daniel*.iii) applied to a fanatic.

85. *Whore in grain*. A thorough, complete whore; dyed in scarlet.

89–90. Cf. operatic *Tempest* (I.i.41–42):

> *Must. within.* Our Vial's broke.
> *Vent. within.* 'Tis but our Vial-block has given way.

92. *Stepony*. A kind of raisin wine, made from raisins with lemon juice and sugar added.

95. *Common-shoar*. Sewer; originally the no-man's land by the shore where filth was allowed to be deposited for the tide to wash away.

96. *tenter Hooks*. Hooks or bent nails by which the edges of cloth are firmly held. The context suggests that the tenter hook poles could be used as ladders.

99–100. Cf. operatic *Tempest* (I.i.51–52): "*All within.* Haul Catt, Haul Catt, &c. Haul Catt, haul: Haul Catt, haul. Below."

103–106. Cf. operatic *Tempest* (I.i.73–79):

> *Enter* Antonio *and* Gonzalo.
>
> [*Trinc.*] Yet again, what do you here? shall we give
> o'r, and drown? ha' you a mind to sink?
> *Gonz.* A pox o' your throat, you bawling, blasphemous,
> uncharitable dog.
> *Trinc.* Work you then and be poxt.
> *Anto.* Hang, Cur, hang, you whorson insolent noise-maker,
> we are less afraid to be drown'd then thou art.

108. *tag-rag and long-tail*. All and sundry. Cf. Pepys, 6 March 1659–60:

> Well, they all went down into the dining-room, where it was full of tag, rag, and bob-tail, dancing, singing, and drinking, of which I was ashamed, and after I had staid a dance or two I went away.

Old Satin, Taffaty, and Velvet. Stephania apparently names some of the prostitutes who are bustling about. *rouze*. Frisk.

114–74. There is a general parallel with operatic *Tempest* (III.iv.62–103), where there is a truce scene between Stephano and Trinculo.

134. *mend the backs of the Chairs*. Advice to stand near the chairs to prepare to use them as weapons, or, possibly, to repair them.

137–38. *to save the great effusion of Christian Chamberly.* Chamberly is urine used for washing; the raiders are apparently tired of getting doused from the chamber pots (cf. lines 43–44 and 57–58 earlier).

141. *Dominion of the Straights mouth.* In Ben Jonson's time the *Streights* consisted of a nest of obscure courts, alleys, and avenues, running between the bottom of St. Martin's Lane, Half-moon (Bedford Street) and Chandos Street (Cf. *Bartholomew Fair* (II. vi.76–77).

142. *Fireship.* A vessel loaded with combustibles to be sent among enemy ships, as used against the Spanish Armada; the term is also applied, as here, to one suffering from venereal disease, a prostitute. Cf. Clodpate in Shadwell's *Epsom Wells* (II.i): "Ud's bud, marry one that would live at *London,* nay at Court; No, I had rather go to Sea in a Fire-ship."

158. *Ling.* Salt fish. *Poys'nous Oyl.* Gamey meat. Oyl seems to be a variation of "olio" here.

166–71. There is a resemblance here to Shakespeare's *Henry the Fifth* (I.ii), when the French ambassadors leave a cask of tennis balls for Henry as an impudent gift from the Dauphin.

177–78. *dyet-drink.* A liquid medicine. Cf. Etherege's *Love in a Tub* (IV.vi), when Betty learns of Dufoy's illness by her discovery of a "bottle of diet-drink he brought and hid behind the stairs."

187. *Nounz.* Wounds.

187–88. *my Bottle.* i.e., her flask. Cf. Shadwell's *The Miser* (I), where Goldingham counts among his unredeemed pledges "a Bauds Silver Aqua-Vitae Bottle."

191–92. Cf. Shakespeare's *Julius Caesar* (IV.iii.130–31): "For shame, you generals! what do you mean? / Love, and be friends, as two such men should be." Hazleton Spencer called attention to the resemblance (*Shakespeare Improved,* p. 95).

196. *Turpentine-pills.* Used as antidote for venereal disease. Cf. Shadwell's *The Virtuoso* (I): "Then says another with great gallantry, pulling out his box of Pills, *Dam-me, Tom, I am not in a condition; here's my Turpentine for my third Clap:* when you would think he was not old enough to be able to get one."

200. *hey Gamer Cook.* Coitus.

204. Cf. operatic *Tempest* (III.iv.52–53), where Trincalo complains about the wine being suddenly changed into water: "There's nothing but malice in these Devils, I would it had been Holy-water for their sakes."

213–14. Cf. operatic *Tempest* (I.i.36): "Hoa up, hoa up, &c."

215–16. *spring a Mine.* Explode a mine.

218. *Butcher-row.* In the Strand; butcher's shambles were located there.

223. Cf. operatic *Tempest* (I.i.92): "*Trinc.* What, must our mouthes be cold then?"

234. *Scanderbeg.* A name given by the Turks to George Castriota (1403–68) the patriot chief of Epirus, which became a common term for a militant warrior. The word is a corruption of "Iskander-beg" (i.e., Prince Alexander).

The Mock-Tempest

240 SD. *It Rains Fire, Apples, Nuts.* Cf. operatic *Tempest* (I.ii.SD 1): *"In the midst of the Shower of Fire the Scene changes."*

Act I, scene ii.

1–4. Cf. operatic *Tempest* (I.ii.1–4):

> *Enter* Prospero *and* Miranda.
>
> *Pros. Miranda,* where's your Sister?
> *Mir.* I left her looking from the pointed Rock,
> At the walks end, on the huge beat of Waters.
> *Pros.* It is a dreadful object.

13. *huckstring.* Huckstering, hustling.
16. *hau.* This apparent misprint may stand for "how" (repeated), or possibly for "man."
18. *Tom-rigging.* Being a tom-rig, or strumpet.
27–29. Cf. operatic *Tempest* (I.ii.19–22):

> . . . Canst thou remember
> A time before we came into this Cell?
> I do not think thou canst, for then thou wert
> Not full three years old.

32–33. Cf. operatic *Tempest* (I.ii.27–28): "What seest thou else in the dark back-ward, / And abyss of Time?"
34–35. Cf. operatic *Tempest* (I.ii.26–27): *"Mir.* Sir, had I not four or five Women once / That tended me?"
39–52. Cf. operatic *Tempest* (I.ii.41–56):

> *Pros.* My Brother, and thy Uncle, call'd *Antonio,*
> To whom I trusted then the manage of
> My State, while I was wrap'd with secret Studies:
> That false Uncle having attain'd the craft
> Of granting suits, and of denying them;
> Whom to advance, or lop, for over-topping,
> Soon was grown the Ivy which did hide
> My Princely Trunk, and suck'd my verdure out:
> Thou attend'st not
>   *Mir.*   O good Sir, I do.
>   *Pros.* I thus neglecting worldly ends, and bent
> To closeness, and the bettering of my mind,
> Wak'd in my false Brother an evil nature:
> He did believe he was indeed the Duke,
> Because he then did execute the outward
> Face of Sovereignty. Do'st thou still mark me?
>   *Mir.* Your story would cure deafness.

42. *Pigeon-holes.* A game in which balls were rolled through holes. "Pigeon-holes" is also a slang term for the stocks.

52. *Kib'd-heels.* Heels sore with chilblains.

53–64. In this passage the phrase starting "so dry he was for sway" in line 53, and the sequence starting from "they hoysted us" in line 62 and continuing through line 64, have no equivalents in the parallel passage from the operatic *Tempest* (I.ii.57–74). However, the Dryden-Davenant *Tempest* (4to, 1670) does include these passages:

> . . . he needs would be
> Absolute *Millan,* and confederates
> (So dry he was for Sway) with Savoy's Duke,
> . . . .

> . . . the very Rats instinctively had
> quit it: they hoisted us, to cry to Seas which
> roar'd to us; to sigh to Winds, whose pity sighing
> back again, did seem to do us loving wrong.

53. *Dry.* Thirsty.

61. *Hyde Park-corner.* Located at the great west end entrance into London, Hyde Park was one of the most well-known promenading places in the city.

66–68. Cf. operatic *Tempest* (I.ii.80–83):

> Some food we had, and some fresh Water, which
> A Nobleman of *Savoy,* called *Gonzalo,*
> Appointed Master of that black design,
> Gave us;

67. *Gregoria Dunn.* Gregory Brandon and his son, Richard (known as "Young Gregory") were hangmen of London from the time of James I to 1649. "Gregory" became a common term for a hangman. Following the death of Richard, Edward Dun became hangman until he died in 1663; Jack Ketch then took over until 1686.

68–70. Cf. operatic *Tempest* (I.ii.94–96):

> . . . here cease more questions,
> Thou art inclin'd to sleep: 'tis a good dulness,
> And give it way; I know thou canst not chuse,

69. *pinck-ey'd.* Squint-eyed.

74–83. Cf. operatic *Tempest* (I.ii.99–111):

> *Enter* Ariel.

> *Ariel.* All hail, great Master, grave Sir, hail, I come
> To answer thy best pleasure, be it to fly,
> To swim, to shoot into the fire, to ride

On the curl'd Clouds; to thy strong bidding, task
Ariel and all his Qualities.
  Pros. Hast thou, Spirit, perform'd to point the Tempest
That I bad thee?
  Ariel.   To every Article.
I boarded the Dukes Ship, now on the Beak,
Now in the Waste, the Deck, in every Cabin,
I flam'd amazement; and sometimes I seem'd
To burn in many places on the Top-mast,
The Yards, and Bore-sprit; I did flame distinctly.
Nay once I rain'd a shower of Fire upon 'em.

Act II, scene i.

The parallel scene is in operatic *Tempest* (I.ii.290–337).
1–7. Cf. operatic *Tempest* (I.ii.290–97):

>   *Dor.* Oh, Sister! what have I beheld?
>   *Mir.* What is it moves you so?
>   *Dor.*   From yonder Rock,
> As I my eyes cast down upon the Seas,
> The whistling winds blew rudely on my face,
> And the waves roar'd; at first I thought the War
> Had been between themselves, but strait I spy'd
> A huge great Creature.
>   *Mir.*   O you mean the Ship.
>   *Dor.* Is't not a Creature then? it seem'd alive.

12–13. Cf. operatic *Tempest* (I.ii.305–06): ". . . till, at last, all side-long / With a great crack his belly burst in pieces."
14–24. Cf. operatic *Tempest* (I.ii.309–18):

> But, Sister, I have stranger news to tell you;
> In this great Creature there were other Creatures,
> And shortly we may chance to see that thing,
> Which you have heard my Father call, a Man.
>   *Dor.* But what is that? for yet he never told me.
>   *Mir.* I know no more than you: but I have heard
> My Father say, we Women were made for him.
>   *Dor.* What, that he should eat us, Sister?
>   *Mir.* No sure, you see my Father is a Man, and yet
> He does us good. I would he were not old.

48–53. Cf. operatic *Tempest* (I.ii.330–37):

> Let you and I look up and down one day,
> To find some little ones for us to play with.
>   *Mir.* Agreed; but now we must go in. This is
> The hour wherein my Father's Charm will work,
>   Which seizes all who are in open air:
> Th' effect of his great Art I long to see,

The Mock-Tempest

Which will perform as much as Magic can.
Dor. And I, methinks, more long to see a Man. [*Exeunt.*]

Act II, scene ii.

The parallel for this scene is in operatic *Tempest* (II.iv) and in the Dryden-Davenant *Tempest* (II.i).

5. *muggin.* A long footless stocking.

6. *switcheld.* Having had sexual intercourse.

21. *the half moon.* A military formation of men or ships drawn up crescent-wise. Very likely referring to the buttocks.

22. *serty'd.* Serried, pressed close together in the ranks.

24. *red listed Reformados.* Red ants. A reformado is a soldier, especially an officer, from a disbanded ("re-formed") unit. "Listed" might mean: (1) striped; or (2) enclosed in or converted into lists for tilting. Since the context emphasizes the movements of the attacking insects, the second meaning might be more likely.

26–27, 33. Cf. Shakespeare's *Hamlet* (I.i.158–64):

> Some say that ever 'gainst that season comes
> Wherein our Saviour's birth is celebrated,
> The bird of dawning singeth all night long:
> And then, they say, no spirit dare stir abroad;
> The nights are wholesome; then no planets strike,
> No fairy takes, nor witch hath power to charm,
> So hallow'd and so gracious is the time.

34. *Cowitch.* Cowage; the stinging hairs of the pod of a tropical plant.

37. *pize.* Pox.

40–53. Cf. operatic *Tempest* (II.iv.52–61):

> *Sung under the Stage.*
>
> 1. *Dev. Where does the black Fiend Ambition reside,*
>   *With the mischievous Devil of Pride?*
> 2. *Dev. In the lowest and darkest Caverns of Hell*
>   *Both Pride and Ambition does dwell.*
> 1. *Dev. Who are the chief Leaders of the damned Host?*
> 3. *Dev. Proud Monarchs, who tyrannize most.*
> 1. *Dev.   Damned Princes there*
>   *The worst of torments bear.*
> 3. *Dev. Who in Earth all others in pleasures excel,*
>   *Must feel the worst torments of Hell.*

47. *Toast.* An excessive drinker.

57–68. Cf. operatic *Tempest* (II.iv.65–72):

> 1. *Dev. Tyrants by whom their Subjects bleed,*
>   *Should in pains all others exceed.*

> 2. *Dev. And barb'rous Monarchs who their Neighbours*
> *invade,*
> *And their Crowns unjustly get;*
> *And such who their Brothers to death have*
> *betrai'd,*
> *In Hell upon burning Thrones shall be set.*
> 3. *Dev. —In Hell, in Hell with flames they shall*
> *reign,*
> *Chor. And forever, for ever shall suffer the pain.*

60. *tipple.* Drink freely.

61. *bubble.* Cheat.

79–87. Cf. operatic *Tempest* (II.iv.79–88):

> 1. *Dev. Who are the Pillars of the Tyrants Court?*
> 2. *Dev. Rapine and Murder his Crown must support!*
> 3. *Dev. —His cruelty does tread*
> *On Orphans tender breasts, and Brothers dead!*
> 2. *Dev. Can Heav'n permit such crimes should be*
> *Attended with felicity?*
> 3. *Dev. No, Tyrants their Scepters uneasily bear,*
> *In the midst of their Guards they their*
> *Consciences fear.*
> 2. *Dev. Care their minds when they wake unquiet will*
> *keep,*
> *Chor. And we with dire visions disturb all their sleep.*

74. *zealous professor.* Religious fanatic.

75. *Canters.* A fanatic who used religious cant. *Cully.* One easily duped.

94. *standing Dish.* One that appears at every meal.

98–99. Cf. operatic *Tempest* (II.iv.92): "*Say, Say, shall we bear these bold Mortals from hence?*"

106–07. Cf. operatic *Tempest* (II.iv.93): "*No, no, let us show their degrees of offence.*"

108. A passage in a later section of the operatic *Tempest* (IV.ii.77–79) uses the same nonce-formula:

> *Trinc. Why then I'll tell thee, I found her*
> [i.e., Sycorax] *an hour ago under an Elder-tree,*
> *upon a sweet Bed of Nettles, singing Tory, Rory, and*
> *Ranthum, Scanthum, with her own Natural Brother*
> [i.e., Caliban].

117. Cf. operatic *Tempest* (II.iv.94–95): "*Let's muster their crimes up on every side, / And first let's discover their pride.*"

121 SD 162. Cf. operatic *Tempest* (II.iv.96–111):

> *Enter Pride.*
> *Pride. Lo here is Pride, who first led them astray,*

> *And did to Ambition their minds then betray.*
> Enter *Fraud.*
> *Fraud.*   *And Fraud does next appear,*
>   *Their wandring steps who led,*
>   *When they from vertue fled,*
>   *They in my crooked paths their course did steer.*
>   Enter *Rapine.*
> *Rapine.*   *From Fraud to Force they soon arrive,*
>   *Where Rapine did their actions drive.*
>   Enter *Murder.*
> *Murder.*   *There long they could not stay;*
>   *Down the steep hill they run,*
>   *And to perfect the mischief which they had begun,*
>   *To Murder they bent all their way.*
>   *Around, around we pace,*
> *Chorus of all.* *About this cursed place;*
>   *While thus we compass in*
>   *These Mortals and their sin.*
>
>   [*Devils vanish.*]

126. *I put out the light.* Three possible senses may be involved: (1) to douse the light as a fillip to sexual frolic; (2) to put out the much-touted "inner light" since it is not really needed; and (3) possibly a thrust at Shakespeare's *Othello* (V.i.7): "Put out the light, and then put out the light." The main point of the jest seems to be at the expense of the Quakers.

129. *by Yea, and by Nay.* A term of contempt for Puritans, especially Quakers. Specifically, it alludes to the famous scriptural injunction against oath-taking (*Matthew,* v.33–37). The phrase is common in the literature of the period. A 1674 broadside entitled *The Quakers Ballad* includes the following stanza:

> *To see holy seed so grand a designer,*
> *As to turn yea and nay into major and minor,*
> *Use language of beast* Concedo *or* Pergo,
> *And tickle their tobies at last with an* Ergo.

A lengthy satiric attack on the Quakers uses the phrase in its title: *The Quakers Art of Courtship: or, The Yea-and-Nay Academy of Compliments* (London, 1710).

129 SD. *Padder.* A footpad, highwayman, or thief.

138. Cf. Shakespeare's *Macbeth* (II.ii.74): "Wake Duncan with thy knocking! I would thou couldst!"

145. At the point in the operatic *Tempest* (III.iv.35–37) when the wine in Trinculo's butt is changed to water, Sycorax and Trincalo have the following exchange:

> *Syc.* This is the drink of Frogs.
> *Trinc.* Nay, if the Frogs of this Island drink such, they
> are the merriest Frogs in Christendom.

146–47. Possibly alludes to Shakespeare's *I Henry IV*, opening sequence (II.iv), where Hal confuses Francis the drawer.

164. *Spirit of Brimstone*. One of the four substances so named by medieval alchemists.

170. *St. James's Fair*. Held in an open space near St. James's Palace, and afterwards in St. James's Market, the Fair was closed by the Puritans in 1651; it reopened at the Restoration, but was suppressed before the end of the reign of Charles II. It opened on the eve of St. James (July 24), and ran for two weeks.

171. *methinks I hear a great she Devil*. Apparently, performances of the *Tempest* during the Restoration involved performers of considerable girth in the roles of the spirits. In the Dryden-Davenant *Tempest* (III.iii), Gonzalo says: "O for a Collop of that large-haunch'd Devil / Who went out last." Also, cf. *The Rehearsal* (II.v): "Udzookers, you dance worse than the Angels in *Harry the Eight*, or the fat Spirits in *The Tempest*, I gad."

172. *Crispe*. The crackling, or crispy rind, of roast pork.

175. *Shalot*. A small onion. *Collop*. A slice of meat.

178. *haugou*. Flavor, spice, sauce.

181. *Shat'lin*. Cf. Pepys, 13 March 1667–68: ". . . at noon all of us to Chatelin's, the French house in Covent Garden, to dinner." There are frequent references to this restaurant in the literature of the period. *Locket*. Locket's, a tavern at Charing Cross, founded by Adam Locket, who died about 1688; quite as well known as Chatelin's. *Olio's*. Meat stews.

186. *Raw-head and Bloody bones*. Imaginary monsters. Cf. Shadwell's *Epsom Wells* (IV.i): "This fellow [i.e., Clodpate] has not yet outgrown the belief of Raw-head and Bloody-bones."

188–203. Cf. operatic *Tempest* (II.iv.131–48):

> Arise, arise! ye subterranean winds,
>   More to disturb their guilty minds.
> And all ye filthy damps and vapours rise,
> Which use t' infect the Earth, and trouble all the Skies;
> Rise you, from whom devouring plagues have birth:
> You that i' th' vast and hollow womb of Earth,
> Engender Earthquakes, make whole Countreys shake,
> And stately Cities into Desarts turn;
> And you who feed the flames by which Earths entrals burn.
> Ye raging winds, whose rapid force can make
> All but the fix'd and solid Centre shake:
> Come drive these Wretches to that part o' th' Isle,
>   Where Nature never yet did smile:
> Cause Fogs and Storms, Whirlwinds and Earthquakes there:
> There let 'em houl and languish in despair.
> Rise and obey the pow'rful Prince o'th' Air.
>
> Two Winds rise, Ten more enter and dance:
> At the end of the Dance, Three winds sink, the rest drive
> **Alonzo, Antonio, and Gonzalo** off.

The Mock-Tempest

This song is one of the notable additions in the operatic *Tempest;* it did not appear in the Dryden-Davenant version.

189. *hinds.* Rustics, boors; a hind is a bailiff or steward on a farm.

199. *flux'd.* Purged.

Act III, scene i.

The parallel scene is in the operatic *Tempest* (II.i). Duffett does virtually nothing with Caliban (although he does insert him into the masque at the end of the play), but instead expands the part of Mother Stephania (Stephano) and the prostitutes, Beantosser and Moustrappa (Ventoso and Mustacho). The setting up of a government by the sailors, with "Duke Stephano" in charge, is paralleled in Duffett's sequence by the inauguration of a "court of justice" with Stephania as judge.

5. *Lambs wool.* A drink made of the juice of roasted apples with spiced ale. Summers called attention to the obscene pun *(Shakespeare Adaptations,* p. 269).

6. *Pasty-fri'd.* Fried into a pie or fritter.

7. *beat Hemp.* To beat the stems of hemp so as to detach the fibre. This was a common prison activity, similar to "beating the rock pile" in the twentieth century.

8. *squeeze.* Empty.

11. *fico.* The "figs."

17. *Crack.* Harlot.

29. *last Dish.* Of wine.

29–32. *as slow, and . . . in a leaky Pump.* This jibe at the Quakers has a basis in the operatic *Tempest* (IV.ii.86–87): "*Trinc.* I fear the Butt begins to rattle in the throat and is departing: give me the Bottle."

33. *her.* The pitcher.

38–40. Cf. operatic *Tempest* (II.ii.18–19): "*Ventoso.* Look! *Mustacho* weeps. Hang losses, as long as we have Brandy left. Prithee leave weeping."

43–44. *staunch thou . . . Jewes-Trump.* "Shut your mouth."

52. *Farendine.* A cloth made partly of silk, and partly of wool or hair.

60. *Taylors Trotter.* A tailor's girl messenger, although the context suggests a male. *Jessimy-butter.* An ointment perfumed with jasmine.

61. *Jessimy-Gloves.* Gloves of a light yellow color. Summers suggests gloves perfumed with jasmine *(Shakespeare Adaptations,* p. 271).

67. *laced Mutton.* Prostitute.

73. *Aunt.* Bawd.

77–78. *is there never a fresh Runlet tap'd?* "Don't you ever get any new prostitutes?" Cf. operatic *Tempest* (II.i.1–2): "The Runlet of Brandy was a loving Runlet, and floated after us out of pure pity"; and 6–7: ". . . Where hast thou laid the Runlet?"

84. *build Sconces.* To run on tick, or credit, especially at an alehouse.

90–91. *as would make the Bells ring backwards.* The sense suggests "in a manner that would really surprise you." Literally, the expression means to ring the bells beginning with the base bell, in order to give alarm of fire or invasion.

104. *Ten go downs upon Re.* This seems like a drinking challenge. A "go down" is a gulp or swallow. "Re" is possibly a nonce word here. Cf. Shakespeare's *Romeo and Juliet* (IV.v.120–21): "I'll re you, I'll fa you; do you note me?"

105. *rem.* Possibly an ellision for "re, mi"; cf. previous note.

106–07. *salt.* Lecherous. *Suburbian.* From the outer parts of the city. *Hackney.* Prostitute.

108. *stood three years at Livery.* To stand at livery is to be kept for the owner, and fed and groomed at a fixed charge.

109. *been hyr'd for 6d. a side on Holydaies.* Cf. operatic *Tempest* (II. i.149–51), where Trincalo says of Caliban: ". . . were I in *England,* as once I was, and had him painted, not a Holy-day fool there but would give me six-pence for the sight of him."

111. *Gillian flirt.* A "gill-flirt" is a young, wanton girl.

115. *the French.* Syphilis.

119. *danc'd naked at the French House.* Cf. Pepys, 30 May 1668:

And here I first understood by their talk the meaning of the company that lately were called Ballers; Harris telling how it was by meeting of some young blades, where he was among them, and my Lady Bennet and her ladies; and their there dancing naked and all the roguish things in the world.

119–20. *Mild-Sixpences.* Milled sixpences, having edges fluted or grooved by the operation of milling. Milled coins were more valuable than the older struck coins, by this time much debased by clipping.

120. *Lerry-come-twang.* A "leery poope" is a fool.

134. *Who storms the Fort in private with a Leathern Gun?* Moustrappa suggests that Beantosser masturbates.

137. *broad Gold.* A Broad-piece (of gold); the name applied after the introduction of the guinea in 1663 to the older coins of the preceding reigns, which were much broader and thinner than the new milled coinage.

138. *Trapes.* A slovenly woman or girl; a slut.

142. *bug words.* Words meant to frighten or terrify.

146. *let acts of Hostility cease.* In a later scene of bickering and quarrel between the low characters in the operatic *Tempest* (III.iv.99), Trincalo refuses to surrender up the butt: "That I refuse, till acts of hostility be ceased."

146–47. Cf. operatic *Tempest* (II.i.49–50): ". . . I was Master at Sea, and will be Duke on Land."

148. Cf. operatic *Tempest* (II.i.25): "*Trinc.* I'l have no Laws."

149–52. Cf. operatic *Tempest* (II.i.55–59):

> *Steph. whispering.* Ventoso, dost thou hear, I will advance
> thee, prithee give me thy voice.
> *Vent.* I'l have no whisperings to corrupt the Election; and

to show that I have no private ends, I declare aloud that I will be Vice-Roy, or I'l keep my voice for my self.

190. *Does the Rebel send word.* Cf. operatic *Tempest* (IV.ii.54), where Trincalo says, "Stephano, give me thy hand, thou hast been a Rebel"; and also line 60, when Trincalo repeats, "Thou hast been a false Rebel."

214–16. Cf. operatic *Tempest* (II.i.72–75):

> *Steph.* Hold, loving Subjects: we will have no Civil War
> during our Reign: I do hereby appoint you both to be my
> Vice-Roys over the whole Island.
> *Both.*[*Ventoso* and *Mustacho*] Agreed! Agreed!

220–21. Cf. operatic *Tempest* (II.i.91–93):

> *Steph.* We have got another Subject now [i.e., *Trincalo*];
> Welcome, Welcome into our Dominions!
> *Trinc.* What Subject, or what Dominions?

222. *Justice of Whorum.* A pun on "justice of quorum," the commission appointing justices of the peace "of whom" certain were specially named.

229. *Mittimus.* An order of imprisonment.

241. *Westminster Wedding.* A whore and a rogue married together.

248–49. *he rob'd me of . . . and a Pewter Squirt.* Cf. operatic *Tempest* (II.i.22–23), where Mustacho, in remembering his wife, says, "She gave me a gilt Nutmeg at parting." *Pewter Squirt.* A "squirt" is a syringe; a pewter squirt might be an enema bottle or a douching bottle.

253–54. *Chuck-office.* "Chuck" is a cant term for prison food. The chuck-office might refer to the prison kitchen.

288. *Limbo.* Prison.

Act III, scene ii.

5. *Coging.* Cheating.

6–10. Cf. the children's prayer:

> Four corners on my bed,
> Four angels there aspread;
> If any danger come to me,
> Sweet Jesus Christ deliver me.

12. *Paganis-me.* Perhaps an affected pronunciation of "paganism."

23. *Bettern.* The bittern, whose breeding cry resembled a "boom."

30. *the yellowes.* Jealousy.

37. *Crouder.* Fiddler.

51–52. Cf. operatic *Tempest* (III.i.26–27):

Sea-Nymphs hourly ring his knell;
Hark! now I hear 'em, ding dong Bell.

47. *battoon.* A stick or cudgel.
49. *Nandy.* Summers suggests a playful diminutive for "Ferdinand" (*Shakespeare Adaptations*, p. 274).
54. *Limbo.* Prison.
58. *Stock-fish.* Cod, split and dried; a term of contempt. *Pilchards.* Small sea fish.
59. *Thornback.* Rag-fish, another term of contempt.
60. *hone.* Whine, moan.
64. *Guly Penno.* Although Summers suggests William Penn, 1644–1718 (*Shakespeare Adaptations*, p. 274), this may well refer to Penn's first wife, Gulielma Maria Springett Penn, 1644–93, who was known as "Guli Penn" (cf. Lucy Violet Hodgkin, *Gulielma, Wife of William Penn*, London, 1947).
65. *him.* Satan.

Act IV, scene i.

1–2. Cf. operatic *Tempest* (II.ii.126): "*Pros.* Now my designs are gathering to a head."
4. *Switchel.* To have intercourse. *giglet.* A giddy, laughing, romping girl.
10–11. Cf. operatic *Tempest* (III.ii.128–29):

> What, *Ariel!* my servant *Ariel,* where art thou?
> *Enter* Ariel.
> *Ariel.* What wou'd my potent Master? Here I am.

12–37. Cf. operatic *Tempest* (III.ii.142–60):

> *Pros.* How do they bear their sorrows?
> *Ariel.* The two Dukes appear like men distracted, their
> Attendants brim full of sorrow mourning over 'em;
> But chiefly, he you term'd the good *Gonzalo:*
> His Tears run down his Beard, like Winter-drops
> From Eaves of Reeds, your Vision did so work 'em,
> That if you now beheld 'em, your affections
> Would become tender.
> *Pros.*   Do'st thou think so, Spirit?
> *Ariel.* Mine would, Sir, were I humane.
> *Pros.*   And mine shall:
> Hast thou, who art but air, a touch, a feeling
> Of their Afflictions, and shall not I (a man
> Like them, one who as sharply rellish passions
> As they) be kindlier mov'd then thou art?
> Though they have pierc'd me to the quick with injuries,
> Yet with my nobler Reason 'gainst my fury
> I will take part; the rarer action is
> In vertue than in vengeance. Go, my *Ariel,*

The Mock-Tempest

Refresh with needful food their famish'd bodies.
With shows and cheerful Musick comfort 'em.

16. *Adsbud.* God's blood.
24. *gally'd.* Vexed, confused.
26. *Coblers wax.* A resinous wax used by shoemakers for rubbing their thread.
27. *Culvers.* A culver is a pigeon.
30. *Pouch.* Mouth.
34. *Case.* A pun on the genitals.
38. *the Play-house.* Summers comments (*Shakespeare Adaptations*, p. 275):

Mr. W. J. Lawrence is of opinion that these references are to the "business" with the banquet in Shadwell's *Tempest* (III, 3), at the Duke's House. The two Spirits who there descend and fly away with the table of meat and fruits were no doubt dressed in some fantastic ape-like shapes with long tails. They are alluded to by Alonzo and Gonzalo as "Devils" and "Fiends". Punchanello would then be the rival manager (of the Duke's Theatre). Mr. Lawrence writes in a private letter to myself: "I feel sure *The Tempest* had never been given anywhere by puppets, unless, indeed, Punch had indulged in some burlesque of the Shadwell production. But this would have taken the wind out of Duffett's sails, and for that reason hardly seems probable".

40-42. Duffett refers in these lines to a sequence involving Prospero and Ariel which occurs early in the operatic *Tempest* (I.ii.147-50):

> *Ariel.* Is there more toyl? since thou dost give me pains,
> Let me remember thee what thou hast promis'd,
> Which is not yet perform'd me.
>   *Pros.* How now, *Moodie?*
> What is't thou canst demand?

44-53. Cf. operatic *Tempest* (I.ii.163-66):

> *Pros.* Thou ly'st, malignant thing! hast thou forgot
> The foul Witch *Sycorax*, who with age and envy
> Was grown into a Hoop? hast thou forgot her?
> *Ariel.* No, Sir.

Duffett seems also to have had I, ii, 181-87 in mind:

> Refusing her [Sycorax's] grand Hests, she did confine thee,
> By help of her more potent Ministers,
> (In her unmitigable rage) into a cloven Pine,
> Within whose rift imprison'd, thou didst painfully
> Remain a dozen years; within which space she dy'd,
> And left thee there; where thou didst vent thy Groans,
> As fast as Mill-wheels strike.

54-58. Cf. operatic *Tempest* (I.ii.203-08):

The Mock-Tempest

> *Pros.* If thou more murmurest, I will rend an Oak,
> And peg thee in his knotty entrails, till thou
> Hast houl'd away twelve Winters more.
> *Ariel.* Pardon, Master,
> I will be correspondent to command,
> And be a gentle spirit.

59–60. *the Conjurers of to'ther House.* The management of the Duke's House.

SD 65. *Nickers.* Marbles.

67–68. Cf. operatic *Tempest* (II.ii.19–21):

> *Pros.* O gentle Youth, Fate waits for thee abroad,
> A black star threatens thee, and death unseen
> Stands ready to devour thee.

69. Cf. operatic *Tempest* (II.ii.33): "Hippolito. Women! I never heard of them before."

78. *Bullet.* Bowls, a bowling game.

79. *Cat, and Trap-ball.* Games in which a ball, balanced on a stick, is flipped into the air and batted with the stick or caught back onto the hollowed stick. In Shadwell's *The Sullen Lovers* (III), Sir Positive-at-All brags of being an expert at cat and trap-ball.

80–89. There is a general similarity here to operatic *Tempest* (II.ii.34–46):

> [*Hip.*] What are Women like?
> *Pros.* Imagine something between young Men and Angels:
> Fatally beauteous, and have killing Eyes,
> Their voices charm beyond the Nightingales,
> They are all enchantment, those who once behold 'em,
> Are made their slaves for ever.
> *Hip.* Then I will wink and fight with 'em.
> *Pros.* 'Tis but in vain,
> They'l haunt you in your very sleep.
> *Hip.* Then I'l revenge it on 'em when I wake.
> *Pros.* You are without all possibility of revenge,
> They are so beautiful, that you can ne'r attempt,
> Nor wish to hurt them.
> *Hip.*   Are they so beautiful?

96. *Lemine.* A mild oath.

112–18. Cf. operatic *Tempest* (II.ii.63–72):

> *Pros.* Go in and read the Book I gave you last.
> To morrow I may bring you better news.
> *Hip.* I shall obey you, Sir.   [*Exit* Hippolito.]
> *Pros.* So, so; I hope this Lesson has secur'd him,
> For I have been constrain'd to change his lodging
> From yonder Rock where first I bred him up,
> And here have brought him home to my own Cell,
> Because the Shipwrack happen'd near his Mansion.

The Mock-Tempest

> I hope he will not stir beyond his limits,
> For hitherto he hath been all obedience:

Also cf. Prospero's remark to Ferdinand (III.vi.101): "Go practise your Philosophy within."

116. *head-piece.* A man of intellect, a "brain."

131. *By never.* A mild oath.

132–37. These lines have a general resemblance to Prospero's lines following Hippolito's exit (III.vi.156–64):

> On what strange grounds we build our hopes and fears,
> Man's life is all a mist, and in the dark,
> Our fortunes meet us.
> If fate be not, then what can we foresee?
> Or how can we avoid it, if it be?
> If by free-will in our own paths we move,
> How are we bounded by Decrees above?
> Whether we drive, or whether we are driven,
> If ill, 'tis ours; if good, the act of Heaven.

Act IV, scene ii.

16–21. Cf. operatic *Tempest* (II.ii.93–96):

> *Dorinda.* Do they run wild about the Woods?
> *Pros.* No, they are wild within doors, in Chambers,
> And in Closets.
> *Dorinda.* But, Father, I would stroak 'em,
> And make 'em gentle, then sure they would not hurt me.

17. *Curl'd.* Adorned with curls.

23. *Scotch Morice.* Morris-dance.

56. *Truss-fayl.* A children's game similar to leap-frog and "Johnny-ride-the-pony."

60–63. Cf. operatic *Tempest* (II.iii.6–7):

> *Dor.* O Sister, there it is, it walks about like one of us.
> *Mir.* I, just so, and has legs as we have too.

64. *Pissabeds.* Dandelions.

65. *Blew Bottles.* Blue corn flowers.

73. *Shock.* A lap-dog.

74–78. Cf. operatic *Tempest* (II.iii.30–33):

> *Pros. within. Miranda,* Child, where are you!
> *Mir.* Do you not hear my Father call? go in.
> *Dor.* 'Twas you he nam'd, not me; I will but say
> My prayers, and follow you immediately.

The Mock-Tempest

93. *kip kap.* Fool.

94. *py you.* Some coarse stage-business is apparently involved here.

101–09. Cf. operatic *Tempest* (II.iii.36–48):

> *Hip. seeing her.* What thing is that? sure 'tis some Infant
> of
> The Sun, dress'd in his Fathers gayest Beams,
> And comes to play with Birds: my sight is dazl'd,
> And yet I find I'm loth to shut my Eyes.
> I must go nearer it—but stay a while;
> May it not be that beauteous Murderer, Woman,
> Which I was charg'd to shun? Speak, what art thou?
> Thou shining Vision!
>   *Dor.* Alas, I know not; but I'm told I am a Woman;
> Do not hurt me, pray, fair thing.
>   *Hip.* I'd sooner tear my eyes out, then consent
> To do you any harm; though I was told
> A Woman was my Enemy.

101–02. *Infant of the Park.* Prostitute.

103. *play at Hemp and Beetle.* "Work the rock-pile" is perhaps the best modern equivalent. To play at hemp is similar to Stephania's "beat Hemp" (cf. note to III.i.7); while to play with a beetle suggests hard labor. A "beetle" is a sledge-hammer for heavy-duty pounding.

104. *fleering.* Sneering.

107. *Trapstick.* Used in the game of trap-ball (cf. note to IV.i.79). *mun.* Man.

112. *Cowes heels.* The foot of a cow or ox stewed so as to form a jelly; or, the dish prepared from this.

112–13. *a Mrs.* A mistress.

113. *Teale.* A small fresh-water fowl.

119. *the Parsly-bed.* Pudendum.

125. *Phoe.* Phooey.

138. *dildin.* A small dildo, or phallus.

149. *keep the door.* i.e., while the tryst is consummated within. Cf. Duffett's *Empress* (ii.277), where Muly Hamet admits: "I did with hands in Pocket door maintain."

152–57. Cf. operatic *Tempest* (III.ii.22–27):

> *Pros.* Cherish those thoughts: you have a gen'rous soul;
> And since I see your mind not apt to take
> The light Impressions of a sudden love,
> I will unfold a secret to your knowledge.
> That Creature which you saw, is of a kind
> Which Nature made a prop and guide to yours.

161–64. Cf. operatic *Tempest* (III.ii.35–38):

> For shortly, my *Miranda,* you shall see
> Another of this kind, the full-blown Flower,
> Of which this Youth was but the Op'ning Bud.
> Go in, and send your Sister to me.

166. *Cursy.* Curtsy.

167-72. Cf. operatic *Tempest* (III.ii.41-46):

> O Come hither, you have seen a man to day,
> Against my strict command.
>> *Dor.* Who I? indeed I saw him but a little, Sir.
>> *Pros.* Come, come, be clear. Your Sister told me all.
>> *Dor.* Did she? truly she would have seen him more
> Then I, but that I would not let her.

173. Cf. operatic *Tempest* (III.ii.83): "What past betwixt you and that horrid creature?"

199-200. Cf. operatic *Tempest* (III.ii.126): "Now my designs are gathering to a head."

200. *hopeing.* Well-intentioned: probably balances "wishing" (199).

Act IV, scene iii.

The opening lines of this scene suggest the possibility that Duffett made use of the Dryden-Davenant *Tempest* (4to, 1670). The main action of the scene, however—the appearance of the table of food on stage and its being whisked away—does not occur in the Dryden-Davenant version, in which this business with the table occurs offstage.

1-7. Cf. Dryden-Davenant *Tempest* (III.iii); (words with emphasis added do not appear in operatic *Tempest*):

> *Gonz.* I am weary, and can go no farther, Sir,
> *My old Bones ake, here's a Maze trod indeed,*
> *Through Forth-rights and Meanders, by your Patience*
> *I needs must rest.*
>> *Alonz.* Old Lord, I cannot blame thee, who am my self
>> seiz'd
> With a weariness to the dulling of my Spirits:
> *Sit and rest.*   [*They sit.*]
> Even here I will put off my hope; and keep it
> No longer for my Flatterers:

10-11. This short speech does not appear in the operatic *Tempest.* Cf. Dryden-Davenant *Tempest* (III.iii): "*Antonio.* Do not for one repulse forego the purpose /Which you resolv'd t'effect."

17. *hock-tide.* The second Monday and Tuesday after Easter Day. In pre-Reformation days money was collected for church and parish purposes. Summers comments (*Shakespeare Adaptations*, p. 277):

The Mock-Tempest

One of the earlier customs (to which reference is made here) was the seizing and binding (by women on Monday and by men on Tuesday) of persons of the opposite sex, who paid a small coin to be released.

23–30. Cf. operatic *Tempest* (III.iii.12–19):

> Dry those eyes which are o'rflowing,
> All your storms are overblowing:
> While you in this Isle are biding,
> You shall feast without providing:
> Every dainty you can think of,
> Ev'ry Wine which you would drink of,
> Shall be yours; all want shall shun you,
> Ceres blessing so is on you.

32. *powder'd Beef.* Salted beef; also, a prostitute.

36–37. Cf. operatic *Tempest* (III.iii.23–24):

> Gonz. O for a heavenly vision of Boy'ld,
> Bak'd and Roasted!

Also cf. (V.ii.239): "*Neptune* and your fair *Amphitrite,* rise"; (242): "Come, all ye *Trytons;* all ye *Nereides,* come"; and (145 SD):

> [Neptune, Amphitrite, Oceanus and Tethys *appear in a Chariot drawn with Sea-horses; on each side of the Chariot, Sea-gods and Goddesses, Tritons and Nereides.*]

38 SD. Cf. operatic *Tempest* (III.iii.SD 25):

> [*Dance of fantastick Spirits, after the Dance, a Table furnish'd with Meat and Fruit is brought in by two Spirits.*]

Downes commented on the stage effects used at this point in the operatic *Tempest,* pointing out that there was one scene "flying away, with a Table Furnisht out with Fruits, Sweetmeats and all sorts of Viands; just when Duke *Trinculo* and his Companions; were going to Dinner" (*Roscius Anglicanus,* reprint, London, 1886, pp. 33–34).

40. *Mackarell.* Betty Mackarell, who apparently played Ariel.

44. *Soop.* Soup.

45 SD. Cf. operatic *Tempest* (III.iii.36 SD): "[*Two Spirits descend, and flie away with the Table.*]"

Act V, scene i.

1–42. This sequence closely parodies the operatic *Tempest* (III.v.1–22):

The Mock-Tempest

Ferd. How far will this invisible Musician
Conduct my steps? he hovers still about me,
Whether for good or ill, I cannot tell,
Nor care I much; for I have been so long
A slave to chance, that I'm as weary of
Her flatteries as her frowns, but here I am—
    Ariel.   Here I am.
    Ferd. Hah! art thou so? the Spirit's turn'd an Eccho:
This might seem pleasant, could the burthen of
My Griefs accord with any thing but sighs.
And my last words, like those of dying men,
Need no reply. Fain I would go to shades,
Where few would wish to follow me.
    Ariel.   Follow me.
    Ferd. This evil Spirit grows importunate,
But I'l not take his counsel.
    Ariel.   Take his counsel.
    Ferd. It may be the Devil's counsel, I'l never take it.
    Ariel. Take it.
    Ferd. I will discourse no more with thee,
Nor follow one step further.
    Ariel.   One step further.
    Ferd. This must have more importance then an Eccho.
Some Spirit tempts to a precipice.
I'l try if it will answer when I sing
My sorrows to the murmur of this Brook.

The echo-device was a popular one. There is an echo-sequence in Butler's *Hudibras* (I.iii.1–20), where Orsin laments his separation from the bear. A little more than a year after *The Mock-Tempest* appeared, Lee's *Gloriana* featured an echo-scene in Act V. A famous echo-scene is in Webster's *The Duchess of Malfi* (V.iii).

9–10. *Scourge-stick of Prophanishness.* Possibly intended as a mock-title for a Quaker pamphlet, as well as an obscene pun.

13. *Bearward.* A bear-keeper or trainer.

13–14. *the Bull and Mouth.* A well-known tavern in Bishopsgate Street. *The Quakers Art of Courtship* (London, 1710), referred to earlier (see note to II.ii. 129), also links the Quakers with this tavern. Part of its title page reads:

> Calculated for the Meridian of the *Bull-and Mouth,*
> and may indifferently serve the Brethren of the
> *Windmill-Order,* for Noddification in any Part of
> *Will-a-wisp-Land.*

Throughout *The Quakers Art of Courtship* Quakers are referred to as "Bull and Mouth people."

14. *Lumbard-street.* Center of banking and mercantile transactions in London.

15. *Westminster.* Originally a separate city, but since swallowed up by modern London, located in the southwest part of the city.

17. *I-will top and scourge thee.* "I will beat and whip thee."

18. *humguig.* Summers suggests "to lash lustily" (*Shakespeare Adaptations*, p. 277).

21. *Dagon, Bell and the Dragon.* Dagon was the god of the Philistines (cf. *I Samuel*). Bell (usually Bel) and the Dragon are Babylonian idols in the apocryphal book of that name who devoured huge sacrifices.

43–44. In the pamphlet, *Songs and Masques in the New Tempest* (1674), the following lines are substituted:

> *Quak.* What's a Clock?
> *Ariel.* Thy nose in my Nock.

Charles Haywood comments on the anomaly of Duffett possibly feeling that the above lines were too salty for the quarto of *The Mock-Tempest* (cf. "The Songs and Masques in the New Tempest: An Incident in the Battle of the Two Theatres, 1674," *HLQ* 19[1955], 43–44).

43–61. Cf. operatic *Tempest* (III.v.23–40):

> [*Ferd.*]   *Go thy way.*
> *Ariel.*   *Go thy way.*
> *Ferd.*   *Why should'st thou stay?*
> *Ariel.*   *Why should'st thou stay?*
> *Ferd. Where the winds whistle, and where the streams creep,*
>   *Under yond Willow-tree, fain would I sleep.*
>   *Then let me alone,*
>   *For 'tis time to be gone,*
> *Ariel.*   *For 'tis time to be gone.*
> *Ferd. What cares or pleasures can be in this Isle?*
>   *Within this desart place*
>   *There lives no humane race;*
>   *Fate cannot frown here, nor kind fortune smile.*
> *Ariel. Kind Fortune smiles, and she*
>   *Has yet in store for thee*
>   *Some strange felicity.*
>   *Follow me, follow me,*
>   *And thou shalt see.*

Act V, scene ii.

1–7. Cf. operatic *Tempest* (III.vi.1–10):

> *Pros.* Advance the fringed Curtains of thine Eyes,
> And say what thou seest yonder.
>   *Mir.*   Is it a Spirit?
> Lord! how it looks about! Sir, I confess
> It carries a brave form. But 'tis a Spirit.
>   *Pros.* No, Girl, it eats, and sleeps, and has such sences
> As we have. This young Gallant, whom thou seest,
> Was in the wrack; were he not somewhat stain'd
> With grief (beauty's worst cancker) thou might'st

The Mock-Tempest

Call him a goodly person; he has lost
His company, and strays about to find 'em.

1. *glout.* Scowl.
5. *yerker.* A kicker, a flogger.
8. *crumptious.* Delightful.
28–36. Cf. operatic *Tempest* (III.vi.13–19):

> *Pros.* It goes on as my soul prompts it: Spirit, fine
> spirit.
> I'l free thee within two days for this.
> *Ferd.* She's sure the Mistris on whom these Airs attend.
> Fair Excellence, if, as your form declares,
> You are Divine, be pleas'd to instruct me
> How you will be worship'd; so bright a beauty
> Cannot sure belong to humane kind.

36. *a long Exercise.* A sexual bout; also, "exercise" meant praying, as a strenuous Puritan activity. Summers cites Mrs. Behn's *The Round-Heads* (II.i), when Lady Disbro refers to "Prayers; from which long-winded Exercise I have of late withdrawn my self"; and Otway's *The Atheist* (V.i), when Porcia says, "My Lover Gratian sighs, and turns up his Eyes like a godly Brother at Exercise" (*Shakespeare Adaptations,* pp. 277–78).
46. *Trencher.* Platter.
60–71. This appears to be a routine parody of Quaker language. Cf. *The Quakers Art of Courtship* (London, 1710), pp. 1–2:

Humh! Humh! Humh! Friends! It may not be amiss, when a Friend undertaketh to speak as touching a *Thing,* the Nicety of the *Thing,* the Subject of the *Thing,* the Consequence of the *Thing;* how far the *Thing* may be according to the *Light,* and how far not according to the *Light;* which is the main *Thing* in Question. The *Thing* that we are now upon, is, concerning the *Word* or the *Thing* called *Compliment* or *Court-ship.*

61. *luck.* Possibly, a misprint for "like."
83. *mouz'd.* To be pulled about, good-naturedly.
86–131. This sequence is based on the operatic *Tempest* (III.vii); (IV.i.191–274); and (IV.iii.1–25).
87. *Nicodemus.* A Puritan, a fanatic.
94–97. The Quakers were well known for their refusal to cooperate with the government, especially in regard to the swearing of oaths of allegiance.
96. *enlightened Weaver.* Summers writes, "The Protestants who came from Flanders and brought with them the woolen manufactory, were much given to singing hymns whilst at their work"; and refers to Falstaff's remark, "I would I were a weaver: I could sing psalms or anything" (*I Henry IV* (I.ii.4); and to Jonson's *Epicoene* (III.iv), when Cutbeard mentions a "cold got with sitting up late and singing catches with cloth-workers" (*Shakespeare Adaptations,* p. 278).

99. *Spand-farthing.* A tossing game; the object of one player was to throw his farthings so close to those of his opponent that the distance between them could be spanned with the hand.

100–06. Cf. operatic *Tempest* (III.vii.8–12):

> But, gentle Youth, as you have question'd me,
> So give me leave to ask you, what are you?
> > *Hip.* Do not you know?
> > *Ferd.*   How should I?
> > *Hip.* I well hop'd I was a Man, but by your ignorance
> Of what I am, I fear it is not so:

100. *Professor.* One who is a believer, who "professes" the faith; cant term for a Puritan.

112–13. Cf. operatic *Tempest* (IV.i.201–02): "*Ferd.* I see your ignorance; / And therefore will instruct you in my meaning."

114–18. Cf. operatic *Tempest* (IV.i.220–23):

> > *Ferd.* I find I must not let you see her then.
> > *Hip.* How will you hinder me?
> > *Ferd.*   By force of Arms.
> > *Hip.* By force of Arms?
> My Arms perhaps may be as strong as yours.

117. *adznigs.* God's nigs; a nig is a coin clipping.

119–21. Cf. operatic *Tempest* (IV.iii.7–8):

> [*They fight a little,* Ferdinand *hurts him.*]
> > *Ferd.* Sir, you are wounded.
> > *Hip.*   No.
> > *Ferd.*   Believe your bloud.
> > *Hip.* I feel no hurt, no matter for my bloud.

132. Cf. operatic *Tempest* (IV.iii.26): "*Pros.* What dismal noise is that?"

134. *betwattl'd.* To be subject to much babbling or chatter. "Twattle" is babble or chatter.

136. *sayo.* This appears as "say" in some copies of the quarto; retained here on the chance that a nonce usage may be intended.

146. *Mother Damnables.* Generic term for a bawd.

147. *Pilgrim Salve.* Slang for excrement; Summers suggests "an old ointment made chiefly of swine's grease and isinglass" (*Shakespeare Adaptations,* p. 278).

149–54. Cf. operatic *Tempest* (IV.iii.79–91):

> *Enter* Miranda *and* Dorinda.
> > *Mir.* My Love! is it permitted me to see
> You once agen?
> > *Pros.* You come to look your last; I will
> For ever take him from your eyes.

The Mock-Tempest

But, on my blessing, speak not, nor approach him.
   Dor. Pray, Father, is not this my Sister's Man?
He has a noble form; but yet he's not
So excellent as my *Hippolito.*
   Pros. Alas, poor Girl, thou hast no Man: look yonder;
There's all of him that's left.
   Dor. Why, was there ever any more of him?
He lies asleep, Sir, shall I waken him?
                [*She kneels by* Hippolito, *and jogs him.*]
   Ferd. Alas! he's never to be wak'd agen.

155–58. Cf. operatic *Tempest* (IV.iii.96–100):

>   *Enter* Alonzo, Gonzalo, Antonio, Ariel (invisible).
>   *Alon.* Never were Beasts so hunted into Toils,
> As we have been pursu'd by dreadful shapes.
> But is not that my Son? O *Ferdinand!*
> If thou art not a Ghost, let me embrace thee.
>   *Ferd.* My Father! O Sinister happiness!

155. *Rumford.* Modern "Romford" is fifteen miles northeast of London.
159–71. Cf. operatic *Tempest* (IV.iii.106–19):

>   *Pros.* You start upon me as
> You ne'r had seen me; have fifteen years
> So lost me to your knowledge, that you retain
> No memory of *Prospero?*
>   *Gonz.* The good old Duke of *Millain!*
>   *Pros.* I wonder less, that thou, *Antonio,* know'st
> Me not, because thou didst long since forget
> I was thy Brother, else I never had been here.
>   *Anto.* Shame choaks my words.
>   *Alon.*   And wonder mine.
>   *Pros.* For you, usurping Prince.
> Know, by my Art, you were shipwrack'd on this Isle,
> Where, after I a while had punish'd you,
> My vengeance wou'd have ended, I design'd
> To match that Son of yours, with this my Daughter.

177. *Quakero shall be hang'd.* Cf. operatic *Tempest* (IV.iii.132): "Your *Ferdinand* shall die."
180. Cf. operatic *Tempest* (IV.iii.148): "Now I can hold no longer; I must speak."
183–90. Cf. operatic *Tempest* (V.i.31–33):

> Then I collected the best of Simples underneath
> The Moon, the best of Balms, and to the wound
> Apply'd the healing juice of vulnerary Herbs.

183–84. *Urganda of Wildo Streeto.* The context suggests that a famous bawd or prostitute is being alluded to. Urganda is an enchantress in the romances of

The Mock-Tempest

Amadis and Palmerin. Great Wild Street, Lincoln's Inn, ran from the Drury Lane end of Great Queen Street to Sardinia Street. This area was well known as a red-light district. Cf. Pope's letter to Cromwell (18 March 1708): "In the town it is ten to one, but a young fellow may find his strayed heart again, with some Wild Street or Drury Lane damsel" (*Correspondence,* ed. Sherburn, 5 vols, Oxford, 1956, I, 42).

186. *Punchanello Alquiffe.* A coarse allusion to the management at Dorset Garden. Summers writes, "Mr. W. J. Lawrence writes of this passage: 'Perhaps the Dorset Garden manager was called Punchanello because he was turning his actors into flying puppets—after the puppet method of the hour' " (*Shakespeare Adaptations,* p. 279).

189. *Suppositorial Ligneous puffe and blow.* This sounds like a comic sort of bellows.

190–233. The reviving of Hippolito in the operatic *Tempest* takes place offstage.

227. *Cat-stick.* A stick or bat used in the games of tip-cat and trap-ball.

228. *Rearer.* A light flatbat or racket used in striking a shuttlecock.

229. *stealers and Pickers.* Fingers and hands. Cf. Shakespeare's *Hamlet* (III.ii. 349), when Hamlet answers Rosencrantz's, "My lord, you once did love me," with, "So I do still, by these pickers and stealers." Cf. *The Booke of Common Prayer* (1549), in "A Catechisme" for "Confirmacion": "To kepe my hands from picking and stealing, ..."

231. *Gigg.* A whipping top.

239–40. *now the man shall have his mare again.* Cf. Shakespeare's *A Midsummer Night's Dream* (III.ii.463): "The man shall have his mare again," says Puck, as he squeezes the herbal juice on Lysander's eyelids.

241–43. Cf. Shakespeare's *Hamlet* (II.ii.33–34): "*King.* Thanks, Rosencrantz and gentle Guildenstern. /*Queen.* Thanks Guildenstern and gentle Rosencrantz."

243–44. Cf. operatic *Tempest* (V.ii.200–01): "*Trinc.* What, more Dukes yet? I must resign my Dukedom; /But 'tis no matter, I was almost starv'd in't."

245. *Moor-fields.* An open space in the northeast part of the city, famous for wrestling, cudgel-playing, train-band musters, and cheap bookstalls. The context suggests that Stephania and the girls will set themselves up at another bawdy-house, somewhere in the Moor-fields.

250. *that man in black.* Prospero, most likely.

252–56. Cf. operatic *Tempest* (V.ii.211–14):

> *Pros.* No matter, time will bring 'em to themselves,
> And now their Wine is gone, they will not quarrel.
> Your Ship is safe and tight, and bravely rigg'd,
> As when you first set Sail.

258–63. Cf. operatic *Tempest* (V.ii.249–52):

The Mock-Tempest

> *Amphitrite.*   *My Lord: Great Neptune, for my sake,*
> *Of these bright Beauties pity take:*
> *And to the rest allow*
> *Your mercy too.*

258. *Cac-Cac-Cac-Cac-Calyban.* Cf. operatic *Tempest* (II.i.198): Caliban's song of freedom includes, "Ban, Ban, Cackaliban."
264–69. Cf. operatic *Tempest* (V.ii.259–60): "*Neptune. So much my* Amphitrite's *love I prize, / That no commands of hers I can despise.*"
264. *Mopsa.* "Sweetie-pie."
270–76. Cf. operatic *Tempest* (V.ii.253–58):

> *Let this inraged Element be still,*
> *Let* Aeolus *obey my will:*
> *Let him his boystrous Prisoners safely keep*
> *In their dark Caverns, and no more*
> *Let 'em disturb the bosome of the Deep,*
> *Till these arrive upon their wish'd-for Shore.*

275. *Beetle.* A pounding instrument.
277–84. Cf. operatic *Tempest* (V.ii.261–66):

> [*Neptune.*]   *Tethys no furrows now shall wear,*
> *Oceanus no wrinkles on his brow,*
> *Let your serenest looks appear!*
> *Be calm and gentle now.*
> *Nept. &   Be calm, ye great Parents of the flouds and the*
> *Amph.   Springs,*
> *While each* Nereide *and* Triton *Plays, Revels, and*
> *   Sings.*

280. *Pigs nye.* A flower, the word often used as a word of endearment. See *Canterbury Tales,* A3268.
282. Cf. Shakespeare's *A Midsummer Night's Dream* (V.i.327): Thisby's lament includes, "His eyes were green as leeks."
283. *Pad.* A foot-pad, highwayman, or robber.
287–94. Cf. operatic *Tempest* (V.ii.267–71):

> *Oceanus.   Confine the roaring Winds, and we*
> *Will soon obey you cheerfully.*
> *Chorus of* ⎫ *Tie up the Winds, and we'll obey,*   ⎧ *Here the Dan-*
> *Tritons*   ⎬ *Upon the Flouds we'll sing and play,* ⎨ *cers mingle*
> *and Ner.* ⎭ *And celebrate a Halcyon day.*   ⎩ *with the*
> *   Singers.*

299–305. Cf. operatic *Tempest* (V.ii.272–81):

> *Nept.   Great Nephew* AEolus *make no noise,*
> *Muzle your roaring Boys*   [AEolus *appears.*]

> *Amph.*   *Let 'em not bluster to disturb our ears,*
>   *Or strike these Noble Passengers with fears.*
> *Nept.*   *Afford 'em onely such an easie Gale,*
>   *As pleasantly may swell each Sail.*
> *Amph.*   *While fell Sea-monsters cause intestine jars,*
>   *This Empire you invade with foreign Wars.*
> *Nept.*   *But you shall now be still,*
>   *And shall obey my* Amphitrites *will.*

299. Cf. operatic *Tempest* (V.ii.286): "*Let all black Tempests cease.*"

308–21. Cf. operatic *Tempest* (V.ii.282–93):

> *AEolus descends. You I'll obey, who at one stroke can make,*
> *With your dread Trident, the whole Earth to quake.*
> *Come down, my Blusterers, swell no more,*
> *Your stormy rage give o'r.*   ⎰ *Winds from*
> *Let all black Tempests cease—*   ⎱ *the four cor-*
> *And let the troubled Ocean rest:* ⎱ *ners appear.*
> *Let all the Sea enjoy as calm a peace,*
> *As where the Halcyon builds her quiet Nest.*
>   *To your Prisons below,*
>   *Down, down you must go:*
> *You in the Earths Entrals your Revels may keep;*
> *But no more till I call shall you trouble the Deep.*

313. *crimson Lace.* Bloody lacerations. See *Macbeth* (II.iii.118).

316–17. The jail ("castle") will be as quiet as it is when most of its clientele are busy at court.

326–30. Cf. operatic *Tempest* (V.ii.294–97):

> [*AEolus.*]   *Now they are gone, all stormy Wars shall cease:*
>   *Then let your Trumpeters proclaim a Peace.*
> *Amph.*   *Tritons, my Sons, your Trumpets sound,*
>   *And let the noise from Neighbouring Shores rebound.*

331 SD. Cf. operatic *Tempest* (V.ii.302 SD):

> [*Here the Trytons, at every repeat of* Sound a Calm,
> *changing their Figure and Postures, seem to sound*
> *their wreathed Trumpets made of Shells.*]

336–40. Cf. operatic *Tempest* (V.ii.298–302): "*Sound a Calm,*" etc.

340 SD. Cf. operatic *Tempest* (V.ii.323 SD):

> [*Scene changes to the Rising Sun, and a number of Aerial*
> *Spirits in the Air,* Ariel *flying from the Sun, advances*
> *towards the Pit.*]

341–48. Cf. operatic *Tempest* (V.ii.303–10):

Nept. *See, see, the Heavens smile, all your troubles are past,*
   Your joys by black Clouds shall no more be o'rcast.
Amph. *On this barren Isle ye shall lose all your fears*
   Leave behind all your sorrows, and banish your cares.
Both. *And your Loves and your Lives shall in safety enjoy;*
   No influence of Stars shall your quiet destroy.
Chor. of all. *And your Loves, &c.*
   No influence, &c.

343–48. The pamphlet, *The Songs and Masques in the New Tempest,* reassigns these lines as follows: 343–44 to "Syc."; 345–46 to "Pimp."; and 347–48 to "Baud."
353–58. Cf. operatic *Tempest* (V.ii.311–16):

  Oceanus. *We'll safely convey you to your own happy Shore,*
     And yours and your Countrey's soft peace we'll restore.
  Tethys. *To treat you blest Lovers, as you sail on the Deep,*
     The Trytons *and Sea-Nymphs* their *Revels shall keep.*
  Both. *On the swift Dolphins backs they shall sing and shall play;*
     They shall guard you by night, and delight you by day.

354. *Stepony.* A raisin wine made from raisins with lemon-juice and sugar added.
356. *Waits.* A small body of wind instrumentalists maintained by a city or town at the public charge.
361–67. Cf. operatic *Tempest* (V.ii.330–36):

  Ariel. *Where the Bee sucks, there suck I,*
     In a Cowslips Bed I lie;
     There I couch when Owls do cry.
     On the Swallows wings I fly
     After Summer merrily.
     Merrily, merrily shall I live now,
     Under the Blossom that hangs on the Bow.

365. *Cullies.* Dupes, those easily cheated.
368–75. Cf. operatic *Tempest* (V.ii.347–52):

    Henceforth this Isle to the afflicted be
    A place of Refuge, as it was to me:
    The promises of blooming Spring live here,
    And all the blessings of the ripening Year.
    On my retreat, let Heav'n and Nature smile,
    And ever flourish the *Enchanted Isle.*

TEXTUAL NOTES

Location File of Extant Copies

Title page: THE MOCK-TEMPEST (*see facsimile*).

Signature collation: 4⁰: A^3, B–H⁴.

Copies are in the following libraries: British Museum (BM), two copies; Bodleian Library (O); Trinity College, Cambridge (CT); Worcester College, Oxford (OW); National Library of Scotland, Edinburgh (EN); William Andrews Clark Memorial Library, Los Angeles (CLUC); Henry E. Huntington Library (CSmH); Beinecke Library, Yale University (CtY); Folger Library (DFo); Library of Congress (DLC); Newberry Library (ICN); University of Chicago Library (ICU); Boston Public Library (MB); Houghton Library, Harvard University (MH); Chapin Library, Williams College, Williamstown, Massachusetts (MWiW); Butler Library, Columbia University (NNC); University of Cincinnati Library (OCU); University of Texas Library (TxU).

Press Variants in *The Mock-Tempest*

Sheet F (outer forme)

Corrected: OCU, CLUC, CtY, TxU, CSmH, DLC, DFo, MWiW, ICU, MH, BM.
Uncorrected: ICN, NNC.
F_1 line 27 Colly-flower] Colly-follwer
F_1 line 32 save] seve (turned letter)
F_1 line 33 other] other other
F_2^v line 36 you] your
F_3 line 27 Cloves] stloves
F_3 line 28 struse] Cruse

Sheet G (outer forme)

Corrected: ICN, OCU, CLUC, CtY, TxU, CSmH, DLC, DFo, MWiW.
Uncorrected: BM, ICU, NNC, MH.
G_2^v lines 5–6 a good Vision] a Vision

The Mock-Tempest

G$_2$^{v} line 7 *Quakero,* nay, but] *Quakero* nay but
G$_2$^{v} line 11 shouldst thou] should, thou [CSmH and TxU have "shouldest, thou"]
G$_2$^{v} line 15 follow'd] followe'd
G$_2$^{v} line 27 thee] the
G$_4$^{v} line 12 say] sayo [OCU, CLUC, CtY, ICU, MH have "say"; TxU, CSmH, DFo, MWiW, NNC, ICN, BM have "sayo"; leaf missing in DLC]

Sheet G (inner forme)

G$_1$^{v} line 3 snach'd] snatch'd
G$_1$^{v} line 5 Fourth] Second
G$_1$^{v} line 16 hath it sweetly] hath he is sweetly [MH corrected with an errata slip]
G$_1$^{v} line 17 write] right
G$_1$^{v} line 26 omitted in uncorrected copies
G$_2$ line 11 Poor] Poo
G$_2$ line 13 omitted in uncorrected copies
G$_4$ line 8 upright] upriȝht [NNC, ICN have "upright"; leaf missing in DLC; other copies retain turned letter]
G$_4$ last line I'le] I'le [NNC, ICN have turned letter; other copies correct; leaf missing in DLC]

Sheet H (outer forme) [Not extensively examined]

Corrected: CLUC, CtY, NNC, BM.
Uncorrected: MWiW, ICU, MH.
H$_1$ line 1 *Prospero!*] *Prospero*
H$_1$ line 9 Paramount.] Paramount
H$_1$ line 28 puffe and blow, which] puffe, and blow which

Substantive Variants

I, i, 66 flye] ye [my own emendation]
IV, ii, 71 you, Sister] you Sister [OCU, CLUC, CtY, TxU, CSmH, DLC, DFo, MWiW, ICU, MH, BM]
                    your Sister [ICN, NNC]
V, i, 9 hath it sweetly] hath he is sweetly [BM, ICU, NNC]
V, i, 10 right] write [ICN, OCU, CLUC, CtY, TxU, CSmH, DLC, DFo, MWIW]
V, i, 20 omitted in BM, ICU, NNC, MH
V, i, 36 Poor] Poo [BM, ICU, NNC, MH]
V, i, 37 omitted in BM, ICU, NNC, MH
V, i, 67 a good Vision] a Vision [BM, ICU, NNC, MH]

The Mock-Tempest

Accidental Variants

I, i, 110 Wenching base] Wenching, base
I, i, 186 bacon face] bacon, face
I, i, SD213 *all, pulling*] *all. pulling*
I, i, 235 Mother, in two minutes 'twil] Mother in two minutes, 'twil
I, ii, 39 mean and] mean, and
I, ii, 41 self to] self, to
I, ii, 65 'scape, Father?] 'scape Father?
I, ii, 76 thee?] the?
II, i, 1 seen, pray?] seen pray?
II, i, 11 at one, Sister? Indeed] at one Sister, indeed
II, i, 21 What, must] What must
II, i, 53 Husband, Sister, how] Husband Sister how
II, ii, 1 *Gonzalo,* Oh] *Gonzalo* Oh
II, ii, 97 *Quakero's* gone] *Quakero's,* gone
II, ii, 115 *Tongue,*] *Tongue.*
II, ii, 122 *left*] *lest*
II, ii, SD124 Quaker. *Sings.*] Quaker *Sings.*
II, ii, 137 *I,* Rapine,] *I* Rapine,
II, ii, 171–72 Devil call] Devil, call
III, i, 33 hear] here
III, i, 37 Look, *Moustrappa*] Look *Moustrappa*
III, i, 52 Farendine he] Farendine, he
III, i, 56 drowning, for] drowning for
III, i, 109 Holydaies, by] Holydaies. by
III, i, 111 has, Mrs.] has Mrs.
III, i, 132 Money she] Money, she
III, i, 211 *thy*] *they*
III, i, 264 away, Jaylor] away Jaylor
III, ii, 26 *Wife,*] *Wife.*
III, ii, 32 *tell*] *tells*
III, ii, 49 *Nandy,*] *Nandy.*
III, ii, 67 Ariel. [*Sings.*] *Thwick,*] Ariel. *Thwick,*
IV, i, 34 touch, a] touch a
IV, i, 88 Colly-flower] Colly-follwer [ICN, NNC]
IV, i, 94 as soon as any other will] as soon other other will [ICN, NNC]
　　　　　　　　 as soon any other will [OCU, CLUC, CtY, TxU, CSmH, DLC,
　　　　　　　　　　　　 DFo, MWiW, ICU, MH, BM]
IV, i, 103 it, a] it a
IV, i, 107 *Hyp.*] *Pros.*
IV, i, 125 Hah, thy] Hah thy
IV, ii, 4 am, the King shall] am the King, shall
IV, ii, 97 Cloves] stloves [ICN, NNC]

IV, ii, 98 abstruse] abCruse [ICN, NNC]

IV, ii, 111–12 abroad, which] abroad. which

IV, ii, 121 ha' got] ha, got

IV, ii, 178 Why, why? Speak out.] Why, why speak out?

IV, ii, 193 too] to

IV, iii, 18 friends] fiends

IV, iii, 45 SD *snatch'd*] *snach'd* [BM, ICU, NNC, MH]

IV, iii, 45 SD *Fourth*] *Second* [BM, ICU, NNC, MH]

V, i, 4–5 Candle of the Socket] Can dleo f the Socket [TxU, CSmH, DLC]

V, i, 69 *Quakero*, nay, but] Quakero nay but [BM, ICU, NNC, MH]

V, i, 77 follow'd] followe'd [BM, ICU, NNC, MB]

V, ii, 7 thee] the [BM, ICU, NNC, MH]

V, ii, 43 Why, did] Why did

V, ii, 44 4to has this in two lines, as follows:

> *Quak.* Nay assuredly, but I hope I shall—
>
> *Quak.* Whose soft Palmes . . .

V, ii, 52 Sister, far, far] Sister far, far

V, ii, 87 hither, discourse] hither discourse

V, ii, 96 upright] "g" turned in OCU, CLUC, CtY, TxU, CSmH, DFo, MWiW, BM, ICU, MH

V, ii, 98 *Hyp.*] *Hey*

V, ii, 122 thee] the

V, ii, 126 I'le] "l" turned in OCU, CLUC, CtY, TxU, CSmH, DFo, MWiW, BM, ICU, MH

V, ii, 136 sayo] say [OCU, CLUC, CtY, ICU, MH]

V, ii, 157 What, my . . . alive?] What my . . . alive,

V, ii, 161 How, my] How my

V, ii, 183 Stay, my] Stay my

V, ii, 189 puffe and blow, which] puffe, and blow which [MWiW, ICU, MH]

V, ii, 212 *Quak.*] *Foran.*

V, ii, 232 *Quak.*] *Faran.*

V, ii, 254 4to repeats "*Pros.*" at beginning of this line.

V, ii, 340 SD going down; *Aurora,*] going down *Aurora,*

Psyche Debauch'd

The Performance

Shadwell's *Psyche* premiered Saturday, 27 February 1674–75 at Dorset Garden.[1] Downes mentions that "It had a Continuance of Performance about 8 Days together it [*sic*] prov'd very Beneficial to the Company," and adds, "yet the Tempest got them more Money."[2] Duffett's *Psyche Debauch'd* appeared soon after, although exactly when is not clear. Nicoll has suggested that it occurred "either during Lent or summer 1675."[3] *The London Stage* supports the possibility of a performance of *Psyche Debauch'd* in August 1675:

> The date of the premiere is not known, but Robert Hooke attended a play on 27 Aug 1675 which might well refer not to *Psyche* but to Duffett's travesty of it. In addition, John Harold Wilson has argued that the reference in the Prologue [i.e., to *Psyche Debauch'd*] to "The new-come Elephant" probably concerns the elephant imported by Lord George Berkeley and sold by 12 Aug 1675 (see The Diary of Robert Hooke, p. 174). The cast also contains a number of "young actors" who might well have had an opportunity to act in a play in the summer vacation.[4]

Although it was common in all three of Duffett's burlesques for men to play some of the women's parts, one of the unusual features of the casting in *Psyche Debauch'd* was the playing of two of the male roles by women: Mrs. Corbett played King Theander, and Mrs. Knepp played Prince Nicholas. *Psyche Debauch'd* might well have made its satiric point. John Harold Wilson has pointed out that the anonymous tragedy, *Piso's Conspiracy,* performed at Dorset Garden during the summer of 1675, makes specific reference to *Psyche Debauch'd.*[5] The prologue refers to play-bills "in Praise o'th' Beauty of Miss-Non-so-Fair" (who was played by Joe Haynes!) and to the interesting possibility that:

> Our Men Players are out of Heart
> Of being seen in a Heroic Part:
> What with Prince Nick, and t'other House Gallants,
> They have run Hero's out of Countenance.

---

[1] *The London Stage*, I, pp. 229–30.
[2] *Roscius Anglicanus* (Reprinted 1886), p. 36.
[3] Nicoll, I, p. 407.
[4] *The London Stage*, I, p. 235.
[5] *Mr. Goodman, the Player*, pp. 41–42.

The Text

The quarto of *Psyche Debauch'd* did not appear until 1678; no mention of it is made in the *Term Catalogues*. The performance of *Psyche Debauch'd* in 1675 makes its publication in 1678 somewhat puzzling. A much more likely time of publication would have been soon after the production, as was the case with Duffett's two earlier burlesques. A possible explanation may lie in the identification of Duffett-the-forger with Duffett-the-dramatist. If Duffett was indeed getting into difficulties with the law, there may have been pressures building up that prevented him from moving into print; however, the legal difficulties we know of are not mentioned until 1677.

Copies of the quarto are not plentiful. The only copies in the United States are at Folger Library (DFo), Yale (CtY), and Huntington Library (CSmH). I have examined the Folger and Yale copies. The Huntington copy is reproduced in the Readex Microprint series, *Three Centuries of British Drama, 1500–1800*. I have examined the British Museum (BM) copy (644.h.6) from a photocopy of the original. Differences within these copies of the quarto are minimal. The colophon of the British Museum copy reads in part: "Printed for *John Smith* in *Great Queen-street*," while the other three copies read, "Printed for *J. Smith* Bookseller in *Great Queen-street*." The card catalog entry for *Psyche Debauch'd* at the Folger Library includes the note: "Wing probably in error when he lists imprint as 'For John Smith' instead of 'For J. Smith.'" It is more likely, however, that Wing (in listing *Psyche Debauch'd* in the *STC*) had seen a copy like the one in the British Museum. In the Yale copy L_1 is lacking and is replaced by photocopies. In the British Museum copy I_3 has inaccurate page numerals. Instead of "61" and "62" this copy has "63" (with the "6" quite blurred) on the recto, and "60" on the verso with a "2" one-quarter of an inch to the right and dropped to the next line. In the Huntington copy the verso of I_3, instead of having page numeral "62," has a blurred "64." Last, in the British Museum copy, the verso of I_4 has the page numeral "64" with the "4" turned.

PSYCHE

Debauch'd,

A

COMEDY,

As it was Acted at the

Theatre-ROYAL

By *T. Duffett.*

LONDON,

Printed for *J. Smith* Bookseller in *Great*
Queen-street, 1678.

PROLOGUE.

Now Fancy's up; lest waiting palls the jest;
Psyche *the second's coming half undrest:*
But in that Garb you like fine Women best.
Let our Rich Neighbours mock our Farce; we know
(Already, th'utmost) of their Puppet-show.   5
Since they 'gainst Nature go, they Heav'n offend,
If Natures purpose then cross Natures end;
Unnat'ral Nature is not Natures Friend.
                [—There's Nature for you.]
As Aesop's *Cat dressed in a Nymph's disguise,*   10
Their gaudy Trifle may at first surprize;
None but the (Dirty-rout) *will like it twice:*
A well drest Frollick once may please the eye;
But Plays (like Women) can't so satisfie.
Ye masked Nymphs can tell, there's something in ye,   15
Besides a painted face that gets the penny:
Yet all the Fame you give 'em, we'l allow
To their best Plays, and their best Actors too.
That is, the Painter, Carpenter, and show
Beaumont, *and* Fletcher, *Poet, and* Devow.   20
But Sirs, free harmless Mirth you here condemn,
And Clap at down-right Baudery in them.
In Epsom-Wells, *for example—*
Are they not still for pushing Nature on,
Till Natures feat thus in your sight is done?   25
Oh Lord!—
Take off their Psyches *borrow'd plumes awhile,*
Hopkins *and* Sternhold *rise, and claim your style;*
Dread Kings of Brentford! *leave* Lardella's *Herse,*
Psyches *despairing Lovers steal your verse:*   30
And let Apollo's *Priest restore again*
What from the nobler Mamamouchy's *ta'n.*
    Let 'em restore your Treble prices too,
To see how strangely still they bubble you,
It makes me blush; and that I seldom do.   35
Now Psyche's *strip'd from all her gay attire,*

TE DE POLYKAGATHOI, Behold the Fire!
But Oh! a long Farewell to all this sort,
Which Musick, Scenes, nor Preface can support.
Yet you admire it, make 'em thankful for't: 40
Alass their Charge was great, and you must pay't.
If they should purchase at a cursed Rate,
The New-come Elephant, and shew't in State;
Get him a Room with Pomp and Lux'ry drest,
Would you pay Crowns a piece to see the Beast?   45
Show some of your good Natures here kind Sirs;
If our Conceit less proud or gay appears,
She's less expensive, and more brisk then theirs.

The Actors Names.

King Andrew,		*Mrs.* Corbett.
Nicholas,	*Princes in love with* None-so-fair,	*Mrs.* Knep.
Phillip,		*Mr.* Charleton.
Bruine, *the White Bear of* Norwich,		*Mr.* Harris
Apollo, *A Wishing-Chair,*		*Mr.* Lyddall.
Jeffrey, *Bruines Man,*		*Mr.* Coysh.
Costard, *A Country-man,*		*Mr.* Poell.
Justice Crabb, (*For the God* Mars,)		*Mr.* Wiltshire.
Tag-rag,	*Common Prisoners.*	
Brazen-nose,		
Tatter'd-hoe,		
Bullbarrow,		
Shrubs-hall,		
Wou'dhamore,	*K.* Andrew's 3 Daughters,	*Mrs.* Rutter.
Sweetlips,		*Mrs.* ———
None-so-fair,		*Mr.* Haynes.
Redstreak, *Costard's Wife,*		*Mr.* Cory.
Twattle,	*Ladies attending on* None-so-fair.	
Glozy,		
Woossat, [*representing* Venus,]		*Mr.* Clarke.
Priests, Masquers, &c.		

THE

MOCK OPERA.

ACT I.

Enter None-so-fair, Twattle and *Glozy.*

Non. O *Glozy!* What a crumptious place is here?
Where none can see one play with ones none Dear.
Under each bush kind Sun doth warm;
Here one may kiss, and laugh, and think no harm:
For Countrey Love has neither joyes nor fears,   5
And Bushes break no Trust, though Walls have ears:
    Gloz. No Missy *None-so-fair,* they are not of *Outalian* mind.
        Man hunts not here for man-kind,
        Wyer on Hare not man prevails,
        Nor are men caught with Pipe like Quails,   10
        No salt is here thrown on their Tails.
    Twat. No Gossip *Glozy,*
You may here sing *Hey down* with every Clown,
        And none will disclose ye,
        As at *London* lewd Town.   15
Poor Rusticks cannot cheat, nor lye nor swear;
Incroach on Neighbours spot of ground,
Or put dumb Creature into Pound;
No *Covent-Garden* Tricks are practis'd here.
    Non. Ah! Gammer *Twattle;* Ah! my poor Lady,   20
I wish I were no Princess born:
But some poor Shepheardess Forlorn,
To sleep all day on Mowes of Hay or Corn.
How green's the Grass? how Fine's the Tree?
How luscious is the Black-berry?   25
    Gloz. But Oh! How sweet's the Company?
    Twat. The Company—
    Non. That—That; Oh goody *Glozy,* Oh Gammer *Twat:*
I'le ne're go home again that's Flat.

Maids are not here confin'd to Rules,   30
As at your Whoresome Boarding Schools.
    Gloz. How silly is the Show and Pomp,
That's practis'd there by every Romp;
First Mock-Wedding's to be seen,
    Twat. And then with great Din, comes Mock-lying In.   35
Mistress of School, must be Midwife, Old Fool;
Mammy, and Dad, and Nurse must be had;
And Cradle and Ladle, and Fiddle-come-faddle,
      You'd think 'em all Mad.
    None. When Gossips are come, and fill up the Room;   40
Glass goes about, till Girles crye out, A ha, a, ah ha.
    Gloz. Drink goes down, Midwife, Run, sport's begun, all undone.
Hold her back, or 'twill crack by my fack.
    Twat. Alack, alack,—Caraways, run *Jack,* Ah, a, a, ha.
    Non. Then she must whine for the Burnt Wine;   45
Stools, Tools and Fools flye about;
And at last comes out great Baby of Clout:
Then Christning comes, and Sugar Plums,
And Mistress Tipling like old Crony:
Gives dainty words as sweet as hony,   50
And all to gets poor Childrens Mony.
    Gloz. Each strives to be in Mistress Books,
Though Purse of Parents bleed, Gadzooks.
    Twat. And when e're they do play Truant,
If she'l say she never knew on't,   55
They do not care one souse, 'gad knows,
How silly Beldams led by th'Nose.
    Non. And then Forsooth we must have Shooes:
    Gods, Divels, and Goddesses,
    Swayns, Satyrs, and Shepherdesses,   60
Soust in dull Rime, and serv'd in several Messes,
    Gloz. Yet glittering Scenes, and Golden Dresses,
Wont make amends for doggrel Verses.
    Non. No, not even there where Dance and Song,
Supported by the Mighty, and the Young,   65
Though practised ne'r so often, ne'r so long,
Though ne'r so much imposed upon the Town,
Their own flat stuffs wrought up to pull them down,
As a great Owl, which on bare stump bawls,
Swell'd with the whooping Musick of his Throat,   70
Down to the wrath of Larks and Linnets falls.
So boasting Scribblers on their Labours doat;
But all their swelling Hopes and Huffs,

Critick out, like Candle puffs;
And then they smoak, and stinck like Snuffs;   75
So School Girls that have in the morn
Been Cock a Hoop, and rul'd the Roast,
E're Noon ev'n like an over-soak'd Toast,
Sinck to the bottom of the Pot of scorn:
These woaful Chances I have lately seen,   80
     And ne'r will go to School agen,
          No not to be a Queen.
     Twattle. Oh *None-so-fair;* sweet *Miss!*
     You need not have run from your good Father, I wis;
For Prince *Phillip,* or Prince *Nicholas,* if you had but said the   85
word, would have marri'd you while one can say what's this?
               How say by that?—
     Gloz. —Well rim'd goody *Twat.*
Not a Prince in the street, but was so loving
He'd a kissed your Elbow to bake in your Oven;   90
So says ev'ry one that knows thee.
     Twat. Well said goody *Glozy:*
Though the Coif of your heart were dry enough, God wot,
You would not let it be smooth'd, while loves Iron was hot,
When loves strong Charms your smoothing-board invirons,   95
You laugh to see poor Princes shake their Irons.
     Non. Not Sugar-cakes, nor Ginger-bread,
Me from this Countrey life shall lead:
The live long day about the Fields we saunter,
Sloes, Black-berries, and Hawes we ne'r shall want here.   100
     At night we'l go a Gooding
     For Bacon, and Kale, and nappy Ale,
     Stout Beef, and figged Pudding.
     Gloz. Ah! but sweet Lady, we want the Ready,—
And we can't fill our Guts, if we buy not,   105
     Twat. Oh! but Lady *None-so-fair,* look ye, d'e see, *Glozy,* will
make them come, and bring it to us with a why not:
     Non. What ayle Gammor *Glozy,* I mar'l what a dickens
Don't all the Fields grow full of Hens and Chickens?
Don't Birds grow upon Trees like Pears, what would she desire?   110
Don't Pyes grow in a little Brick-house close by the Fire?
     Twat. And somtimes *Missey* we'l trudge a nutting.
     Non. Faith, Gammor *Twattle* that was well put in:

               She Sings.

          Then the Nymphs *and the* Swains
          Shall trip it o're the Plains,   115

               – 159 –

And crown me with Garlands of Roses,
And marry me with a Rush ring:
Then how we will firck it, caper, and jerk it } sing and
Under the green Wood Tree. } dance.

Gloz. Very right—*Oh* sweet *None-so-fair!*   120
None-so. Princes have no such joys as these
When they sit down to Pork and Pease.
What Crowding's this my ears do pull?
With which the empty Air is full.   } *Musick is heard.*
    Twat. Oh! Gads-lidikins now I know,   125
This is *May-day* in the morning, ho.
    Non. Oh! is it so, then let's go straight away,
For I'le be Lady of *May.*   *exeunt all.*

Enter Costard *and* Redstreak.

    Redstr. O lo! O lo! Costard, who dost thou think is come
hither—now?—   130
    Costard. —Who, who, vor the mercies sake?
    Redstr. —Guess *Costard,* guess.
    Costard. —Gammer Bunch the Carret-Woman?
    Redstr. Noa, noa, noa.
    Cost. Cicely Pountrinckets the Tripe-Wife?   135
    Red. Pshaw waw; who but Princess *None-so-fair* our Landlord
King *Andrews* youngest Daughter—
    Cost. Then have mercy on us, we shall see bad times;
For I believe she's run away from School.
    Redst. Twittle Twattle, what if she be? what have we to do   140
With state business—perhaps she's run away *Incognito* with
her Fathers consent—
    Cost. Now she's here, the short and the long on't is, we must
chuse Her Lady of May.—
    Red. Yes by my Fay. —And we'l have a Masque, and   145
Crouder shall be *Pan,* and he must sing in resitantivy;
Great *Psyche* go dress up the silly Rogues,
And then Piper shall be *Chorus,* and he shall sing:
Now *Pan* with his fooling has made a fair hand.
    Then there must be Symphonie.   150
    Cost. Shan't I be Symphonie, *Redstreak?*
    Red. Hold thy tongue, Wilta? Lord to bless us; what rowly
powly, all fellows at Foot-ball? The Symphony? No, Symphony
must be a woundy cranck, short, tall, squat vellow with rusty
Musick; and he must cry like a Bird: and then we must have   155
An Eccho—

Cost. Oh! there's an Eccho down at hollow Banck. I'le call
it Presently.—
    Redstr. No no, we'l make an Eccho of our own.
    Cost. How? prythee *Redstreak* how?   160
    Redstr. Why look thee: One must be Voice, and another
must be Air, and another must be Rock; then voice must talk
Soundly to Air, and beat her against Rock; and Rock must
Beat her back again; and then Air must cry out, and scold
With Voice, and that's Eccho—Let me alone for Plot; If   165
you will but work up the Sense and Passion, as they say;
Go, and let every Mothers Child about it, and I'le entertain
Princess *None-so-fair* the while. —Yonder she comes.
                                       exit Costard.

            Enter None-so-fair, Twattle *and* Glozy.

    Non. Gammar *Redstreak*, I make bold.
    Red. So I am told,   170
Sweet Princess *None-so-fair.* Bring in Wickar-chair,
Twattle and *Glozy;* Cheeks shall be rosy.
       For I have good Fuddle,
    Twat. —Mum Ducks in the puddle,
    Gloz. —Gad-speed, Gammar *Redstreak.* We'l drink, till our   175
heads-ake,
    Twat. —And we'l have some Chat,
    Red. —Marry why not?
    Non. —What Crouding's this I hear?
    Red. An entertainment which our head Hinds do for you prepare.
    Twat. She fibs, they do't once a year, whether your at home or   180
here.
    Red. O Dear! 'tis for the nonce by Cocks bones.
    Non. Well, well, be quiet, I say be quiet twice and once.

Enter a Countrey Crouder, *followed by a Milk-maid with her
       Payl dressed up as on* May-day. —*After them a company of
       Morris-dancers, a Sylvan, and a* Dryad—

    Red. A Masque so please your Worship, *Madam;*
Their Garments should be better, if we had e'm.
Pan come sing. God *Pan, Chorus!* Oh *Symphony!* where's   185
Your rusty Musick; so, so, 'tis well; what are You?
    Syl. I am a *Sylvan—Dry.* And I am a Dryad Dame.
    Red. Come Cheer up.—

Pan sings.

Great None-so-fair, *King* Andrews *Daughter dear,*
Whom we do worship, but our Dame doth fear;   190
For why? you come to eat up our good Chear.
   Here's Cake, Bread, and Pruin,
     And eke more are stewing.
     Then pray now be doing.

Chorus.

{ *And* Cisly, *and* Dolly *shall trip it around,*   195
{ *And* None-so-fair *shall have a dainty green Gown.*

Sing Damzels, Sing, and jolly Lads Sing loud,
When Swains be blith, the Nimphs should not be proud,
But foot it featly after every Croud.
     And when you are weary,   200
     Lye down and be merry,
     Till cheek's red as Cherry.

Chorus.

{ Croudero, *and* Piper *shall sing and shall play,*
{ *And* None-so-fair *shall be Lady of* May.

A Dance of Morris-Dancers, Milk-maid. &c.

Red. So, so, well done, well done all; *Ha, ha, ha,* it makes   205
my heart leap in my Belly for joy--homely Countrey sport,
Now could I weep for pure hearts ease, to see how
towardly they are; and how my good man *Costard* looks so
sprunt I warrant ye. *Chorus, Symphonie, Pan;* stand to your
Fittles, can you be merry sweet Princess? Eccho; where's   210
Eccho, Rock, Ayr, Voice? Oh *dull, dull!*
 Non. Fret not thy self sweet *Redstreak.*
 Red. Oh Lord your Worship,—a pax take ye;
Come, or I'le fetch you in with a Hedge-stake,
For Courtesie you have no Peer.   215
 Nonsy. Methinks 'tis most serene and clear.
 Red. Serene and clear, that I'le remember I warrant ye:
Then if that you do please to sit,
Old Nick take you, for a Company of lazy patches.
We have more sport to show you yet.   220

I.   Psyche Debauch'd

Voice, Ayr, Rock, do'e hear?
Hold up your heads, and do't most serene and clear.

{ Voice sings and beats Ayr against Rock—Rock beats her }
{ back again, and makes her cry out like an Eccho. }

Song.

Voice. *How do Maids cry, when they lose what they value so dear?*
Rock. —*What they value so dear,*
Ayr. —*O dear!*   225
Voice. —*And then the poor Fellow does sigh like a Lass,*
Rock. —*O does sigh like a Lass,*
Ayr. —*a Lass.*
Voice. —*Beauties like meadows are mow'd, and they pass,*
Ayr. —*does are mow'd, and they pass,*   230
Rock. —*They pass.*
Voice. —*Then what have they left for to offer at here?*
Ayr. —*for to offer at here?*
Rock. —*at here.*

Chorus of All.

Dayzy Roots do mar the growth;   235
And Marjorum is good for Broath.
But Beef 'tis makes us lusty,
I love thee Sue, *I'le take my Oath,*
Then why art thou so crusty?
Thou shalt have Eggs and Clary,   240
          Faddle Fiddle,
          Hey down Diddle.
          Faith let's be merry.

Exeunt all the Dancers singing.

Red. It may be sweet Princess, you like not this Solemn
Musick, *Faddle Fiddle, hey down Diddle.* —I value not my   245
self upon the Wit, but the fitness of the words; for Air and
Melody.

Faddle Fiddle hey down Diddle,
          Faith let's be merry.

I have skill though I say't, that shudn't, as they say for the   250
Jews Trump-Citizen, and Trump-Marine, I'le turn my back

to none, though some have been bred up many years to't;
I my self chalk'd out the way to the Tune-Maker: I know I
have many Foes, that say I make not what I own, but mum
for that: This Rare *Opera* is all mine I'le swear; but for   255
the Dress and Trim, give the Divel his due, I am beholding
to the most Serene and clear Monsieur *Stephen,* the Kings
Corn-cutter, and so you are all, for he put me upon't.
        Now if that you'l walk in to close up all,
        We'l have a most Serene and clear Rank Ball.   260
                         Exit Redstreak.

   Non. Oh happy silly life, what sports are here?
Noise without noise, grief without care;
Joys without joyes, and frights without fear.
E'r all the World, me from this life shall hall;
I'l cry, lie down in ground, and kick and sprawl.   265

     Enter Ambition, *an Aldermans Wife;* Power, *Schoolmistress;*
        Plenty, *an Ale Wife;* and Peace, *a Zealot.*

     Plen. See where she is, Oh! Missy y'are a Fine Princess
to run away from your Friends so.—
    Pow. You put your Father, King *Andrew* into a fine twitter
twatter.
    Amb. I come to fetch you from this life of Beast,   270
To grand Solemnity of City Feast;
Leave smoaky Cot, and Cake-bread tough,
There's Custards hot, and Fools enough:
Leave Tib and Tom, for good House-holder,
There's Capon fat, and Mutton shoulder.   275
Leave Eldern whistle, Gut of Cats,
For City Horn-pipe and Waits;
By me ev'n Mrs. *Steward* you shall sit,
Whose Lilly hand carves every bit.
And tells the price to show housewifely Wit,   280
Lump shall be carri'd home too in Kerchief Wallet;
Or else it shall go hard in faith la, shall se't,
By me to noble thoughts you shall be brought,
And all the Arts of City Madam taught.
Locket on Arm, Ring on Finger,   285
Of Bobs too, in each ear a Clinger;
With fingers end, or Diamond Ring to play,
And cry, Oh Lord! when you have nought to say:
Finely to stretch, or show the pouting lip,
I'le teach you when to cry foro'th, or sip;   290

I'le teach you how to filtch and spend
Dull Husbands muck on courtly Friend;
Yet with grave mouth to rail at th'other end
Of this wild Town.—
Leave boars with limbs more stiff and hard then Oak,   295
And think of ruling sparks in Camlet Cloak;
Fresh Sweet-hearts every day new love shall swear:
And in all junckets, who but *None-so-fair?*
Come, come, wed rich retailing Prince; be Great,
Sit finely drest in Shop, serve God, and cheat.   300

    Pow. I from your silly life do you invite,
I, whose dread Scepter every child does fright;
Presents, and Fasting dayes are my delight.
If *None-so-fair* will back to School with me,
None of my Girls shall eat so much as she;   305
And so that I may get the Pence,
With any Prentice, Lord, or Footman Prince,
I'le give her leave to run away from thence.

    Plenty. Is this a place for *None-so-fair?*
As stately Painted Ale-house is fitter farr,   310
Come, go with me, and keep my splendid Barr.
                Princess, thou shalt Govern there,
                Luxurious Ale, and double Beer.
Thy heart in precious Brandy thou shalt soak;
In clouds of strong Mundungus smoak,   315
Hid like a Goddess thou shalt lye,
Till thou art comely, Plump, and fair as I;
With ease, Fat Bub, and Virtuous Luxury.

    Peace. And I, that thy delights may never cease,
Will steel thy soul with an audacious peace.   320
                And lift up every sence,
                With zealous Impudence:
When envious People rail, thou shalt reply,
The Saints have suffered still, and so must I.
Let vicious Innocence be all thy care,   325
Such peace becomes chast wanton *None-so-fair.*

    Nonsy. Blest are the Rich, and Happy, eke are those
That never saw Lord-Mayors Puppet Shows;
Nor like clean Beasts stood chewing cribs,
Till Coat was burnt from Rump with Squibs,   330
Ambition ne'r shall stick to my ribs.
       Power, in vain you huff and brag;
       Since I have given School the bag,
       Catch me there again, and cut off my leg.

Plenty has told a tempting tale,   335
But in the mind I am I'le drink no Ale.
Peace notably has spoak, but pains must loose;
Girls know more now e'r they can tye their shooes.
                  You have your answers,
                  And may be gone Sirs.   340
    Plenty. —How say by that?
    Power. —She knows not what for her self is good:
Therefore let's force her up between Dorsers,
And carry her home in spight of her blood a.
      Come *Mrs. Minx.*   345
    Nonsy. —I won't, goodly stincks,
    Amb. —I Faith, but you shall a.
    Non. —I defie you all, a Grandjurie of Furies.
Oh Mrs. Ambition, pity my Condition.
Power, Oh Power, let me stay but one hour.   350
Gammar *Plenty* I'le Saint ye sweet face; goody *Peace,*
Pity my case Furies, Divels, Plagues; Bastard, help *Redstreak.*
Help *Costard;* oh here's Prince *Nicky,* I Faith he'll lick ye.

    Enter Prince Niclas, *and* Amb. Pow. Plent. *and* Peace *run off.*

    Nick. Since Queans are gone that came eftsoons to humble ye,
Oh let me now anon hear my last Doom most humbly.   355
    Nons. The first request I did command,
      Was, that you should not hunt me out:
The next request you understand,
Will make you hang your ears, and pout.
My peace you here come for to break,   360
      After my back, why should you sneak?
    Nick. —Cows that do fill our Guts can't long be hid,
      Though Mice run into holes, none see,
      When they have eat our Bread and Cheese,
      And stinck most basely when they'r dead.   365
Sweet Cow you hide your Teats in vain,
Though your full Udder fills anothers pan,
Give me some stroakings to ease my pain.
    Non. Prince *Nick* buckle of girdle turn,
For Milk of mine you ne'r shall churn.   370
Without's my skin, but mind's within;
Though you my hand may find, you cannot reach my mind.
    Nick. Will You on you take just such blame,
As *Ciss* did lay upon her Dame;
Make faults to punnish them? Oh fie for shame!   375

     If Dame should give her Fish to fry,
     She must give Butter by and by.
Let *Ciss* without Butter do what she can,
If she no Butter has, she burns the Pan:
Butter to save, she does Dame offend,   380
Who gave her Butter then to no end.
Cisses unbutter'd things may get her kicks,
For all her Maggots and her drop-nos'd tricks.
Butter can't err, *Ciss* out o'th'way may turn:
Though *Ciss* may fret, yet Butter cannot burn.   385
     Non. Butter good Dames have still allow'd enough,
But Maids turn Butter into Kitchin-stuff:
So when they saw their Butter thrown away,
They put their Butter under lock and key.
     Nick. —If Dames Engine by *Ciss* must govern'd be,   390
And Butter spent—For what a Devil serves she?
Must Maids dry Chops be butter'd, they'l ne'r keep touch,
Though they are ayl'd with Butter ne'r so much.
Oh *None-so-fair!* sweet Dame I am your man,
My heart's unbutter'd burning in your Pan,   395
Without some Butter, it can never move:
Oh Butter it with Butter of your love.
     Non. Against your self sweet Prince y'have said too much,
I'le keep my Butter since you can't keep touch.
Go somewhere else, and make your greazy puns,   400
I love no butter'd Fish, nor butter'd buns.
     Nick. —Butter, Oh sweet Butter; ease my hissing smart,
And Butter *None-so-fairs* unbutter'd heart.

Enter Prince Phillip.

     Nick. Prince *Phillip,* here, that mighty lout,
Gad then 'tis time to look about.   405
     Non. Oh you sneaking Prince, what would have had?
     Phil. Oh thou little Devil! I love thee like mad:
And chill take thee at a venture hab nab.
     Nick. Fierce love full soon must die I think,
And vanish like abortive slink.   410
     Phil. My love's zoo bomination strong,
That 'twill hold buckle and thong;
And if dozn't get thee vurder aveel,
Shat zee' can strick vyre with my steel.
     Nick. —Gods—   415
     Phil. —Gods—and Devils!

Thee talk'st of Courage, if th'hast any,
Here be the Cudgels, let's have a veny.
    Nick. I don't care much if I have one touch.

They play Cudgels.

    Non. —Princes, hold, for all your Squablin   420
Cannot purchase my Tantablin.
    Phil. Adzboars Prince *Nick,* cham yours.
If *None-zo-vair* zay do't, chill buss thy root.
    Nick. —Prince *Phillip,* for fair Trollop,
Whose voice might bear of whelp beguile a,   425
Or Bread and Butter beg from Child a,
I'm thine—
    Non. —The next command of mine, in brief
Is after me no more to sniff.
Princes farewell, without or and if.   430
    Nick. —So sad are the commands that you do give,
That without meat or drink I cannot live.
    Phil. Your mind that upon our veirce wrath prevails,
Can when you please, make hot or cool your nails.
exit None-so-fair.

Enter Woudhamore *and* Sweet-lips.

    Phil. But Zee, Zee, laud to bless us, if here been't hur   435
Zusturs now. —Come Prince *Nick,* let's budge.
    Sweet. Great Princes, wither d'ye sneak from this place?
    Woud. To *None-so-fair,* their Calf with a white face.
    Sweet. I wonder what Princely virtues you can see in her,
i'faggs.
Can she make Butter, and Cheese, and Egs?   440
    Woud. She's a Bastard, some Village Hind got her under a
Hedge, when our Royal Mother was overtaken at a Wake.
Love us, Princes, here's your true beauty.
    Phil. There's your Anchovies.
    Woud. Here's a Cherubimical Face, mark how my Eyes roll.   445
Here's a Languishing look, Ah!—
    Phil. Odzboars my Stomach begins to wamble at her.
    Woud. Here's a foot like a Fairy, and a leg like a Lapwing.
    Phil. Look Prince *Nick,* chil wager a Groat there's zomething
at the end of thick leg,—there's your Anchovies.   450
    Sweet. Here's your white Hounds Tooth.
    Woud. Here's your Illustrious *Persian* Hawk-Nose.

Sweet. Here, here, here's your generous wide Nostrils,
you may see my Brains work through e'm when I'm in passion.
    Phil. Con yo Whistle and Dance *Barnaby?* 455
    Both. Ay, ay.—
    Phil. Con yo zing a new Ditty?
    Both. Ay, ay, ay.—

SONG.

> *God Cupid, Oh fie, O fie, Oh fie,*
> *God Cupid Oh fie, Oh fie,* 460
>   *I am vexed full sore,*
>   *Oh! thou Son of a Whore.*
> *Take pity on me or I dye, I dye,*
> *Take pity on me or I dye.*
>   *My face is Pale and wan,* 465
>   *My blood is turn'd to a jelly;*
> *In my heart I have a great pain,*
> *Oh! Oh! how I long for a man,*
> *With a Sol, my, fa, la, lang tre down derry.*

    Phil. Oh Prince *Nick,* ch'ad lever ha one o'th theze 470
then a Cow, o' Ten groats. —Con ye milk a dreelegg'd Stool?
live vive Months upon the droppings of your Nose? and lye with
no body but your own Husbands?
    Both. Ay, ay, any thing for Husbands.
    Phil. Then give me your hands,—good buy to ye 475
with all my heart—

                              Exit Phillip.

    Woud. Oh! Villanous Clown, I think we are abus'd.
    Sweet. Were ever Ladies bright so us'd?
Surely there's more of honour in Prince *Nicklas.*
    Woud. He looks like a Gentleman, sure he'l tickle us. 480
    Nick. Sweet lips, and wou'd hamor you each, and both,
May keep your Princely wind to cool hot broth.
You know your Cheer, and may go chew your Cuds,
For I'le have *None-so-fair,* or lye ith' Suds,
This is my dire resolve, witness ye Gods. 485

                              Exit Nicklas.

    Sweet. Rot her beauty, while the case is thus,
No *Crouder* e'r will Fiddle us.
    Woud. Each day she can command a several King,
As if the Gods, to do more had nothing
>   But to make Kings for her,
>   Oh laud, Oh lack, Oh dear. 490

With strayning I am almost burst, hey ho;
What shall we do? for all our Cake is doe.
> *Sweet.* Well I will straight complain to Mother *Wosset.*
And she shall Snuff a Candle in her Posset;   495
Brick Wall her Temple does Inviron,
Back-door too is fenc'd with spikes of Iron.
>> Oh! Mother *Wossat,* you that can
>> By Circles dark, and deep, trappan,
>> The heart of any Jill or Jan.   500
Oh! help us to debauch this Jade,
Or her coy tricks will marr thy Trade.
> *Woud.* No Citizen will pawn his Cloak;
No Country Squire will love one stroak,
And how can then thy Chimny smoak?   505
>> Nay, if things go on so odly,
>> All the Gallants will turn godly.
And then for Bub thou maist go choak.
> *Sweet.* Rowse mightily *Woossat,* Mantle done,
Thy hagship Venge, or Credits gone,   510
Make hast, and let's know off, or on.

> *Horrid Musick heard in the Air.*

> *Woud.* Ha! what powerful Melody appears?
And snatches thus our ears?

> Woossat *appears in a Charriot drawn by two Brooms.*

> *Sweet.* The Charriot of the Goddess comes,
Drawn by a Brace of well grown Brooms.   515

> Woossat *sings.*

>> *Fair Damzels I have heard you prate,*
>> *You shall have Husbands soon or late.*
> *I am as mad as any Dog to find,*
> *Y'have had so little good of humane kind,*
>>> *But there's the more behind.*   520
> *I will so order* Nonsey's *Princely louts,*
> *You shall be satisfi'd and leave your pouts:*
>>> *With* Nonsey *now is Daddy dear*
> *And hand in hand th'are gone to wishing Chair,*
>>> *Good fortune for to hear.*   525
> *That Rogue will very civil prove to me,*

For Witch and Juggler never disagree:
  To you and me so kind he'l prove,
    That when you feel his love,
You'l give half piece to buy him fring'd glove.   530
                                          Woossat ascends.

Sweet. Great Beldam, me thy hagship thank,
And now methinks I in wondrous Cranck.
    Woud. While young we'l to loves Altar bow;
And when w'are old be ev'n as thou.

          Enter King Andrew, None-so-fair,
          Twattle, Glozy, *and Attendants.*

K. And. Daughters, by the love that you do bear me,   535
And the duty which I owe you, hear me:
Cease your brawling, and your Twittle Twattle.
At the *Rose* let's call in, and drink a loving bottle.

          Then we'l to the wishing chair,
          If that don't ease your cares,   540
          I'le give you both my Royal ears,
            I think that's very fair.
          None-so-fair's agreed sweet Lady,
          Will you deny poor harmless Daddy?
          What er' you wish for you will have,   545
          Else say King Andrew *is a knave.*

Non. Cheer up Sisters, why should you look so gloomy?
What er' the wishing chair shall say:
The King and That I will obey,
Else may this liquor ne'r go through me.   550
    K. And. Come let's not on each other stare,
But hye us to the wishing chair:
That will set all right in a minuit,
Or else I think the Devil's in it.
So swimmingly we'l carry matters,   555
All pristine Poets that come after's,
To sing Heroick love and slaughters,
Shall write of King and his three Daughters.
                                          Exeunt.

          The End of the First Act.

ACT II, scene i.

Enter Wossat *and* Bruine.

Woss. Son *Bruin* mind your hits, I say mind your hits; this
                    young cold Harlottry *None-so-fair,* must be sous'd,
and touz'd, do'e mark me? she must be tumbl'd and jumbl'd;
she must, I say it, or else the Noble Science of Wenching will
grow obsolete, and all our Famous Function may starve; for   5
after that, who will pity poor decay'd old Gentlewomen that
carry Letters? or suffer Tours, Points, Paint, or Patches,
to be brought to their Chambers? And you of the Illustrious
Society of Pimping, may hang if you have Courage enough
to deserve it; or dye in holes like poyson'd Ratts; You   10
will be shouted through the Street, like strange Dogs with
horns at their tails, pump'd and baited like Spirits that steal
children; every Cuckold will have a snap at your Carkasses.
    Bru. Then one comfort will be, that our miseries will be
short liv'd, for those Beasts you talk of swarm so thick, that   15
'twill be impossible to pass one Street without being worried
to death. Every publick Assembly looks like a Picture of the
Creation before man was made, fill'd up with variety of
Creatures, that show all Horns and Tails.
    Woss. 'Tis for our honour, know, that I will revive the   20
Sect of *Adamites,* renew the *Family of Love,* and make the
slavery of Marriage so out of fashion, that a Man and Wife
shall be show'd about, and wondred at as much as an *Herma-*
phrodite, an entire *Egyptian* Mummy, or a Cat with two tails.
    Bru. I know, Mother, your Interest with the Gentry is   25
great, there is hardly a Noble Family, where one of your
Order does not lye hid under the shape of a Couzen, House-
keeper, Wayting Woman, Chamber-Maid, or the like.—
    Woss. That I learn't from my Brother on the other side of
the water, whose Emissaries are all disguis'd; his precepts   30
and mine agree in most circumstances. We had rather allow
20 Whores then one wife to those of our order; I will bring
up here that old *Scotch* Custom, that every Lord of the
Manour shall have the first nights dalliance with the Bodies
of all his Vassals.   35
    Bru. That will assure you the hearts of all the great Ones,
and keep the others from Marriage, so your business is done.
    Woss. But first let *None-so-fair*'s business be done.
    Bru. I dare not; she is King *Andrews* best beloved daughter.

Woss. Were she the skin between his brows, I'de not   40
spare her; do't or forswear thy Office.—

Bru. That I could easily do, for 'tis not now worth keeping;
if there's any new piece worth Money, a Father, Brother, or
some Relation, Usurps our office, and reaps the profit.

Woss. 'Tis too true, and 'tis unconscionable, that Christians   45
should turn Canibals, and feed upon their own flesh and blood,
my case is even as bad too; I that have spent my Youth to gain
experience, must in my Age be Nos'd, and have my Bread taken
from my Teeth, by every Black brow'd Baggage, that leaps into
the publick Practice of procuring, e'r they know the mystery   50
of jilting; nay, too often learn both together.

Bru. In the City they dare not use two Trades at once;
but in the Suburbs they may do any thing.—

Woss. Your Midwife, who is related to our Craft, as a
Phisician is to a Mountebank—for we make work for them   55
to finish, though we Lay six to their one—suffers none to
profess their Art till they have been Deputies seven years.—
Well, things and things must be mended; but first to the
point, King *Andrew*s three Daughters are coming to the
wishing Chair: the two elder are mad for Husbands, their   60
business is done to our hands.—

Bru. Quite contrary; for if they Marry they'l renounce you.

Woos. No! Though ordinary people that pretend not to
the Modish, Marry to live sullen, that is, chast; others know
better things; your Gentleman stands now as much for the   65
priviledge of keeping a Miss after Marriage, as a Woman
with a Portion does for a Joynture: Ay! and inserts it into
that Covenant. —Make us thankful, we live in a loving
Age,—but to the point—*None-so-fair,* by my means is
resolved to wish the White Bear of *Norwich* to be her Husband;   70
thinking, which is indeed true, that there is no such thing,
though we have frighted silly people into that belief, to
cheat them the better.

Bru. Oh! now I find your meaning, that White Bear I
will be; and the King being possest with a Reverence to   75
our Juggling wishing Chair; shall himself bring her to my Arms.

Woss. Very good; but least she should be stubborn, let
Jeffery be ready to assist you in your pious design.

Bru. If we can but wheedle them into an awful faith.

Woss. Why? should not the speech of a Chair, do as much   80
as *Apollo*'s tripod, a Spirit in a Wall; or the eyes of Images
moved with Wires? let all be Grave and Solemn, for that's

the chief support of Counterfeit worship: and let your
expressions be in Greek, or any unpractis'd canting Gibberish.

    Bru. Enough, I'le warrant the bus'ness.   85

    Woos. This Musick tells their approach, let's dispatch and
attend them in.—

[Act II, scene ii.]   *Soft Musick.*

      The Scene drawn, discovers the wishing Chair.

Enter a Boy in a Surplice, dancing, follow'd by two women
bearing a Chaffing dish between them, and smoaking Tobacco;
after them comes the Chief Priest in a Fools-coat, his Train
supported by two in like habit, two Priests in Surplices
follow them; then come two Judges playing on Jewes-trumps
followed by a Cardinal, playing on a Childs Fiddle; two in
grave habits follow him playing on Childrens Pipes; then
comes a Major beating a little Drum; after him the King,
leading *None-so-fair.* Prince *Nick* and *Sweet-lips, Phillip*
and *Woudhamore* attended—with Guards &c. They pass round
the Stage, and place themselves on each side, and the Chief
Priests before the Chair, and the two in Surplices on each
side.

                Song.

      Let Maudlin *lovers that are in despair,*
      And musty Virgins at their latest Pray'r,
      To be freed from their troubles, come hither.
             And Widows, whose fires
             Of unnatr'all desires   5
      Have parch'd up their faces like leather.

                Chorus.

      We'l dry up their tears, and ease all their Care,
      With a delicate thing called a new wishing chair.

      Of crackling tell-tale Wicker *'tis not made,*
      Which loves dear Secrets has too oft' betray'd.   10
      To this Chair so much Vertue is given
                That when you are in
                At the turning a pin,
      You will think you are going to Heaven.

Chorus.   *We'l* &c.   15

   With offerings laden, to the chair make hast,
   Before the precious time of wishing's past.
   For when once the kind Engine is falling,
      You must bear your pain,
      Till the time come again 20
   Though you rend the moist Clouds with your bawling.

Chorus.   *We'l dry up your tears.* &c.

 The Priests bow, and mutter to the Chair; then turn to
the People.

Song.

   Son of Latrona, *thou great rogue,*
   Here's None-so-fair *her grief to disimbogue.*
   The Jade is skittish, full of treachery 25
   But wilful rude, and loath to try.

Chorus.

   Loe, here's the Fool King Andrew *too,*
   Let's cheat them firmly er' they go.
   Let's cheat, &c.

Chief Priest. —The Sacred Chair vouchsafes that all 30
Upon all four should to him fall.

    All fall on their hands.

Chair. Hoh, hoh, hoh, hoe, hoe, hoe:
Ch. P. —Your offerings are accepted, stand by my Cronies,
Till we have finished all the Ceremonies.

    Chair roars.

   Ha! the mystick Chair begins to frown, 35
   All that have wealth, must lay it down.
   Keep nought of Pride, or Riches near you,
   Least Chair in wrath to pieces tear you.

 They all lay down their Money, Swords, &c. which the
Priests gather up.

Song by the two Priests.

1. *Pr. Thou pickst the Butchers knife out of his mouth,*
Thou robst a poor old woman of her tooth.   40
    2. *Pr. —Thou didst the monstrous Flesh-flies to destroy,*
Who bred the Maggots which did Beef o're run.

Chorus.

Thou sly, and bauling Thief, go on with joy,
Their Money, Swords, and Hats are all our own.

A Dance by the two Priests.

Song.

1. *Pr. By* Germain Princess, *that notorious cheat.*   45
    2. *Pr. By* Cressets *memory we thee intreat,*
Thou wouldst with noise, and show blind all their eyes.
    1. *Pr. Least they our silly* Opera *despise,*
Chorus of both. *—Least they our silly* Opera *despise.*

Chorus.

$\left\{\begin{array}{l}\end{array}\right.$ *Now Croudy mutton is come out of France,*   50
Tom Thimble has made show compleat,
Jewes-Trumps, and Cymbals sound, and let us dance,
Since Wool is small, let cry be great.

A Dance.

The Invocation.

2. *Pr. —James Naylor, Pope Joan, Wat Tyler, Mall Cutpurs,*
Chocorelly.
    All Answer. —Help our *Opera,* because 'tis very silly.   55
    2. *Pr. —Massaniello, Mosely, Jack-straw, Jantredisco,*
Pimponelli.
    Ans. —Help our *Opera,* because 'tis very silly.
    2. *Pr. —Hocus-pocus, Don Quixot, Jack Adams, Mary Ambry,*
Frier Bungy, William Lilly.—
    Ans. Help our *Opera,* because 'tis very silly.
    2. *Pr. Carpentero, Paintero, Dancero, Musickero, Songstero,*
Punchanelly.   60
    Ans. Help our *Opera,* because 'tis very silly.

Chorus. *First Sung, and then Sung and Danc'd to.*

> *Some shall hollow, some Dance and Sing,*
> *Hey ding, ding, ding, hey ding, ding,*
> *Omn'a bene—Omn'a bene.*
> *Ding, ding, ding, with hey ding, ding ding,*   65
> *With hey, &c.—*

The Chief Priest seats None-so-fair *in the Chair, it Thunders*
and Lightens; the Chair sinks, and in its place a dreadful shape
arises, and sayes.—

> The Princess to the Chair is pleasing,
> And all her troubles now are easing.

The Chief Priest turns over his head, and the other two Priests
take the little Boy in the Surplice, and whip him while they

Sing this.

> *He took him by the Lilly Frock,*
>> *And scourged him full sore;*   70
> *A long half hour by the Clock,*
>> *Alack a day therefore,*
> *While Youth doth last, the changes Ring,*
> *With a ding dong, ding dong ding,*
> *When Youth is flown, and Age is come,*   75
> *The Clappers down, the Bell doth groan:*
> *And call you to a sad long home,*
> *With a heavy, heavy, heavy boam, boam.*

The Chief Priest rises and waves his Wand thrice.

Ch. Pr. Comorah whee, Comorah whee, Comorah whee.
All answer, bowing. Shoolimocroh, Shoolimocroh, Shoolimocroh.   80
Ch. Pr. —Kiss *Betty.*
All answer, bowing. —Pollykagathoy.—

It Thunders and Lightens, the Priest waves his Wand, all
squat down—the dreadfull shape sincks, and the Chair rises
kissing None-so-fair,—*and she immediately comes out of it.*

Ch. Pr. Behold the Chair.—[*All rise up hastily and bow.*]
Now *None-so-fair* has had her wish,

And first you shall hear what it is;   85
And after we will sacrifice a—Fish.
    K. And. Oh Sir! we humbly do beseech
To know who shall her Husband be,
For that our very Ears do itch;
And if you please we fain would see.   90

    It Thunders and Lightens extreamly, and then the Chair
    delivers this Oracle.—

    Lead None-so-fair *to yonder Wood,*
    Where Lovers howle like Beasts for Food,
    There she must sigh, and weep a good.
        And so you there must leave her,
        For the White Bear of Norwich *must have her.* 95
    To her he will be very Civil,
    Be gone, 'tis vain to huff or snivil.

    K. And. O fie, O fie, O laud, O me forlorn,
Would I had dy'd e'r I was born;
        I have spent my Youth fair,   100
        To get a wife for a Bear.
    Woud. Lippy, I could leap out of my skin for joy.
Mother *Woossat,* a brave Beldam! she has keep'd her word.
    Sweet. Nothing vexes me, but that I must be Aunt to her
litter of Cubs. —We shall have roaring Nephews.—   105
    K. And. Troop, troop, if I keep in this dreadful mind,
I will come back, but I'le leave my life behind.
    Nick. Hold, hold, King *Andrew* stay, be wise I say,
        And don't the Gods obey;
If 'twere good that *None-so-fair* were given to the Bear,   110
        You should hear'd on't before y'had known't.
    Phil. But if 'tis bad, then 'tis not good, we know what's what.
We must not shed the guiltless blood,
        Yet *None-so-fair,* poor Sheep, must go to pot:
Cods, you wou'd be veaz'd, wo'r you z'ard in your kind,   115
Vor y'are never half an hour in a mind.
    Nick. King—be not cheated nor cullied, King; I'le be hang'd
if there is not a live thing in the wishing Chair, didn't you
see how *None-so-fair* was tickl'd, did not she spin like a
Top, and stand upon her head like a Juggler; 'tis a damn'd   120
Son of a Whore Chair, and he lyes, and I am not satisfi'd.—
    Ch. Pr. Oh Sir, take heed, for Crimes like this,
The Sacred Chair has Rods in piss.

K. And. When wishing Chair his Silence broak,
I do believe Tom-tumbler spoak.   125
    Ch. Pr. The wonders of our wishing Chair, prov'd by
Miracle, and that shews the truth of the power of the wonder.
    Nick. The Power is governed by the Order, which commands
the Power and the Order, Rules the Beauty which
governs the Order, which is found ty'd fast to the end of   130
the Creation, in a long round Chain; and things, and things
loose fast upon one another, I don't know howish, like
bunches of Paper at a Kites tail, and so by a plain orderly
method of Power and Order, and Order without Power,
and Power without Order; and no Power, and no Order,   135
and no Order, but a kind of Dis-orderly Powerful Order.
           The fixed World is drawn, confin'd at large;
           As men in Ropes ty'd loose, tugg Western Barge.
    Ch. Pr. You and your Nature are meer Ignorance,
But we appear to wise foreseeing chance.   140
    Nick. If Nature is less then Miracle, when Heaven uses
Supernatural Miracle; the Gods declare their Power less,
because Miracle is greater then Nature; —But if the Gods
make children, when Natures Instrument is out of tune:
They use no Nature, because Nature without Nature is   145
not Nature, but Miracle Unnatural, miraculous Nature.
    Phil. There's your Anchovies, *Priest*—'twas woundy
well spoak. And zooe if this be granted, the Gods can, but
they wo'not; because they would, but they cannot, and
they wo'nt, and they cannot, and they cannot, and they   150
wo'nt, and zo.
           They'le ne'r be mad, because they'r not long in a mind,
           Az a deaf Hostess can't zee, because she's blind.
    Ch. Pr. Avaunt, you scoffing Blades, avaunt,
The Thundring Gods begin to Rant.   155

*It Thunders, and Lightens, the Chair sinks, and the Priests,
and all their Attendants run off the Stage.*

    Phil. What dost think, we be wild *Irish;* and will run away,
Because the Clouds be troubl'd with the wind cholick,
Odzboars, dost think chill lose my Coin, and my Parcel?
    Non. The Gods and wishing Chair, we must obey,
And I will go, because I cannot stay.   160
    K. And. —Come my sweet Pigs-nie, let's make hast;
If bear eats thee for his breakfast,
As I'm a sinner, he shall have me for a dinner.

Nick. Thus great ——— was betray'd,
And *Psyche* taken from her Dad,   165
Though Princess huff'd, and swore like mad.

Exeunt all but Phillip.

Phil. —All gwon, zure 'tis a Bawdy-house,
Vor there cham twoald they use you thus,
Be vengeance cranck, till you are snoring drunk,
And then away shirks Money, Cloaths, and Punck.   170
The Gods may well rain Golden showr's,
Into the Laps of Paramours:
Credit is theirs, but cost is ours;
Ch'ave not one penny left my drouth to quench;
If this be Religion; give me a Wench. There's your Anchovies.   175

Exit Phillip.

ACT II, scene iii.

A Wilderness.

Enter King Andrew, Sweet-lips, Woudhamore, *and* None-so-fair.
Non. O Royal Dad! See how he blubbers;
Kings should not whine so like great lubbers.
K. And. O slip! O Daughter mine! where art thou gadding?
I ne'r shall hear thee more sing with a fadding.
Oh! that could grave thee hadst thou put in,   5
Before by me thou wer't begotten:
Why should the Gods be so barbraous?
Oh! that t'hadst dy'd in Natures Ware-house,
Then Death that cunning old Shop-lifter,
From stall of eyes had never snift her.   10
Non. —Your sniv'ling melts me, so that I
Shall be quite dead before I dye.
K. And. Oh ye Gods!
I've many a day paid Scot, and lot,
And well I'm serv'd now, am I not?   15
Non. —Oh! Sir begone, begone, I say,
For if you tarry here,
My life it will soon sneak away:
And cheat the Gods, and eke the bear.
Sisters two I leave you here,   20
To keep you clean and sweet.
Be good unto my Daddy dear,
For so 'tis very meet.
Each week let him have shirt full clean,

Let head be comb'd, and wash'd his face,   25
Let holes be mended in hosen,
    Himself can't do't, you see, alass.
Sir, On my knees I you beseech,
    To leave me now alone.
For why my Elbows both do itch,   30
    Till you are fled, and gone.
O! Budge away from this place flat, all,
For if the Bear should come, have at all.
Bw'y Daddy for ever and a day.
    K. And. —Mine own dear Hussey do not so say,   35
Bespeak a place for me below there:
For I'le come down some time or other,
And do'e hear, remember me to your Mother.

                        Exeunt all but None-so-fair.

    Non. For all so well I hid my fears,
Deaths Calumny my face besmears,   40
Laud what a quiddie am I in i'fack; i'fack,
You may wring the shift upon my back:
If 'twere but Flesh and Blood I would not fear,
But to be touz'd by nought, but clawes and hair,
Hair, stiffer then an old mans Beard,   45
Would make the stoutest Vizard here afeard.
    Why should I speak so; the Chair told me the Bear would be
kind to me; I'le shut my eyes, and think, 'tis some Gallant in
Masquerade with Fur'd-Coat on, but then he can't cry like a
discreet soft Courtier—do'e know me now? no, he'll roar boh,   50
ho, ho, and fall on like a Drunken Soldier at the Sack of a
City.

              Enter Phillip *and* Nicklas.

    Phil. O hoe! here she is—pluck up Heart, O Grace! here,
take my muckinder, and dry thy ey'n, cham the Blood O'the
Phillips! ne'r a Dog in the Village can zay—blacks mine   55
eye—but in the way of love and honesty, and av'ore the Bear
shall eat one bit o've thee,
    Princess, Chill beat my Oaken Plant to th'stumps.
    Don't windle zoo, but leave thy doleful dumps.
    Nick. —Let Guts and Garbage feed white Bears,   60
Poor strolling Cracks and Wastcoteers:
Not Gods, but cheating Crew of juggling Chair,
Are mad to make a Meal on Royal Gueer.
    Non. I will not hear the Sacred Chair abused.

Nick. —Poor harmless Rogue! how sadly he's misused?   65
Great Princess, since grim *Bruins* coming,
No longer here let's stay Caps thrumming.
Come jog along with us good Fellows,
We will regale you at next Ale-house.
And of one kiss of *Bona Robas,*   70
Bears, Gods, nor Divels, shall not bob us.
    Non. No more, great Sirs, waste Court-ship here,
You take the wrong sow by the ear,
For by Lord *Harry* I'le ne'r marry,
And when I do, it shan't be you,   75
             Therefore, go to.

        A Roaring within as of a Bear.

    Phil. Odzboars, Prince *Nick!* Vast, here's the Anchovies.
    Nick. Bear up, *Phillip,* bear up.
    Phil. Ay, ay, but don't hunch me zoo, chill warn't vor one.
    *A Roaring again, the Bear enters, seizes the Princess, and
sincks with her, while* Jeffry *with a switch beats off the
Princes.*

        The End of the Second Act.

          ACT III, scene i.

    Enter Pavers *with Beaters on their shoulders, and their
Master with his measuring Rod.*

            SONG.

      You tough brawny Lads, that can live upon stone;
          And skin the hard Flint for good Liquor:
    Let love to the Idle and wealthy begone,
         And let Preaching alone to the Vicar;
    Let all be made plain, with your Strikers and Thumpers,   5
    And when your works done, we'l about with the Bumpers.

    The little blind God, of which lovers do prate,
         Makes all that adore him grow lazy,
    For counterfeit blessings he long makes you wait,
         And with sighs and diseases he pays ye.   10
    But he you serve now, with your Strikers and Thumpers,
    When the work's done, will about with the Bumpers.

1. *Pav.* The Walks are all gravell'd, and the Bower shall be
prepar'd for the Bear and *Nonsey.*

2. *Pav.* But e'r we go in, let the Drinking begin,   15
And then we will Thump it agen.

Chorus.

With full double Pots,
Let us liquor our throats.
And then we'l to work with a hoh, ho, ho,
But let's drink e'r we go, let's drink e'r we go.   20

Mast. Then toss up your liquor, and to labour make hast,
The time is too precious to wast.

Chorus. —*With full double,* &c.

1. *Pav.* Here, *Harry.*
2. *Pav.* —Here, *Will.*
3. *Pav.* —Old True-penny still.   25
All. —While one is drinking, another should fill.
3. *Pav.* —Here's to thee, *Peter,*
4. *Pav.* —Thanks, honest *Phil.*
All. —Let's lustily swill, and while one is drinking,
another should fill.

Chorus. —*With full double,* &c.

Mast. Dispatch, or the Bear, or the Princess will chide,   30
For Love can no hindrance abide.

1. *Pav.* There's more need of drinking, drinking, then kissing,
by ods.
We'l bouse it in spight of the Gods.

Chorus. —*With full double,* &c.

A Dance, and all run off.

Enter Bruin *and* Jeffry.

Bru. Brave Boys all, 'tis as well done as if I had chalk'd out   35
the way my self; and it had been doing 16 whole Months, by the
excellent approved, great, most Famous, Ingenious, Industrious,

careful Society of *More-fields;* well, *Geffery,* what dost think of
my Missy *None-so-fair!*

    Jeffry. Think! Oh she's the delicat'st but of Mans meat that   40
e'r lips were laid to, or legs laid over; she's an Armfull for
one of the Gods, for *Jupiter* himself in his Altitudes.

    Bru. In his Altitudes—what's that?

    Jeffry. Why that's drunk as David's Sow, with *Nector* and
Ambrosia, which is stout Mum and Brandy the Gods drink upon   45
Holy-dayes. But Sir, is not *None-so-fair* a little soft childish,
no wiser then she should be?

    Bru. I though thou hadst known better; all cunning Amorous
Women put on a modish seeming Innocent Ignorance, that they may
have pleasure without loss of reputation. 'Tis a modest way of   50
wooing, and as pleasant to the hearers, as great lyes ingeniously
made, and seriously told, for things that come nearest Truth, and
are not so, are most taking.

    Jeffry. Therefore, young Gallants are so much pleased with being
like Gentlemen; and the total of all the praise they would give a   55
Friend, ends in—Gad, in short he's much like a Gentleman, the
Divel take me, much like a Gentleman?—

    Bru. Ay! that is, he Swears, Drinks, Games, and Whores, which
are no more the true accomplishments of a right Gentleman then
Huffing and speaking loud Nonsence are of the Gods, whatever our   60
Friends, the Fopps, and the Poets, which are much like one
another, say to the contrary.—

    Jeffry. Apollo, the wishing Chair, told me—

    Bru. Pox take that liquorish Rogue, he has been beforehand,
he'l have a hand in every sack,—what did he say?   65

    Jeffry. When he kiss'd her, she cry'd—Oh laud! why do'e
kiss a body so, I'le tell my Father, so I will.—

    Bru. Ay, and thrust out her lips as 'twere to push him away,
when 'twas only to kiss closer?—

    Jeffry. And when he talk'd a little,—I don't know howish,   70
you know of that same,—she look'd so wistly, and Innocently
in his face.

    Bru. As Ignorant People do on one that speaks a Forreign
Language.—

    Jeffry. Ay, and repeated ev'ry strange word so harmlessly,   75
and cry'd—what's that now?

    Bru. And was as curiously inquisitive, as if she were learning
a new stitch on her Sampler.—

    Jeffry. And look'd with such Religious Languishing Eyes.

    Bru. Religious Languishing Eyes?   80

    Jeffry. Ay, as if she were at Prayers.

Bru. Thou incorrigible Fool—If a Woman looks so, though
in the Church, thou maist swear her thoughts are in the very
Altitudes of Love. —Her heart's drunk with it, and her eyes
reel, and are dazl'd. Her dying Eyes! think thyself into an   85
Amorous extasie, and I'le tell thee how thou lookst.

Jeffry. Gad, and so I will.

Bru. Now, now, now, there's your Religious, languishing,
drunken, dying Eyes.

Jeffry. Oh, oh, aha.—   90

Bru. There's your Anchovies, as Prince *Phillip* says.

Jeffry. I'le swear 'tis very pretty, but why won't you appear
to her like a Gentleman?—

Bru. No, no, when she sees me in this invisible shape, like
a Prince, she'l think I'm a God, and will make her a Lady.   95
When love thus storms a Fort, and enters by force, he plunders
freely, and imposes what conditions he will; but when he comes
sneaking, and creeping like a Boy after a Butterfly, Ten to
one but she flies off, and he falls into the next Ditch; for
where love is in motion, like Water thrown on the ground,   100
'twill fall into the first hollow place it finds.

       My love comes, *Jeffry* to your Post, away,
       Take care that none disturb our Play;
       'Twill be your own another day.

Exeunt Bruin *and* Jeffry *several ways.*

ACT III, scene ii.

   *The Scene chang'd to an Arbour dress'd up with gaudy
Play-games for Children.*

Enter None-so-fair *alone.*

Non. Oh, what a bewitching sight is here, a finer place can't
be seen in a Summers day. —Oh! my tother goodness, it
looks like an Orange stuck with Cloves, or a Pudding full
of Plums, as who should say, come eat me; 'tis the very *Virginy*
Pepper of Nature, where the Spicy tast of all Shows is   5
bound up in one fine sight. Was this made for a Slaughter-
house? no, 'tis more like an *Opera* then a *Bear-Garden;* 'tis
as fine as to Day and to Morrow, sure 'tis the Countrey-house
of some City God; I was brought hither above ground too,
as if I had flown in the Air: —Oh happy *Nonsey.* —But stay,   10
if the Gods should play the Jacks with me, and show me

Roast-meat, to thrust the Spit in my Guts? —No, no, let
nothing trouble thee, little *Nonsy*, th'are better bred, and
scorn to be so base. —But if some fine God should come in a
great Periwig, and red and green Ribbons, and swear he loved   15
me like a Divel, and all that—there's your Anchovies, as
Prince *Phillip* says.

Bruin *within sings.*

Bru. *Sweet, open the Door, and let me come in a,*
For to go a wooing, I now begin a.
Non. *I'le open, and open, and open again,*   20
Then I prythee sweet heart come in.

O Melody most ravishing!
I could for ever hear it sing.
Oh if thou hast the Bowels of a Man a!
Tune up thy Pipes, and sing again a.   25

Bruin *within.*

Bru. *Oh fair Maid! be not affraid: For I am come a wooing,*
Thou art mine, and I am thine own sweet heart, and Bruin.
Non. Once more, Oh box my ears once more!
If er' I heard the like, I'm the Son of a Whore.
Bru. Hey ding a ding, muck and Trash,   30
Little Misse *None-so-fair* has a white Elbow,
Oh take all my dross! but give me the Lass,
For I want a new sheath to my Bilbow.
Non. With a hey tralil, and ho tralil, my Elbow does itch,
Which makes me cry still: 35
Oh give me thy Dross! and thou shalt have the Lass,
And a Dainty fine sheath for thy Bilboe.
My heart's provok'd by some Divine Bauble,
And all my Blood is turn'd to a Caudle.
Bru. All Play-games that e're be brought,   40
For love or Money, I'le give my Honey,
She shall have all the World in thought.
Non. —O Dear! O dainty!
Bru. —O sweet and twenty!
Non. —When shall I my Charmer know?   45
Bru. —Too morrow to mo.
Non. —I'm affraid,
Bru. —Fie fair Maid.

– 186 –

Non. —Hey I'm sad, and I'm glad,
Bru. —Why all's paid I'gad.   50
Non. —By this great guift, thou art some Goddy,
Bru. —Thou shalt perceive, I am no Noddy.
Non. —Come in then my Dear hoddy doddy.

A Dance of Bears, among which is the white Bear of Norwich,
*and at the end of the Dance his shape flyes off, and he appears
dressed like a* Cupid.

Non. Oh what a glorious thing was here, in shape of ugly Bear.
Oh what hands! what legs are there?   55
But Oh the face! and oh the hair!
And Oh that he were mine own dear!
  Bru. The Bear I am,
  Non. Pray Gad be Jon.
  Bru. For all you are so cranck and prety,   60
The Chair has sent me here to eat ye.
  Non. Oh eat me quickly! and Oh eat me long!
For and Oh! I am not sickly, but Ah! I am not young.
  Ah! I'm very tender by my troth,
  Oh! I long to leap into thy mouth.   65
    In thy dear kidnies I'le inhabit,
    And make a Burrough like a Rabbit.
Oh! no other love shall thence me ferret,
Ah! I will not hurt thee, do not fear it.
    But like gentle Viper some-   70
    Times to pretty mouth I'le come,
Hounds-teeth to pick; on eyes to gaze,
And view thy comely maple face:
Then turning round in wainscot jawes,
And sliding down rough corral Throat.   75
      There in loves sweets I'le stewing lye,
      Till all dissolv'd in love, I dye.
My mind boils over with the thought,
  Bru. My fair,
  Non. —my Love,
  Bru. —my Dear,
  Non. —my Dove.
  Bru. My Honey,
  Non. —my Bunny,
  Bru. —my Croney,   80
  Non. Let me approach ye,
  Bru. —Let me make much o'ye—

Non. Oh let me kiss that pretty pretty dimple!
Bru. My love is willing, but she's wondrous simple.
Non. Ah how I long! Oh how I am stung!
Ah I feel your headed steel!   85
Oh how it smarts! Ah how it tickles!
Ah the softness! and Oh the prickles!
Ah how it cleaves my heart in pieces!
    Now, now, Oh now it increases.
    Now my Blood begins to be at peace,   90
    I'le warrant you, 'twas all up in my face.
Oh the sweets of the pain! Ah the pain of the pleasure!
Ah the griefs! Oh the joys without measure!
    Bru. Is this cold *Nymph* without heart like Iron?
Her face doth tempt, but tricks do tyre one,   95
My stomacks full, but she's more eager,
Then Soldier coming from long leaguer.
    Non. Oh the Trance in which I've been!
Ah that 'twould 'till Death remain!
But Oh 'twill never, never come again!   100
    Bru. Allonz, my Dear, I am thy Bear,
Cheer up I say, I have it for ye,
With nought but love I will not marry.
    Non. Ah Laud, Sirs, did you ever see the like? what have
you done to me? well, y'are a naughty Bear, I believe y'are   105
a Witch; do virtuous Princess use to be so—Poor thing I
was never so before, and I would do nothing mis-becoming
the Rank, Quality of King *Andrews* daughter—
    Bru. Oh well dissembled Ignorance!
    Non. Your hand bewitch'd me, but your eyes; Oh those   110
Inchanting eyes! I never saw such eyes, nor felt such eyes,
nor heard such eyes, nor understood such eyes. Oh those
delicate! dear, long, round, twinckling, pincking, glazing,
leering, sneering Sheeps eyes of thine.
        O look away, they pierce me so,   115
        I know not wher' I feel or no.
    Why do'e gape so amorous? zee,
    Would you have any thing of me?
    Bru. Oh yes, I am soust too in loves pickle,
Salt tears down cheeks like Mil-stones trickle;   120
My heart in Stomach there would rest,
As brooding Rook does on soft nest;
And while for food it there sits calling,
With bit of pity, thou must stop his yawling:
Oh give me thy pretty thing.   125

And when that pretty thing thou givest to me,
I'le burn its Tail, that it may fly from me.
    Non. Oh take it then! Oh catch it quickly,
Staying with me 'tis grown so sickly,
It melts too fast, unless your help withstands,   130
'Twill dye away, and lye upon my hands;
Oh it flutters, Ah it pants, yet, yet I hav't,
Oh Sir dispatch, dispatch, if you would sav't,
Sir, Sir, Sir, now, now, Oh now it tingles at my fingers ends,
'Tis gone, 'tis gone, run, fetch it back again: 135
Oh I shall dye unless thou giv'st me thine.
                            Exeunt running.

Scene chang'd.

Enter the Princes, Nicklas *and* Phillip.

    Phil. Prince *Nick,* cham zick ove this zokring work;
Che wonder where the Vengeance scab do lurk,
Why wuss mon she's but one o' my Naunts:
There vore lets squot, and leave theez murrin Jaunts;   140
    Nick. All ground's too hot for me to tarry on,
Till I have got my Princely Carrion;
Though Fortune is froppish, still we hope well,
Phil, be not moapish, but ask all Pe-o-ple.
    Phil. May be she's zunning on zome odrous mixion,   145
Choud teaz her ifz cou'd vind the Vixon;
    Nick. Had she none but we to put her tricks on.
    Phil. A vowdry tit; come *Nick,* lets zlip hence,
When luch zares pride wull pay her odd vip'ence;
Yet white Bears a Beast, if he hurt imp Royal.   150
Though Bear have Feast, let wishing Chair pay all:
Let's hye us to'm straight, and bumbast the bony Witch,
Che doubt thick Chair had vurst lick ove her hony Critch.
    Nick. Mums the word, least he by flight prevent us;
Let's gallop straight on pair of nimble Tentoes.   155
                        Exeunt.

The Scene chang'd to the Arbour.

Enter None-so-fair.

    Non. Laud, what have I done, I reek like a new shot gun.
Heigh hoe, a kind of shameless shame I feel;

– 189 –

But I feel something else that joyes me still,
And does that other feeling quite out-feel:
I can't repent now for my blood,   160
Sure things so sweet must need be good,
Besides to love is to obey a God,
The things so Sacred, and so kind to boot:
That I will roar it out—again I'le do't.
Here comes the little loving Rogue,   165
Now do I blush like a blew Dog;
What shall I do, I am rapt, Oh! I shall have my fit again, for
something catches me fast by the inclination.—
Oh, you Divel, you Ah!

She sings this.

The more I look, the more I like, beauty breeds my hearts delight.   170

   Bru. Poor virtuous loving Princess,
At first she seem'd to loath loves pleasant bub,
And now she's all for empting of the Tub.
   Non. Though I'm so fond of one ne'r seen before,
I hope you do not think I am a Whore;   175
         Yet least that I should prove with Child,
And you should run away therefore,
         I pray Sir, be so meek and mild,
To tell me like a trusty Trojan,
Both what's your Name, and where's your Lodging.   180
   Bru. I am a great Prince, my Estate lyes in the new *Utopia*.
I am chief commander of all the Padders, Jugglers, Priggers,
Ditchers, Bulkers, and Pickpockets. To me all those merry
Greeks pay Tribute, which shall come into thy Fob; all the
beautious Doxies, Dells and Drabs, shall obey thy back, and   185
admire thy magnificence.
   Thou shalt be both my pretty *Romp* in Luxury and Pomp.
Thy eyes shall watch while thy ears are ravished, and all thy
other Senses shall dance *Bobbing-Joan* for joy. I'le keep thee
in thy Hair, and thy Slippers; thou shalt eat like a Cameleon,   190
and drink like a Flitter-mouse; thy House shall be made of
one intire Sugar-Plum, out of which thou shalt every day
eat thy passage like a lovely Viper out of his Dams Belly,
thy Closet shall be furnished with Sun-beams, thy Cloaths
shall be all Marmalade powdered with Caraways for spangles,   195
thy Bed shall be made of a great Blue-Fig, and thy Curtains
of Dyet-bread Paper, where thou shalt lye like the Lady in

the Lobster 'till I come to dress thee with the Vinegar of love,
and the Nutmeg of Luxury, thy Coach shall be of some fine
new Trangam—which we'l study for—   200
    Non. Oh I am rapt again!
    Bru. Thou shalt have a Dog and a Parrot, and when th'are
sick, thou shalt have a Physitian and a Surgean for them.
    Non. Oh! I am rap't again—but what if they should dye?
    Bru. Then thou shalt mourn o're thy dear Cur, like a   205
grave Person of quality; put thy woman in black, and convey
it with a Train of Hakneys to the Sepulchre of his stinking
Ancestor in Pomp and Luxury. —But my dear Bunting I tell
thee one thing.
        Ask not my mighty name, for that once known,   210
        Like fairy pence thy Trump'ry will be gone:
        If *Newgate*-keeper once should smoak us,
        Thy Bear must vanish with a hocus.
    Non. But Love, Honey, won't you let my Sisters visit me?
truly they are not adopted Sisters, but of my true Royal   215
Flesh and Blood; and I would fain show my Pride and Luxury.
For Bravery without being seen, is like *John* come kiss me
without dancing, or a Bell without a Clapper, for it makes
no noise.—
    Bru. My *Jeffery* shall for them hye,   220
And fetch them hither by and by.

Enter Jeffery.

    Bru. Hoe, *Jefferey,* Hoe, make hast, and go
Hunt for great Sisters high and low.
Thou'lt find the stately *Trape's* tyr'd with Travel,
Out of surbated trotters picking gravel,   225
Or at some Farmers door a resting haunches,
And singing smutty Ballads for Bread and Cheese.
    Jeff. The Quean looks shy on't, will she bob? will she come?
    Bru. The *Nymph* is plyant, done is job, word is mum.
    Jeff. Blouzes I fly to call as fast as hoofs can fall,   230
        I'le bring them hither with their Fardels,
        Or leave them there, it will go hard else.
                               Exit Jeffery.
    Bru. I hope your Sisters are no setters,
And come to tempt you with Love-letters:
If you let any other—at my Charges,   235
My fresh tap'd love will turn as sowr as Verjuice.
But let that pass—

Now prick up ears, let eyes stare hard,
Let all thy Senses stand on Guard.
That I may catch them unprepar'd.   240
Till *Jeffry* do thy lineage bring,
We'l go, and hunt the pretty thing.

Exeunt.

ACT III, scene iii.

Enter Wishing-Chair *and* Jeffry.

Wish. And how, and how, do things and things fit? does
she melt like Snow in his arms? and make the Rogue think
there's Fire in his bosom? —does the little Vermine twine
about him like a tame Snake? and make her tongue seem
forked with swift motion?   5
Jeffry. Why all these questions Friend, and ask'd with
such envious curiosity? because you made the first discovery,
you thought the Natives would truck with no other. —Y'are
out; you only touch'd upon the Coast, he has sail'd up the
River, discovered the In-land,—planted a Colony, and   10
settl'd the Trade of Furs.—
Wish. Oh Rogue! 'tis a dainty spot of Ground, Woods,
Rivers, Mountains, over which is plac'd a Sky always serene
and clear. Well the Dog has his day.
Jeffry. —Ay and He'l not lose a minuit of it.   15
Wish. I shall ne'r forget, the pretty skittish thing did so
snatch away my kisses, and throw them back again with such
a furious kind Scorn. —Pray let me go now, won't you? —and
then imbrac'd me so fiercely, as if she had wish'd, the Divel
take me if I did. —Ah! she pressed, like fresh Curds newly   20
put into the Cheese-frame. —Oh *Jeffry! Jeffry!*
Jeffry. Oh Friend! Friend! you have had your time,
and must now live upon your *Alforges;* like a great Monkey
chew the Cud, for you must be a clean Beast in spight of
your teeth. I over-heard the Puissant Princes make dangerous   25
resolves against your dear life. Prince *Phillip* will be at
your Anchovies; i'faith, *Bruin* thinks fit that you repair to
our Pallace the new Musick-house, you know where, for
your Worships safety,—and to incourage you, heark ye—
I am sent for two fresh Frollicks, the two elder Sisters.   30
Wish. Art thou so? —enough—I am for the *Straights.*

Enter Gammer Redstreak.

— 192 —

Jeffry. Hold, hold, here's a Packing-penny, she comes to
wish for a Famine, that Corn may sell dear.

Wish. Or a foul disease on those that Robb'd her Hen-roost,
Pox upon her brown Bread *Phisnomie,*—lets go.   35

Jeffry. Not a foot Sir 'till this old Jade's curry'd; y'are
bound by Oath to refuse none.—

Wish. Prithee *Jeffry,* be favourable, dispence.

Jeffry. On, on, Sir, will you perform, or shall I complain;
remember.   40

      Wee'l dry up your tears, and ease all your Care,
      With delicate thing call'd a new wishing Chair.

Let the good Woman be satisfied; now will I go find her
Husband, and send him hither immediately. Dear mischief, how
I love thee.   45

                             Exit Jeffry.

Red. Ah blessing on his good heart, he speaks most Serene
and clear, he's a very notable Man I'le warrant you; —and
whoever says Gammar *Redstreak* hath no Judgement? Hy hee
and for all your whim whams, they prate and prate, but give
me something has some savour; and say, and hold, Gadslidikins,   50
I'le not be trampl'd on by the Proudest. —I have
known the time when my penny was as White, and round,
as the best fiddle faddle of them all; Oh the tumbling, and
rumbling there was then, I'le warrant you my Linnen was so
touzl'd, and mouzl'd, 'twou'd do ones heart good to see't.   55
But now like an old crack'd Groat, whose stamp's worn out;
none will take me, they say I am not current. —But I'le fit
'em, for I'le wish my self a Queen, and this House full of
Money in my Pocket.

Wish. And the Devil in thy Chattering Chops.   60

Red. Ay, your worships: and a new Husband every time
I change my Apron.—

Wish. And a new Disease ev'ry time thou tun'st thy Clack.

      Enter Jeffry *and* Costard *observing them.*

Jeffry. See how close they are, an honest Man, and an
Headborough.   65

Cost. Oh Trumpet, Oh Hilding, I have been her true and natural
Husband any time this twenty Year, up zitting and down-lying.
Ah how she bumbast him, out thou Carrion!—

Red. Show your favour Sir, and when I am a Queen you shall be
my head Hind.   70

Wish. Some kind mischief deliver me, from this she Dragon.

– 193 –

Red. I shall make a rare Queen, and bring good houswifry
into fashion; for I'le make all the *Masques,* and *Chorus's,* and
Simphonies my self, *With a Fiddle Faddle, hey down diddle,*
faith let's be merry.   75

Cost. How Pestilent Jocund the lown is; well, my heart
leaps against my teeth, like a Rat against the Wyers of a
Trap. —I'le be with thee in the twinckling of a Cabbage,
I'le scoure thy Crab-lanthorn with a witness, look to't, I'le
swing thy Croudledum, I will.—   80

Jeffry. Dispatch then, for the Show will be past else; I would
fain get the Rogue some soure sawce to his sweet bit.

Cost. Ah! how she sneers like a Mare that has spy'd her stray
Coult. —do, do, Ring all in, chill Ring noon about thy Pate
presently.   85

                                                    Exit Costard.

Jeffry. So the dull Larrum's wound up, I would fain stay
to hear it clatter; but I must seek *Sweetlips* and *Woudhamore.*

                                                    Exit Jeffry.

Wish. Well I am mollifi'd, thou shalt see the Show; the
Woman is decent, cleanly, and sound I'le Warrant; hang't,
we must not always expect Beautious Women; stay here a   90
little, thou pritty Rogue; I begin to have a mind to her;—
ha, old True penny.

                                                    Exit Wish.

Red. Now for me, I'le be a Queen or a Lady at least; and
King *Andrew's* Three Daughters shall be my Maids, and I'le
have a high Seat in the Church, and the Chaplain shall pray   95
for his virtuous Patrons. —Then I'le have the head-ach, and
be very sick, that I may receive Visits in my Bed, Oh! there's
no way like it to draw on Sutors; they know a poor weak
Woman that lyes there on purpose, has no power to deny.—
One that I know, drest her self in six several dresses to catch   100
her Sweet-heart, but nothing pleas'd her, I'le warrant you,
'till she fucust her face, blanch'd her hands, put on a rich suit
of Night Linnen, and went to Bed; where she lay like a
Queen Apple upon a Tod of Wool, and the Patches look'd
for all the World like Birds pecks, which show the Fruit is   105
Rotten-ripe; and what do'e think? the Whore-Son snuffed
up his Nose, and cry'd he did not love brown crust in Milk;
a proud Jack. I'le make a Law that every man shall be hang'd
that refuseth a Woman; ay and 'tis high time, for we have
been even so kind to'm, that they use us as they do Rackets   110
at Tennis, when they have exercised their Bodies and
thump'd their Balls,—dress, and away; but my Lady

Redstreak, won't be serv'd so ifaith. —After Dinner the
Steward shall set things right with me in my Closet, and the
Gentleman of the Horse, or some spruce fellow shall Fiddle
me asleep. Oh *Redstreak,* didst thou ever think to come to
this? But if this should be a lye, now I'm bravely served.— 115

The wishing Chair is discover'd.

Oh there's the Chair, I cannot hold 'till the Gentleman
comes. —Oh a Queen, a Queen and 80 Husbands, and this
House full of Money, O lo, O lo, whither am I going? 120

The Chair sinks with her,—and Costard *enters
ridiculously Arm'd.*

Cost. Whaur, whaur, whaur? —Ha, gwon, shark'd away,
Oh mischief, Oh *Costard,* Oh Cuckold—budding, budding.
I feel 'em budding. —Oh Beast, I'le kill thee with my horns;
a Cuckold in my old days, I'le draw thy Colts Tooth with a
vengeance. 125

Exit Costard, *and Enter wishing Chair, and* Redstreak.

Red. A thousand thanks to your worship. I have not seen
so fine a Show this seven years.—
Wish. A tough carrion, she draws like a Whirl-pool, and
would kill a Man as easily as a Cat sucks the breath of a Child:
Go thy ways old Mumpsimus, the mark's in thy mouth still. 130

Enter Costard.

Cost. Now, Courage, for the Blood of the *Costards,* Ile
mow them off both in the middle, so swiftly that they shall
stand still, and never think th'are dead.
Wish. No, no more at this time, I thank your Queen-ship.
Cost. Ah umh! she clings like a rotten Egg to a Pillory; 135
yes pray do, and I'le watch the grins like the head of a
dead Horse. Scoundrel, snarle-chops, Beezom-Beard, come
out, come out, if thou darest. —O Laud!
Red. I'm undone, as a man would undo an Oyster, my
natural good man is here, and there's Murder in his looks. 140
Wish. What art thou? what dost stare at? wilt fight, ha?
Cost. 'Pranter, aye 'Pranter; no, my tongue's my own, and
God save the King's no Treason, my Blood's up, and I'le—

Wish. What wilt thou do? —who wouldst fight with?
Cost. Zate there cham as cunning's the Devil, and won't tell.   145
Wish. Dam ye for a beetle-headed Dog.

Costard *runs out.*

Cost. Oh Sir! Sir! Sir!
Red. Oh good Sir! *Wishing-Chair* sit down, for I know
he'l come again, and if I don't put this out of his head, he
won't leave a whole bone in my skin.—   150

The Chair *claps down,* Redstreak *sits in it, and* Costard
returns.

Red. And I wish, and I wish, that my dear Husband *Costard.*
Cost. How! wishing in the *Chair* for me? odz pretious, if
this been't a good Woman, the Devil's a Hog.—
Red. I wish, that my good Husband *Costard* were married
to King *Andrews* eldest Daughter, though I were dead and   155
rotten, I should rejoyce for't a thousand year hence, if I
could remember't.
Cost. Poor *Redstreak,* my own true Spouse, —'twere
better I were hang'd, then thee wert dead: what a villanous
Beast was I to think ill of her? no, thee art my Princess, and   160
I had rather lose the best Horse in my Team, then lose my Wife.—
Red. Ay, that thou hadst all, I dare swear.
Cost. No, zately, these two of them cost me zeaven and
twenty Shillings a piece, but prythee *Redstreak* let me wish
for thee now, and requite thee in thy own Coyn. —a woundy   165
fine *Chair.* —a *Wishing-Chair* do'e call it, Laud to see the
Art of man, by your leave—Odzvish, and eeles, what

[*When he tryes to sit, the Chair moves, and he falls down.*]

has it no Bottom? —yes it has, why what a muxon did I
vall through the *Chair,* or the *Chair* through me? let me zee;
zoo cham in now, and I wish, and I wish,   170

[*The Chair strikes him a blow on the ear.*]

What's that vor, *Redstreak?* ha is't no more then a word and a
blow, —what a Vengeance!
Red. Laud Husband I didn't touch you.—
Cost. Wilta lye to come o' this side,—so now I wish, and
I wish.—   175

[*The Chair strikes him on tother side.*]

What a pox ayles the Woman-bones? O' me, wouldst be leather'd,
ha?

    Red. Truly Husband I never touch'd you.

    Cost. Never touch'd me? why thou Whore-Son Scab, come
and stand before, and look me in the face. —So now   180
I wish, and I wish.

[*The Chair picks his Pocket.*]

Bones O me, Wife! there's a live thing in my Pocket,—why,
Woman, all my money's vanished.

    Red. That can't be, man, vor there's no kirsen Soul here but
thee and I; —but if it be gwon, sit thee down, and wish for   185
me.

    Cost. Stand thee behind the Chair then, and zee that nothing
molest me. —And I wish, and I wish,—Oh lo, and I wish
that—Oh! I will have my wish in spight of the Devil, and
I wish—Oh Bones! O me! Oh gogs nouns thou drab! she has   190
run a rifle into my Posterity, but chill pay thee vor't with
a witness.

    *She pushes him into the Chair, who holds him fast, while both
beat him.*

    Red. Out thou Carl, thou Beast to use a Woman so, the
Wrong-way, Dunder-nose, Dog-bolt, Limber-twist, I'le
teach thee to spoile a Woman.   195

    Cost. Oh Murther! Fellony, Salt and Batter, the Devil
and the Witch will murther me.

    Enter Princes Nicklas *and* Phillip.

    Phil. Now *Nick* for the honour of Knight-hood let's stand to
our Pan-puddings, here's the white Bear, and the Wishing-Chair:
have at 'em by guess.   200

    Nick. Oh *Nonsy,* Lady mine! inspire my Arm with Knightly
prowess to fight this dreadful Battel. This trenchant Blade
I draw, and now have at all.

    Red. O mercy! mercy! passion o' me, their naked Tucks
upon a Woman.   205

    The Chair *and* Costard *sink, the Princes cut off* Redstreaks
head, clap it on a Sword, and go off singing.

Good Christians Rejoyce,
With glad heart, and with Voice:
The white Bear is dead,
And here is his head.

The End of the Third Act.

ACT IV, scene i.

Enter two men—Neighbours.

1. *Neighbour.* Don't you see a great noise somewhere?
just like an Eccho coming from a Playn, where are no Woods,
Hills, or Valleys to make it.
    2. Ay, ay, 'tis because the Princes have kill'd the Bear,
and every mothers Child is gone out to meet them.   5
    1. The Princes are fine Blades, ifaith 'specially Prince
Phillip for Quoyts, or Cudgels, turn him loose. —Well now,
Maids may live and marry, when they can get Husbands.
    2. Ay, and we may hope to hear of a Maid in the ten's
again, before they were affraid of being given to the Bear,   10
that Maiden-heads were as cheap as stinking Fish.
    1. I have heard much of these Maiden-heads, prythee
what are they like?
    2. Like? —why they are so like nothing, that there is
nothing like them.—   15
    1. If the Bear was kill'd but half an hour ago, as it seems
by the story, how could the triumphal Arch be built, and
all this Pomp and Luxury be prepared to entertain the
Prince?—
    2. The way was chalk'd out by some Poet; or perhaps it   20
was done by Nature, and the Gods.
    1. Nature and the Gods, they had other Fish to fry, they
have been together by the ears all this day about Princess
None-so-fair; But heark, the Eccho draws near from the
Playn: Let's take our places, least we lose the Show.   25
                                      Exeunt.

    Enter the Princes Riding in Triumph on Hobby-horses,
the Womans-head carried on a Spear, attended with many on
Horse-back; and a Foot with Banners, and Trails, Drums,
and Trumpets, &c.—After they have passed round the
Stage, and taken their places; One sings a Ballad, and all
throng about him.

Song.

Prick up your ears, for, and that you may hear,
A Battel so dreadful, 'tween Princes and Bear,
                    Oh Christian Pee-pel!
This Beast was so hungry, and also right fell,
                    he eat youth, and baggage,   30
                    like Salt, Beef, and Cabbage,
'twas dolefull to look on, and ruefull to tell.

Chorus.

                    But now the Bear's dead,
                    And here is his head,
By which you may see, all is sooth that I said,   35
Therefore rejoyce, sing, and dance all, and some
With a lum, trum, tum, trum, tum, &c.

Dark was the Air, as if Welkin *were sick,*
When bloody minded rose Phillip, *and* Nick,
                    Quoth Nicolas, *I think,*   40
The Fight will be doubtful, then first let us drink.
                    Prince Phillip *by and by,*
                    Did fill out the Brandy.
And Courage did swell up, as Bottle did shrink.

Chorus.

                    But now the Bear's dead, &c.   45

Brandishing Blades with Bottle and Bag,
These Princes went boldly to find out the Drag-
                    gon-Bear I do mean.
And catch'd him devouring of two pretty men,
                    They stole both behind him,   50
                    And e'r he could mind them,
They cut him, and slash'd him agen and agen.

A Dance performed by two men and a Bear, showing
the manner of the Princes killing the Bear.

Song.

You Champions great, that kill'd the Beast,
Shall drink, and eat still of the best,

For him you slew with Swords sharp dint,   55
Car'd not one Fig for Jack o'lent.
But star'd, as if he would cry forth,
When Boy with Clapper cry'd shooh shoh.

Chorus.

Among Knights errant, you shall not
Give place to any, but Quixot.   60

1. While we their Praises are hum drumming,
See where Mother *Wossat*'s coming.

Mother Woossat *flies over the Stage, and calls Justice* Crab,
who comes out in his Charriot.

Woss. [*knocks.*] Is Justice *Crab* within?
Crab. What wouldst thou, mortal?

Song.

Woss. Justice! Oh gentle Justice Crab!   65
Crab. Why makes my Croan this doleful moan?
Who dares affront my beauteous drab?
Woss. My sister Redstreaks *dead,*
Crab. Is sister Redstreak *dead?*
Woss. —Ay! ay!   70
Crab. What mortal did the direful deed!
Woss. Proud Springal Princes made her bleed,
                    And said
          They cut off Bruines *head,*
   Oh! If thou yet canst prise   75
   The Amber *dropping from my eyes;*
   If all the Pensions I have paid,
   And jobs that thou hast Gratis had,
   Have any dent in Noddle made:
   Let None-so-fair *thy Fingers feel,*   80
   And all that did my Redstreak *kill.*

Crab. —From thy dear Chops,
          Such Kindness drops.
Still so much influence from thee rains,
Thou shalt command my heart and brains,   85
I'le pay those saucy Princes for their pains,

I'le give them a Posset,
Dare make their tricks thus at,
My poor Mother *Woossat.*
                Little Constable,   90
                Come with Painted bauble,
                And send off the Rabble.
Sumptuous their Throne is, but I'le make a Carr on't,
Crabs word alone is more powerful then Warrant.

                    Chorus.

        Let the stripplings and lasses be lustily curried,   95
                Ay, and let their good Graces,
            To limbo, to limbo, to limbo, be hurri'd.
        Woossat *and* Crab *fly out, a little Spirit rises, and beats*
off the Princes and Attendants.   *Exeunt all.*

        ACT IV, scene ii.   *Enter* Nicklas *and* Phillip.

Nick. What bloody Rogues were these?
                And we not run each Mothers Son
                Had gone to Little ease.
    Phil. A curse on thick Whoreson with the Painted Rod,
Sure 'twas some Divel, or some God.   5
    Nick. Prince *Phillip,* there was never Knight errant famous
without being enchanted; nor Opera notorious without Gods,
and Divels: hast thou observ'd the numerous Caves and Walks,
in your dry White Cheese?—
    Phil. Ay your tickle crack Cheese.   10
    Nick. In one of those Cheeses was a Knight of *Wales*
Enchanted Seven years; and through those dangerous wayes
he Travel'd, and destroy'd all the Heathen Knights, that like
little Vermine devour'd the fat of it.—
    Phil. Ah! mischief on the Heathen Knights, and the   15
Welch Knight too, they tickled the Cheese so between e'm,
that no goodness has been in't ever since.—
Yet 'spight of Hell wee'l search from Ventures,
Till Nymph distressed, is freed from Tenters.

        Enter Woudhamore *and* Sweetlips.

    Woud. Now luck! Husbands, or something to eat, we beseech   20
thee.
    Sweet. If they won't have us, let's ravish them. —Save

your Princes, still whining after your Pin-box, are there no
more Maids but *Maukin?*
We might e'r this have got fire out of flints,   25
Some brinded Wolf, *Phils* Father was, I wot,
On some she Rock, relentless thee he got.
    Woud. My *Nickies* dam was some rough Bear,
And Tigre fierce was sure his sire;
Oh pity thy despairing Trull.   30
    Sweet. O let me buss my *Phils* fair Gull.
    Woud. Cloud not those Lanthorns clipped eyes,
If *Nickie* frowns poor *Woudha.* dyes;
Pity my heart in loves fire roasting;
Such pretty Bees sure should have no sting.   35
    Sweet. Thou little Princox be more mild,
Oh how it joyed me when it smil'd.
    Nick. Indeed sweet Ladies, you but loose your labour.
    Phil. You may as soon catch a Hare with a Tabar.
    Woud. Is it so? Lippy we are out. —Gad, we must be   40
more brisk; these Fellows are for the down-right way.—
    Sweet. Courage then, la, la, la, come thou little pouting
Villain, I will order thee for thy dissembl'd cruelty.—
    Phil. Bless us, what's the matter with the Woman? let me
alone.   45
    Sweet. Dam your pettish frowns. come, here's a Guinny.—
    Woud. Since *Nonsies* devour'd by the Bear, 'tis no
inconstancy to chuse again.—
    Nick. That whim won't pass Madam! we search'd every
cranny of the Beast, and found no sign of her.   50
    Sweet. If she lives, you have been constant to her too long,
for by the new modish Articles of faithful Love, 'tis no sin,
nor inconstancy, to quit one Mrs. or Gallant, for another, as
often as you will, so you have but one at once. Come, come,
a George will gain the Lad, as well as the Lady—here take   55
Money.
    Nick. Y'are an insolent audacious hectoring Pugg, and
I'le have you kick'd if you do not leave us presently.—
    Sweet. Come poor Green-sickness Rascals, they do not
know what's good for themselves, let's away with them.   60
    Phil. Help, help, a Ravishment. —Y'are a brace of
saucy foul Mouth'd, Rampant, *Tatterdemalion* Princesses,
and—
    Nick. And so we take our leave,
    Phil. Ay, and so we take our leave.   65
                          Exeunt Princes.

Woud. Never were Poor Princesses so distressed for Husbands.

Sweet. Princes! No, there's no Princely Virtue in their
Blood.

Woud. Dam 'em, a Prince would no more refuse a handsom
Woman, than a Lyon would hurt a Prince.   70

Sweet. Frozen Joy, Slaves let them be hang'd.

Woud. Hang'd 'gad; and so they shall for killing mother
Redstreak, for all they made the silly People believe 'twas
the Bear.

Sweet. Let's give notice to the Officers, and have them   75
seiz'd; when they are in durance, their tough stomacks will
soon melt.

Enter Jeffery.

Woud. We'l do't,—but stay, here's fresh game, he's right
I'le warrant, I know by his leering eye.—

Sweet. Then he's mine, for I saw him first.   80

Woud. Another word like that condemns thee.

Sweet. If y'are so Tyrannical, I'le stroll alone.

Woud. Stay, the stripling has something to deliver.

Jeffry. Queen *None-so-fair,* (Ladies most splendiferous)
Intreats you both would come, and dine at her house.   85
And after that, great hearts to solace,
She'l show you ev'ry Nook o' th' Pallace.
My Master loveth her most fervent,
I'm *Jeffry* his man, and your Servant.

Woud. Oh Fortune! luck! our hopes are melted,   90

Sweet. Were ever Princesses so jilted:
None-so-fair, a Queen.—

Woud. Let's send to Jaylor, er' bad news spread further,
That surly Princes may be seiz'd for murther.
None-so-fair a Queen.—   95

Jeffry. —True I'le assure ye.

Woud. Come, Let's behold her Pomp, and eke Luxury,
And let Heroick love be turn'd to Fury.
To Jaylor we'l send Porter as we go by,
A Queen! i'faith we'l tickle her Toby.   100

                                                    Exeunt.

[Act IV, scene iii.]

The Scene chang'd to None-so-fair's *house.*

Enter None-so-fair, Sweetlips, *and* Woudhamore.

Woud. Say no more, the Treat was splendid.
    Sweet. But where's your kind good man I wonder?
Of all your Pomp let's see the Founder.
    Non. Stay you here a little tinie,
And I'le go call my loving Ninny: 5
Love, Honey, Chuck, Duch, so hoe, il o ho, ho, ho.
    Woud. Our Sister Queen has an excellent voice to call
Harvest-men to Dinner.—
Oh Cross, untoward Fate! Ay that thou art!
Must she all pleasure have, and we all smart?   10
    Sweet. Like Image on house-top th'hast put her,
And we must crawl like Ducks in gutter.
    Woud. And see her Finery, Oh Rot her!
Such earthen Dishes, such scull Bason,
Table so scrubb'd, you may see face on,   15
Such shining Platters, Shelves with lace on.
Such Pots so scour'd with Sand and Whiting,
Monarch had n'r such Kitchin to delight in.
    Sweet. Her Man, her Maid, her Dog, her Cat too,
At Dinner dresser thump'd like Tattoo: 20
Strong-bub in Closet, and all that too.
    Woud. We thought she'ad given Crow a pudding,
And Luxury is just a budding;
And we to see't must come a gooding.
    Sweet. I cannot live to see this thing long,   25
A Curse on Mother *Woossat*'s flim flam,
Are these the Fruits of flattering sing song?
    Woud. Well, luck may turn, what's more ficle then chance?
Come let's Club our Sculs, and plot Vengeance,
Her strolling jilting tricks, we'ltell'o   30
And make her trusty *Roger* yellow.

Enter Bruin *and* None-so-fair.

He comes, i'faith a witty fellow.
    Sweet. Oh happy Mauks! if I could reach the rope of her
heart, I would strangle her with't.
    Woud. A brave fellow! he stands like a Tree, and his legs   35
look like *Hercules*'s Pillars.—
    I'le sell my Cloaths from my back,
    To buy love-Pouder for his sake.
    Sweet. I'le poyson my dear Sister Crack,
E'r I this Gallant thing will lack,   40
I must speak to him Servant Jack.

Woud. Hold, when I have supp'd with *Margret Trantum,*
With goodly thing you may play Rantum;
Till then ifacks y'are like to wantum.

Bru. Ladies, first, y'are very wellcom; and secondly, I hope   45
to give you all content.—
For Sisters sake my beautious Gipsie,
On whom Prince *Bruin* casteth Sheeps eye,
You shall bouze gratis till y'are tipsie;
On stately shank rest tyr'd ham trulls,   50
And you shall see my tricks and gambols.
Hisco flisco whisco fibribisco fosco posco, sebosco larasco
velasco, trumdle fundle, bundle hundle, tantarra dundle—
surgito surgitote.—

The Scene drawn, and many Statues discover'd in several
postures.

Woud. O *Lippy,* what stone works here?   55
Bru. He that looks so like a despairing lover, is *Peter*
Whiffle, eldest Son of the Countess of *Puddle dock,* he
espoused the Puissant *Landabridas* Queen of Sluts, and
hang'd himself because she would not wear fine cloaths, and
have a Gallant.   60
Woud. Alas poor *Peter,* I would not have been so unkind
as Queen *Lamberdas.*
Bru. Those two are Polynicky, Nicampoops, two valorous
Princes of Fairy-land; they div'd through Apivel to Hell,
for the love of Piss-kitchin Daughter of King *Easie-pate,*   65
passed through Fire and Water, without spoiling their
Cloaths or Perriwiggs; and are now good sufficient House-
keepers in *Elizium.*—
That's *Rablays,* the grave French Philosopher, that grew
mad with Writing the Second part *Tom Thum* in Heroick   70
meetre.
Woud. Well, he did his indeavour, though he missed his
Province.
Sweet. Oh *Woudha. Woudha.* if this Image were in a warm
Bed, I'e be hang'd if I did not fetch life in him, and make   75
him wagg.
Bru. When a house is on fire, the Lame, Sickly, and Lazy,
frisk as if they had a swarm of Hornets about them.—
  Green Sickness Girle can lift huge trunck,
  But Blade with Loves flame scorch'd and shrunk,   80
  Will do much more for charming Punk.

These stones compell'd by Amorous *Bruin,*
Shall Sing and Caper to some *Tuin.*
Mark how dull Statue kicks and Winces.
And all for love of *Nonesy* Princess.   85

Bruin *Sings like a* Walloon, *and Playes on a* Cimball *and
all the Images move.—*

Bru. Now you shall hear the Images sing in praise of the
most Heroick and Magnificent Sciences of Wenching, and
Drinking. —A Ditty fit for Sphears, and Quires of Cupid,
          when Gods are deaf, and Princes grow stupid.
My dear *Nonesy* set them in the way.—   90

SONG.

Let Taffy *go seek for his bliss in a Leek,
And* Teag *in hot Isquebagh slobber.*
Jocky *be doing with Oatcakes and Sowing,
And sup up their brave Bonny clabber.*

Chorus.

But let Misses and Gallants, make use of their Talents,   95
  To be Wise, is to love and be drunk;
For drink, and that same will get you a name,
  When your healths and Estates are all sunck.

Let sullen old Men keep their beesom Beards clean,
  Let Slaves strive for Honour and Riches,   100
Let Widgeons *debate our Religion and State,*
  And Matrons be sober as Witches.

Cho. *But let Misses,* &c.

Let's drink and be clapp'd till our Shin-bone fore scrap'd,
  And gems deck our faces all over,   105
Till Palsies and Cramps, make our eyes shine like Lamps,
  For such is the true drunken lover.

Cho. *But let Misses,* &c.

A Warlike Dance, and then Exeunt all but None-so-fair,
  Sweetlips *and* Woudhamore.

Non. Now Sisters did not I rise with my back upwards
met this what do'e call him?—   110
    Woud. Ay! what do'e call him indeed? I'le be hang'd if he
does not deal with the Divel—Second me *Lippy.*—
    Sweet. No, no, the Divel he isn't so good a Scholar, 'Tis
some pitiful juggling Jack-pudding, some strolling Tumbler.
    Woud. When he grows a little weary of you, he'l strip you,   115
and leave you; nay, say y'are oblig'd to him, for teaching
you a modish Trade, by which you may come to keep your
Coach, if you have any Fortune.—
    Non. I won't despair, since the Proverb's on my side,
Fools have Fortune, and Cracks have luck,—I can pretend   120
to both by vertue of my Education.—
    Woud. If his Highness were true and trusty, why should he
hide his Title?
    Non. Oh say no more, I tremble all over!

Enter Jeffry.

    Jeffry. Madam great Sisters must be packing,   125
My Master finds some Trenchers lacking.
    Non. How, Royal Sisters grown light finger'd?
Of Princesses was e'r so foul a thing heard;
Richer Goods in house could not be chosen,
Odznigs they cost two groats a dozen.   130
    Woud. How steal your Trenchers? Traps, marry come up here,
I find we should pay sauce, if we should sup here.
    Sweet. 'Tis not gentilely done, Faith, Sister *Nonsy.*
    Woud. And if we had you out, i'gad we'd trounce ye.
    Non. Minxes cease your idle prittle prattle,   135
And render back my Goods, and Chattle.
    Woud. Minxes—a ha—let's give her battle.
    Sweet. We'l thump bewitching eyes black and blue,
Put tricks on Daughters of King *Andrew.*

They fight. Enter Bruin.

    Jeffry. Great Master comes with arms a kimboe,   140
    Bru. Take filching Madams hence to Limbo
Hence, or thy self shalt strait for them go.
    Woud. Must we that have sent Princes thither, go our selves?
    Hear me Justice, if there's any;
    Let's not be long without company.   145
    Bru. Away with them.

Sweet. As by's own Bull was kill'd *Phalaris*,
W'are sent to Prison by *Will. Harris.*
                    Exeunt Jeffry, Sweetlips, and Woudhamore.

Bru. This was an an Intrigue of love and state; poor Ladies,
they stole no Trenchers, but I heard Baggages contrive.—   150
                    To undermine Prerogative,
                    And to seduce if they were able,
                    My Importance comfortable,
                    Before I'm weary of Bauble.
Non. To Prison sent for filching Trencher-Plate,   155
When we had none in house,
        Oh too too late;
        I do begin to smell a Rat.
Ah wo is me! poor little mouse.
Bru. Why frowns? my beautious dear,   160
Thy Forheads muffl'd in black pouts,
Like warlike Steed in Fun'ral clouts,
That did eftsoons both prance and neigh,
And briskly fell to Oats and hay,
As if he promised a fair day.   165
But strait in black dog'd masters Course,
My dear looks sad as morning Horse.
Non. Poh! you prate, and prate, but you don't love me.
Bru. Love thee, ungrateful Imp! Ah curse on thy jealous
Noddle, another word I'le squeeze thee like a Custard,   170
                    Devour thee without Salt or Mustard.
    Ha, my Princess sniv'ling, who has disbused thee, Pydy
tell me, if I have ought can give thee ease; I swear, 'tis thine
now by this Cheese, the Oath of Gods.
Non. Enough, and if 'tis Truth, tell me thy name, Oh   175
charming youth!
Bru. Heavens! Powers! Oh hold!
Non. Nay, nay, you have sworn.
I must have all the Secrets that are thine.
Bru. Must I my Secretest Secret then resign?   180
Non. Why should you keep your Secret? and yet take mine?
Bru. Prythee *Nonsy* ask any thing else?
Non. No, nothing.
Bru. The Devil take me if—
Non. Is this your love? miserable unhappy Princess, perjur'd   185
dissembling men! before you had me, you swore any thing.—
You use poor Women, as Children do Bubbles; you spare for
no water of Sighs, nor black Soap of Oaths, till you have

blown us up with the Reed of your love, and then you cast
us off to break in the wide World. —Ah! that ever   190
I poor vertuous Lady should live to see this day! Oh! ho,
ho.

    Bru. Well if like a wall-ey'd Hare, you won't see right
before you, but run into the noose, take your ill fortune.—
    Non. Ay let me have it.   195
    Bru. Shall I speak?
    Non. Ay, ay, I say.
    Bru. Then I shall you say?
    Non. Odslifelykins, ay I say.
    Bru. Consider.—   200
    Non. I'le be hang'd first, when did a longing Woman
consider? What, what? Oh quickly.
    Bru. I am.
    Non. Heart, blood and bones, what are you?
    Bru. Yet be wise,   205
    Non. I will not be wise, nor hear, nor see, nor speak till
I know.
    Bru. I am *Deval.*
    Non. Bless us all—
    Bru. That French Prince of the Padders, that was thought   210
to be hang'd, I have liv'd ever since in this disguise, because
I would not quite break the kind Ladies hearts, to see me
hang'd twice.
        But now must fly for thy folly least I am caught,
        And pawn my pretty *Nonesy* for the shot.   215

    Exit Bruin, *claps on the Bears skin, and flies over the Stage—*

    The Scene chang'd to a Tavern.—

        Enter two Drawers.

    1. I come, I come, did you call Sir? ha where's the Gentle-
man that pays the reckning? look to the door *Harry.*
    2. What's the matter?—
    1. A Crack, a Crack; to pay here in the Flower Pot?
    2. Eleven and three pence; a Pox, I know her, she plies at   220
the *Pagean.*
    Non. O gen'rous Youth speak not untruth,
I am a Princess of King *Andrews* stock in sooth.—
    Right Valiant Knights spare my Honour, and do what

you please, but use your Victory with discretion, for Fortunes   225
Wheel is still turning.—

    1. Knights Honour and Fortune, 'gad she's mad.

    2. Didst find any Honour about her?

    1. No, no Honour. —If women have any such thing, they
hide it so cunningly that none can find it. —*Harry,* thou   230
knowest we melted down a Silver Tankard to sodder up
Cisses crack'd Honour; let's swear she stoll it, and clap a
strong House upon her back to keep her warm.

    2. But first, let's strip her; come strip, strip.—

    1. Ay, ay, this is she stoll our Silver Tankard; come strip.   235

Non. Oh the lovely Prince?

    1. How, the Prince? 'gad she speaks Treason, lock her up
and call the Constable—away.—

Exeunt Drawers.

Non. Oh my dear Prince, why wouldst thou fly hence, and
let thy loving Romp be stripp'd from all her Pomp.   240

        Sure in my mind 'twas much unkind,

        To shark away and leave your love behind:

        What ever now is thy design,

        I'm sure when *Nonsie*'s dead, he'l whine,

        Crost love and grief to make an end 'o,   245

        I'le break my neck out at a Window.

    King Andrews *Ghost rises Crown'd, and* Redstreak *with
her head in her hand—attended with two Spirits.*

Song.

        Oh stay thy foul and bad intent,

          Dame chance doth smile and frown,

        When heels more high then head are sent,

          That's upward that was down,   250

        And None-so-fair *shall have her Bear,*

K. And. —*Shall have her Bear,*

Redstr. —*Shall have her Bear.*

Chorus.

        And None-so-fair *shall have her Bear,*

        And none shall have the sweet Beast but her.   255

        Woossat will come for, and to chide,

          From mischief fly a main,

>   *For all must obey that are ty'd,*
>   *Till they are freed again,*
> Cho. *And* None-so-fair, &c.   260

                    The Song ended, they Vanish.

Non. Why should I fly dear Dad, and eke
Ghost of *Redstreak?*
I've nothing stoll upon my Soul,
Else wou'd I n'r might speak.

                Woossat flies down in her Chariot.

Wooss. Dares *None-so-fair* with eyes of Cat,   265
Look on Queen hag the dread *Woossat?*
So Impudent not make a Cursy,
Bend stubborn hams, or 'gad I'le force ye.
    Non. What have I done? dread Witch should seeking Ruin.
    Wooss. Debauch'd my Son, my first begotten *Bruin,*   270
Taught envious men to burn my Thatch,
    Nail Horse-shoe under hatch.
    Nay strove by your enchanting eye,
    To be a greater Witch then I.
    Non. If Beauty be fault in me, 'tis Heavn's decree,   275
I do not paint truly, as you may see;
He took my pretty thing for his Rantidla,
I did not ask him first indeed la.
    Wooss. Dare's Minx to prate to me so proudly?
Thinking to choak my hate with loudy: 280
No, thou shalt never get whole hence,
But to Prison; *Volens, Nolens,*
To dye for Treason and Insolence.
                                    Woossat flies away.

        Enter Drawers, and Whistles.

    1. *Draw.* Princess, so hoe Princess!
If you have ought to say dear Crack, be short,   285
    Black Guard won't stay.
    Non. Oh well a day! I must away to Pluto's Court,
    Oh State of Greatness variable!
    Oh luck of Princess miserable!

        The End of the Fourth Act.

ACT V.

A common Prison confused.

A great noise heard—Singing, Shreeking, Groaning,
Roaring, and Ratling of Chains.

Enter many common Prisoners, among which, Tagrag, Brazen-
nose, Tatter'd-hoe, Shrubs-hall, Bull-barrow, *bringing in the*
Princes and Princesses.—

All cry out. —Garnish, garnish, garnish,
   Tag. Come, disburse, disburse.
   Nick. As I'm a true Prince, our Exchecquers were rob'd by
these miscreant Knights, that brought us to this Fortress.
   Tag. Strip, strip then, and go like an Eastern Monarch   5
half naked.—
   Braz. Ay, ay, cast off superfluous Trappings, they'l
harbour vermine to destroy the Microcosm.
   Bull. Come my dainty Damzels, you must pay for Entrance
too into our thrice nasty, and right dread Society.   10
   Tag. Skink away, sheer, drink, do'e hear not a rag of
Provaunt, and then we'l have a Song; and after that, erect
our mock-Court of Justice, and cast your Destinies: Cheer
up, if you dye like Birds on Trees, you shall be cut down
like Flowers, and your Funerals shan't cost you 2 *d.* you shall   15
be intom'd in a Ditch on the publick charge.
   Come, a Song, a Song. —Princess *Nonsy,* put in your
Treble at *Rome;* be a *Roman.*—

Song.

Be jovial, be jovial, each Lad,
Great Dukes of the Dungeon, and Knights of the Pad;   20
    Now the Jaylor from hence is,
    We are all great Princes.
Let's sing, let's laugh, let's drink, and be mad.

Chorus.

Along, and along, mirth have its swing,
   For older or younger, there's none can live longer   25
   Then Fortune is pleased, and the King;
Then let's merrily sing, and dance in a string,
Then let's merrily sing, and dance in a string.

This Pallace, and all is our own,
Our lodging's provided, the Rent is paid down.   30
    Every Shop's our Exchecquer,
    Each purse is our debtor,
We alwayes gain who ever's undone.
Cho. *Along, &c.*

The Treasures the Husband does lend,   35
Treats on his doxy, we briskly do spend.
    Ay, and when we are chain'd here,
    She steals the remainder.
And kindly comes to visit her Friend.
Cho. *Along, &c.*   40

   A Dance perform'd by Prisoners under Gallos's.

   Tag. Now let's Adjourn to our Sessions house, and bring
our new Prisoners to Trial.

          Exeunt all but Princes and Princesses.

   Phil. A pox o' your zeeking Ventures, cham as dumpish as
a new shrouded Tree. —What course must we take now?
   Nick. Course? why I think 'tis better to be freed, and   45
Marry the Princesses, then be hang'd.—
   Phil. Why, I think zoo too, but then who must be hang'd
for killing Mother *Redstreak?* —Justice must be satisfi'd.
   Nick. Justice may be better satisfied with Marriage then
hanging—for 'tis now the greater punishment.   50
   Phil. Have you any 'Tority vor what you zay?
   Nick. 'Tority, no, but I have reason—is not it better
to go to Heaven in a string, then be a Gally Slave, and be
chain'd to one seat all ones life?—
   Phil. Then do thee go to Heaven in a string, and let me   55
be Marri'd.
   Nick. Thank you for that, 'faith what a well meaning
Fool is this? —I tell thee 'twas not *Redstreak,* but the Bear
we kill'd.
   Phil. The Bear—Odzboars 'twas as errant a Woman as   60
my mother, and all the neighbours know she was right.—
   Nick. Then she was Enchanted?
   Phil. Enchanted! Ah, if this should be a lye, we are
bravely serv'd.--
   Nick. Why may not a beast be turn'd to a Woman? we   65
see Women every day turn'd to Beasts.

Woud. Y'are rightly serv'd, for a couple of Dander Nos'd
Princes as you are; if y'had Marri'd us, you might both have
been King *Andrews* by this time.—

Non. Why, has our poor sneaking Daddy kick'd up his   70
heels? Ah dismall merry Tragedy, I thought somthing would
follow when I saw his Ghost, and heard the Crickets sing so
dolefully.

Woud. Your tricks broak his heart, for when he heard we
were sent to Prison for stealing Trenchers, he sigh'd, eat   75
a great piece of Bread and Butter; and departed as quietly
as any sucking Pig.

> *The Scene drawn, discovers the Court of Rogues with*
>   *attendants.*

Phil. Stint, stint, the Cwourtz zet, what must I zay, Prince
Nick?

Nick. Why say she kill'd her self *volens nolens,* in her   80
own defence.

Phil. Bolens nolens,—a pox on your *bolens nolens.*—

Tag. Bulbarrow, set the Prisoners to the Bar. —Read
their Indictment.

Braz. No, no, let's over-rule that formality, and proceed   85
to Sentence.

Tag. First, for fashions sake, though we have most prudently
determin'd to hang them, whatever they can say—ask them
the usual question.—

Shrub. —Guilty or not guilty? why don't you answer?   90

Tag. Give 'em time, I know my face is terrible; for a Judges
leering smile is as certain a sign of death, as walking in
Sir *John Broads* Exchange all Dinner time, is a sign of an
empty pocket; Come Gentlemen Rogues, you that look as sour as
small Beer after Thunder; You with the Ember face.   95

Braz. You stand as if you were doing pennance for stealing
a Pudding out of your neighbours Wives-Kettle.

Tag. Or making Composition for killing your Father, or
eating Eggs on a Fasting day, which are equal Crimes
among the Learned,—answer, in what shape did thy Friend   100
the Devil appear, when he advis'd thee to act this horrid
bloody inhumanity?

Braz. Inhumane, untoward, unhandsom; Brother, inforce
the charge, *Tatter'd-ho:* unhandsome, unwholesome.—
I say unwholesom, for I have believ'd 'twill cost thee   105
thy life; Villanous, unlucky—*Tagrag?*

Tag. Unlucky, pitiful, most pitiful crime of—of What's
the Crime Brothers?—

Braz. By my Commission I know not, but that's all one,
our business is to Judge, and hang the offenders; let the   110
Crimes alone, if we destroy them, our Trade will be at
an end.—

Tag. Come, confess, confess your Crime, and you shall
have the favour to ride to the Gallows in a Coach.

Nick. —Sir.—   115

Bull. —Sir! You must say my Lord.

Tag. Ha, who's that whisp'ring? —*Bullbarrow*—Sirrah!
how darst thou be of Counsel against the King? thou bloated
Jewish villain, that dost lye and batten in the Blood of poor
Prisoners, like a Hog in his own mire? —Dar'st thou be of   120
Counsel against the King?

Braz. Against the King a Jaylor would betray the Gods,
if Prisoners had Money to bribe him to't; tye him up.—

Bull. Ah! I beseech your good Lordships, I only Instructed
him to give you your just Titles, because I know several   125
have been hang'd for omitting them. —Pray your
Honours.

Tag. Sirrah, no more of this,—Hatchet-face, speak you;
guilty, or not guilty?—

Phil. She kill'd her self, *volens nolens* in her own defence,   130
ask Prince *Nick* else?—

Tag. Ask Prince *Nick.*—

Phil. —Ay—All King *Andrew*'s Household can bear me
Concord, I was bred up in the Vear of my vather and mother.

Shrub. Guilty or not guilty?—   135

Phil. I zay cham not guilty, Prince *Nick* draw'd me in
like a young Wench to a Nunnery. —*Volens, Nolens.*

Tag. So, so, Prince *Nick* draw'd thee in, and Squire Catch
shall draw thee out: Come Prince *Nick,* what say you
Prince *Nick?* speak out Prince *Nick;* quickly Prince *Nick,*   140
you'r in a fine pickle Prince *Nick.*

Nick. I say I am the the man that kill'd the Bear, that stole
the Princess; that broke the heart of King *Andrew.*

Tag. Brave! this is the Horse that come of the Mare, that
eat the Oats that grew in the Field, that was bought with   145
the Money that *Jack* stole. —Well Prince *Nick.* —Bring in
the Bears-head there.

The Womans head set on the Table.

Nick. Now let my malicious adversaries hang their ears,
and eat one another as hungry Dogs devour dirty Puddings.
Behold my Lords; if this be not the Bear's head, I'm the   150
Sophy of *Persia.*

Tag. I never met a more Intricate business, if any here
was acquainted with our defunct Sister, whether Bear or
Woman, let them discourse the head.—

Woud. I and my Sister *Lippy* know, this is the head of honest   155
Gammar *Redstreak,* and this we will swear; because those unworthy
Princes refused to marry us.

Tag. Gentlemen, your Opinions; is it the Bear's, or the
Woman's head?

All. The Womans, the Womans.   160

Tag. Prince *Nick!* you hear the Sentence of the Court
Prince *Nick!*

Nick. The Court's bewitch'd, and the head's enchanted.

Tag. Sirrah! you grow saucy, tye up Prince *Nick.*

Nick. Why may not the Bears-head be chang'd to a   165
Womans, as well as Mambrino's Helmet to a Barber's bason,
or a notorious Fellon to your Lordships? let the head deny it
if it dares.

*The hands lift up the head, and it speakes, and then flies
up in the Air.*

> Lament and be sad,
> *Redstreak* is dead;   170
> And here is her head.
> Prince *Nick,* and *Phil,*
> Did me kill.

Nick. Oh I confess! I confess! pray hang me quickly,
least the head should do me some mischeif.   175

Tag. Take 'em away, I knew this would do, 'tis not the
first time Ghosts have appear'd to hang their Murtherers.

                                    Exeunt Princes Nick and Phil.
Set those she-Monsters to the Bar.

Tatterd. Brother, it grows late, and I have no sweet-meats
to nibble on, which I think as becoming the gravity of a   180
Judge, as a Tooth-pick the Solemn State of a Spanish Grandee.—
Pray let the Court over-rule all they can say, and proceed
to Sentence; for my stomack is maukish.

Tag. Be it so; I'le give directions to the Jury in a wise
speech according to Custom, and then we'l adjourn the Court.   185

Gentlemen of the Jury, it was an Ancient saying among

the noble *Romans,* and worthy of everlasting Fame; set
the Hares Head against the Goose-Jiblets, and 'tis a right
worthy custom among those modern *Heroes:* that Collar-Beef
to put a layer of fat, and a layer of lean, and what is   190
all this for, but to teach us to mix Mercy with Justice?—
We are here met together, and for what are we met together?
to lye (like *Diogenes* lazily) in a Tub, 'till the Sun cures
the disease of State? No, we must set our hand to the
Plough tail, let every one pluck a hair from the thick bushy   195
Beard of Malefactors, and the Chinn of mischief will soon
be bald; as *Poor Robbin* has it in his modern Philosophy:
We have discover'd a Wasps Nest of Hornets to you, 'tis
your part to set the Brimstone of Justice on fire, and
smother them with the smoak of Correction. —Two are found   200
Guilty, of stealing most Feloniously Gammer *Redstreaks* head
from her shoulders, so much to her Detriment, that she will
hardly ever be her own Woman again. —This appears as
clear to the eye of reason, as if it were written with the
Rain-bow on the South wind.   205
        The two eldest Daughters of King *Andrew,* of notorious
memory, are in for stealing Trenchers. —You must find them
Guilty, because We the mouth of the Law determine it; If
any grumblings of Conscience arise within you, the Court
over-rules them; *Psyche* the 2d. also Miss *Nonsy* shall be   210
freed, because her Predecessor *Psyche* the first was, though
both (for running from their Fathers; and practising publickly
what their Sisters did but wish well to) deserve more punishment then they. —Now dispatch! and as *Socrates* says—what
you do, do quickly—I read your Sentence in your looks;   215
The Princes have already suffer'd, and for your Ladies
errant, the Sentence of the Court is, that you never be
marri'd, but allow'd the Conversation of all men through
a Grate without touching any; to Lasses of your Complexion,
I think this is as bad as drawing Water in a Cieve, or being   220
hang'd in Chains alive; away with them.

        Exeunt all but None-so-fair. *The Scene changes.*

    Non. Must I for using what's my own,
            In Hellish hole be left alone;
            With pinches, and pricks of pin,
            Be rack'd all day, all night with din?   225
            With Hempen cord, have great Toe cramp'd,
            By Dog of *Newgate* thump'd and stamp'd;

By Rogues and Vermine kept from sleep,
While some do roar, and some do weep.
Oh *Woossat* harsh, Prince *Bruin* cruel,   230
To sneak away from precious Jewel:
Yet in these horrours I could sing,
Had I again my pretty thing.

Song.

Let Beauty triumph o're despair,
For none are cruel to the Fair;   235
The Crooked, the Old, and deformed shall be,
From cares and affronts never free;
But the Youthful, the pretty and kind,
In a Prison some pity will find,
For all are to Love, and to beauty inclin'd.   240

One gives her a Bottle of Brandy, and Sings—this.

Come hither, and take this Bottle of Nantz,
'Twill make mother Woossat *soon leave off her rants,*
For I know she is one of my Naunts.
          Though she's hot as a Codling,
          'Twill make her straight Maudlin.   245
She'l sip, she'l sigh, she'l swear, she'l sing, and she'l melt,
She'l kiss thee, and groan for the pains thou hast felt.

Chorus.

Alass my poor Nonsy *I grieve for thy smart,*
For though an old Woman be never so tart;
A dram of the Bottle will soften her heart.   250

Song.

Thy Sisters must howl, for the Trenchers they stole,
          And the Princes are in the Pit-hole.
                    There they shall stay,
                    For ever and a day.
          But Nonsey *shall straight go to play,*   255
1. —*Make hast poor* Nonsey,
2. —*Make hast poor* Nonsey,
Both. —*Make hast poor* Nonsey *to* Bruin,
1. —*For* Nonsey *shall injoy her pretty thing.*

2. —*For* Nonsey &c.—   260
Both. —*For* Nonsey &c.—
             Chorus of all. *make hast poor* Nonsey.
                        make &c.—
                        make—
                        For Nonsey.   265

Non. Now I am so glad and so sorry, I don't know which
Leg to set foremost. —My Sisters were two crabbed vixons to
me, yet their Sufferings put out the lighted Tinder of my
joy, but then the Steel of my love strikes new Fire into the
Tinder-box of my Inclination, and makes my natural affection   270
glow again; I shall injoy my Bear for ever. Oh happy
Nonsey! —yet this was a horrible merry Tragedy, O lo!
the Princes, *Nicklas* and *Phillip,* here again!—

             Enter Princes Phil. *and* Nick.

Nick. No, we are but their Ghosts.
Non. Their Ghosts, Oh! 'tis well you say so your selves,   275
for no-Body would believe it from any other,—what makes
you come to me?
Nick. We vow'd at our Death's to come, and tell you what
place we were at.
Non. Poor loving Ghosts, tell me quickly then?—   280
Nick. Immediately after we were dead, we found our
selves in a Bower; made all of Wishes pav'd with thoughts,
where at a Table of Heigh-hoes sat King *Andrew,* and Mother
Redstreak at Dinner; they had a *Phaenix* boil'd with a Dish
of love Raptures, and drank nothing but Spirit of Extasie,   285
we sat down with them, and Six Gods attended us: after
Dinner we slept upon a Couch of Virginity, imbroyder'd all
over with Kings smiles; then walking by a Fountain of
Fruition, who should we see but King *Andrew* and his Queen
at Hey-gammer-Cook in a Grotto of Innocence.   290
Non. Oh most ravishing delights! but why is *Phillip*'s
Ghost so mopish?
Nick. He would have been kind to Gammar *Redstreak,*
and she threw a Glass of extasie in his Chops. —One thing
dear Princess we must intreat of you, that you will sing that   295
Ingenious Song of the delights of the Bottle three and thirty
times, and make as many Cursy's to the West; for till that is
done, our Soul's won't be free of *Elyzium.*

Non. Upon my Honour, I'le do't, though I were to give
my self a thump in the back ev'ry time. —For example.   300

Song.

The delights of the Bottle, and the Charms of a drab,
When they pour out their pleasures will make a man mad.
All the night in deep Healths, and loud Curses is spent,
Which the dull silly Fop the next day does repent.
And Love's sweet debauch in a moment is gone,   305
But leaves a damn'd Pox to last all the life long.

Love and Wine rule the Swords that shed so much Blood.
All the World, but for them, would grow vertuous and good.
Were it not for the Witchcrafts of Wenching and Wine,
Madam—would be poor, and my Lord would be fine.   310
But she now keeps her Coach, and can live without thinking,
And damns her Debauch with his Wenching and Drinking.

Nick. Enough, enough, dear Princess; farewel, when
thus you do, Think of us two.
Phil. Dear Princess, Farewel. When thus you do, think of   315
us two, For I'm a Ghost, though I stood so like a Post.
Non. Farewel, two such loving Ghosts were never found
—On English Ground.

The delights of the Bottle &c. —Oh how I begin to be
weary! If this will make Mother *Woossat*'s heart chearful?   320
sure 'twill refresh me? —Princess thy good health, —*Nonsy*
I'le pledge thee six go-downs, —humming stuff upon my
honour. Princess, where is this sold Princess? Asking questions
Nonsy! —Time's precious: Ah poor loving Ghosts! —*The*
delights of the Bottle &c. You had hard Fortune; but there's   325
one above knows all. Oh my head swims! and I grow faint
with strength. —My dear Bear farewell. —*The delights of*
the Bottle.—

[She falls asleep.]

Enter Bruin.

Bru. Where is my love? where is my dear?
O lemine I think she's here!   330
Where are thy eyes? thy pretty eyes,
Look how thy love poor *Bruin* cries.

She's dead, she's dead, she's dead,
Oh! whither art thou fled?
Oh Mother *Woossat!* Oh cruel Death!   335
Oh! who has stop'd thy spicey breath?
Oh pretty *Nonsy!* Oh hapless *Bruin!*
Oh fie! Oh dear! Oh me! Oh thee! Oh hear!
   Thy sobbing houling Bear.
Oh *Woossat* Mother! since tha'st kill'd my joy,   340
I will thy Imps and sucking Toads destroy.
Thy Charmes and Pictures all shall perish too;
And what so e'r thou dost, I will undo.

          Woossat *flies down in her Charriot.*

   Wooss. So Insolent, why, what a Murrain?
You'l find the stink the worse for stirring.   345
   Bru. I will revenge my dear *Nonesee,*
On Justice *Crab,* and eke on thee.
What Hellish Teen? what Devilish Ire,
Made thee leave *Nonsey* in the mire?
   Wooss. For her you did neglect my Trade,   350
And when to *Wishing-Chair* I call'd for aid,
You wheedl'd him to be your Bawd.
   Bru. Oh save my love! my *Nonsy* save,
And I'le for ever be thy Slave.
I'le trot to Carriers ev'ry week,   355
Fresh Countrey Ware for thee to seek.
         And when thou hast'm,
I'le bring thee ev'ry Gallants Custom.
   Wooss. Pry'thee stint thy silly talk,
Thou mayest as well turn Cheese to Chalk.   360
   Bru. Oh my *Nonsey!* Oh my heart Blood and Guts!
Oh save my dear! Oh save my Queen of Sluts!
Thou stony-hearted Witch, is this so much?
Think, what fine *Nymphs* I did for thee debauch?
   Wooss. Thou prat'st in vain, the cruel Dye is cast,   365
   Bru. Oh cruel Mother! whither in such hast?
I'le show thy tricks, and all thy conjuring Art;
And make thee ride in Triumph in a Cart.
No Gallant e'r shall rap at dore,
And without Man, in vain is Whore.   370
   Wooss. Th'art insolent; I'le hear no more.

         Woossat *Enters into her Charriot.*

Bru. Inhumane *Woossat* do not run,
And let thy Son be quite undone.
I thee conjure, don't leave her thus,
By thy beloved *Incubus.*   375
Thy publick Drabs, and private dores,
Thy little Bottles, and great scores:
Thy much Impudence, and no shame,
By all thy sports and by that same:
Oh stay the Cart! stay the Cart! stay the Cart.   380

> *He lays hold, and is drawn up, till he pulls down the Charriot.*
> *Justice* Crab *is driven in, in a Wheel-barrow.*

Bru. O ho, here's Justice *Crab!* now by this light,
He'l do me right.
Dear Soul, I beg you'l check the Hag,
And read her a Lecture for abusing her *Hector.*
  Crab. Matron of love, be kind to bauling Imp,   385
And let him have his am'rous shrimp.
If *Hector* be disgruntl'd, Trade is broken,
He'l make thy mischiefs known by tale and token.
Redstreak and the King, you made dye,
And caused the Princess sad Tragedy.   390
Both Sisters ruin'd by your Plot,
If *Nonsy* too should go to Pot.
He'd blaze all this about the Town,
And make thy very house pull'd down.
  Wooss. Shall he have mortal only to his use?   395
When Pomp and State ne'r so much bigger?
Can't keep frail *Missy* to one trigger:
No, 'tis to credit Trade, and House abuse;
Besides she'l eat Bread out of mouth;
I will not suffer't, 'faith, and troth.   400
  Crab. Nonsey's business shall be done,
She's mortal, therefore may be wone;
No, *Missy* was ever true to one.
  Wooss. Then *Nonsy* rise, rise my sweet punck;
She seemed dead, yet was but drunk.   405
Rise from thy Chair as soft as Couch,
And turn to Arms of loving Slouch.

> None-so-fair *Wakes.*

Non. Wha, wha, what's the matter? who's there? Not

guilty, Not guilty my Lord *Tagrag*, Heigh ho, I wish you
were all hang'd for waking me. Gods! have I my pretty thing   410
again?

    Bru. Thou hast, Oh let me hug and buss it!
Thanks to great *Crab,* and Mother *Woossat.*

    Non. I have? —Oh let me hug and buss it!
Thanks to great *Crab,* and Mother *Woossat.*   415

    Crab. Come jolly lovers, let's be trudging;
Ile see you both safe in your lodging.
There kiss and take your fill of dodging:
First to my Hall, for there are coming
A Crew of jovial youth's a mumming.   420
So well you shall be treated there,
That ev'ry Youth, and Damzel here,
Shall envy joys of Youth and Bear.

                                Exeunt all.

    The Scene open'd, discovers a Crew of Bachanals *dressed with
Ivy, and Vine-leaves, drinking, and laughing: beyond them a
company of Lovers adorn'd with Garlands of Roses,* &c, *in a
pleasant Grove.*

              Song by the *Bacchanals.*

    While this is a singing, *Bacchus* rises, riding on a
Hogshead dressed with Vine-branches and Ivy.

        Time's an old Rascal, he never will stay,
        Yet in spite of his Scythe, and his Glass;   425
        He that flies from his liquors an Ass.
        Boy, drink away, Boy drink away.

              Song by the Lovers.

    While this is singing, *Cupid* flies down on the Stage.

Ah! Charming, Fair, Divine, Ice, Flames & Darts,
Nymph, Goddess, beauties, shrine, O eyes and hearts!
Stars, Suns, and Diamonds, Roses, and Lillies,   430
Damon! Alexis! *Oh* Cloris! *Ah* Phillis!
Powr's, Gods, and Fates, Oh pity, joy, and pain,
Languish alass, Fears, Hopes, Smiles, and Disdain.
Oh cruel Nymph! *Ah unrelenting* Swayn!

Psyche Debauch'd

Bacchus *sings.*

While this is singing, all the *Bacchanals* come on the Stage.

> *Come my Sons of the Grape, while your faces outshine*   435
> *The Sun in the Sky, with the juice of the Vine.*
> *Let the pale whining lover*
> > *discover*
> *How sad are the Chains, and how pleasant are mine.*

Cupid *sings.*

While this is singing the lovers come on the Stage.

> *Come happy Lovers, come, and tell,*   440
> *The joys that in your Bosom's dwell.*
> *The pleasures of the hands and eyes,*
> *How ev'ry look and touch surprize,*
> *Let your perswasive Language prove,*
> *There is no Paradise but Love.*   445

Chorus of all.

> *We come to dye or win the Field,*
> *For hearts with Love and* Bacchus *fill'd,*
> *Can fight, and fall; but never yield.*

A Dance of Bacchanals, and Lovers.

A Song by a Lover.

> *When* Caelia *my heart did surprize,*
> *In an Ocean of grief my fair Goddess did rise;*   450
> *And like Christal dissolv'd, the tears flow'd from her eyes.*
> *From her beautiful Cheeks, all the Roses withdrew,*
> *And she look'd like a Lilly o'rladen with dew.*

> *How sweet did her sorrow appear?*
> *How I trembl'd, and sigh'd, and for every tear,*   455
> *Made a vow to the Gods, and a Prayer to her,*
> *Oh how soft are the wounds we receive from the fair!*
> *But the joys and the pleasures there's none can declare.*

> *What panting, and fainting, I feel,*
> *When imbracing her feet before* Caelia *I kneel:*   460

Oh how dear are her smiles! and how sweetly they kill?
Ev'ry minute I dye with the thoughts of her Bliss,
And she breaths a new life in each languishing kiss.

                    O Love let us still wear the Chain,
Let no Passion, but love in our fancies e'r reign,   465
Let us often be cur'd, and ne'r freed from our pain.
All the pleasures of Wine to the Sense are confin'd,
But 'tis Love is the Noblest delight of the mind.

SONG by a *Bacchanal*.

Lovers grow pale, and Beauties grow stale;
And their pleasures end all like an old Winters tale.   470
But the Beauties of Wine do still sparkle and shine,
And make all that love it and drink it Divine.

Love makes you old, e'r thirty is told,
But the aged, and cold, become active and bold,
Look as plump, and as brisk as the Grape that's unprest,   475
When their heads with the Spirit of Wine are possest.

The Clouds open, and from the inner part of the Heaven,
escends *Jupiter* in his Charriot drawn by Eagles.

Jupiter *sings*.

Let Love and Wine no more contend,
To whose high Pow'rs all Mortals bend.
Before this Assembly, where are
The Amorous, the Youthful, and Fair,   480
Make an end of your long doubtful War.

Chorus.

Why should you quarrel? and fiercely complain?
All the World is your own, & your Rites would maintain:
But without one another, you neither can Reign.

A Chorus of *Cupid* and *Bacchus*.

Let Hermes *the Herald of Heaven, and Fame;*   485
The Union of Cupid, *and* Bacchus *proclaim.*

Trumpets are heard a far off, the Heavens divide; and
from the furthest end *Mercury* flies down attended by Fame,
and the whole Heaven appears adorn'd with Angels, &c.
and Musick.—

Mercury *sings*.

> *To all, and to Singular in this great meeting,*
> *The weighty Gods,* Cupid *and* Bacchus, *send greeting.*
> *Whereas by some Poets a wicked design*
> *Of difference, was raised between Love and good Wine.*   490
> *They now do declare*
> *An end of the War,*
> *And the hearts of all Mortals will equally share.*

Chorus.

> *When Beauties are cruel to banish your care,*
> *From Love to the Charms of* Bacchus *repair,*   495
> *And when* Bacchus *inflames you with too hot a Fire,*
> *To the pleasures of Love for assistance retire.*

A Catch sung in three parts, and danc'd. By Bacchanals and Lovers.

> *Let's love, and drink, and drink, and love, and drink on,*
> *What have we else in this dull World to think on?*
> *But still to love, to drink, and love, and drink on?*   500
> *Let's love, and drink, and drink, and love for ever,*
> *And let each* Nymph *be made a kind believer.*
> *For he that loves, and drinks, will ne'r deceive her.*

Enter two *Elizian* Princes, and dance through Hoops.
The Dance ended,
Mercury *speaks to the Audience.*

Although the War 'twixt Love and Wine is done,
We dare not triumph, 'till your pleasure's known;   505
For here the very Gods your Powers own.
If all that Love and Drink loud plaudits ring,
The joyful Gods, and Nymphs again shall sing,
    Sing. —And *Nonsy* shall injoy her pretty thing.

F   I   N   I   S.

EPILOGUE.

Like *Cunning Wives to cheat you to your Bliss,*
We took the Garb and Humours of your Miss.
As gay,—as vain, and ayery we are grown;
And you, as brisk; as young Gallants came on:
And look as dull as they, now th' Act is done.   5
Since Non-sense, Noise, and Show still bear the Bell,
As wise Physicians do with Mad-men deal,
We humour you, to make you sooner well.
If this won't take—
T'insure our future charge, and Credit too,   10
As undertakers for great Volumes do;
We'l paint your Coats of Arms o'r ev'ry Scene,
And dedicate 'm t'ye to draw you in.
   Poor Nonsy *dreading the approaching storm,*
Sits trembling like a Hare within her Form: 15
While Criticks swarm from ev'ry part o'th'Town,
Prepar'd with Damning noise to run her down:
She fears no Gen'rous Hunters, for they come
Only for sport, and would prevent her Doom.
She fears no snarling Fops, though ev'ry foot,   20
Like eager Lovers they will put her to't,
Still hunting close, and snatching at her Scut;
No, only sneaking Poachers, she can dread;
That with their long-tail'd Mungrils hunt for Bread,
And lurk in holes to knock her on the head.   25
You Gentlemen that for your pleasure came,
Let not those creeping Vermine kill your game:
Give her fair Law, and while in view she flies,
You swelling hopes and sweet delights will rise:
But when you paunch her, all your pleasure dies.   30
Keep up your sport; and to prevent our sorrow,
Save her this night, and run her down to morrow.
Non-So. —*Now to the Misses, thus poor* Nonsy *bends,*

To leave no stone unturn'd to gain our ends.
You She-Weavers, that without lawless Engines, come;   35
Engines—
That like dark Lanthorns lurk in little Room,
And manage twenty Shuttles with one Loom:
While honest Lab'rers that can use but one,
For want of work lye still, and are undone.   40
Let all your Tools be stirring for your Aid,
Or we will burn your Engines, and destroy your Trade.

ANNOTATIONS

All quotations from Shadwell's *Psyche* in the annotations that follow are taken from Vol. II of *The Complete Works of Thomas Shadwell,* edited by Montague Summers, 5 vols., London, 1927.

Prologue.

Duffett's Prologue closely follows the Epilogue to Shadwell's *Psyche.*
1–4. These lines appear in an altered form in the version of this prologue included on page 93 in Duffett's *New Poems, Songs* (1676):

> *Psyche* debauch'd, poor Soul! she made great hast,
>   I knew the jilting Quean could never last
> Five weeks, she (must perhaps decay more fast)
> —As our friend *Nicander* has it.
> Whilst our rich neighbors mock our Farce, we know.

4–5. Cf. Shadwell's Epilogue (16–17): *"Whilst our rich neighbours mock us for't, we know / Already th' utmost they intend to do."* Shadwell's reference to "rich neighbours" is most likely to the French, who had produced *Psyché* in 1671. Shadwell's *Psyche* was an adaptation of the French version.
6–9. Cf. Prince Nicander's remark in Act I of Shadwell's *Psyche:* "If we 'gainst Nature go, we Heav'n offend, / Who made that Nature to pursue its end." There may also be a glance at Shadwell's own comment in his Preface: *"Good Comedy requiring much more Wit and Judgement in the Writer, than any rhyming, unnatural Plays can do."*
10–14. Duffett's *New Poems, Songs* (p. 94) prints these lines in a different version:

> As *AEsop's* Cat drest like a Lady, this
> At first surpris'd, now where's the gaudy Miss
> You saw, and knew, and left her in a trice?
> None but the Dirty Rout would like her twice.
> Their well-drest frolick once may please the Eye.

10. *Aesop's Cat.* Demonstrating that one's real nature will always shine through a disguise, the fable concerns a young man so enamoured of his cat that Zeus grants that it be changed into a maiden; however, because she still chases rats Venus changes her back into a cat.

12. Cf. Shadwell's Epilogue (24): "*The dirty Rout would damn 'em* [i.e., farces] *in a Fair.*"

15–16. Cf. Shadwell's Epilogue (11–12): " . . . *Gallants you can tell, / No foreign Stage can ours in Pomp excel.*"

17–18. Shadwell's Epilogue (18–19): "*Yet all the Fame you give 'em we allow, / To their best Plays, and their best Actors too.*" The lines again refer to the French.

19–20. Cf. Shadwell's Epilogue (1–3):

> *What e'er the Poet has deserv'd from you,*
> *Would you the Actors for his faults undo,*
> *The Painter, Dancer, and Musician too?*

20. *Devow.* Anthony DeVoto, who ran a puppet-show at Charing-Cross, the open space at the top of Whitehall. Not only was DeVoto well-known for his puppets, but in November 1672 he was permitted to perform drolls and interludes with living actors (cf. George Speaight, *The History of the English Puppet Theatre*, London, 1955, pp. 73–91).

21–26. Cf. Shadwell's Epilogue (20–28):

> *But, Sirs—*
> *Good Plays from Censure here you'll not exempt,*
> *Yet can like Farces, there below contempt*
> *Drolls which so coarse, so dull, so bawdy are,*
> *The dirty Rout would damn 'em in a Fair:*
> *Yet Gentlemen such Stuff will daily see;*
> *Nay, Ladies too, will in the Boxes be:*
> *What is become of former modesty?*
> *Yet—*

23. *Epsom-Wells.* In Shadwell's *Epsom Wells* (V.i), Bisket and Fribble indulge in some peeping-tom antics, observing their own wives having intercourse with Kick and Cuff.

27. Cf. a slightly different version of this line in Duffett's *New Poems, Songs* (p. 95): "Let's take off *Psyche*'s borrow'd plumes a while."

28. *Hopkins and Sternhold.* John Hopkins and Thomas Sternhold began publishing metrical translations of the Psalms in 1547. They are referred to here as prototypes of monotony and dullness.

29. *Kings of Brentford.* The famous duo who appear in *The Rehearsal* (II.ii). *leave Lardellas hearse.* Lardella's funeral is depicted in *The Rehearsal* (IV.i).

30. *Psyches despairing Lovers.* Cf. previous note.

31. *Apollo's Priest.* The first part of Act II of Shadwell's *Psyche* presents an elaborate ceremony at Apollo's shrine with a chief priest officiating.

31–32. *. . . restore again / What from the nobler Mamamouchy's ta'n.* Edward Ravenscroft's *The Citizen turn'd Gentleman* (D.G. July 1672) was reissued in 1675 as *Mamamouchi.* Summers notes that "The scene to which reference is here made is the burlesque investiture of old Jorden as a mamamouchi" (*Works*. I, p. cxx). Duffett is comparing Shadwell's scene at the temple of Apollo to the famous "mamamouchi" sequence, and suggesting that the latter, for all its absurdity, is nobler than Shadwell's pretentiousness.

33–34. In Duffett's *New Poems, Songs* (p. 95), these lines appear in a slightly altered form: "Let them restore your treble prices too; / To see how strangely they did bubble you." *bubble.* Cheat. *Treble prices.* Nicoll lists the premiere of *Psyche* as costing three times the usual price (I, p. 348).

37. *TE DE POLYKAGATHOI.* One of the cries uttered by the crowd of people at the shrine of Apollo in *Psyche* (II), in response to the chief priest's invocations to Apollo. This is a slight garble for Polloi kagathoi [for kai agathoi]— many and good. Shadwell has it in Greek, and correctly.

38–39. Cf. Shadwell's Epilogue (31–32): "But Oh a long farewell to all this sort / Of Plays, which this vast Town can not support." Remarks like this, and the general tone of the Preface, suggest that Shadwell was glad to be done with *Psyche*.

39. *Preface.* Shadwell's Preface to *Psyche* is his apologia for his part in the opera. For comment on the Preface see "Note on Text" above.

43. *The New-come Elephant.* This may refer to the elephant imported by Lord Berkeley and sold by 12 August 1675 (mentioned in *The London Stage*, I, p. 235). Rochester's poem, "My Lord All-Pride" (1679) includes the lines (23–26):

> So have I seen, at Smithfield's wond'rous fair,
> When all his brother-monsters flourish there,
> A lubbard elephant divert the town
> With making legs and shooting off a gun.

(Poem included in *Poems on Affairs of State*, Vol. I: 1660–78, ed. George deF. Lord, New Haven, 1963, pp. 414–15.)

47–48. Cf. Shadwell's Epilogue (33–34): "*If you could be content th' Expence to bear, / We would improve and treat you better ev'ry year.*"

Act I.

1–6. Cf. *Psyche* (I), opening lines (*Works*, II, p. 283):

> *Psyc.* How charming are these Meads and Groves!
> The Scene of Innocence and Artless Loves;
> Where Interest no discord moves.
> No stormy passions can the mind invade,
> No Sacred Trust is violated here.

1. *crumptious.* "Scrumptious," i.e., delightful. Summers suggests that it was said with a lisp (*Works*, I, p. cxix).

2. *ones none Dear.* "None" is an obsolete variant of "own." Cf. the following

from "Prologue to *The Armenian Queen*" in Duffett's *New Poems, Songs* (p. 85.): "At last he finds his nown dear *Phillis* laid in some close shade."
7. *Outalian.* Foreign. Cf. Dryden's *Sir Martin Marr-All* (IV.i.99–100): "*Moody. . . .* they are no *Englishmen,* but some of your *French Outalion* Rogues." Writing about Duffett in his edition of *The Rehearsal* (Stratford-upon-Avon, 1914), Summers quotes this word as "Oatalian" and calls it a pun on Oates and the Popish Plot (p. xxi); and refers to it in the same way in his edition of Shadwell (*Works,* II, p. cxix). The spelling in the quarto seems to me clearly to indicate a "u" rather than an "a" as the second letter of the word. Although the quarto of *Psyche Debauch'd* was not printed until 1678, the play was produced in 1675 when the pun that Summers claims to see would have made little sense.
8–11. Cf. *Psyche* (I, p. 283):

> 1. *Lady.* Man does not here his own kind fear,
> Traps are for Wolves and Foxes made,
> And Toils for Beasts, not Men, are laid;
> Man is not here by Man betray'd.

19. Cf. *Psyche* (I, p. 283): "For in this happy place no Court-like Arts are taught."
38. *Fiddle-come-faddle.* Triviality.
44. *Caraways, run Jack.* Possibly, this is a nonce phrase; but it may refer to Garraway's, a noted coffee-house in Exchange or Change Alley, Cornhill.
45. *Burnt Wine.* Hot wine.
47. *Baby of Clout.* A doll made of cloth.
52–53. Cf. *Psyche* (I, p. 284): "Each strives who shall his Monarch lead, / Though at the price of his own Father's Head."
56. *souse.* A draught or gulp.
64–82. Cf. *Psyche* (I, p. 284):

> 1. *Lady.* Yet there the Mighty are not prosp'rous long,
> Though ne'r so cunning, ne'r so strong;
> Though ne'r so much endear'd to th' Crown:
> Fresh Favourites succeed and pull them down.
> *Psyche.* As a black Cloud which the gross Earth exhales,
> Swell'd and opprest with its own weight,
> Down to the Earth rent with fierce Lightning falls:
> So splendid Fav'rites in their envy'd height,
> Big with the swellings of their Pride and Pow'r,
> Do seldom scape the dismal hour,
> When by some new-rais'd Meteors torn,
> They from the highest pinacle of fate,
> Fall to the most dejected state,
> And, from the Idols of the World, become the scorn.
> These troubles in my Father's Court I've seen,
> And ne'r can wish to be a Queen.

77. *Cock a Hoop*. A state of elation. Cf. these lines from the early part of
Butler's *Hudibras* (I.iii):

> For Hudibras who thought h' had won
> The field, as certain as a gun,
> And having routed the whole troop,
> With victory was cock-a-hoop.

78. *over-soaked Toast*. One who drinks to excess.

79. *Pot*. Pit, abyss.

89–91. Cf. *Psyche* (I, p. 284):

> 2. *Lady*.   Not one who can a Prince in Greece be call'd,
> Who is not by your Eyes enthrall'd:
> Each Prince great *Psyche* does adore,
> And pity from her heart implore.

93–103. Cf. *Psyche* (I, p. 284):

> 1. *Lady*.   But you with all their charms unmov'd remain,
> And smile when every Captive shakes his Chain.
> *Psyche*.   Not all the Pomp of Courts can e'r remove
> Me from the Pleasures of the quiet Grove:
> Each pretty Nymph to me her Tribute yields
> Of all the fragrant Treasure of the Fields.
> Garlands and Wreaths they bring
> From the sweet bosom of the Spring.

93. *Coif*. Skull-cap.

100. *Sloes*. Plums. *Hawes*. The fruit of the hawthorn.

101. *Gooding*. Begging.

102. *nappy*. Foaming.

104. *the Ready*. "The ready rhino"; immediately available cash.

118. *firck*. Beat, stir, move.

123–24. Cf. *Psyche* (I, pp. 284–85): "What Harmony is this which fills the
Air? / And does my Senses charm?"

SD 129. *Costard, Redstreak*. There are no parallels for these characters in
Shadwell's *Psyche*.

146. *Crouder*. "The village performer on the crwth or crowd, a primitive kind
of fiddle" (Edward J. Dent, *Foundations of English Opera*, p. 122).

152–53. *rowly powly*. Pell mell.

154. *woundy cranck*. A very lusty fellow.

161–68. Shadwell's abilities as dramatist-librettist-adapter-musician seem to be
glanced at here.

173. *Fuddle*. Booze.

174. *Mum Ducks in the puddle*. Possibly a nonce formula used as a toast while
drinking.

179. *Hinds.* Rustics, boors.

181. *Cocks.* God's.

189–90. Cf. *Psyche* (I, p. 285): "Pan. *Great* Psyche, *Goddess of each Field and Grove,* / *Whom every Prince and every God does love.*"

195–96. Cf. *Psyche* (I, p. 285): "Chorus. *And* Pan, *who before all here did command,* / *Now resigns all his Empire to* Psyche's *fair Hand.*" Shadwell includes elaborate stage-directions at this point:

> [They all kneel, and sing the *Chorus.*]
> [While the following *Symphony's* playing, *Pan*
> Crowns her with a Garland, his Attendants
> present her with Fruits, Flowers, &c.]
> A short *Symphony* of Rustick Musick, representing the
> Cries and Notes of Birds. Then an Entry danc'd by
> four *Sylvans* and four *Dryads* to rustick Musick. At
> the end of the Dance, the *Dryads* upon their Knees
> present *Psyche* with Fruits and Flowers; and the
> *Sylvans* present her with Wreaths of Lawrel, Myrtle
> and Cyprus. Then *Exeunt Sylvans & Dryads.* Then a
> short *Symphony* of Rustick Musick, representing an
> *Echo.* The *Dryads* and *Sylvans* presenting their
> Offerings. One sings.

209. *sprunt.* Brisk.

210. *Fittles.* Fiddles?

214. *Hedge-stake.* Fence-post.

219. *patches.* Boobies.

SD 222. Duffett also has fun with an echo-sequence in *The Mock-Tempest,* when *Ariel badgers Quakero* (V.i).

223–34. Cf *Psyche* (I, pp. 285–86):

> 1. Voice. *Great* Psyche *shall find no such Pleasure as here,*
> Echo.   *no such Pleasure as here*
>   *as here.*
> 2. Voices. *Where her dutiful Subjects shall all stand in awe*
> Echo.   *shall all stand in awe*
>   *in awe.*
> 3. Voices. *Her Frowns and her Smiles shall give us all Law,*
>   *shall give us all Law*
>   *all Law.*
> 4. Voices. *And from us of Rebellion she need have no fear*
>   *she need have no fear*
>   *no fear.*

240. *Eggs and Clary.* Clary is a sweet drink consisting of a mixture of wine, clarified honey, and various spices, as pepper and ginger. The eggs were probably "roasted," or hard-cooked, to be eaten with the clary.

245–58. These lines represent a pasticho of Shadwell's remarks in the Preface and in the Epistle Dedicatory to *Psyche*. For lines 245–47 and 250–54 (p. 280) compare these from the Preface:

In all the Words which are sung, I did not so much take care of the Wit or Fancy of 'em, as the making of 'em proper for Musick; in which I cannot but have some little Knowledge, having been bred for many Years of my Youth to some Performance in it. I chalked out the way to the Composer . . .

For lines 254–55 (p. 278) compare these from the Epistle Dedicatory:

I have . . . met with some Enemies, who . . . endeavour to persuade him [the King] that I do not write the Plays I own, or at least, that the best Part of them are written for me;

For lines 255–58 (p. 280) compare these, again from the Preface:

The Scenes were painted by the ingenious Artist, Mr. Stephanson. *In those Things that concern the Ornament or Decoration of the Play, the Great Industry and Care of Mr.* Betterton *ought to be remember'd, at whose desire I wrote upon this Subject.*

251. *Jews Trump-Citizen, and Trump Marine*. A large obsolete musical instrument of the viol kind, single-stringed and played with a bow, and producing a tone like that of a trumpet.

258. *Corn-cutter*. One who cuts corns on the feet.

261–65. Cf. *Psyche* (I, p. 286):

> *Psyche.* Oh happy Solitude! Oh sweet Retreat!
> Free from the noise and troubles of the Great!
> Not all the wealth of all the World shall charm
> Me from this calm retirement here.
> Where I enjoy all pleasure, know no fear,
> No Joy can her surprize, nor Danger can alarm.

264. *hall*. Obsolete form of "haul."

270–72. Cf. *Psyche* (I, p. 286): "*Ambition.* We come t' invite you from your vicious ease, / To Courts, where glorious Actions are perform'd."

272. *Cake-bread*. Bread made in flattened cakes.

276. Cf. *Psyche* (I, p. 286): "Leave lazy Groves for active Palaces." *Eldern whistle*. A whistle made of elder wood. *Gut of Cats*. Fiddle.

277. *Waits.* A small body of wind instrumentalists maintained by a city or town at the public charge.

278. A possible paraphrase here is: "Through my help you'll sit at table as if you were the steward's wife."

281. *Lump.* A lump of expensive food, or perhaps, of money.

283. Cf. *Psyche* (I, p. 286): "By me to noble thought may be inflam'd."

296–98. Cf. *Psyche* (I, p. 287):

> To think of Ruling Kings, not silly Swains,
> Each day your Beauty a new Captive gains,
> And in all Courts no other Beauty's nam'd.

296. *Camlet.* Rich fabric; camel or hair of the angora goat.

298. *junckets.* Parties, get-togethers.

299. *retailing Prince.* A merchant.

301–08. Cf. *Psyche* (I, p. 287):

> *Power.* I from your Solitude do you invite
> And I am she for whom all Monarchs fight,
> *Power,* Mankind's supreme delight,
> Fair *Psyche* to the Court, come follow me,
> Numbers of Tributary Kings shall kneel to thee.
> What e're can be within the prospect of thy Thought,
> Shall instantly to thee by humble Slaves be brought.

304. *back to School.* i.e., boarding-school.

309–18. Cf. *Psyche* (I, p. 287):

> *Plenty. Psyche,* this lonely Desart quit,
> The Scene of homeliness and poverty:
> A splendid Palace does your state befit,
> Where you shall be adorn'd by me,
> With all the Treasures of the East and West.
> Thy life shall be but one continu'd Feast,
> And every Prince shall be thy Guest:
> All delicates I'll find for thy content,
> Which Luxury, inspir'd by Wit, can e'r invent.

315. *Mundungus.* Tobacco.

318. *Bub.* Drink, strong beer.

319–26. Cf. *Psyche* (I, p. 287):

> *Peace.* And I to crown all these,
> Will give you everlasting Peace;
> Peace that no Fiends shall ever harm,
> Nor the mad tumults of Mankind allarm:
> My Olive still shall flourish where you are,
> For Peace should always wait upon the fair.

324. *The Saints.* The Puritans.

327–38. Cf. *Psyche* (I, p. 287):

> *Psyche.* Happy are they who know Ambition least.
> I'm only safe and quiet, while my breast
> Is not with base ambitious thoughts opprest,
> Too turbulent to let poor mortals rest.
>   O'er all my Tyrant Passions Power I have,
> And scorn that Pow'r which can but rule a Slave.
>   The use of mighty Riches is but small;
> Besides I, nothing coveting, have all.
>   Peace, with such vain Companions never dwells,
> She's only safe in humble Groves and Cells.

329. *cribs.* Provender.

330. *Squibs.* Fire-crackers. The image here suggests a country bumpkin having a practical joke played on him: a string of fire-crackers being lit and dropped into his pocket.

343. *Dorsers.* Not clear; a "dosser" is a houseless vagrant.

345–53. The rhymes in these lines suggest that this sequence may have been intended as verse.

348. *Furies.* At this point in *Psyche*, I, Envy, along with six Furies, drives off the allegorical panelists. Several stanzas are sung.

354–61. Cf. *Psyche* (I, p. 288):

> *Nicander.* Madam, I to this Solitude am come,
> Humbly from you to hear my latest Doom.
>   *Psyche.* The first Command which I did give,
>   Was, that you should not see me here:
>   The next Command you will receive,
>   Much harsher will to you appear.

362–401. Cf. *Psyche* (I, pp. 289–90):

> *Psyche.* Shall no conceal'd retirement keep me free
> From Loves vexatious importunity?
> I in my Father's Court too long endur'd
> The ill which I by absence thought t'have cur'd.
>   *Nicander.* Planets, that cause our Fates, cannot be long
>   [obscur'd,
> Though Comets vanish from our sense,
> When they've dispers'd their fatal influence,
> And nothing but the sad effects remain,
> Yet Stars that govern us, wou'd hide themselves in vain.
> The momentary Clouds must soon be past,
>   Which wou'd their brightness overcast.
>   *Psyche.* Why should *Nicander* thus pursue in vain
> Her, o'r whose mind he can no Conquest gain:
> For though my Body thus abroad you see,
> My Mind shall stay within and keep its privacy.

Nicander. Blame not the passion you yourself create,
Which is to me resistless as my Fate:
      Can *Psyche* own such Cruelties,
As vainly Priests impute to Deities?
To punish the Affections they inspire,
As if they'd kindle to put out a fire.
If from the Gods we any gifts receive,
Our Appetites of Nature they must give.
Let Priests for Self-denial then contend,
If we 'gainst Nature go, we Heav'n offend,
Who made that Nature to pursue its end.
Nature's desires Heav'n's known prescriptions are,
Of greater certainty than others far:
Priests Inspirations may but Dreams be found,
Th' effects of Vapors or of Spleens unsound:
But Nature cannot err in her own way,
And though Priests may, she cannot lead astray.
   Psyche. Nature the Gods first uncorrupted made,
But to corruption 'twas by Man betray'd;
Which when so much exorbitant they found,
What first they had made free, they justly bound.
   Nicander. If Nature be not what the Gods first meant,
Then pow'rful Man defeated Heavens intent.
If the Gods Engine of the World must be
Mended by them, how did they then forsee?
Must men, like Clocks, be alter'd to go right?
Or though wound up by Nature, must stand still?
Must we against our own affections fight,
And quite against the Bias bend the will?
   Psyche. Against your self y'have pleaded all this time;
If not to follow Nature be a crime,
Mine so averse to Love by Heav'n is made,
She above all by me shall be obey'd.
   Nicander. Nature incites all humane kind to love;
Who deny that, unnatural must prove.

401. *butter'd buns.* Harlots, prostitutes.

SD 404. *Prince Phillip.* The southern dialect Duffett employs in Prince Phil's speech is similar to that employed by Ben Jonson throughout *A Tale of a Tub*.

404–05. Cf. *Psyche* (I, p. 290): "How, *Polynices*, my great Rival here! / This is the only way I him can fear."

408. *hab nab.* Hit or miss.

409–10. Cf. *Psyche* (I, p. 290):

> *Nicander.* Such violent and sudden love
>   Perhaps must soon remove:
>   'Tis frail as an abortive Birth.

410. *slinck.* An abortive or premature calf or other animal.

411–14. Cf. *Psyche* (I, p. 290):

Polynices. That which I have for that illustrious face,
Is Sympathy, not lazy Love,
The Steel the Loadstone does as soon embrace,
And of it self will ne'r remove.

418. *veny.* A hit or thrust in fencing.

420-21. Cf. *Psyche* (I, p. 291): "Princes, let your untimely Discord cease; / If my Esteem you'd gain, conclude a Peace."

421. *Tantablin.* A tart, or round piece of pastry.

422-23. Cf. *Psyche* (I, p. 291): "So absolute is your Command, / That I my Rival will embrace."

423. *root.* Phallus.

424-27. Cf. *Psyche* (I, pp. 291-92):

> *Nicander.* Your Voice may still the Fury of the Winds,
> Or calm the most distemper'd Minds:
> Wild Beasts at your Command in Peace would be,
> When you make Rivals thus agree.

428-40. Cf. *Psyche* (I, p. 292):

> The next command I give, must be,
> Not to invade my privacy.
> Princes, farewel, you must not follow me.
> *Nicander.* So sacred are the dread commands you give,
> From you my death I humbly wou'd receive.
> For I can scarce hear this and live.
> *Polynices.* Your breath mens minds to any thing may move,
> When you make Rivals one another love.　　[*Exit* Psyche]
> But see! her envious Sisters do appear,
> Whose anger less than love we fear.

> *As they are going off in haste,*
> Enter Cidippe *and* Aglaura.

> *Cidippe.* Great Princes, whither do you fly so fast?
> *Aglaura.* 'Tis to their Idol *Psyche* by their haste.
> *Cidippe.*　　What Prince-like virtue can you find
> In her poor and groveling mind?

439. *i'faggs.* In faith.

441-43. Cf. *Psyche* (I, p. 292):

> *Cidippe.* Her Beauty like her Mind is vulgar too.
> Like the dull off-spring of some Village-Pair,
> She might perhaps some Shepherds heart subdue,
> But should, poor Thing, of Princes looks despair.

444. *There's your Anchovies.* Prince Phil's uniquely pungent epithet.

447. *Odsboars.* God's boars. *wamble.* Rolling or uneasiness of the stomach in nausea.

448. *leg like a Lapwing.* Possibly, long-legged.

452. *Persian Hawk-Nose.* Fashionably "hooked."

455. *Dance Barnaby.* To dance to a quick movement, to move quickly. Cf. Etherege's *Love in a Tub* (V.ii): "Sir Nicholas Cully. Widow, here is music; send for a parson, and we will dance Barnaby within this half-hour." Perhaps the term had reference to sensual matters as well.

481. *Sweet lips and wou'd hamor you each.* There may be a printing error here. Perhaps the girls' names should simply be spelled out, but I have let the text stand since there may be an intended, although confused, play on words.

482–85. Cf. *Psyche* (I, p. 292):

> *Nicander.* Farewel—Such blasphemies we must not hear,
> Against the Goddess we adore.
> *Polynices.* So beautiful to us she does appear,
> That none shall ever charm us more.

484. *lye ith' Suds.* Go down the drain; remain in an unfinished state or condition.

486–89. Cf. *Psyche* (I, pp. 292–93):

> *Cidippe.* Blasted be her Beauty, and her charms accurst,
> That must our ruine bring;
> I am almost with Envy burst,
> To see each Day she can command a King.

495. *Posset.* Hot milk and wine.

496. *Temple.* Brothel.

498–503. Cf. *Psyche* (I, p. 293):

> *Venus!* redress the Wrongs which she has done:
> She may in time insnare your Son.
> She such an Idol by Mankind is made,
> Your Pow'r no more will be obey'd;
> Your Sacred Beauty they'll neglect,
> Your Deity will have no more respect.

499. *Circles dark, and deep.* There is a suggestion here of magic spells, and also of coins. *trappan.* Swindle.

504–30. Cf. *Psyche* (I, pp. 293–94):

> *Aglaura.* No Incense more will on your Altars smoke,
> No Victims more will burn,
> Each Prince her Worshipper will turn.
> Let this your great Divinity provoke;
> Revenge your self, and take our Part,

Psyche Debauch'd

Punish her stubborn Heart,
And by your utmost Fury let her smart.
                    [*A Symphony of soft Musick.*]
Cidippe. What divine Harmony is this we hear!
            Such never yet approach'd my Ear!
[Venus *descends in her Chariot, drawn with Doves.*]
Aglaura. See, *Venus's*, Chariot hovering in the Air;
            The Goddess sure has heard our Pray'r.
Venus sings. With Kindness I your Pray'rs receive,
            And to your Hopes Success will give.
        I have with Anger seen Mankind adore
        Your Sister's Beauty, and her Scorn deplore:
            Which they shall do no more.
        For their Idolatry I'll so resent,
        As shall your Wishes to the full content.
            Your Father is with Psyche *now;*
        And to Apollo's *Oracle they'll go,*
            Her Destiny to know.
        I by the God of Wit shall be obey'd,
        For Wit to Beauty still is subject made:
            He'll so resent your Cause and mine,
            That you will not repine,
        But will applaud the Oracle's Design.

524. *wishing Chair.* This is Duffett's equivalent for Apollo's oracle. A crooked fortune-telling device is suggested. Later, as we shall see, the Wishing-Chair is involved in some sexual titillation with Mother Redstreak (III,iii).
530. *fring'd glove.* Ornamented with fringe.
531–52. Cf. *Psyche* (I, p. 294):

            Cidippe.   Great Goddess, we our thanks return,
                        We after this no more shall mourn.
            Aglaura. Your sacred Pow'r for ever we'll obey,
            And to your Altars our whole Worship pay.
                                [Venus *ascends with soft Musick.*]
            Enter Theander *with his Followers, and* Psyche *with two Ladies.*
            Theander.   Daughters, no more you shall contend,
                        This happy day your strife shall end:
            The Oracle shall ease you of your care;
                        We to the Temple will repair,
                            And *Psyche* will obey,
                        Whate're the *Delphick* God shall say
            And—
            Whate're *Apollo* shall command, shall be,
            I swear by all the Gods, perform'd by me.
                Psyche. And on my Knees I make this solemn vow,
            To his Decree I will devoutly bow.
                        Let his commands be what they will,
                            I chearfully will them fulfill.
                Theander. Let's to *Apollo's* Temple then repair,
            And seek the God with Sacrifice and Pray'r.
                                        [*Exeunt omnes.*]

– 241 –

532. *in wondrous Cranck.* In high spirits.

538. *the Rose.* The Rose Tavern in Russell Street was a noted place of debauchery.

Act II, scene i.

This sequence does not parallel Act II, scene i, of Shadwell's *Psyche,* in which two sets of "despairing lovers" commit suicide by jumping off a cliff. This is one of the modifications by Shadwell of the French version by Corneille-Moliere-Quinault, and it is apparently intended as a portentous preface to the judgement of Apollo's oracle against Psyche. Duffett chose instead to introduce Wossatt and Bruine, his counterparts to Shadwell's Venus and Cupid.

3. *touz'd.* Handled roughly.

7. *Tours.* Taffeta. *Points.* Laces.

12. *pump'd.* Drenched under a pump.

21. *Adamites.* Nudists and / or apostles of free love. *Family of Love.* A sect which originated in Holland and gained many adherents in England in the sixteenth and seventeenth centuries. They held that religion consisted chiefly in the exercise of love, and that absolute obedience was due to all established governments, however tyrannical.

40. *Were she the skin between his brows, I'de not.* I have emended this from the quarto's "her brows" on the basis of common sense.

51. *jilting.* Swindling.

69–73. Mother Wossatt plans to trick None-so-fair into a marriage with Bruine apparently in order to get some control over her.

70. *the White Bear of Norwich.* Bruine's disguise sounds like it might allude to some contemporary freak from a side-show. Norwich was then the second city in the kingdom, famous for textiles and puppet-shows. Cf. Prologue to Etherege's *Love in a Tub:*

> For if you should [i.e., prejudge the play], we and our
> > comedies
> Must trip to Norwich or for Ireland go;
> And never fix, but, like a puppet-show,
> Remove from town to town, from fair to fair,
> Seeking fit chapmen to put off our ware.

81–84. These lines suggest what some of the stage effects in the Dorset Garden production of *Psyche* must have been like; they also refer to the expressions used in Greek as incantatory ejaculations by the Chief Priest. *Apollo's tripod.* Act II of *Psyche* opens with the stage direction:

> *The Scene is the Temple of* Apollo Delphicus, *with*
> *Columns of the* Dorick Order, *inrich'd with Gold,*
> *in the middle a stately Cupolo, on the top of it*
> *the Figure of the* Sun; *some distance before it*

Psyche Debauch'd

an Altar lin'd with Brass; under it a large Image
of Apollo, before which stands the Tripod.

Act II, scene ii.

This scene designation is not included in the quarto. It is indicated here for
two reasons. First, the action shifts markedly from the conversation between
Mother Wossatt and Bruine to the scene with the mock-oracle. Second, although the quarto only indicates one scene-break, it reads at that point (p. 28,
E² verso): "ACT II. SCENE III." Perhaps the sequence at the mock-oracle was
intended to be so marked.
SD 1. Cf. *Psyche* (II.i, pp. 294-95):

> *Enter in a Solemn Procession, the Chief Priest Crown'd*
> *with Lawrel in a white Vestment, over that a Purple*
> *Gown. over that a Cope embroidered with Gold, over*
> *all a Lambs-skin Hood with the Wool on: He has four*
> *Boys attending, two before, two behind, clad in*
> *Surplices, and girt with Girdles of Gold: the first*
> *carrying a golden Censor with Myrrhe, Frankincense,*
> *and sweet Gums, &c. The second a Barley Cake, or*
> *Barley Meal, with Salt, upon a golden Service. The*
> *third a golden Cruise, full of Honey and Water. The*
> *fourth a large gilt Book emboss'd with Gold. After*
> *them six Priests, with Books of Hymns, clad in Surplices*
> *and embroider'd Copes. Then Men with Wind-Instruments,*
> *clad in Surplices, all crown'd with Wreathes of Lawrel.*
> *After them* Nicander, Cidippe, Polynices, Aglaura,
> Theander, Psyche. *Then a Train of Ladies. All the*
> *Women with their faces cover'd with white Veils. After*
> *all* Theander's *Attendants and Guards in their*
> *Procession. This following Hymn is sung in* Chorus.

Jewes-trumps. Large obsolete musical instruments of the viol kind, that were
single-stringed and played with a bow, and which produced a tone like that of
a trumpet.
1–14. Cf. *Psyche* (II.i, p. 295):

> Chorus. *Let's to Apollo's Altar now repair,*
>   *And offer up our Vows and Pray'r;*
>   *Let us enquire fair* Psyche's *destiny.*
>   } *The Gods to her will sure propitious be,*
> Repeat. } *If Innocence and Beauty may go free.*
> Chief Priest. *Go on, and to the Altar lead.*
>   Chief Priest *turns to the People, and sings on,*
>   *This hallow'd ground let no one tread,*
>   *Who is defil'd with Whoredom, or with Bloud,*
>   *Lest all our Pray'rs should be for them withstood.*
>   *Let none be present at our Sacrifice,*
>   *But of an humble uncorrupted mind.*

> *The God for wicked men will all our vows despise,*
> *And will to all our wishes be unkind.*

23–29. Cf. *Psyche* (II.i, p. 295):

> Chief Priest. *Son of* Latona *and great* Jove,
> *In* Delos *born, which thou so much dost love:*
> *Great God of Physick and of Archery,*
> *Of Wisdom, Wit and Harmony;*
> *God of all Divinations too,*
> Chorus of Voices ⎱ *To thee our Vows and Pray'rs are due,*
> and Instruments. ⎰ *To thee our, &c.*
> [Chief Priest kneels, kisses the
> Altar, then rises and sings.]

25. *skittish.* Playful.

39–44. Cf. *Psyche* (II.i, pp. 295–96):

> Chief Priest. *Thou gav'st the cruel Serpent* Python *death,*
> *Depriv'dst the Giant* Tyrion *of his breath:*
> *Thou didst the monstrous* Cyclops *too destroy,*
> *Who form'd the Thunder, which did kill thy Son.*
> Chorus. *Thou light of all our life, and all our joy,*
> *Our Offerings with our hearts are all thine own.*
> [Chief Priest kneels, and kisses the
> Altar again.]

41. *Flesh-flies.* Flies which deposit their eggs in dead flesh.

45–49. Cf. *Psyche* (II.i, p. 296):

> Chief Priest. *By sacred* Hyacinth, *thy much lov'd Flower,*
> *By* Daphne's *memory we thee implore,*
> *Thou wou'dst be present at our Sacrifice,*
> *And not our humble Offerings despise.*

45. *Germain Princess.* Possibly, some notorious bawd.

46. *Cresset.* Again, possibly a bawd, or rogue.

48. *our silly Opera.* While this refers derisively to Shadwell's *Psyche*, it can be taken in another way. Just as Duffett utilized the "Macbeth Epilogue" to cast a mock-magic-spell defending his travesty of Settle from a possibly condescending audience, so here he utilizes the incantations from Shadwell's sequence with the oracle to weave a similar spell protecting *Psyche Debauch'd*.

50–53. Cf. *Psyche* (II.i, p. 296):

> Chorus of ⎫ *And we for ever will thy praise advance,*
> Voices and ⎪ *Thou Author of all Light and Heat.*
> Instruments. ⎩ *Let Pipes and Timbrels sound, and let them*
> *dance.*
> *Each day our worship we'll repeat.*
> *Each day, &c.*

– 244 –

50. *Croudy mutton come from France.* The point here seems to be that Shadwell's *Psyche* derives from an unpromising original. "Croudy" is meal and water stirred together so as to form a thick gruel.

51. *Tom Thimble has made show compleat.* While this may refer to Shadwell, who adapted the French version of *Psyche,* it may possibly be a more pointed reference to Betterton, who is credited with the production, and who instigated the adaptation. At the end of his Preface (p. 297) Shadwell says:

> *In those Things that concern the Ornament or Decoration of the Play, the great Industry and Care of Mr.* Betterton *ought to be remember'd, at whose desire I wrote upon this Subject.*

53. *Since Wool is small, let cry be great.* That is, since the real merit of *Psyche* is negligible, let noise and show, such as music, singing, dancing, and elaborate scenery cover up for it.

54–61. Cf. *Psyche* (II.i, p. 296):

> *Chief Priest. Jupiter, Juno, Minerva, Saturn, Cibele.*
> *Response.* Be propitious to our Vows and Prayers.
> *Chief Priest. Mars, Bellona, Venus, Cupido, Vulcanus.*
> *Response.* Be propitious, &c.
> *Chief Priest. Bacchus, Pan, Neptunus, Sylvanus, Fawnus,*
>   *Vertumnus, Palaemon.*
> *Response.* Be propitious, &c.
> *Chief Priest.* All ye Gods, Goddesses, and all the Powers.
> *Response.* Be propitious, &c.

54. *James Naylor.* One of the more controversial of the early Quakers (1617–60), he proclaimed himself the Messiah in 1656, and was arrested, tortured by being branded and having a spike driven through his tongue, and imprisoned for two and one-half years in Bridewell. Duffett also pokes fun at Quakers in *The Mock-Tempest* in his treatment of Quakero, the counterpart for Ferdinand. *Pope Joan.* Fabled in the Middle Ages to have succeeded Leo IV in 855. The legend went that Joan conceived a violent passion for a monk named Folda, and in order to be near him assumed the garb of a monk. Being clever and popular, she was elected pope, but was discovered through her giving birth to a child during her enthronization. *Wat Tyler.* Leader of the Peasant's Revolt in southern England in 1381. *Mall Cutpurs.* The familiar name of Mary Frith (ca. 1585–1660), a roaring girl, who frequently dressed as a man, and who was well-known as a thief. *Chocorelly.* A nonce-Italian?

56. *Massaniello.* Tommaso Aniello, a Neapolitan fisherman, led a revolt in July, 1647, and ruled Naples for nine days. The name was well-known in England. D'Urfey's *Massaniello* (1699) is in two parts; and cf. the Epilogue to William Chamberlayne's *Wits Led by the Nose* (1678):

Like Massanello's *our kind Judges sit,*
Cry down the Play, because they hate the Wit:

Mosely. Mother Mosely was a well-known bawd who was involved with the Earl of Shaftesbury. *Jack-straw.* The name (or nickname) of one of the leaders of the Peasant's Revolt of 1381. *Jantredisco.* This sounds more obviously like a nonce-Spaniard name, rather than a real one. *Pimponelli.* An illustrious pimp? 58. *Jack Adams.* A notorious forger and counterfeiter. *Mary Ambry.* An English folk-Amazon. According to a ballad, she disguised herself as a soldier at the siege of Ghent in 1584. *Frier Bungy.* Friar Bungay, the companion of Friar Bacon in the adventure of the Brazen Head. *William Lilly.* An English astrologer and prophet (1602-81).

60. Duffett gives tribute in this line to the "non-literary" contributors to the Dorset Garden production of *Psyche.*

62–65. Cf. *Psyche* (II.i, p. 296):

> Chorus. *To* Apollo *our Celestial King,* ⎰ The Dancers mingle
> *We will* Io Paen *sing* ⎱ with the Singers.
> Io Paen, Io Paen,
> Io Paen *will we sing:*

64. *Omn'a bene.* All's well.

67–78. This sequence, involving the seating of None-so-fair in the chair and the whipping of the little boy, has no parallel in Shadwell's *Psyche.*

SD 79–90. Cf. *Psyche* (II.i, pp. 296–97):

> *The Chief Priest kneels at the Altar. The Boys*
> *stand about him. The Priest takes the* Libamina
> *from the Boys, after a little Pause. One Priest*
> *rises and waves a Wand. Then all fall on their*
> *knees.*
> 1 *Priest.* Favete linguis, favete linguis, favete linguis.
> 2 *Priest. (rises, waves a wand)* Hoc agite, hoc agite, hoc agite.
>   *Chief Priest rises, and turns to the people.*
> *Chief Priest. (with a loud Voice)* ΤΊΣ ΤΗ ΔΕ
> *Response of all.* ΠΟΛΛΟΊ Κ'ΑΓΑΘΟΙ. [See note to I.i.37 above.]
>   *Chief Priest turns and kneels at the Altar again. The Boys*
>   *run out and fetch, one a Flambeaux, the other little*
>   *Fagots of* Cedar, Juniper, &c. *The Priest rises and lays*
>   *them on the Altar. All but the Chief Priest and Boys are*
>   *kneeling, intent upon the Altar without speech or motion.*
>   *As soon as the fire is kindled, which the Priest does*
>   *himself with the Flambeau.*
> *Chief Priest. (with a loud voice)* Behold the Fire.
> *All but the Chief Priest fall flat on their faces, then*
>   *rise again. The Boys reach the* Libamina *to the Chief*
>   *Priest:* 1. *The Censor, with Gums, which he offers.* 2.
>   *The Barley Cake, which he strews with salt, then lays*
>   *it on the Fire. Then sprinkles the Honey and Water on*

the Fire. Chief Priest waves his Wand to Theander *and*
Psyche, *who draw near, and kneel just behind.*
Chief Priest. Now ask the God the thing for which you came,
And after that we'll sacrifice a Ram.
Theander. That we may know, we humbly pray,
Who shall *Psyche's* Husband be.
　　　　She will most cheerfully obey
　　　　Her Destiny, and your Decree.

79. *Comorah whee.* Possibly nonsense. "Cummer" is Scottish for aged mother or gossip; "comor" is equivalent to "gather together."
80. *Shoolimocroh.* Again, possibly nonsense. A "shooler" is a beggar or loafer; "mocher" can mean to trifle or to work in the dark.
81. *Betty.* A name of contempt given to a man who interferes with the duties of female servants, or occupies himself in female pursuits.
82. *Pollykagathoy.* ΠΟΛΛΟΊ Κ'ΑΓΑΘΟΙ. "Many and one."
SD 91–107. Cf. *Psyche* (II.i, pp. 297–98):

　　　　It Thunders and Lightens again, the Image trembling,
　　　　and in Convulsions, with a very loud and hollow
　　　　Voice, utters these following Lines.
　　　　Apollo. You must conduct her to that fatal place,
　　　　　　Where miserable Lovers that despair,
　　　　　　With howls and Lamentations fill the air;
　　　　A Husband there your Daughter shall embrace.
　　　　　　On *Venus* Rock upon the Sea,
　　　　　　She must by you deserted be:
　　　　　　A poys'nous Serpent there She'll find,
　　　　By Heav'n he *Psyche's* Husband is design'd.
　　　　　　　　[At this they all start, affrighted.]
　　　　Theander. Gods! that I e'r should live to see this day.
　　　　　　'Tis for some great offence
　　　　Of mine, that thou art to be snatch'd from hence.
　　　　　　Oh take my life, and let her stay.
　　　　But 'tis in vain to ask, we must obey:
　　　　For which I'll weep my hated life away.
　　　　Cidippe. Venus has kept her word, and she shall be
　　　　　　Much more ador'd by me,
　　　　　　Then any other Deity.
　　　　Aglaura. Now my fair Sister must a Serpent have,
　　　　　　'Stead of a Nuptial Bed, a Grave.
　　　　　　Now she shall suffer for her Pride;
　　　　Our Love and Hate will now be satisfi'd.

91–92. *yonder Wood, Where Lovers howle.* Before Psyche is delivered over to the serpent (and rescued by Cupid) at the end of Act II, Shadwell inserted a sequence depicting the suicide of two sets of "despairing lovers."
106–23. Cf. *Psyche* (II.i, p. 298):

Psyche Debauch'd

Theander.　　　　Lead on; and with a funeral pace,
　　　　　　　　For I in that unhappy place
Must bury all my joy, and leave my life behind.
　Nicander.　　　　Stay but a moment, stay;
You will not sure this Oracle obey.
　　　　　　　　Consider and be wise:
If it be good *Psyche* to Sacrifice,
You were oblig'd to't without this command,
And we the action should not then withstand.
　Polynices.　If bad, then Heav'n it self can't make it good;
All good and ill's already understood.
Heav'n has forbid the shedding guiltless blood.
If good and ill anew it has design'd,
The Gods are mutable, and change their mind.
　Nicander.　Be not by this Imposture, Sir, betray'd,
By this dull Idol which the Priests have made:
Too many Cheats are in the Temple found,
Their fraud does more then piety abound:
They make the senseless Image speak with ease
　　　　　　　　What e'r themselves shall please.
　Chief Priest.　Do not the sacred Image thus profane,
Which will revenge it self, and all its Rites maintain.

115. "Gods, you would be driven off (veaz'd) were you so hard in your kind."
123. *Rods in Piss.* Punishment in store.
125. *Tom-tumbler.* An imp or devil.
126–60. Cf. *Psyche* (II.i, pp. 299–300):

　　　　　Chief Priest. By Miracles the pow'r of Heav'n is known.
　　　　　Polynices. Heav'ns power is more by setl'd order shown.
The beauty of that order which is found,
To govern the Creation in a round,
The fix'd uninterrupted Chain, whereby
All things on one another must depend;
This method proves a wise Divinity,
As much as should the Gods on earth descend.
　　　Chief Priest. You speak from Nature, which is ignorance;
But we to inspiration must advance.
　　　Nicander. If, Priest, by Means not nat'ral Heav'n declares
Its will, and our obedience so prepares;
The Gods by this their weakness wou'd confess,
What you call Miracles wou'd make them less.
If something without Nature they produce,
Nature is then defective to their use:
And when by that they cannot work their end,
My Miracle their Instrument they mend.
　　　Polynices. If this be granted, Priest, by this we find,
The Gods foresee not, or else change their mind.
But Heav'n does nothing to our sense produce,
But it does outward Nat'ral Causes use.
Fools trust in Miracles, and Fools ne'r doubt:
'Tis ignorance of Causes, Priest, makes Fools devout.
　　　　　　　　　　　　[Thunders again.]

Psyche Debauch'd

Chief Priest. Be gone, profane and wicked men,
You have provok'd Heav'ns wrath again.

Heav'n does again to you in Thunder speak!
   Nicander. 'Twas nothing but a petty cloud did break;
What, can your Priesthoods grave Philosophy
So much amaz'd at common Thunder be?
   Psyche. We should obey without these Prodigies;
I to Heav'ns Will my own will sacrifice.

156. *be wild Irish.* Superstitious, primitive.

161–66. Cf. *Psyche* (II.i, p. 300):

> *Theander.* Joy of my Life, let's to the fatal place,
> Where thine and all my sorrow is design'd:
> When thee the pois'onous Serpent shall embrace,
> Assure thy self I'll not stay long behind.
>   *Polynices.* Thus the great *Agamemnon* was betray'd,
> And *Iphigenia* thus a Victim made.

161. *Pigs-nie.* See note to *The Mock-Tempest* (V.ii. 280).

169. *cranck.* Vigorous.

Act II, scene iii.

1–2. Cf. *Psyche* (II.i, p. 302): "*Psyche.* Oh! stop those Royal Fountains: Tears are things, / Which ill become the Majesty of Kings."

4. *fadding.* Being busy about trifles.

5–15. Cf. *Psyche* (II.i, p. 303):

> *Theander.* Oh that I'd never seen thy much-lov'd face,
>   And that thou'dst perish in the womb:
> I had not led thee to this fatal place,
> Thy Father had not brought thee living to thy Tomb.
>   *Psyche.* Your sad complaints so soften me,
>   My heart will melt to that degree,
> That I shall have none left when death I see.
>   *Theander.* Heav'ns! what could thus your cruelty provoke?
> Your Altars, by my bounty, daily smoke.
>   With Fat, with Incense, and with Gums:
>   Nor have you wanted *Hecatombs.*
>   And must I thus rewarded be?

16–23. Cf. *Psyche* (II.i, p. 303):

> *Psyche.* Good Sir, be gone, the will of Heav'n obey.
>   Besides, if you should longer stay,
> Before the Serpent comes, my life will steal away.
> Weigh not your loss, but what you have remain;
> You have the comfort of my Sisters left.
>   Who will your drooping Age sustain,
>   When y'are of me bereft.

Psyche Debauch'd

Sisters, be good, and to my Father give
        All comfort, and his grief relieve;
He, from you Two, much pleasure may receive.

34. Cf. *Psyche* (II.i, p. 304): "Farewell for ever—."
35–52. Cf. *Psyche* (II.i, p. 304):

> *Theander.*   Say not so,
> For I to Death will go:
> My Soul to-Morrow shall meet thine below.
>   [*Exeunt all but* Psyche.]
>   *Psyche.* Ev'n now grim Death I slightly did esteem;
> With the wrong end o' th' Glass I look'd on him,
> Then afar off and little he did seem:
>   Now my Perspective draws him near,
> He very big and ugly does appear.
> Away—it is the base false Glass of Fear.

54. *muckinder.* Handkerchief.
59. *windle.* Lose strength or vigor; dwindle.
60–64. Cf. *Psyche* (II.i, p. 304):

> *Nicander.* What Heav'n commands is surely good,
> Heav'n has declar'd 'gainst shedding human Blood.
> Boars, Rams and Bulls will serve *Apollo's* turn,
> Whilst Gums and Incense on his Altars burn:
> 'Tis to the Priests that you are sacrific'd.
>   *Psyche.* I must not hear the Oracle despis'd.

61. *Cracks.* Prostitutes. *Wascoteers.* Low-class prostitutes.
63. *Gueer.* Gear.
71. *bob.* Cheat.
72–75. Cf. *Psyche* (II.i, p. 305):

> *Psyche.* Why for my Preservation shou'd you strive?
> For neither my Affection e'er cou'd move.
> Though Heav'n for that wou'd suffer me to live,
> No Prince on Earth cou'd ever make me love.

SD 80. Cf. *Psyche* (II.i, p. 305):

> [*The Earth opens, infernal Spirits rise and
> hurry the Princes away. Two* Zephyri *descend
> and take* Psyche *by each Arm, and fly into
> the Clouds with her.*

Act III, scene i.

SD 1. Shadwell's stage-directions at this point (p. 306) give an indication of
the elaborateness of the original production of *Psyche*:

Psyche Debauch'd

The Scene in the Palace of Cupid, Compos'd of wreath'd
Columns of the Corinthian Order; the Wreathing is
adorn'd with Roses, and the Columns have several little
Cupids flying about 'em, and a single Cupid standing
upon every Capital. At a good distance are seen three
Arches, which divide the first Court from the other part
of the Building: The middle Arch is noble and high,
beautified with Cupids and Festoons, and supported with
Columns of the foresaid Order. Through these Arches is
seen another Court, that leads to the main Building,
which is at a mighty distance. All the Cupids, Capitals
and Inrichments of the whole Palace are of Gold. Here
the Cyclops are at work at a Forge, forging great
Vases of Silver. The Musick strikes up, they dance,
hammering the Vases upon Anvils.

Paviers. Pavers, street-repairers.

1–34. These lines, with some minor variations, are included in Duffett's *New Poems, Songs* (pp. 115–18). The most interesting of these differences is the information that the song was *"Set by Mr.* Marsh *junior"*; also, the opening verses in the *New Poems, Songs,* version are sung by the "Master."

1–12. Cf. *Psyche* (III, p. 306):

> Vulcan *sings.* Ye bold Sons of Earth, that attend upon Fire,
> Make haste with the Palace, lest Cupid should stay;
> You must not be lazy when Love does require,
> For Love is impatient, and brooks no delay.
> When Cupid you serve, you must toil and must sweat,
> Redouble your blows, and your labour repeat.
> The vigorous young God's not with laziness serv'd,
> He makes all his Vassals their diligence show,
> And nothing from him but with pains is deserv'd;
> The brisk Youth that falls on, and still follows his blow,
> Is his favourite still. The considerate Fool,
> He as useless lays by for a pitiful Tool.

5. *Strikers and Thumpers.* Paving instruments.

13–34. Cf. *Psyche* (III, pp. 306–07):

> 1 Cyclops. This Palace is finish'd, and the other shall be
>   Made fit for his small Deity.
> 2 Cyclops. But fire makes us cholerick, and apt to repine,
>   Unless you will give us some Wine.
> Chorus.   With swinging great Bowls,
>   Let's refresh our dry Souls,
>   And then we'll to work with a Clink, clink, clink;
>   But first let us drink, but first let us drink.
> Vulcan. Let each take his Bowl then, and hold it to his nose,
>   Then let him redouble his blows.
> Cyclops. Nay, stint us not so, but let each take his two,
>   And twice as much as we can do.

Chorus.   *With swinging great Bowls,*
            Let's refresh, &c.
Vulcan. *Ye Slaves, will you never from drunkenness refrain?*
            Remember Ulysses *again.*
Cyclops. Ulysses *is a Dog, were he here he shou'd find,*
            We'd scorn him, and drink our selves blind.
Chorus.   *With swinging great Bowls,*
            Let's refresh, &c.
                    [They take their Kans in their hands.]
Pyra. *Here,* Harpes, *to you.* Harp. *Here,* Brontes, *to you,*
            And so take each Cyclops *his due.*
Bron. *To thee,* Steropes. Ster. Pyracmon, *to thee.*
Omnes. *And thus in our Cups we'll agree.*
Chorus.   *With swinging great Bowls,*
            Let's refresh, &c.
Vulcan. *Be gone, or great Jove will for Thunder-bolts stay,*
            The World grows so wicked each day.
Cyclops. *He has less need of Thunder than we have of Wine:*
            We'd drink, though great Jove should repine.
Chorus.   *With swinging great Bowls,*
            Let's refresh, &c. [The Cyclops dance again.]

35–39. Duffett might have had two spots of Shadwell's *Psyche* in mind in this brief passage. Part of line 35 is similar to *Psyche* (III, p. 307): "*Cupid.* You are my best of Servants, y'have done well." The rest of line 35, and line 36, are based on remarks in Shadwell's Preface (p. 280): "I chalked out the way to the Composer"; and his mentioning that with the exception of the concluding songs the play "was all done Sixteen Months since."
38–42. Cf. *Psyche* (III, p. 307):

> Say, *Zephyrus,* how do you like my Love?
> *Zephyrus.* Her Beauty does all mortal forms excel,
> She should be snatch'd from Earth to reign above.

More-fields. Moorfields was an open space to the north of Holborn where puppet-shows, wrestling and other sports were held.
40. *but.* Butt.
42. *in his Altitudes.* Drunk.
44. *drunk as David's Sow.* This alludes to the folk tale about a Welshman's tipsy wife who fell asleep in the hog-pen.
45. *Mum.* Liquor, strong drink.
63. We know from a later sequence (III.iii.16–21) that Wishing Chair has enjoyed the favors of None-so-fair (apparently during the liturgical whoopee of the sequence at the oracle in II.ii). The reader must keep in mind that Wishing Chair ("Apollo") is a character in the play; since he speaks few lines, it is easy to lose track of this fact.
71. *wistly.* Intently.

79. Cf. *Psyche* (III, p. 309): "Those sweet, those piercing am'rous eyes."

92–104. Cf. *Psyche* (III, p. 307):

> But why do you a humane shape now wear?
> Why will you not your self a God appear?
> *Cupid.*   At first, invisible I'll be.
>   Then like a Prince I will be seen;
>   Me like a God when she shall see,
>   I'll make her my Immortal Queen,
> When Love thus slily his approaches makes,
>   He takes fast hold, and long will stay;
> But if by storm he once possession takes,
> His Empire in the heart will soon decay.
>   Here comes my Love, Away,
> And to her honour dedicate this day.
>   [*Exeunt* Cupid *and* Zephyrus.]

Act III, scene ii.

This scene designation is not indicated in the quarto. I have added it because the sequence that begins here is a clearly self-contained unit.

1–17. Cf. *Psyche* (III, p. 308):

> *Psyche.* To what enchanted Palace am I brought,
>   Adorn'd beyond all humane thought?
> Here Art and Natures utmost powers conspire,
>   To make the Ornament entire.
> Where e'r I turn me, here my dazl'd eye
> Does nought but Gold, or precious Gems descry:
>   This is sure some divine abode,
>   The splendid Palace of some God:
> And not a Den where Humane bloud is spilt.
> This sure was never for a Serpent built.
>   I am at this no less amaz'd,
> Than at my sudden passage to the place.
>   With wonder round about I've gaz'd,
> And, which is strange, I've seen no humane face.
> 'Tis sure some Aery Vision which I see,
> And I to this imaginary height
>   Was rais'd by Heav'n in cruelty,
> That I might suffer a severer Fate.
> I on a Precipice of hope was plac'd,
>   That so my fall might greater be,
> And down with violence I shall be cast
> To th' bottom of despair, th' Abyss of misery.
> Where is the Serpent? when will he appear?

11. *play the Jacks.* To play the knave, to do a mean trick.

18–19. The speech-tag indicating that these lines belong to Bruine is omitted in the quarto. These lines have a source in *Psyche* (III, p. 308): "*Cupid.* The Serpent which you must embrace is near."

22–25. Cf. *Psyche* (III, p. 308):

> *Psyche.* What Divine Harmony invades my Ear?
> This is a voice I cou'd for ever hear.
> O speak again, and strike my ravish'd sense
> With thy harmonious excellence!

28–29. Cf. *Psyche* (III, p. 308): "No object of my sense could e'r / Transport me till this hour."

39. *Caudle.* A warm drink consisting of thin gruel mixed with wine or ale, sweetened and spiced, given chiefly to sick people.

40–42. Cf. *Psyche* (III, p. 308):

> *Cupid.* Whatever can be pleasant but in thought,
> Shall for my Love be sought:
> This shall her Palace, here her Empire be;
> She shall have Sovereign command o'r that and me.

46. *Too morrow to mo.* A nonce-formula for "tomorrow."

51. *guift.* Gift.

53. *hoddy doddy.* A short and dumpy person; a hen-pecked man.

54–58. Cf. *Psyche* (III, p. 309):

> *Enter* Cupid *and takes her up.*
> Oh Heaven! what glorious thing is this I see?
> What unknown Deity?
> His shape is humane, but his face divine;
> He calls me Love: but ah! would he were mine.
> *Cupid.* I am the Serpent Heav'n for you design'd.

59. *Pray Gad be Jon.* A mild oath.

60. *cranck.* Lusty, vigorous.

73. *maple face.* Spotted; a face mottled like the grain of maple.

84–93. Cf. *Psyche* (III, p. 309):

> *Psyche.* There's no request of yours I can withstand.
> Oh I am stung! what's this I feel?
> It is no pointed Steel:
> 'Tis such a pretty tingling smart,
> Now it invades my heart.
> Oh it encreases on me still,
> And now my blood begins to chill.
> But, Oh the pleasure! Oh the pain!
> And, Oh! might both a thousand years remain!

97. *leaguer.* Military engagement.

Psyche Debauch'd

110–24. Cf. *Psyche* (III, pp. 309–10):

> Those sweet, those piercing am'rous eyes,
> That can so easily a heart surprize.
> Oh, may my breast this poison ne'r forsake!
> I'm sure no Antidote I'll take.
> Why do you sigh? are you transported too?
>> *Cupid.* As you by me, so I am charm'd by you.
>>> Oh let my wandring heart find rest
>>> Within thy soft and snowy breast.
>>> Thou must to me thy heart resign,
>>> And in exchange I'll give thee mine
> And when my heart within thy breast does sit,
> Thou must be kind, and nurse, and cherish it.

113. *pincking*. Narrow, peering.

125–36. Duffett uses two passages from *Psyche* (III) as the basis for these lines:

> And when to me that pretty thing thou'lt give,
> I'll use't so kindly, 'tshall not fly away.
>> *Psyche.* Then take it, for with me it will not stay.
>>> [*They kiss.*]

and from a few lines (p. 310) before this passage:

> *Psyche.* Oh! how mine [i.e., my heart] flutters; yet I
>>>> hold it fast,
>> It beats till it self will tire;
> 'Twill lose it self with violent desire:
> Do what I can, it will be gone at last.
> Oh give me thine, for mine will fly away;
> Ah give it me! for if you longer stay,
>> Mine will be gone, and I shall die.
> Pray let your heart the want of mine supply.

137. *zokring*. Possibly "suffering," or "exhausting."

138. *the Vengeance scab*. "Vengeance" is being used as an intensifier. The sense here is "the darn rascal."

139. *wuss*. Know. *Naunts*. Aunts.

143. *froppish*. Peevish, fretful.

145. *zunning on zome odrous mixion*. "Sunning (resting) on some smelly manure pile (mixen)."

148. *a vowdry tit*. A "forward," "bold" minx or hussey?

149. *luch zares*. When "luck soars?"

155. *Tentoes*. Ten toes.

156–80. Cf. *Psyche* (III, p. 310):

> What have I done! I am to blame;
> I blush and feel a secret shame:

Psyche Debauch'd

But I feel something which o'rcomes that sense.
I'm charm'd with so much excellence!
Some Power Divine thus animates my bloud,
And 'twere a sin, if that should be withstood.
Your sacred form so much does move,
That I pronounce aloud, I love.
How am I rapt! what is it thus does force
My Inclination from its proper course?
I was to love an open enemy;
But now the more I look on Thee,
The more I love. My first surprise
Is heightened still by thy bewitching eyes.
Cupid. Love's debt was long deny'd by thee,
But now h'as paid himself with usury.
Psyche. Should I to one I know not be thus kind,
To one who will, perhaps, unconstant be;
Pray let me so much favour find,
To let me know who 'tis has conquer'd me.

166. *blush like a blew Dog.* Not to blush at all.
172. *bub.* Strong drink.
173. *empting of the Tub.* "Going all the way."
181–200. Cf. *Psyche* (III, p. 311):

I in this Region a vast Empire have;
Each Prince you've seen, compar'd to me's a Slave.
To me all *Grecian* Princes Tribute owe,
Which they shall pay to you.
A thousand Beauties shall be still at Hand,
Waiting for thy Command;
And, without Envy, they shall thee adore.
The Pomp, which here thou shalt enjoy, is more
Than e'er was seen in Earthly Prince's Courts:
And Pleasures here shall be
Beyond all mortal Luxury;
Our Recreations shall be heav'nly Sports.
And to such splendid Joys I thee invite,
As do the Gods on Festivals delight.
But first thy Palate thou shalt satisfie,
Thy Ear shall then be ravish'd, then thy Eye;
And all thy other Senses thou shalt feast:
Here I will entertain, and thou shalt be the Guest.

181. *the new Utopia.* Probably alluding to "gang-land"; possibly glances at Edward Howard's *The Six Days Adventure, or the New Utopia* (1671).
182. *Padders.* Robbers, highwaymen. *Jugglers.* Tricksters. *Priggers.* Thieves.
183. *Ditchers.* The context suggests this may refer to robbers who hide out in ditches.
183–84. *merry Greeks.* Roisterers.
184. *Fob.* Pocket.
185. *Dells.* Wenches. *obey thy back.* Do your will.

189. *Bobbing-Joan.* An old dance tune.

196. *a great Blue-Fig.* A delicacy.

197. *Dyet-bread Paper.* Diet bread is bread prepared for invalids or persons with a special diet. Diet bread paper may simply refer to the paper (tissue paper?) the bread was wrapped in.

197–98. *the lady in the Lobster.* In Act III of Shadwell's *The Sullen Lovers,* Sir Positive-at-all is credited with having written a play entitled *The Lady in the Lobster.* The context suggests the phrase may refer to the easy life.

200. *Trangam.* A knick-knack, toy or gewgaw.

201, 204. Cf. *Psyche* (III, p. 312): "*Psyche.* How am I rap't! what pleasures do I find!"

210–13. Cf. *Psyche* (III, p. 311):

> But pray beware of Curiosity,
> > Lest it shou'd ruin Thee and Me.
> > You must not yet know who I am;
> > I will in Time disclose my Name.

212. *smoak.* Detect.

214–22. Cf. *Psyche* (III, p. 312):

> My Love, I have but one request to thee;
> > Two Sisters I have left behind,
> > I hope my Love will be so kind,
> > That they the Witnesses may be
> Of all my pomp and my felicity.

217–18. *John come kiss me without dancing.* Probably, to kiss without preliminaries.

224. *Trape's.* A slut.

225. *surbated.* Footsore.

228. *bob.* Have intercourse.

230–42. Cf. *Psyche* (III, p. 312):

> *Zephyrus.* I'll fly as quick as thought,
> They suddenly shall to this place be brought.
> > [*Exit* Zephyrus.]
> *Cupid.* My Dear, let them not here much time employ,
> > For I must thy whole heart enjoy.
> From me, my Love, not one poor thought must stray,
> For I have given thee all my heart away.
> > But now prepare thy Ears and Eyes,
> > For I thy senses will surprise.
> > Along with me, and thou shalt see
> > What Miracles in Love there be.

230. *Blouzes.* Beggar wenches.

233. *setters.* Decoys who spy on intended victims.

236. *Verjuice.* The acid juice of unripe fruit.

Act III, scene iii.

20–21. *she pressed . . . / . . . the Cheese-frame.* "She felt as soft and succulent as newly pressed cheese."

23. *Alforges.* Cheek pouch of a baboon, and what is stored there.

28. *our Pallace the new Musick-house.* Possibly a jesting allusion to the theatre at Dorset Garden.

31. *the Straights.* This was the name of a nest of obscure courts, alleys, and avenues, running between the bottom of St. Martin's Lane, Half-moon (Bedford Street), and Chandos Street.

32. *Packing-penny.* A penny given at dismissal.

36. *curry'd.* Beaten, swindled, won over.

46–59. Mother Redstreak's speech is very similar to the one by Mother Stephania in *The Mock-Tempest* (III.i.68–95).

49. *whim whams.* Odd fancies.

50. *Gadslidikins.* God's little eye-lids.

52. *penny.* Face, fanny?

53. *fiddle faddle.* Chatter-box. Also, since "to fiddle" is slang for sexual caressing, perhaps "fiddle faddle" refers to the female's sex organs.

56. *Groat, whose stamp's worn out.* A coin whose imprint or markings have worn out.

57. *fit.* Accommodate.

63. *tun'st thy Clack.* Start to talk.

65. *Headborough.* A parish officer similar to a petty constable.

66. *Trumpet.* Strumpet? *Hilding.* A good-for-nothing, jade or baggage.

68. *bumbast.* Beat on the posteriors. *him.* Costard himself.

70. *Hind.* A bailiff or steward; also a rustic, a boor.

76. *lown.* Strumpet.

78. *twinckling of a Cabbage.* "Cabbage" here is a humorous substitution.

79. *Crab-lanthorn.* A lantern burning oil from the carap or crab-nut.

80. *Croudledum.* Cranium.

84. *Ring noon about thy pate.* Vigorous blows on the head. "To ring noon" derives from the cook's signal that dinner is ready.

86. *Larrum.* Old Mother Redstreak is compared to a rusty alarm clock.

102. *fucust.* Beautified with cosmetics. *blanch'd.* Whitened with powder.

104. *Tod of Wool.* A twenty-eight pound weight of wool. *Patches.* Small pieces of black silk or court plaster (i.e., silk coated with plaster) used on women's faces to hide blemishes or as decorations.

115–16. *Fiddle me asleep.* There is a sexual pun.

124. *I'le draw thy Colts Tooth.* Possibly "I'll dismember you."

130. *Mumpsimus.* Old fogey.

137. *Beezom-Beard.* Broom beard.

142. *'Pranter.* Ranter?
163. *zately.* Surely?
165. *woundy.* Extremely.
167. *Odzvish.* God's fish.
168. *muxon.* Ordure (mixen)?
174. *Wilta lye.* "Will you lie."
176. *leather'd.* Thrashed.
179. *Scab.* Scoundrel.
184. *kirsen.* Christian.
190. *gogs nouns.* God's wounds.
194. *Dog-bolt.* A contemptible fellow. *Limber-twist.* One who is pliable. *Dundernose.* Blockhead.
198–99. *stand to our Pan-puddings.* Hold our ground.
204. *Tucks.* Swords.

Act IV, scene i.

SD 1. Cf. *Psyche* (III, p. 312):

> The Scene changes to the principal Street of the City, with
> vast numbers of People looking down from the tops of
> Houses, and out of the Windows and Balconies, which are
> hung with Tapestry. In this Street is a large Triumphal
> Arch with Columns of the Dorick Order, adorned with the
> Statutes of Fame and Honour, &c. Beautified with Festoons
> of Flowers; all the Inrichments of Gold. Through this
> Arch, at a vast distance, in the middle of a Piazza, is
> seen a stately Obelisk.

1–11. Cf. *Psyche* (III, p. 312):

> 1 *Man.* What shouts are those that echo from the Plain?
> 2 *Man.* The Stranger-Princes have the Monster slain:
> The People the victorious Champions meet,
> And them with Shouts and Acclamations greet.
> 1 *Man.* Our freedom these brave Conqu'rors have restor'd,
> The bloud of Men no more shall be devour'd;
> No more young Ladies shall be snatch'd away
>   To be the cruel Serpents prey.

9. *ten's.* Teens.
16–21. Duffett is alluding to the elaborate stage scenery of the Dorset Garden production of *Psyche*. Also, cf. these lines from *Psyche* (III, p. 313):

> 2 *Man.* For this the large Triumphal Arch was built,
> For this the Joyful People meet in throngs,
> The Princes Triumph for the bloud they spilt,
> And celebrate the Conquest with loud Songs.

They in this place a Sacrifice prepare,
To pay their vows and thanks to th' God of War.

20. *The way was chalk'd out by some Poet.* Duffett seemed unable to forget Shadwell's remark in the Preface to *Psyche* (p. 280): "I chalk'd out the way to the Composer."
SD 26. Cf. *Psyche* (III, p. 313):

> Enter the Priests of *Mars*, one carrying the Serpents Head
> upon the Spear, all of them having Targets, Breast-
> plates, and Helmets of Brass. Then the Praesul, having
> a Trophy of Arms carry'd before him. Then *Nicander*,
> *Polynices*, *Cidippe*, *Aglaura*, Train and Guards. The
> Priests sing this following Song, and dance to't.

26–52 SD. Cf. *Psyche* (III, pp. 313–14):

> > *Let us loudly rejoyce,*
> > > *With glad heart and with voice;*
> > *For the Monster is dead,*
> > *And here is his head.*
> > *No more shall our Wives*
> > *Be afraid of their Lives,*
> > *Nor our Daughters by Serpents miscarry.*
> > *The Oracle then*
> > *Shall bestow them on Men,*
> > *And they not with Monsters shall marry.*
> > *Let us lowdly rejoyce*
> > *With glad heart and with voice;*
> > *For the Monster is dead,*
> > *And here is his head.*
> Praesul sings. *Great God of War to thee*
> > *We offer up our thanks and pray'r*
> > *For by thy mighty Deity*
> > *Triumphing Conquerours we are.*
> Chorus.   *Thou'rt great among this heavenly race,*
> > *And onely to the Thunderer giv'st place.*
> Praesul.   *Jove is thy father, but does not exceed*
> > *Thy Deity on any score.*
> > *Thou, when thou wilt, canst make the whole world bleed,*
> > *And thou canst heal their breaches by thy power.*
> Chorus. *'Tis thou that must to Armies give success,*
> > *That thou must Kingdoms too with safety bless,*
> > *Thou that must bring, and then must guard their peace.*
> They dance, striking their Swords upon the Targets, showing
> the postures of their Swords Kettle-Drums beating, and
> Trumpets sounding: Whilst the Praesul and the rest pre-
> pare the Altar, and kindle the Fire.

46–52. Princes Nick and Phil apparently discovered Mother Redstreak "at play"

with Wishing Chair and Jeffry, and, mistaking her for the White Bear of Norwich, decapitated her.

56. *Jack o'lent.* An insignificant or contemptible person; a figure of a man set
up to be pelted, especially as practised during Lent.

61–97 SD. The parody of the parallel passage in Shadwell is quite close in these
lines. Cf. *Psyche* (III, p. 314):

Praesul sings.	*While we to Mars his praises sing,*
	A Horse, th' appointed Victim, bring.
	[*Mars* and *Venus* meet in the Air in
	their Chariots, his drawn by
	Horses, and hers by Doves.]
Venus sings.	*Great God of War, if thou dost not despise*
	The power of my victorious eyes,
	Reject this Sacrifice.
	My Deity they disrespect,
	My Altars they neglect,
	And Psyche *onely they adore,*
	Whom they shall see no more.
	Have I yet left such influence on your heart,
	As to enjoyn you wou'd take my part.
	By some known token punish their offence,
	And let them know their insolence.
Mars.	*So much your influence on me remains,*
	That still I glory in my chains,
	What ever you command, shall be
	A sov'reign Law to me.
	These saucy Mortals soon shall see
	What 'tis to disrespect your Deity.
	To show how much for you I them despise,
	Since they with Venus *dare contend,*
	Ye powers of Hell your Furies send,
	And interrupt their Sacrifice.
	[*Mars* and *Venus* fly away.]

Furies descend and strike the Altar, and break it, and
every one flies away with a fire-brand in's hand.

66. *Croan.* Crone.

72. *Springal.* Youthful, young.

75. *prise.* Prize, value.

76. *Amber.* Tears?

87. *Posset.* Hot milk curdled with ale.

91. *Painted bauble.* A court jester's baton.

93. *make a Carr on't.* Possibly, an allusion to the prisoners' "cart."

95. *curried.* Beaten.

Act IV, scene ii.

1–7. Cf. *Psyche* (III, pp. 314–15):

Psyche Debauch'd

1 *Priest.*	What dreadful prodigies are these!
	Hence from this bloudy rage let's flie,
	And in his Temple let us try
If we his angry Godhead can appease.	
Nicander.	What Magick Charms do this sad place infest,
And us in all our actions thus molest?	
Polynices.	The pow'r of Hell it sure must be
	That thus against us wages war;
	For when fair *Psyche* we wou'd free,
It still does mischiefs against us prepare.	
But no Enchantment yet our courage binds,	
No accidents can alter valiant minds.	

4. *Painted Rod.* This refers, apparently, to the chief priest's wand.

9. *dry White Cheese.* Prostitutes.

10. *tickle crack Cheese.* More prostitutes.

11–12. *a Knight of Wales Enchanted Seven years.* Possibly, an absurd variation of the legend of St. David of Wales having slept seven years in the enchanted garden of Ormandine (and being redeemed by St. George).

18–19. Cf. *Psyche* (III, p. 315): "*Nicander.* In spight of Hell we will go on in quest / Of our lov'd *Psyche,* who is charm'd from hence."

18. *Ventures.* Dangers.

19. *Tenters.* Distress. The expression "being on tenter-hooks" is alluded to.

20–65. This sequence parallels a passage in *Psyche* (III, p. 315), but the resemblance is general rather than specific.

23. *Pin box.* Shorty, shrimp.

24. *Maukin.* A woman of the lower classes.

31. *Gull.* Mouth, orifice.

32. *Lanthorns clipped eyes.* Narrowed eyes, as though enclosed in a lantern.

36. *Princox.* A saucy or conceited young fellow.

39. *catch a Hare with a Tabar.* Proverbial for "perversely ineffectual."

47–50. Cf. *Psyche* (III, p. 315):

> *Aglaura.* Envy it self will sure confess,
> Our Beauties and our Vertues are not less,
> Then the mean Idol's you so much adore,
> And whom ye never can see more;
> The monster you have slain did her devour.
> *Polynices.* We by his rav'nous Maw did find to day,
> The Monster had not yet made her his prey.

55. *a George.* A half crown (bearing the image of St. George).

57. *Pugg.* Harlot.

59. *Green-sickness.* An anaemic disease affecting young women at puberty.

73–77. Cf. *Psyche* (III, pp. 315–16):

> *Aglaura.* I have a trusty Villain which I'll send,
> Who in disguise shall their unwary steps attend;

And then an Ambush shall for them be laid,
That their base Lives may be to us betray'd.
   Cidippe. The Pow'rs of all this Kingdom we'll engage,
To sacrifice their Lives to our insatiate Rage.
   Aglaura. They dearly shall by their Example show,
How soon rejected Love to dangerous Rage can grow.

76. *durance.* Imprisonment.
78–101. This sequence has no parallel in *Psyche.*
82. *stroll.* Solicit as a prostitute.
100. *Toby.* Buttocks.

Act IV, scene iii.

The quarto does not give this sequence a scene designation.
SD 1. Cf. *Psyche* (IV, p. 316):

> The SCENE *is a stately Garden, belonging to the Mag-*
> *nificent Palace seen in the former Act. The great*
> *Walk is bounded on either side with great Statues*
> *of Gold standing upon Pedestals, with small Fig-*
> *ures of Gold sitting at their Feet: And in Large*
> *Vases of Silver are Orange, Lemon, Citron, Pome-*
> *granate; and behind Myrtle, Jassamine, and other*
> *Trees. Beyond this a noble Arbour, through which*
> *is seen a less Walk, all of Cypress-Trees, which leads*
> *to another Arbour at a great Distance.*

1–3. Cf. *Psyche* (IV, p. 316):

> *Aglaura.* Enough the Splendor of your Court we've seen;
> Such ne'er was known by any earthly Queen.
>   *Cidippe.* But we your conqu'ring Lover wou'd behold,
> Of whom such charming Stories you have told.

4–6. The parallel passage in *Psyche* (IV, p. 316) runs to eighteen lines, involving an ecstatic description by Psyche of what it is like to love, and to be
loved by, Cupid.
9–10. Cf. *Psyche* (IV, p. 317): "*Aglaura.* What cursed Fate is this, that did
ordain, / That she shou'd have such pleasure, we such pain?"
11–12. Cf. *Psyche* (IV, p. 317):

> *Cidippe.* Base Fortune! that on *Psyche* wou'd bestow
>   So vast a share of happiness,
> And give her elder Sisters so much less,
> That she shou'd be so high, and we so low.

11. *Image on house-top.* Decorative statue or weather-vane?

13–31. Cf. *Psyche* (IV, p. 317):

> *Aglaura.* Such glory yet no Monarch ever saw;
> Such humble Vassals, such obedient awe,
> Such shining Palaces yet ne'r have been
> Such pomp the Sun in all his progress ne'r has seen.
>   *Cidippe.* A thousand Beauties wait for her command
> As many heavenly Youths are still at hand:
>   And to our envious eyes she chose
>   These hated objects to expose.
> *Aglaura.* When we to our great joy believ'd,
>   That she destroy'd had been,
> Oh how the Ridling God has us deceiv'd;
> We see her here like some immortal Queen,
> Whom all her subjects serve not, but adore.
>   *Cidippe.* Oh! I shall die with envy: say no more,
> But of some quick revenge let's meditate,
>   To interrupt their happy state:
>   Let's by some Art cause fatal Jealousies
>   Between these prosperous Lovers to arise.

14. *scull.* White as a skull?

17. *Whiting.* A preparation of finely powdered chalk, used for whitewashing and cleaning plate.

20. *dresser thump'd like Tattoo.* "Tattoo" is a signal made by beating on a drum or by a bugle call. The context suggests it is a call to dinner.

21. *Strong bub.* Beer.

22. *given Crow a pudding.* Died.

24. *gooding.* Begging.

26. *flim flam.* Nonsense, humbug.

29. *Club our Sculs.* Rack our brains.

SD 32–41. Cf. *Psyche* (IV, p. 317):

> *Enter* Cupid and Psyche, *with many Attendants.*
> *Aglaura.* They're here: What divine Object strikes my eyes?
> *Cidippe.* What heavenly thing does my weak heart surprise?
> *Aglaura.* Her hated sight I can no longer bear.
> *Cidippe.* Oh with what Joy I could her heart-strings tear!
> *Aglaura.* This is the goodliest Creature Heav'n e're made;
> And I will summon Hell up to my aid.
>   But I will Psyche's life destroy;
> And I will then this God-like Youth enjoy.
>   *Cidippe.* When I am dead, he may be had by thee:
> But know, *Aglaura,* I'll ne'r live to see
> This goodly thing enjoy'd by any one but me.

33. *Mauks.* "Maukin," i.e., a drudge.

38. *love-Pouder.* An aphrodisiac.

39. *Crack.* Prostitute.

41. *speak to him Servant Jack.* To speak condescendingly.

42. *Trantum.* Trickster.

43. *Rantum.* Rantum-scantum, disorderly; also, slang for copulation.

44. *ifacks.* In faith.

45-51. Cf. *Psyche* (IV, pp. 317-18):

> *Cupid.* Ladies—
> You such a welcome in this place shall find,
> As fits the greatness of your Sisters mind;
> And by your entertainment I will show,
>   What I to my lov'd *Psyche* owe:
>   For her shall Quires of *Cupids* sing,
> For her the Sphears shall their loud Musick bring.

52. *larasco.* There is a character named Larasco in Duffett's *The Spanish Rogue.*

54. *surgito, surgitote.* Arise, arise!

56-57. *Peter Whiffle.* Whiffle is something light or insignificant.

57. *Puddle dock.* Originally, a watering place for horses on the Thames at Blackfriars. Cf. Lucia in Shadwell's *Epsom Wells* (II.i): "I had rather be Countess of Puddledock, than Queen of Sussex."

58. *Landabridas.* Lindabrides is the heroine of the romance, *The Mirror of Knighthood,* but the name became a common name for a loose woman.

62. *Lamberdas.* Apparently, a humorous misspelling of *Landabridas* (see preceding note).

63. *Polynicky, Nicampoops.* Polynices and Nicander are the two devoted lovers of Psyche in Shadwell's play.

64. *div'd through Apivel to Hell.* At the end of Act IV of Shadwell's *Psyche,* the princes *"Arm in Arm fling themselves into the River,"* their wet suicide inspired by Psyche's being dragged below by Furies. Their ghosts appear in Act V, which is set in Hell. *Apivel.* A nonce term?

65. *Piss-kitchen.* A kitchen-maid.

69-71. *Rablays . . . meetre.* The allusion is comically apocryphal. Cf. Emilia to poet Ninny in Shadwell's *The Sullen Lovers* (III): "I had rather read the History of *Tom Thumb* than the rest of your Poems."

74. *Woudha. Woudha.* The quarto's spelling here can be taken as an abbreviation, or as a shortened "nickname."

79. *Green Sickness.* An anaemic disease affecting young women at puberty.

85 SD. *Sings like a Walloon.* A Walloon is a speaker of a French dialect in southeast Belgium. To sing like a Walloon might mean either to sing unintelligibly, or to sing like a psalm-singing weaver. Many of the Flemish immigrants in places like Norwich were Protestant textile workers.

86-90. Cf. *Psyche* (IV, p. 318):

> Now see what is to *Psyche*'s beauty due,
> And what th' Almighty pow'r of Love can show:
> These senseless Figures motion shall receive;
> *Psyche*'s bright beams can life to Statues give.

Psyche Debauch'd

[*Ten Statues leap from their Pedestals, and dance.*
Ten Cupids *rise from the Pedestals, strew all the*
Stage with Flowers, and fly all several ways.
During the Dance, Cupid *and* Psyche *retire.*

91–107. Cf. *Psyche* (IV, p. 318):

> *Let old Age in its envy and malice take pleasure,*
> *In business that's sower, and in hoarding up treasure:*
> *By dullness seem wise, be still peevish and nice;*
> *And what they cannot follow, let them rail at as vice.*
>
> *Wise Youth will in Wine and in Beauty delight,*
> *Will revel all day, and will sport all the night.*
> *For never to love, wou'd be never to live,*
> *And Love must from Wine its new vigour receive.*
>
> *How insipid were life without those delights,*
> *In which lusty hot Youth spend their dayes and their nights;*
> *Of our nauseous dull beings we too soon should be cloy'd,*
> *Without those bless'd joys which Fools onely avoid.*
>
> *Unhappy grave Wretches who live by false measure,*
> *And for empty vain shadows refuse real pleasure;*
> *To such Fools while vast joys on the witty are waiting,*
> *Life's a tedious long journey without ever baiting.*

91. *Taffy.* A Welshman.

92. *Teag.* An Irishman.

93. *Jocky.* A Scotchman.

99. *beesom Beards.* Broom beards.

101. *Widgeons.* Simpletons.

109. Cf. *Psyche* (IV, p. 319): "Psyche. Now Sisters! how do you approve my Dear?" *with my back upwards.* Aroused; the metaphoric allusion is to a cat arching its back when agitated.

111–12. Cf. *Psyche* (IV, p. 319): "Cidippe. Why does he still conceal his name? / It argues little love, or else much shame."

114. *juggling Jack-pudding.* Mountebank, confidence-man. *Tumbler.* One who allures or inveigles persons into the hands of swindlers.

115–18. Cf. *Psyche* (IV, pp. 319–20):

> *Aglaura.* This violent Love may soon decay,
> And he for some new Mistress may
> Your easie heart betray.
> *Cidippe.* When he shall please to frown,
> You from this heighth are suddenly thrown down:
> And when he thus shall have abandon'd you,
> On whom will you inflict the vengeance due?

Psyche Debauch'd

119–21. This seems to be compressed from *Psyche* (IV, p. 319):

> I have my Love, and that's enough for me.
> My life is one continued Extasie.
>> His love to me is infinite,
>> Each moment does transcend
> Ages of common gross delight,
> For which dull sensual Men so much contend.

120. *Cracks.* Prostitutes.

124–26. Cf. *Psyche* (IV, p. 320):

> *Psyche.* How I'm amazed! Oh my poor trembling heart!
>> *Enter* Zephyrus.
> *Zephyrus.* My Lord commands your Sisters must depart,
> And none must his commands deny.

130. *Odznigs.* God's nigs; Nigs are coin clippings. *groats.* Silver fourpences.

131. *Traps.* Trapes, a slattern or prostitute.

132. *pay sauce.* Pay dearly.

141. *Limbo.* Prison.

143. *we that have sent Princes thither.* Sweetlips and Woudhamore have informed the police that Princes Nick and Phil have cut off Redstreak's head (cf. IV.ii.75–77; 93–94; 99); the Princes have now apparently been taken.

147–48. There is more melodrama in the exit the Princesses make in *Psyche* (IV, p. 320): "*Both offer to stab at Psyche, as she looks another way, and are snatch'd away by Zephyri.*" *Phalaris.* The story goes that Phalaris the Tyrant ordered a brazen bull made for the execution of criminals. Phalaris had the inventor who created the bull baked to death in it as its first victim. Sweetlips claims Phalaris was baked! *Will. Harris.* The actor who played the part of Bruine. He played the part of Morena in Duffett's *The Empress of Morocco.*

160–65. Cf. *Psyche* (IV, p. 321):

> What is't disturbs my *Psyche's* mind?
> What fatal change is this I find?
> Such a black storm me-thinks hangs on thee now,
> As I have seen upon the Mornings brow;
> Which blushing first had promis'd a fair day,
> But strait did nought but dark-swol'n Clouds display.

161. *black pouts.* Mournful looks?

162. *clouts.* Rags.

166. *black dog'd.* Ill-humored.

167. *morning.* Mourning.

169–74. Bruine's impassioned plea here is based on two of Cupid's speeches. Cf. *Psyche* (IV, p. 321):

Psyche Debauch'd

Cupid.   I love thee too at such a rate,
No Mortal can approach my height.
What is it can produce thy grief?

and:

By thy victorious eyes,
Which govern now the heart they did surprise;
By th' Gods inviolable Oath I swear,
By Styx, all thy commands shall be to me
Sacred, as Heav'ns decree.

172. *Pydy.* Sweetie-pie.

175–77. Cf. *Psyche* (IV, pp. 321–22):

By this all fear of coldness you remove,
And then you'll tell me now, who 'tis I love.
Cupid. Heav'n!

180–81. Cf. *Psyche* (IV, p. 322):

Cupid. Must I my fatal secret then resign?
Psyche. Can you keep your heart, and yet take mine?

188. *black Soap of Oaths.* Strong oaths.

192. *wall-ey'd.* Dim-sighted.

199. *Odslifelykins.* God's little life.

208–15 SD. Cf. *Psyche* (IV, pp. 322–23):

Cupid. Know then, my self a God I must declare,
Whom all the other Deities obey:
    All things on Earth, Hell, Water, Air,
Must to my God-head their Devotion pay.
I am the God of Love, whom, to thy Cost,
Thy foolish Curiosity has lost.
By this thou dost my Love to Anger turn,
And must in fatal Desolation mourn.
    I from thy once lov'd Eyes must fly;
For 'tis ordained by cruel Destiny,
Which rules o'er all the Gods and me,
That for thy Folly I shou'd thus abandon thee.

Cupid *flies away. The Garden and Palace vanish, and* Psyche
*is left alone in a vast Desart, upon the brink of a
River in a Marsh full of Willows, Flags, Bulrushes, and
Water-flowers; beyond which is seen a great open Desart.*

208. *Deval.* Claude DuVal, a highwayman, executed at Tyburn in 1667.

219. *Crack.* Prostitute. *the Flower Pot.* An inn in Bishopsgate.

221. *the Pagean.* Apparently, an inn or tavern.

232–33. *clap a strong House upon her back.* Get her into trouble.

239–42. Cf. *Psyche* (IV, p. 323):

> *Psyche.* Oh! whither art thou fled, my Dear?
> Why hast thou left me here?
> Of all my glorious Pomp I am bereft,
> And in Despair am in a Desart left.
> Oh my Misfortune! Oh my Crime!

242. *shark away.* Steal away.

243–78. Cf. *Psyche* (IV, pp. 324–25):

> *Psyche.* No longer these Misfortunes I'll endure;
> Of all such Wounds Death is the sovereign Cure.
> In this deep Stream, that softly by does glide,
> All my Misfortunes and my Faults I'll hide.
>   [*She offers to throw her self into the River. The
>   God of the River arises upon a Seat of Bul-
>   rushes and Reeds, leaning upon an Urn. The
>   Naiades round about him.*

The God sings.	*Stay, stay; this Act will much defile my Streams:*
	With a short Patience suffer these Extreams.
	Heav'n has for thee a milder Fate in Store;
	The Time shall be when thou shalt weep no more.
	And yet fair Psyche *ne'er shall die.*
1 Nymph.	*She ne'er shall die.*
2 Nymph.	*She ne'er shall die.*
Chorus.	*She ne'er shall die;*
	But shall be crown'd with Immortality.
	But shall be, &c.

>   The Gods sing again.
> Venus *approaches; from her Anger flie;*
> *More Troubles yet your Constancy must try:*
> *But th' happy Minute will e'er long arrive,*
> *That will to you eternal Freedom give;*
> *And yet fair* Psyche *ne'er shall die.*

1 Nymph.	*She ne'er shall die.*
2 Nymph.	*She ne'er shall die.*
Chorus.	*She ne'er shall die.*
	But shall be crown'd with Immortality.
	But shall be, &c.

> *Psyche.* I need not fly, I have done no Offence;
> I'm strongly guarded by my Innocence.
>   [Venus *descends in her Chariot.*
> *Venus.* Dares Psyche before me appear?
>   From my dread Wrath you scorn to flie:
>   'Tis Impudence, not Constancy.
> I'll bend your stubborn Heart, and make you fear.
>   *Psyche.* Dread Goddess! How have I
> Provok'd so your unwonted Cruelty?

Venus. You did usurp my Honours; Men to you
Did give that Worship, which to me was due:
For you they did my Deity despise,
And wou'd have rais'd up Altars to your Eyes.
    Psyche. Is Beauty then (Heav'n's Gift) a Fault in me?
It is a Fault I cannot help, you see.

246 SD. The appearance of the ghosts, according to Clinton-Baddeley, "marks the first important appearance of that famous burlesque character" in English burlesque drama (*The Burlesque Tradition in the English Theatre After 1660*, p. 42).

267. *Cursy.* Curtsy.

269. *dread Witch should seeking Ruin.* The sense seems to be: "that such a dread witch as you should seek my ruin."

277. *Rantidla.* Toy?

279–83. Cf. *Psyche* (IV, p. 325):

Venus.   Dare you with me expostulate?
I'll make you feel the worst Effects of Hate:
    My Pow'r you fatally shall know,
And for your Insolence to Hell shall go.
                         [Venus *flies away.*]

280. *loudy.* Noise.

282. *Volens, Nolens.* Willing or unwilling.

SD 284. *Whistles.* Men with whistles?

Act V.

SD 1. Cf. *Psyche* (V, p. 327):

> The SCENE represents Hell, consisting of many burning
> Ruins of Buildings on each Side: In the foremost
> Pieces are the Figures of *Prometheus* and *Sisyphus,*
> *Ixion* and *Tantalus.* Beyond those are a great Number
> of Furies and Devils, tormenting the Damned. In the
> Middle arises the Throne of *Pluto,* consisting of
> Pillars of Fire; with him *Proserpina;* at their feet
> sit *Minos, AEacus,* and *Rhadamanthus.* With the Throne
> of *Pluto* arise a great Number of Devils and Furies,
> coming up at every Rising about the House. Through
> the Pillars of *Pluto*'s Throne, at a great Distance,
> is seen the Gate of Hell, through which a Lake of
> Fire is seen; and at a huge Distance, on the farther
> Side of that Lake are vast Crowds of the Dead, waiting
> for *Charon*'s Boat.

1. *Garnish.* Money extorted from a new prisoner.

12. *Provaunt.* Allowance of food.

12–13. *erect our mock-Court of Justice.* There is a sequence involving a mock-court of justice in Duffett's *The Mock-Tempest* (III.i.141–291).

19–40 SD. Cf. *Psyche* (V, p. 327):

> *To what great Distresses proud* Psyche *is brought!*
> *O the brave Mischiefs our Malice has wrought!*
> *Such Actions become the black Subjects of Hell:*
> *Our great Prince of Darkness who'er will serve well,*
> Chorus. { *Must to all Mortals, nay, Gods, shew their Spight,*
> { *And in Horror and Torments of others delight.*
> *How cool are our Flames, and how light are our Chains,*
> *If our Craft or our Cruelty Souls enow gains!*
> *In perpetual Howlings and Groans we take Pleasure;*
> *Our Joys by the Torments of others we measure.*
> Chorus. *To rob Heav'n of the Fair is our greatest Delight,*
> *To Darkness seducing the Subjects of Light.*
> *How little did Heav'n of its Empire take care,*
> *To let* Pluto *take the Rich, Witty, and Fair:*
> *While it does for it self Fools and Monsters preserve,*
> *The Blind, Ugly and Poor, and the Cripple reserve!*
> Chorus. *Heav'n all the worst Subjects for it self does prepare,*
> *And leaves all the best for the Prince of the Air.*
> [A Dance of Furies.]

20. *Pad.* Robbery on the highway.

44. *a new shrouded Tree.* A tree lopped of its branches.

49–50. Prince Nick is suggesting that he and Prince Phillip marry "princesses" Sweetlips and Woudhamore as an alternative to conviction by the court. The girls would no doubt change their testimony if the boys would agree to marry them.

51. *'Tority.* Authority.

53. *go to Heaven in a string.* To be hanged.

67. *Dander Nos'd.* "Lame-brained."

70–71. Cf. *Psyche* (IV, p. 323) where the news of Theander's death is reported by a soldier:

> *Soldier. We of your Royal Father are bereft,*
> *Who you the Heirs of this great Kingdom left;*
> *So much he for the Loss of* Psyche *griev'd,*
> *That he by Death his fatal Grief reliev'd.*

83–221. This mock-trial sequence has no parallel in *Psyche.*

93. *Sir John Broads Exchange.* Possibly, a nonce-location.

94–95. *as sour as small Beer after Thunder.* Small beer is weak beer. There was a belief that beer changed to vinegar by the action of the thunder.

98. *making Composition.* Making payment.

104. *Tatter'd-ho: unhandsome, unwholesome.* This sounds like it might have been intended as an interruption by Tatter'd-ho in which he starts to parrot the words of Brazen-nose. The quarto version is here reproduced.

Psyche Debauch'd

142–46. Cf. the nursery rhyme, "This is the house that Jack built."

149. *dirty Puddings.* Guts or entrails cast off in a slaughtering.

165–66. *Bears-head . . . Barber's bason.* In *Don Quixote* the barber is caught in a shower and claps his brazen bason on his head. Don Quixote insists that this is the enchanted helmet of the moorish king, Mambrino, which was pure gold and which rendered its wearer invulnerable. Mambrino appears in Ariosto's *Orlando Furioso.*

183. *maukish.* Having a nauseated taste.

189. *Collar-Beef.* Rolled beef.

211. *her Predecessor Psyche the first.* Shadwell's *Psyche.*

220. *Cieve.* Sieve. In *Psyche* (V) the sisters must sift water eternally.

222–29. Cf. *Psyche* (V, p. 328):

> *Psyche.* Does my too criminal Love deserve this Pain?
> Circled with Horror must I here remain?
> Through thousand Terrors I have been convey'd,
> With dismal Yellings, Shrieks and Groans dismay'd:
> O'er troubled Billows of eternal Fire,
> Where tortur'd Ghosts must howl, and ne'er expire:
> Where Souls ne'er rest, but feel fresh Torments still,
> Where furious Fiends their utmost Rage fulfill,
> Tossing poor howling Wretches to and fro,
> From raging Fires into eternal Snow.

The stage direction that Duffett puts at the beginning of None-so-fair's sad lament suggests that she is alone on the stage (*"Exeunt all but* None-so-fair"), but after line 240 we read "One gives her a Bottle of Brandy." Apparently, the first stage-direction refers to the mock-Court, which retires; the prisoners, very likely, remain.

226. *With Hempen cord, have great Toe cramp'd.* Possibly, an allusion to prison sandals.

230–31. Cf. *Psyche* (V, p. 328): "Oh cruel *Venus!* Wilt thou ne'er relent? / Canst thou of Love such an Example make?"

232–33. Cf. *Psyche* (V, p. 328): "I could endure the Horrors of this Place, / Could I again behold his much lov'd Face."

234–40. Cf. *Psyche* (V, p. 329), where the parallel sequence is sung by Pluto:

> *Pluto*   *Refrain your Tears; you shall no Prisoner be;*
> *sings.*   *Beauty and Innocence in Hell are free:*
>   *They're Treasons, Murders, Rapes and Thefts, that*
>   *bring*
>   *Subjects to th' infernal King.*
>   *You are no Subject of this Place:*
>   *A God you must embrace.*
>   *From Hell to Heav'n you must translated be,*
>   *Where you shall live and love to all Eternity.*

SD 241. *One gives her a Bottle of Brandy.* In *Psyche* (V) Pluto and Proserpina give Psyche a *"Treasury divine"* which will win for her the good graces of Venus. Also cf. following note.

241–65. Cf. *Psyche* (V, p. 329):

> Proserpine. Psyche, *draw near: with thee this present take,*
> *Which, giv'n to* Venus, *soon thy Peace will make:*
> *Of Beauty 'tis a Treasury divine,*
> *And you're the Messenger she did design:*
> *Lost Beauty this will soon restore,*
> *And all Defects repair.*
> *Mortals will now afresh her Beams adore,*
> *And ease her Mind of Jealousie and Care.*
> *No Beauty that has this can e'er despair.*
> Pluto. *Here are your Sisters, who your Life once sought:*
> *Their Malice to this Place has* Psyche *brought,*
> *And against her all these dire Mischiefs wrought.*
> *For ever here they shall remain,*
> *And shall in Hell suffer eternal Pain:*
> *But* Psyche *shall a Deity embrace.*
> Proserpine.   *Be gone, fair* Psyche!
> Pluto.   *Be gone, fair* Psyche!
> Both.   *Be gone, fair* Psyche, *from this place!*
> Chorus }   *For* Psyche *must the God of Love embrace.*
> of all. {   *For* Psyche *must the God of Love embrace.*

241. *Nantz.* Brandy from Nantes.

243. *Naunts.* Aunts.

244. *Codling.* Roasted apple.

252. *Pit-hole.* Grave.

266–77. Cf. *Psyche* (V, p. 330):

> *Psyche.* In vain, poor Sisters, I deplore your Fate,
> Though living you pursu'd me with your Hate:
> 'Tis a dark Cloud upon my Happiness;
> But I'll strive to forget what's past redress.
> Were't not for this, my Joys I could not bear:
> Immoderate Joy would overthrow,
> Were it not ballasted with Care.
> My Love! I shall enjoy thee now,
> Together we shall happy be,
> And live and love to all Eternity!
> *Enter the Ghosts of* Polynices *and* Nicander
>   [Psyche *starts.*]
> This was a dismal Tragedy!
> These are the Prince's Ghosts we see.
> Oh! what sad Chance has brought you down to me?

280. Cf. *Psyche* (V, p. 330): "*Psyche.* Poor Ghosts! Why would you suffer for my Sake?"

Psyche Debauch'd

280–90. Cf. *Psyche* (V, p. 331):

> *Psyche.* Stay, Princes! and declare where, and what 'tis,
>   This everlasting Place of Bliss?
> *Nicander.* In cool sweet Shades, and in immortal Groves,
> By Chrystal Rivulets, and eternal Springs;
> Where the most beauteous Queens and greatest Kings
> Do celebrate their everlasting Loves.

290. *Hey-gammer-Cook.* Coitus.

301–12. The parallel sequence is the concluding song in *Psyche* (V, p. 338):

> *Bacchus. The Delights of the Bottle, and the Charms of good*
>   *Wine*
>   *To the Pow'r and the Pleasures of Love must resign:*
>   *Though the Night in the Joys of good Drinking be past,*
>   *The Debauches but till the next Morning will last.*
> Chorus to Hautboys and Rustick Musick of *Maenades* and
>   *AEgipanes.*
>   *But Love's great Debauch is more lasting and strong;*
>   *For that often lasts a Man all his Life long.*
>   [A Returnello again.]
> *Bacchus. Love and Wine are the Bonds, which fasten us all,*
>   *The World but for these to confusion would fall:*
>   *Were it not for the Pleasures of Love and good Wine,*
>   *Mankind for each Trifle their Lives would resign.*
> Chorus. *They'd not value dull Life, or would live without*
>   *thinking;*
>   *Nor would Kings rule the World but for Love and good*
>   *Drinking.*
>   [A Returnello again.]

313–18. The rhymes in these lines suggest they may have been intended as verse. Also, cf. the parallel passage in *Psyche* (V, p. 332):

> *Polynices.* For ever without you we must remain.
>   And now we must no longer stay,
>   Lest we contribute to your Pain,
> And your immortal Happiness delay.
> Farewell for ever, and remember me.
> *Nicander.* Farewell for ever, and remember me!
>   [*Exit* Nicander *and* Polynices.]
>   *Psyche.* Farewell! Such Friends and Rivals ne'er were found.
> How much am I by Love and Honour bound.   [*Exit* Psyche.]

318. It would seem that the princes exit at the end of this line.

319–28. Cf. *Psyche* (V, p. 332):

> *Psyche.* These Lovers must for ever in my Thoughts remain;
>   And would for ever give me Pain,
> Did not the Thoughts of him my Mind employ,

Psyche Debauch'd

Who'll banish all my Cares, and will compleat my Joy.
But ah! my Sufferings have transform'd me so,
　　My decay'd Face and languid Eyes,
　　My ruin'd Beauty he'll not know;
Or if he does, he will my Looks despise.
But I have here a sacred Treasury,
　　Which all my Ruins may repair;
Since it can make *Venus* her self more fair,
Is't an Offence if it be us'd by me?　　[*She opens the Box.*]
Oh! What dark Fumes oppress my clouded Brain!
I go, and never shall return again.
Farewell, my Love, for ever fare thee well.　　[*She swoons.*]

330. *lemine.* A mild oath.
333–45. Cf. *Psyche* (V, p. 333):

　　She's dead! she's dead! O whither art thou gone?
　　O Tyrant Death! what has thy bold Hand done?
　　O cruel Mother, whose insatiate Rage
　　Could thee against such Innocence engage!
　　Thou hast by this all Ties of Duty broke;
　　　　No longer I'll endure thy Yoke:
　　My filial Duty to Revenge shall turn,
　　You soon shall feel what to my Pow'r you owe;
　　With hopeless Love you shall for ever burn,
　　Your unregarded Pains no Ease shall know:
　　You still shall rage with Love, and to Despair shall bow.
　　　　Venus *descends in her Chariot.*
　　Venus. What Insolence is this I hear?
　　This from a Son I can no longer bear.

344. *Murrain.* Plague.
346–52. Cf. *Psyche* (V, p. 333):

　　For thee, dear *Psyche,* full Revenge I'll take,
　　And of my Mother first I'll the Example make.
　　What hellish Rage provok'd you to this Deed?
　　Whom Monsters would have spar'd, you have made bleed.
　　Venus. You suffer'd her my Glory t' invade;
　　And when I call'd *Apollo* to my Aid,
　　You did the fraudulent God suborn.

353–54. Cf. *Psyche* (V, p. 334):

　　Oh my lov'd *Psyche!* Oh my only Joy!
　　Oh give me her! my Duty I'll retain;
　　Your Son for ever shall your humblest Slave remain.

355–60. Cf. *Psyche* (V, p. 334):

　　Oh give me her, I'll all my Pow'r resign.
　　　　Here take my Quiver, take my Darts;

Psyche Debauch'd

> You, when you please, shall rule all Hearts:
> You shall the pow'r of Love to that of Beauty join.
> *Venus. Psyche* and you have so provok'd my Hate,
> Your Pray'rs as soon may alter Fate.

355. *Carriers.* Setters, or lookouts.

356. *Countrey Ware.* Girls from the country to be inveigled into prostitution.

361–64. Cf. *Psyche* (V, p. 334):

> Ah think what Pity to your Son is due!
> Think but what Wonders he has wrought for you!
> How many Hearts he has wounded for your sake!
> Remember this, and then some Pity take.

366–70. Cf. *Psyche* (V, p. 334):

> *Cupid.* Oh cruel Murdress! I will take her Part,
> And will revenge my self upon your Heart;
> Against your Breast I'll sharpen every Dart.
> You in Despair shall languish and decay;
> Those feeble Charms y' have left shall fly away:
> Languid shall be your Looks, and weak your Eyes,
> Your former Worshippers shall your faint Beams despise.
> No Lover more you e'er shall gain,
> I will be deaf, when ever you complain;
> Without Love's Pow'r, all Beauty is but vain.

371–80 SD. Cf. *Psyche* (V, p. 335):

> *Venus.* Farewell, you insolent and daring Boy:
> A living *Psyche* you shall ne'er enjoy.
>   [*She mounts her Chariot, and flies away.*]
>   *Cupid.* Oh cruel Mother! do not fly;
> Oh think how great must be that Misery
> Makes an Immortal Being wish to die!
> Spight of my self I must for ever live,
> And without her eternally must grieve:
> You I conjure by all the heav'nly Race,
> By all the Pleasure of each stol'n Embrace;
> By the most ravishing Moment of Delight
> You ever had, free from your Husband's Sight,
> By all the Joys of Day, and Raptures of the Night,
> Return, return.
>   [Venus *being almost lost in the Clouds,*
>   Cupid *flies up and gets into her*
>   *Chariot, and brings her back.*]

SD 381–423. Cf. *Psyche* (V, pp. 335–36):

> Jupiter *appears upon his Eagle.*
> *Cupid.* But lo! the mighty Thund'rer does appear,

Psyche Debauch'd

To him your Cruelty I will reveal:
To the great *Jupiter* I now appeal.
Soul of the World, I beg you'll do me right,
Against my savage Mother's Rage and Spight.
    Jupiter. Goddess of Beauty, you must gentle grow,
        And your severe Decree recall;
T'almighty Love the Universe must bow,
And without him must to confusion fall:
On Earth no Prince, in Heav'n no Deity,
        Is from his pow'rful Scepter free.
Do not the God of Union provoke,
Lest Heav'n and Earth feel his revenging Stroke.
Should he the utmost of his Rage employ,
He might the Frame o'th' Universe destroy.
    Venus. Should he a Mortal for his Wife embrace,
And by this hated Match blemish my heav'nly Race?
    Jupiter. Psyche to him shall equal be,
She is no Mortal, she shall never die;
For I will give her Immortality.
    Venus. This puts a happy end to all our Strife.
Psyche, arise; from seeming Death return,
And with my Son enjoy immortal Life,
Where you shall ever love, and never mourn.
                      [Psyche *revives*.]
    Psyche. Who is it calls me from Death's silent Night,
        And makes me thus revisit Light?
Oh Gods! Am I again blest with thy Sight!
    Cupid. For ever both your God-heads I'll adore,
Who did my *Psyche* to my Arms restore;
Nor Hell nor Heav'n shall make me quit thee more.
    Psyche. Do I again view thy Celestial Face!
    Cupid. Do I again my Dear, my Love embrace!
    Jupiter. Come, happy Lovers, you with me shall go,
Where you the utmost joys of Love shall know:
    Amongst the Gods I *Psyche* will translate,
And they shall these blest Nuptials celebrate:
        In Honour to them, I will summon all
        The Pow'rs of Heav'n to keep a Festival.

392. *go to Pot.* To go to the lowest "pit" of ruin.

394. *And make thy very house pull'd down.* Duffett's *The Mock-Tempest* opens with an elaborate sequence depicting the pulling down of a bawdy-house.

397. *trigger.* Boyfriend?

402. *wone.* Won.

420. *a mumming.* Performing dumb-shows; the sense here suggests "to go partying."

423 SD. Cf. *Psyche* (V, p. 336):

> *The* SCENE *changes to a Heaven. In the highest Part is*
> *the Palace of* Jupiter; *the Columns and the Ornaments*
> *of it of Gold. The lower Part is all fill'd with* Angels
> *and* Cupids, *with a round open Temple in the midst of*

Psyche Debauch'd

*it. This Temple is just before the Sun, whose Beams
break fiercely through it in divers Places. Below the
Heavens, several Semicircular Clouds, of the Breadth of
the whole House, descend. In these Clouds sit the
Musicians, richly Habited. On the front Cloud sits
Apollo alone. While the Musicians are descending, they
play a Symphony, till Apollo begins, and sings, as
follows.*

424–503. There is something here it would be pleasant to know more about.
The theme of this masque is exactly that of the one near the end of Act II in
Shadwell's *Timon of Athens* (DG January 1678). Although verbal similarities
are not close, and the identical theme could be coincidental, there are still three
possibilities: this masque in *Psyche Debauch'd* might have suggested Shadwell's
masque; Shadwell might have used his material earlier; Duffett might have
added this in 1678.

485–93. Cf. *Psyche* (V, p. 339):

> Apollo. *But to Love, to Love the great Union they owe;*
> *All in Earth and in Heav'n to his Scepter must bow.*
> A general Chorus of all the Voices and Instruments. The
> Dancers mingle with the Singers.
> *All Joy to this Celestial Pair,*
> *Who thus by Heav'n united are:*
> *'Tis a great Thing, worth Heav'ns Design,*
> *To make Love's Pow'r with Beauty's joyn.*

504–09. Cf. *Psyche* (V, p. 339):

> *Jupiter.* For ever happy in your *Psyche* be,
> Who now is crown'd with Immortality;
> On Earth Love never is from Troubles free,
> But here 'tis one eternal Extasie:
> 'Mongst all the Joys which Heav'n and Earth can find,
> Love's the most glorious object of the Mind.

Epilogue.

In *New Poems, Songs* (p. 96), Duffett has the following (rather short) alternate
epilogue to *Psyche Debauch'd:*

> Now to get off, gadzooks, what shall we do?
> 'Tis plain, my friends, that we have chous'd you too.
> Our *Psyche* that so pleasantly appears,
> Has prov'd as very a jilting Crack as theirs.
> When your high hopes for Beauty were prepar'd,
> To meet a common ill-drest thing 'tis hard;
> But pardon us and your resentments smother,
> We promise you e'r long a touch with t'other.

23. *Scut.* A short tail.
30. *paunch.* Puncture; punch.
35. *She-Weavers.* Independent prostitutes.

TEXTUAL NOTES

Location File of Extant Copies

Title page: PSYCHE DEBAUCH'D (*see facsimile*).

Signature collation: 4⁰: *A*², B–L⁴, M².

Copies are in the following libraries: British Museum (BM); Bodleian Library (O); Worcester College Library, Oxford (OW); Henry E. Huntington Library (CSmH); Beinecke Library, Yale University (CtY); Folger Library (DFo).

Substantive Variants (all are editorial changes)

II, i, 40 his brows] her brows
II, iii, 72 waste] was't
II, iii, 77 *Phil.* Odzboars, Prince *Nick!* Vast, here's the Anchovies.]
                      Phil. Odz-boars Prince *Nick,*
                      Ston. Vast, here's the Anchovies.
III, i, 63 Chair, told me] Chair told me,
IV, ii, 77SD *Enter* Jeffery.] in 4to included in line 79:
                      I'le warrant, I know by Enter *Jeffery* his leering eye.

Accidental Variants (most are editorial changes)

Prologue, 39 Musick, Scenes,] Musick Scenes
Prologue, 38–40, 41–43 Brackets not in BM.
I, i, 14 ye,] ye; [BM]
I, i, 106 *Glozy,* will] *Glozy* will
I, i, 113 well] we'll
I, i, 157 Banck. I'le] Banck I'le
I, i, 170 told,] told.
I, i, 178 hear?] hear, prepare [4to repeats "prepare" from line 180]
I, i, 189 None-so-fair, *King*] *Nonesofair King*
I, i, 220 yet.] yet?
I, i, 244 Princess, you] Princess. You

Psyche Debauch'd

I, i, 265SD *Schoolmistress;*] *Schoolmistress,*
        Ale Wife;] *Ale Wife,*
        Peace, *a*] Peace *a*
I, i, 288 Oh Lord!] Oh! Lord
I, i, 291 spend] spend,
I, i, 293 end] end.
I, i, 295 limbs more] limbs, more
I, i, 314 soak;] soak,
I, i, 315 smoak,] smoak;
I, i, 346 won't, goodly] won't goodly
I, i, 350 *Power,* Oh] *Power* Oh
I, i, 351 face; goody *Peace,*] face, goody Peace,
I, i, 352 case. Furies,] case, Furies
I, i, 353 *Nicky,* I] *Nicky* I
I, i, 353SD Niclas, *and*] Niclas and
I, i, 370 churn.] churn
I, i, 404 here, that] here that
I, i, 420 Princes, hold, for . . . Squablin] Princess, hold for . . . Sqaublin,
I, i, 424 *Phillip,* for] *Phillip* for
I, i, 439 her, i'faggs.] her i'faggs.
I, i, 443 us, Princes] us Princess
I, i, 476SD *Exit Phillip.*] *Exit. Phillip*
I, i, 489 nothing] nothing.
I, i, 493 doe.] doe.
I, i, 549 King and] King, and
I, i, 556 after's,] after's.
II, i, 3 touz'd, do'e] touz'd do'e
II, i, 4 must, I] must I
II, i, 20 know, that] know that
II, i, 25 know. Mother, your] know Mother your
II, i, 27 Order does] Order, does
II, i, 28 Woman] Women
II, i, 30 water, whose . . . disguis'd;] water:whose . . . disguis'd,
II, i, 39 *Bru.*] *Bou.*
II, i, 42 keeping;] keeping,
II, i, 51 nay, too] nay too
II, i, 55 Mountebank—for] Mountebank;—for
II, i, 56 one—suffers] one,—suffers
II, i, 64 chast; others] chast. Others
II, ii, SD1 Surplice, dancing,] Surplice dancing,
        King, leading] King leading
II, ii, 2 *Pray'r,*] *Pray'r.*
II, ii, 5 *desires*] *desires.*
II, ii, 11 *given*] *given.*

II, ii, 23 Latrona, *thou*] Latrona *thou*

II, ii, 27 Loe, here's] Loe here's

II, ii, 43 *Thief, go*] *Theif go*

II, ii, 45 Princess, *that*] Princess *that*

II, ii, 54 *Wat*] *Wat.*
        Mall] *Mall.*

II, ii, 58 *Bungy, William*] *Bungy. William*

II, ii, SD62 *then Sung and Danc'd to.*] *then Sung, and Danc'd to.*

II, ii, 84 *None-so-fair* has] *None-so-fair,* has

II, ii, 114 Sheep, must] Sheep must

II, ii, 117 King—be . . . cullied, King;] King be . . . cullied King;

II, ii, 145 Nature is] Nature; is

II, ii, 147 Anchovies, *Priest*] Anchovies; *Priest*

II, ii, 148 spoak. And . . . granted, the] spoak, and . . . granted; The

II, ii, 154 Avaunt, you] Avaunt you

II, ii, 158 Odzboars, dost] Odzboars dost

II, ii, 161 Pigs-nie, let's make hast;] Pigs-nie let's make hast,

II, ii, 162–63 breakfast./ As I'm a sinner, he] breakfast:/ As I'm a sinner. He

II, iii, 1 Dad! See how he blubbers;] Dad, see, how he blubbers,

II, iii, 15 serv'd now] serv'd, now

II, iii, 19 bear.] bear,

II, iii, 27 see, alass.] see alass.

II, iii, 32 flat, all,] flat all,

II, iii, 45 then an] then, an

II, iii, 47 me the] me, the

II, iii, 50 Courtier—do'e] Courtier, do'e
        no, he'll] no He'll

II, iii, 53–54 here, take] here take

II, iii, 55–56 zay—blacks mine eye—but] zay, blacks mine eye; but

II, iii, 57–58 thee,/ Princess, Chill] thee./ Princess Chill

II, iii, 58 stumps.] stumps,

II, iii, 66 *Bruin's*] *Bruc'us*

II, iii, 67 here let's] here, let's

II, iii, 70 *Bona Robas,*] *Bona Robas.*

III, i, 3 *Idle and*] *Idle, and*

III, i, 27 4. *Pav.* —Thanks,] 4. —Thanks

III, i, 35 chalk'd] chalk

III, i, 37 great, most] great most

III, i, 38 well, *Geffery,*] well *Geffery,*

III, i, 40 delicat'st but] delicat'st, but

III, i, 45 Mum and Brandy the] Mum, and Brandy; the

III, i, 46 Holy-dayes. But] Holy-dayes, But

III, i, 49 Women put] Women, put

III, i, 50 reputation. 'Tis] reputation, 'tis

III, i, 52 Truth, and] Truth; and
III, i, 55 praise they] praise, they
III, i, 56 in—Gad,] in.—Gad,
 Gentleman, the] Gentleman; the
III, i, 59 Gentleman then] Gentleman; then
III, i, 60 Huffing and] Huffing, and
 Nonsence·are] Nonsence, are
III, i, 63 me—] me,—
III, i, 66 cry'd—Oh] cry'd Oh
III, i, 76 cry'd—what's] cry'd what's
III, i, 83 Church, thou] Church; thou
III, i, 84 Love. —Her] Love —Her
III, i, 85 daz'ld. Her dying Eyes! think] daz'ld her dying Eyes, think
III, i, 100–01 ground, 'twill] ground: 'twill
III, ii, 1 Oh, what] Oh what
III, ii, 4 me; 'tis] me 'tis
III, ii, 5 tast of] tast, of
III, ii, 6 sight. Was] sight; was
III, ii, 7 *Opera* then] *Opera,* then
III, ii, 13 thee, little] thee little
 bred, and] bred; and
III, ii, 16 that—there's] that; there's
III, ii, 18 Bru. *Sweet, open*] *Sweet open*
III, ii, 101 Allonz, my Dear, I] Alonz my Dear I
III, ii, 103 naught but] naught, but
III, ii, 104 Laud, Sirs,] Laud Sirs,
III, ii, 105 well, y'are] well y'are
III, ii, 111 felt such eyes,] felt such eyes;
III, ii, 112 eyes. Oh] eyes, Oh
III, ii, 113 long, round,] long round,
III, ii, 127 me.] me;
III, ii, 143 froppish, still] froppish still
III, ii, 144 *Phil,* be] *Phil.* be
III, ii, 148 tit; come *Nick,* lets] titcome *Nick* lets
III, ii, 150 Royal.] Royal,
III, ii, 153 Critch.] Critch,
III, ii, 154 word, least . . . us;] word least . . . us,
III, ii, 156 Laud, what . . . gun.] Laud what . . . gun,
III, ii, 183 Pickpockets. To] Pickpockets, to
III, ii, 184 Fob; all] Fob, all
III, ii, 187 Pomp.] Pomp,
III, ii, 188 Thy eyes shall watch while] thy eyes shall watch; while
III, ii, 189 joy. I'le] joy, I'le
III, ii, 210 known,] known;

III, ii, 222 *Bru.*] *G. Pri.*
III, iii, 2–3 think there's] think, there's
III, iii, 8 thought the] thought, the
III, iii, 10 River, discovered] River; discovered
                            Colony, and] Colony; and
III, iii, 18 you? —and] you? and
III, iii, 25 teeth. I] teeth, I
III, iii, 27 Anchovies; i'faith,] Anchovies, i'faith
III, iii, 29 safety] safely
III, iii, 38 *Jeffry,* be] *Jeffry* be
III, iii, 39 Sir, will] Sir will
III, iii, 44 immediately. Dear mischief, how] immediately, dear mischief how
III, iii, 50 something has] something, has
III, iii, 65–66 4to runs these lines together:
                    Headborough Cost: Oh Trumpet, Oh Hilding, I have been
III, iii, 72 make a rare Queen,] make rare a Queen,
III, iii, 101 her, I'le] her; I'le
III, iii, 101–02 you, 'till] you 'till
III, iii, 108 Jack. I'le . . . Law that] Jack, I'le . . . Law, that
III, iii, 111 Bodies and] Bodies; and
III, iii, 121 Ha, gwon,] Ha gwon,
III, iii, 126 worship. I] worship, I
III, iii, 137 Horse. Scoundrel,] Horse, Scoundrel
III, iii, 142 'Pranter, aye 'Pranter; no, my] 'Pranter aye 'Pranter, no my
III, iii, 145–46 4to runs these speeches together:
      Cost. Zate there cham as cunning's the Devil, and won't
      tell *Wish:* Dam ye for a beetle-headed Dog.
III, iii, 162 Ay, that . . . all, I] Ay that . . . all I
III, iii, 163 No, zately,] No zately
III, iii, 176–77 leather'd, ha?] leather'd ha?
III, iii, 179 me? why . . . Scab,] me, why . . . Scab?
III, iii, 182–83 why, Woman, all] why Woman all
III, iii, 184 be, man,] be man,
III, iii, 201 *Nonsy,* Lady] *Nonsy* Lady
III, iii, 205SD sink, the Princes cut] sink the Princess, cut
III, iii, 209SD The End of the Third Act.] not in 4to
IV, i, 52SD men and a Bear, showing] men, and a Bear showing
IV, i, 64 thou, mortal?] thou mortal?
IV, i. 76 *eyes;*] *eyes.*
IV, i, 77 *paid,*] *paid?*
IV, i, 95 *lasses*] losses
IV, ii, 29 sire;] sire,
IV, ii, 46 come, here's] come here's
IV, ii, 53 another, as] another; as

IV, ii, 66 *Woud.*] omitted in 4to

IV, ii, 67 Princes!] Princes.

IV, ii, 69 'em, a] 'em a

IV, ii, 73 believe 'twas] believe, 'twas

IV, ii, 86 that, great] that great

IV, ii, 90 luck! our] luck our

IV, ii, 97 Come, let's] Come Let's

IV, iii, 32 comes, i'faith] comes i'faith

IV, iii, 42 Hold, when] Hold when

IV, iii, 45 Ladies, first, y'are] Ladies first y'are

IV, iii, 55 Lippy, what] lippy what

IV, iii, 57 *Whiffle,* eldest] *Whiffle* eldest

IV, iii, 80 shrunk,] shrunk;

IV, iii, 108 *But*] *Yet*

IV, iii, 133 done, Faith, Sister *Nonsy.*] done Faith Sister *Nonsy:*

IV, iii, 139SD *They fight. Enter* Bruin.] They fight, —*Enter Bruin.*

IV, iii, 149 state; poor] state, poor

IV, iii, 162 clouts,] clouts.

IV, iii, 168 Poh! you] Poh you

IV, iii, 169 thee, ungrateful] thee ungrateful

IV, iii, 202 consider? What,] consider./ *Non.* What,

IV, iii, 220 her, she] her she

IV, iii, 265 Cat,] Cat?

V, i, 28 *merrily*] *merily* [DFo]

V, i, 43-44 dumpish as a new] dumpish a new

V, i, 47 Why, I] Why? I

V, i, 49 *Nick.*] *Giok.* [CSmH, BM]

V, i, 70 Why, has] Why has

V, i, 72 Crickets] Circkets [CSmH, BM]

V, i, 75 Trenchers, he] Trenchers; he

V, i, 78 zay, Prince] zay Prince

V, i, 96 pennance for] pennance, for

V, i, 103 unhandsom;] unhandsom,

V, i, 106 Villanous, unlucky—*Tagrag?*] Villanous unlucky *Tagrag.*

V, i, 122 King a] King, a

V, i, 123 to't; tye] to't, tye

V, i, 135 *Shrub.* Guilty or not guilty?] shrubsh: guilty or not guilty.—

V, i, 159-60 These lines are run together in the 4to:
  Woman's head? All the Womans the Womans

V, i, 207 memory, are] memory are

V, i, 209 you, the] yow. The

V, i, 214 says—what] says what

V, i, 215 quickly—I] quickly?—I

V, i, 217 errant, the] errant. The

V, i, 273 *Nicklas* and *Phillip*,] *Nicklas,* and *Phillip*
V, i, 371 insolent; I'le] insolent I'le
V, i, 380SD *up, till*] *up; till*
V, i, 419 coming] coming.
V, i, 422 here,] here;
V, i, 431 Damon!] *Damon*
V, i, 432 *pity, joy*] *pity joy*
V, i, 447 *fill'd,*] *fill'd.*
V, i, 472 it and] it, and
Epilogue, 3–5, 6–8, 20–22, 28–30. Brackets not in 4to; inked in on DFo.
Epilogue, 11 do,] do.
Epilogue, 21 to't,] to't.

BIBLIOGRAPHY

Adams, William Davenport. *A Book of Burlesque, Sketches of English Stage Travestie and Parody.* London, 1891.

Arber, Edward. *The Term Catalogues, 1668–1709.* 3 vols. London, 1903–06.

Benét, William Rose, ed. *The Reader's Encyclopedia.* New York, 1948.

Biographia Dramatica. Edited by David Erskine Baker, Isaac Reed, and Stephen Jones. 3 vols. London, 1812.

Bond, Richmond P. *English Burlesque Poetry, 1700–1750.* Cambridge, Mass., 1932.

Bowers, Fredson. *A Supplement to the Woodward and McManaway Checklist of English Plays 1641–1700.* Charlottesville, Va., 1949.

Brewer's Dictionary of Phrase and Fable. New York, n.d.

Butler, Samuel. *Hudibras.* Edited by John Wilders. Oxford, 1968.

Calendar of State Papers, Domestic, 1677–78. London, 1911.

Chamberlayne, William. *Wits Led by the Nose.* London, 1678.

Chandler, Frank W. *The Literature of Roguery.* 2 vols. Cambridge, Mass., 1907.

Cibber, Colley. *The Rival Queans.* Dublin, 1729. Facsimile reprint, with Introduction by William Peterson, in *Lake Erie College Studies* 5. Painesville, Ohio, 1965.

Clinton-Baddeley, V. C. *The Burlesque Tradition in the English Theatre After 1660.* London, 1952.

Cotton, Charles. *Scarronides: or, Le Virgile Travestie.* London, 1664.

———. *Scarronides: A Mock-Poem.* London, 1665.

Cunningham, Peter. *The Story of Nell Gwynn.* London, 1908.

Davenant, Sir William. *The Dramatic Works of Sir William Davenant.* Edited by James Maidment and W. H. Logan. 5 vols. London, 1872–74. Reprint. New York, 1964.

Dent, Edward J. *Foundations of English Opera.* Cambridge, 1928. Reprint. New York, 1965.

Dictionary of National Biography. Edited by Sir Leslie Stephen and Sir Sidney Lee. 22 vols. Oxford, 1917.

Dobrée, Bonamy, ed. *Five Heroic Plays.* London, 1960. Contains a reprint of the 1673 quarto of Settle's *The Empress of Morocco* ("sculptures" are not included).

Downes, John. *Roscius Anglicanus.* London, 1708. Reprint. London, 1886.

Doyle, Anne Therese. *The Empress of Morocco: A Critical Edition of the Play and the Controversy Surrounding It.* Ph.D. dissertation, University of Illinois, 1963. This edition contains Settle's *The Empress of Morocco;* the *Notes and Observations* on *The Empress of Morocco* (1674), attributed to Crowne, Dryden, and Shadwell; Settle's reply, *Notes and Observations on The Empress of Morocco Revis'd* (1674); and a reprint of Duffett's *The Empress of Morocco.*

Dryden, John. *The Poetical Works of Dryden.* Edited by George R. Noyes. Rev. ed. Boston, 1950.

———. *The Works of John Dryden.* Vols. I, VIII, IX. General editor H. T. Swedenberg, Jr. Berkeley, 1956, 1962, 1966.

Duffett, Thomas. *The Amorous Old-woman.* London, 1674. Ascribed to Duffett by Langbaine.

———. *Beauties Triumph.* London, 1676.

Bibliography

————. *The Empress of Morocco*. London, 1674.

————. *The Mock-Tempest*. London, 1675.

————. *New Poems, Songs, Prologues and Epilogues*. London, 1676.

————. *Psyche Debauch'd*. London, 1678.

————. *The Spanish Rogue*. London, 1674.

Etherege, Sir George. *The Dramatic Works of Sir George Etherege*. Edited by H. F. B. Brett-Smith. 2 vols. Oxford, 1927.

Farmer, John S., and W. E. Henley. *Slang and its Analogues*. 7 vols. London, 1890–1904.

Fielding, Henry. *The Covent-Garden Tragedy*. London, 1732.

Furnivall, Joseph, ed. *New Shakespeare Society Papers*. Fourth Series. London, 1886.

Gagey, E. M. *Ballad Opera*. New York, 1937.

Genest, John. *Some Account of the English Stage, from 1660 to 1830*. 10 vols. Bath, 1832.

[Gildon, Charles.] *The Lives and Characters of the English Dramatick Poets*. London, 1699.

Gussey, George Robert. *After the Tempest*. Los Angeles: University of California, 1969. Special publication of the Augustan Reprint Society.

Harbage, Alfred. *Sir William Davenant, Poet Venturer 1606–1668*. Philadelphia, 1935.

Haywood, Charles. "*The Songs and Masques in the New Tempest:* An Incident in the Battle of the two Theatres, 1674." *Huntington Library Quarterly* 19 (1955): 39–56.

Hazlett, W. Carew. *Second Series of Bibliographical Collections and Notes on Early English Literature 1474–1700*. London, 1882. Reprint. New York, 1961.

Hodgkin, Lucy Violet. *Gulielma, Wife of William Penn*. London, 1947. Author is sometimes listed as "Lucy Violet Holdsworth."

Howard, James. *The English Monsieur*. London, 1674.

[J. M.] Untitled note on Duffett's *The Empress of Morocco*. *Notes and Queries*. 3rd Series, 12 (July 27, 1867):63.

Jonson, Ben. *Ben Jonson*. Edited by C. H. Herford and Percy Simpson. 11 vols. Oxford, 1925–52.

Kavanaugh, Peter. *The Irish Theatre*. Tralee, 1946.

Langbaine, Gerard. *An Account of the English dramatick poets*. Oxford, 1691.

Lawrence, W. J. *The Elizabethan Playhouse*. First Series. London, 1912.

Lewis, Peter Elvet. "The Three Dramatic Burlesques of Thomas Duffett." *Durham University Journal* 58 (1966):149–56.

McManaway, J. G. "Songs and Masques in '*The Tempest*' [c. 1674]." *Theatre Miscellany: Six Pieces Connected with the Seventeenth Century Stage*, pp. 71–87. Oxford, 1953.

Nicoll, Allardyce. *A History of Restoration Drama, 1660–1700*. 4th ed. (Vol. I of *A History of English Drama 1660–1900*.) Cambridge, 1952.

North, Roger. *Roger North on Music*. Edited by John Wilson. London, 1959.

Notes and Observations on The Empress of Morocco. London, 1674. Usually attributed to Crowne, Shadwell, and Dryden.

Novak, Maximillian E. *The Empress of Morocco and Its Critics*. Los Angeles: University of California, 1968. Special publication of the Augustan Reprint Society.

O'Dell, George C. D. *Shakespeare from Betterton to Irving*. 2 vols. New York, 1920.

The Oxford English Dictionary. Edited by James A. H. Murray et al. 12 vols (plus a supplementary volume). Oxford, 1933. Reprint. 1961.

Partridge, Eric. *A Dictionary of Slang and Unconventional English*. 6th ed. New York, 1967.

Pepys, Samuel. *Diary*. Edited by Henry Wheatley. 8 vols. London, 1893–99.

Philips, Ambrose. *The Distrest Mother*. London, 1712.

Philips, (Mrs.) Katherine. *Pompey, a Tragedy*. London, 1663.

Bibliography

Poems on Affairs of State. Vol. I, 1660–1678. Edited by George deF. Lord. New Haven, 1963.

Pope, Alexander. *Correspondence.* Edited by George Sherburn. 5 vols. Oxford, 1956.

The Quakers Art of Courtship: or, The Yea-and-Nay Academy of Compliments. London, 1710.

The Quakers Ballad. London, 1674.

Ravenscroft, Thomas. *Pammelia, Deutromelia, Melesmata.* Edited by MacEdward Leach. Reprint of first editions of 1609 and 1611. Philadelphia, 1961.

Settle, Elkanah. *The Empress of Morocco.* London, 1673.

———. *Notes and Observations on The Empress of Morocco Revis'd.* London, 1674.

Shadwell, Thomas. *The Complete Works of Thomas Shadwell.* Edited by Montague Summers. 5 vols. London, 1927.

———. *Psyche, a Tragedy.* London, 1675.

Shakespeare, William. *The Complete Works of Shakespeare.* Edited by Hardin Craig. Chicago, 1951.

Smith, Dane Farnsworth. *Plays About the Theatre in England.* New York, 1936.

Spencer, Christopher, ed. *Five Restoration Adaptations of Shakespeare.* Urbana, 1965. This edition includes both Davenant's *Macbeth* and the operatic *Tempest* of 1674.

Spencer, Hazleton. *Shakespeare Improved.* Cambridge, Mass., 1927.

Speaight, George. *The History of the English Puppet Theatre.* London, 1955.

Summers, Montague. *A Bibliography of the Restoration Drama.* London, 1934.

———. *The Playhouse of Pepys.* New York, 1935.

———. *The Restoration Theatre.* London, 1934.

———, ed. *Shakespeare Adaptations.* London, 1922. Reprint. New York, 1967. This edition includes the Davenant-Dryden *Tempest* of 1670, and Duffett's *The Mock-Tempest.*

Sutherland, James. *English Satire.* Cambridge, 1958.

Thornbury, George Walter. *Old and New London.* 6 vols. London, n.d.

Van Lennep, William. *The London Stage 1660–1700.* Part I of *The London Stage 1660–1800.* Carbondale, 1965.

Villiers, George (Duke of Buckingham). *The Rehearsal.* Edited by Montague Summers. Stratford-upon-Avon, 1914.

Waller, Edmund et al. *Pompey the Great.* London, 1664.

Wheatley, Henry B., and Peter Cunningham. *London Past and Present.* 3 vols. London, 1891.

Wilson, John Harold. *Mr. Goodman, the Player.* Pittsburgh, 1964.

Wing, Donald. *A Short Title Catalogue of Books . . . 1641–1700.* 3 vols. New York, 1945–51.

Woodward, Gertrude L., and James G. McManaway. *A Checklist of English Plays 1641–1700.* Chicago, 1945.

Worcester, David. *The Art of Satire.* Cambridge, Mass., 1940. Reprint. New York, 1960.

W[right], J[ohn]. *Thyestes and Mock Thyestes.* London, 1674.

Wright, Joseph. *The English Dialect Dictionary.* New York, 1898–1905.